6. Can a local account be used in a trust relationship? Explain.

7. In a complete trust domain model that uses 4 different domains, what is the total number of trust relationships required to use a complete trust domain model?

Exam Questions

The following questions are similar to those you will face on the Microsoft exam. Answers to these questions can be found in section Answers and Explanations, later in the chapter. At the end of each of those answers, you will be informed of where (that is, in what section of the chapter) to find more information..

1. ABC Corporation has locations in Toronto, New York, and San Francisco. It wants to install Windows NT Server 4 to encompass all its locations in a single WAN environment. The head office is located in New York. What is the best domain model for ABC's directory services implementation?

   A. Single-domain model

   B. Single-master domain model

   C. Multiple-master domain model

   D. Complete-trust domain model

2. JPS Printing has a single location with 1,000 users spread across the LAN. It has special printers and applications installed on the servers in its environment. It needs to be able to centrally manage the user accounts and the resources. Which domain model would best fit its needs?

   A. Single-domain model

   B. Single-master domain model

   C. Multiple-master domain model

   D. Complete-trust domain model

5. What must be created to allow a user account from one domain to access resources in a different domain?

   A. Complete Trust Domain Model

   B. One Way Trust Relationship

   C. Two Way Trust Relationship

   D. Master-Domain Model

Answers to Review Questions

1. Single domain, master domain, multiple-master domain, complete-trust domain. See section, Windows NT Server 4 Domain Models, in this chapter for more information. (This question deals with objective Planning 1.)

2. One user, one account, centralized administration, universal resource access, synchronization. See section, Windows NT Server 4 Directory Services, in this chapter for more information. (This question deals with objective Planning 1.)

6. Local accounts cannot be given permissions across trusts. See section, Accounts in Trust Relationships, in this chapter for more information. (This question deals with Planning 1.)

Answers to Review Questions: For each of the Review and Exam questions, you will find thorough explanations located at the end of the chapter.

Exam Questions: These questions reflect the kinds of multiple-choice questions that appear on the Microsoft exams. Use them to become familiar with the exam-question format and to help you determine what you know and what you need to review or study more.

Suggested Readings and Resources

The following are some recommended readings on the subject of installing and configuring NT Workstation:

1. Microsoft Official Curriculum course 770: *Installing and Configuring Microsoft Windows NT Workstation 4.0*

   • Module 1: Overview of Windows NT Workstation 4.0

   • Module 2: Installing Windows NT Workstation 4.0

2. Microsoft Official Curriculum course 922: *Supporting Microsoft Windows NT 4.0 Core Technologies*

   • Module 2: Installing Windows NT

   • Module 3: Configuring the Windows NT Environment

3. *Microsoft Windows NT Workstation Resource Kit Version 4.0* (Microsoft Press)

   • Chapter 2: Customizing Setup

   • Chapter 4: Planning for a Mixed Environment

4. Microsoft TechNet CD-ROM

   • *MS Windows NT Workstation Technical Notes*

      • MS Windows NT Workstation Deployment Guide – Automating Windows NT Setup

      • An Unattended Windows NT Workstation Deployment

5. Web Sites

   • www.microsoft.com/train_cert

Suggested Readings and Resources: The very last element in each chapter is a list of additional resources you can use if you wish to go above and beyond certification-level material or if you need to spend more time on a particular subject that you are having trouble understanding.

W9-COA-066

Use of the Microsoft Approved Study Guide Logo on this product signifies that it has been independently reviewed and approved in complying with the following standards:

- ◆ Acceptable coverage of all content related to Microsoft exam number (70-087), entitled (Microsoft Internet Information Server 4.0 Exam).
- ◆ Sufficient performance-based exercises that relate closely to all required content.
- ◆ Technically accurate content, based on sampling of text.

MCSE

Second Edition

Internet
Information
Server 4

New Riders

Dave Bixler

MCSE Training Guide: Internet Information Server 4, Second Edition

Copyright ® 1999 by New Riders Publishing

All rights reserved. No part of this book shall be reproduced, stored in a retrieval system, or transmitted by any means, electronic, mechanical, photocopying, recording, or otherwise, without written permission from the publisher. No patent liability is assumed with respect to the use of the information contained herein. Although every precaution has been taken in the preparation of this book, the publisher and author assume no responsibility for errors or omissions. Neither is any liability assumed for damages resulting from the use of the information contained herein.

International Standard Book Number: 0-7357-0865-7

Library of Congress Catalog Card Number: 99-62817

Printed in the United States of America

First Printing: May 1999

03 02 01 00 99   7 6 5 4 3 2 1

Interpretation of the printing code: The rightmost double-digit number is the year of the book's printing; the rightmost single-digit number is the number of the book's printing. For example, the printing code 99-1 shows that the first printing of the book occurred in 1999.

Trademarks

All terms mentioned in this book that are known to be trademarks or service marks have been appropriately capitalized. New Riders Publishing cannot attest to the accuracy of this information. Use of a term in this book should not be regarded as affecting the validity of any trademark or service mark.

Internet Information Server 4 is a registered trademark of Microsoft Corporation.

Microsoft is a registered trademark of Microsoft Corporation in the United States and other countries. New Riders Publishing is an independent entity from Microsoft Corporation, and not affiliated with Microsoft Corporation in any manner. This publication may be used in assisting students to prepare for a Microsoft Certified Professional Exam. Neither Microsoft Corporation, its designated review company, nor New Riders Publishing warrants that use of this publication will ensure passing the relevant exam.

Warning and Disclaimer

Every effort has been made to make this book as complete and as accurate as possible, but no warranty or fitness is implied. The information provided is on an "as is" basis. The author and the publisher shall have neither liability nor responsibility to any person or entity with respect to any loss or damages arising from the information contained in this book or from the use of the CD or programs accompanying it.

EXECUTIVE EDITOR
Mary Foote

ACQUISITIONS EDITOR
Amy Michaels

DEVELOPMENT EDITOR
Chris Zahn

MANAGING EDITOR
Sarah Kearns

PROJECT EDITOR
Caroline Wise

COPY EDITOR
Kelli Brooks

INDEXER
Lisa Stumpf

TECHNICAL EDITORS
Thomas Houser
Marc Savage

SOFTWARE DEVELOPMENT SPECIALIST
Jack Belbot

PROOFREADER
Sheri Replin

LAYOUT TECHNICIANS
Darin Crone
Cheryl Lynch

Contents at a Glance

Table of Contents

6 Monitoring and Optimization   229

PART II: Final Review

PART III: Appendices

About the Author

Dave Bixler is a Senior IT Consultant with one of the largest systems integrators in the United States. He has been working in the industry for the last 12 years, working on network designs, server implementations, and network management. Lately, Dave has focused on Internet technologies, including DNS and Web servers, information security, firewalls, and a 6000-user Virtual Private Networking (VPN) implementation. Dave has also worked on a number of Macmillan books as an author, technical editor, or book reviewer.

Dave's industry certifications include Microsoft's MCPS and MCSE, as well as Novell's CNE for NetWare versions 3.x, 4.x and IntranetWare, ECNE, and MCNE. Dave also has IBM's PSE, Check Point Software's CCSE, and 3Com's 3Wizard Master certifications. (He takes plenty of certification tests!)

Dave lives in Cincinnati, Ohio, with his very patient wife Sarah, sons Marty and Nicholas, and two Keeshonds, Zeus and Arcus.

About the Technical Editors

Marc Savage, MCT, MCSE, is presently working as a Senior Microsoft Technical Instructor for PBSC Computer Training Centres in the Ottawa, Canada branch. He has recently served as project leader for the Implementation of Windows NT Workstation and Microsoft Office 97. He has also been assisting with courseware design and implementation.

Thomas Houser is an MCSE who holds the MCP+I certification. He and his family live in northwest Louisiana where he is employed as an administrator at Clement Industries. He has been there over five years. Prior to employment there, he had earned a degree in Computer Aided Drafting and Design from Northwest Louisiana Technical College. While attending NLTC, he earned the Robert C. Byrd scholarship. Clement Industries, Inc., was first in steel dump trailer manufacturing and first in aluminum dump trailers for 1998. He can be reached at thomas@clementind.com.

Dedication

I would like to dedicate this book to my parents, Jane and Loring. I would not be writing books today without their guidance through my formative years. Thanks, Mom and Dad, for putting up with me through all the "fun" times. No dedication would be complete without including my wife Sarah and sons Marty and Nicholas, the reasons I got into this line of work in the first place.

Acknowledgments

No project of this type gets done without the help and support of many people. The folks that got me through this project include:

Amy Michaels, Acquisitions Editor. Thanks for the opportunity and challenge this project represents. I couldn't have done it without your support.

Chris Zahn, Development Editor. Chris is the man who made all my input into a real book. Thanks, Chris, this would not have ended up being a book were it not for you!

Marc Savage, Technical Editor. Marc is the man who keeps me honest project after project. Thanks again Marc…once again, I couldn't have done it without your expertise!

Thomas Houser, Technical Editor. This is the first time I've had the pleasure to work with Thomas, but his comments and insights on IIS helped make this a much better book. Thanks, Thomas.

My sisters Susan, Laura, and Amy, whose names have now graced three of my books. You're the best sisters I ever had.

Davin Kuenzi, a blast from the past. The most methodical thinker I have ever met, and probably ever will. Hi, Davin!

Finally, another huge thanks to my wife and sons. Sarah, Marty, and Nicholas…thanks for putting up with me through yet another book!

Tell Us What You Think!

As the reader of this book, *you* are our most important critic and commentator. We value your opinion and want to know what we're doing right, what we could do better, what areas you'd like to see us publish in, and any other words of wisdom you're willing to pass our way.

As the Executive Editor for the Certification team at New Riders Publishing, I welcome your comments. You can fax, email, or write me directly to let me know what you did or didn't like about this book—as well as what we can do to make our books stronger.

Please note that I cannot help you with technical problems related to the topic of this book, and that due to the high volume of mail I receive, I might not be able to reply to every message.

When you write, please be sure to include this book's title and author, as well as your name and phone or fax number. I will carefully review your comments and share them with the author and editors who worked on the book.

Fax: 317-581-4663

E-mail: certification@mcp.com

Mail: Mary Foote
Executive Editor
Certification
New Riders Publishing
201 West 103rd Street
Indianapolis, IN 46290 USA

How to Use This Book

New Riders Publishing has made an effort in the second editions of its Training Guide series to make the information as accessible as possible for the purposes of learning the certification material. Here, you have an opportunity to view the many instructional features that have been incorporated into the books to achieve that goal.

CHAPTER OPENER

Each chapter begins with a set of features designed to allow you to maximize study time for that material.

List of Objectives: Each chapter begins with a list of the objectives, as stated by Microsoft.

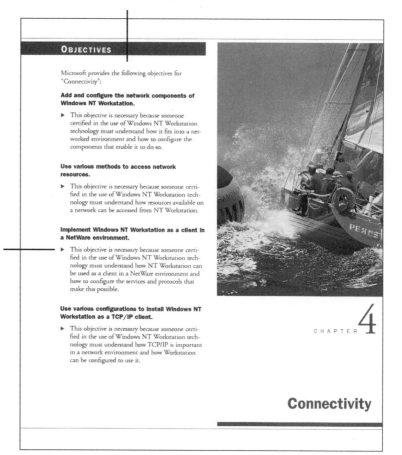

Objective Explanations: Immediately following each objective is an explanation of it, providing context that defines it more meaningfully in relation to the exam. Because Microsoft can sometimes be vague in its objectives list, the objective explanations are designed to clarify any vagueness by relying on the author's test-taking experience.

OBJECTIVES

Microsoft provides the following objectives for "Connectivity":

Add and configure the network components of Windows NT Workstation.

▶ This objective is necessary because someone certified in the use of Windows NT Workstation technology must understand how it fits into a networked environment and how to configure the components that enable it to do so.

Use various methods to access network resources.

▶ This objective is necessary because someone certified in the use of Windows NT Workstation technology must understand how resources available on a network can be accessed from NT Workstation.

Implement Windows NT Workstation as a client in a NetWare environment.

▶ This objective is necessary because someone certified in the use of Windows NT Workstation technology must understand how NT Workstation can be used as a client in a NetWare environment and how to configure the services and protocols that make this possible.

Use various configurations to install Windows NT Workstation as a TCP/IP client.

▶ This objective is necessary because someone certified in the use of Windows NT Workstation technology must understand how TCP/IP is important in a network environment and how Workstation can be configured to use it.

CHAPTER 4

Connectivity

OUTLINE

Chapter Outline: Learning always gets a boost when you can see both the forest and the trees. To give you a visual image of how the topics in a chapter fit together, you will find an outline at the beginning of each chapter. You will also be able to use this for easy reference when looking for a particular topic.

STUDY STRATEGIES

▶ Disk configurations are a part of both the planning and the configuration of NT Server computers. To study for Planning Objective 1, you will need to look at both the following section and the material in Chapter 2, "Installation Part 1." As with many concepts, you should have a good handle on the terminology and know the best applications for different disk configurations. For the objectives of the NT Server exam, you will need to know only general disk configuration concepts—at a high level, not the nitty gritty. Make sure you memorize the concepts relating to partitioning and know the difference between the system and the boot partitions in an NT system (and the fact that the definitions of these are counter-intuitive). You should know that NT supports both FAT and NTFS partitions, as well as some of the advantages and disadvantages of each. You will also need to know about the fault-tolerance methods available in NT—stripe sets with parity and disk mirroring—including their definitions, hardware requirements, and advantages and disadvantages.

Of course, nothing substitutes for working with the concepts explained in this objective. If possible, get an NT system with some free disk space and play around with the Disk Administrator just to see how partitions are created and what they look like.

You might also want to look at some of the supplementary readings and scan TechNet for white papers on disk configuration.

▶ The best way to study for Planning Objective 2 is to read, memorize, and understand the use of each protocol. You should know what the protocols are, what they are used for, and what systems they are compatible with.

As with disk configuration, installing protocols on your NT Server is something that you plan for, not something you do just because it feels good to you at the time. Although it is much easier to add or remove a protocol than it is to reconfigure your hard drives, choosing a protocol is still an essential part of the planning process because specific protocols, like spoken languages, are designed to be used in certain circumstances. There is no point in learning to speak Mandarin Chinese if you are never around anyone who can understand you. Similarly, the NWLink protocol is used to interact with NetWare systems; therefore, if you do not have Novell servers on your network, you might want to rethink your plan to install it on your servers. We will discuss the uses of the major protocols in Chapter 7, "Connectivity." However, it is important that you have a good understanding of their uses here in the planning stage.

Study Strategies: Each topic presents its own learning challenge. To support you through this, New Riders has included strategies on how to best approach studying in order to retain the material in the chapter, particularly as it is addressed on the exam.

INSTRUCTIONAL FEATURES WITHIN THE CHAPTER

These books include a large amount and different kinds of information. The many different elements are designed to help you identify information by its purpose and importance to the exam and also to provide you with varied ways to learn the material. You will be able to determine how much attention to devote to certain elements, depending on your goals. By becoming familiar with the different presentations of information, you will know what information will be important to you as a test-taker and which information will be important to you as a practitioner.

Objective Coverage Text: In the text before an exam objective is specifically addressed, you will notice the objective is listed to help call your attention to that particular material.

Warning: When using sophisticated information technology, there is always potential for mistakes or even catastrophes that may occur through improper application of the technology. Warnings appear in the margins to alert you to such potential problems.

EXAM TIP

Only One NTVDM Supports Multiple 16-bit Applications Expect at least one question about running Win16 applications in separate memory spaces. The key concept is that you can load multiple Win16 applications into the same memory space only if it is the initial Win16 NTVDM. It is not possible, for example, to run Word for Windows 6.0 and Excel for Windows 5.0 in one shared memory space and also run PowerPoint 4.0 and Access 2.0 in another shared memory space.

Exam Tip: Exam Tips appear in the margins to provide specific exam-related advice. Such tips may address what material is covered (or not covered) on the exam, how it is covered, mnemonic devices, or particular quirks of that exam.

Note: Notes appear in the margins and contain various kinds of useful information, such as tips on the technology or administrative practices, historical background on terms and technologies, or side commentaries on industry issues.

---

8   Chapter 1   PLANNING

INTRODUCTION

Microsoft grew up around the personal computer industry and established itself as the preeminent maker of software products for personal computers. Microsoft has a vast portfolio of software products, but it is best known for its operating systems.

Microsoft's current operating system products, listed here, are undoubtedly well-known to anyone studying for the MCSE exams:

- Windows 95
- Windows NT Workstation
- Windows NT Server

NOTE

Strange But True Although it sounds backward, it is true: Windows NT boots from the system partition and then loads the system from the boot partition.

Some older operating system products—namely MS-DOS, Windows 3.1, and Windows for Workgroups—are still important to the operability of Windows NT Server, so don't be surprised if you hear them mentioned from time to time in this book.

Windows NT is the most powerful, the most secure, and perhaps the most elegant operating system Microsoft has yet produced. It languished for a while after it first appeared (in part because no one was sure why they needed it or what to do with it), but Microsoft has persisted with improving interoperability and performance. With the release of Windows NT 4 which offers a new Windows 95-like user interface, Windows NT has assumed a prominent place in today's world of network-based computing.

WINDOWS NT SERVER AMONG MICROSOFT OPERATING SYSTEMS

► As we already mentioned, Microsoft has three operating system products now competing in the marketplace: Windows 95, Windows NT Workstation, and Windows NT Server. Each of these operating systems has its advantages and disadvantages.

WARNING

Don't Overextend Your Partitions and Wraps It is not necessary to create an extended partition on a disk; primary partitions might be all that you need. However, if you do create one, remember that you can never have more than one extended partition on a physical disk.

Looking at the presentation of the desktop, the three look very much alike—so much so that you might have to click the Start button and read the banner on the left side of the menu to determine which operating system you are looking at. Each offers the familiar Windows 95 user interface featuring the Start button, the Recycling

STEP BY STEP

5.1 Configuring an Extension to Trigger an Application to Always Run in a Separate Memory Space

1. Start the Windows NT Explorer.

2. From the View menu, choose Options.

3. Click the File Types tab.

4. In the Registered File Types list box, select the desired file type.

5. Click the Edit button to display the Edit File Type dialog box. Then select Open from the Actions list and click the Edit button below it.

6. In the Editing Action for Type dialog box, adjust the application name by typing **cmd.exe /c start /separate** in front of the existing contents of the field (see Figure 5.15).

FIGURE 5.15
Configuring a shortcut to run a Win16 application in a separate memory space.

Step by Step: Step by Steps are hands-on tutorial instructions that walk you through a particular task or function relevant to the exam objectives.

Figure: To improve readability, the figures have been placed carefully so they do not interrupt the main flow of text.

---

14   Chapter 1   PLANNING

You must use NTFS if you want to preserve existing permissions when you migrate files and directories from a NetWare server to a Windows NT Server system.

Windows 95 is Microsoft's everyday workhorse operating system. It provides a 32-bit platform and is designed to operate with a variety of peripherals. See Table 1.1 for the minimum hardware requirements for the installation and operation of Windows 95. Also, if you want to allow Macintosh computers to access files on the partition through Windows NT's Services for Macintosh, you must format the partition for NTFS.

MAKING REGISTRY CHANGES

To make Registry changes, run the REGEDT32.EXE program. The Registry in Windows NT is a complex database of configuration settings for your computer. If you want to configure the Workstation service, open the HKEY_LOCAL_MACHINE hive, as shown in Figure 3.22.

The exact location for configuring your Workstation service is

    HKEY_LOCAL_MACHINE\System\CurrentControlSet\Services\
    LanmanWorkstation\Parameters

To find additional information regarding this Registry item and others, refer to the Windows NT Server resource kit.

This summary table offers an overview of the differences between the FAT and NTFS file systems.

In-Depth Sidebar: These more extensive discussions cover material that perhaps is not directly relevant to the exam, but is useful as reference material or in everyday practice. In-Depths may also provide useful background or contextual information necessary for understanding the larger topic under consideration.

CASE STUDIES

Case Studies are presented throughout the book to provide you with another, more conceptual opportunity to apply the knowledge you are developing. They also reflect the "real-world" experiences of the author in ways that prepare you not only for the exam but for actual network administration as well. In each Case Study, you will find similar elements: a description of a scenario, the Essence of the Case, and an extended Analysis section.

CASE STUDY: REALLY GOOD GUITARS

ESSENCE OF THE CASE

Here are the essential elements in this case:

- need for centralized administration
- the need for WAN connectivity nation-wide
- a requirement for Internet access and e-mail
- the need for Security on network shares and local files
- an implementation of Fault-tolerant systems

SCENARIO

Really Good Guitars is a national company specializing in the design and manufacturer of custom acoustic guitars. Having grown up out of an informal network of artisans across Canada, the company has many locations but very few employees (300 at this time) and a Head Office in Churchill, Manitoba. Although they follow the best traditions of hand-making guitars, they are not without technological savvy and all the 25 locations have computers on-site which are used to do accounting, run MS Office applications, and run their custom made guitar design software. The leadership team has recently begun to realize that a networked solution is essential to maintain consistency and to provide security on what are becoming some very innovative designs and to provide their employees with e-mail and Internet access.

RGG desires a centralized administration of its

continues

Essence of the Case: A bulleted list of the key problems or issues that need to be addressed in the Scenario.

Scenario: A few paragraphs describing a situation that professional practitioners in the field might face. A Scenario will deal with an issue relating to the objectives covered in the chapter, and it includes the kinds of details that make a difference.

CASE STUDY: PRINT IT DRAFTING INC.

continued

too, which is unacceptable. You are to find a solution to this problem if one exists.

ANALYSIS

The fixes for both of these problems are relatively straightforward. In the first case, it is likely that all the programs on the draftspeople's workstations are being started at normal priority. This means that they have a priority of 8. But the default says that anything running in the foreground is getting a 2-point boost from the base priority, bringing it to 10. As a result, when sent to the background, AutoCAD is not getting as much attention from the processor as it did when it was the foreground application. Because multiple applications need to be run at once without significant degradation of the performance of AutoCAD, you implement the following solution:

1. On the Performance tab of the System Properties dialog box for each workstation, set the Application Performance slider to None to prevent a boost for foreground applications.

2. Recommend that users keep the additional programs running alongside AutoCAD at a minimum (because all programs will now get equal processor time).

The fix to the second problem is to run each 16-bit application in its own NTVDM. This ensures that the crashing of one application will not adversely affect the others, but it still enables interoperability between the applications because they use OLE (and not shared memory) to transfer data. To make the fix as transparent as possible to the users, you suggested that two things be done:

1. Make sure that for each shortcut a user has created to the office applications, the Run in Separate Memory Space option is selected on the Shortcut tab.

2. Change the properties for the extensions associated with the applications (for example, .XLS and .DOC) so that they start using the /separate switch. Then any file that is double-clicked invokes the associated program to run in its own NTVDM.

Analysis: This is a lengthy description of the best way to handle the problems listed in Essence of the Case. In this section, you might find a table summarizing the solutions, a worded example, or both.

CHAPTER SUMMARY

KEY TERMS

Before you take the exam, make sure you are comfortable with the definitions and concepts for each of the following key terms:

- FAT
- NTFS
- workgroup
- domain

This chapter discussed the main planning topics you will encounter on the Windows NT Server exam. Distilled down, these topics revolve around two main goals: understanding the planning of disk configuration and understanding the planning of network protocols.

◆ Windows NT Server supports an unlimited number of inbound sessions; Windows NT Workstation supports no more than 10 active sessions at the same time.

◆ Windows NT Server accommodates an unlimited number of remote access connections (although Microsoft only supports up to 256); Windows NT Workstation supports only a single remote access connection.

Key Terms: A list of key terms appears at the end of each chapter. These are terms that you should be sure you know and are comfortable defining and understanding when you go to take the exam.

Chapter Summary: Before the Apply Your Learning section, you will find a Chapter Summary that wraps up the chapter and reviews what you have learned.

EXTENSIVE REVIEW AND SELF-TEST OPTIONS

At the end of each chapter, along with some summary elements, you will find a section called "Apply Your Knowledge" that gives you several different methods with which to test your understanding of the material and review what you have learned

---

APPLY YOUR KNOWLEDGE

This section allows you to assess how well you understood the material in the chapter. Review and Exam questions test your knowledge of the tasks and concepts specified in the objectives. The Exercises provide you with opportunities to engage in the sorts of tasks that comprise the skill sets the objectives reflect.

Exercises

1.1   Synchronizing the Domain Controllerys

The following steps show you how to manually synchronize a backup domain controller within your domain. (This objective deals with Objective Planning 1.)

Estimated Time: Less than 10 minutes.

1. Click Start, Programs, Administrative Tools, and select the Server Manager icon.

2. Highlight the BDC (Backup Domain Controller) in your computer list.

3. Select the Computer menu, then select Synchronize with Primary Domain Controller.

12.2   Establishing a Trust Relationship between Domains

The following steps show you how to establish a trust relationship between multiple domains. To complete this exercise, you must have two Windows NT Server computers, each installed in their own domain. (This objective deals with objective Planning 1.)

Estimated Time: 10 minutes

1. From the trusted domain select Start, Programs, Administrative Tools, and click User Manager for Domains. The User Manager.

FIGURE 1.2
The login process on a local machine.

2. Select the Policies menu and click Trust Relationships. The Trust Relationships dialog box appears.

4. When the trusting domain information has been entered, click OK and close the Trust Relationships dialog box.

Review Questions

1. List the four domain models that can be used for directory services in Windows NT Server 4.

2. List the goals of a directory services architecture.

3. What is the maximum size of the SAM database in Windows NT Server 4.0?

4. What are the two different types of domains in a trust relationship?

5. In a trust relationship which domain would contain the user accounts?

Exercises: These activities provide an opportunity for you to master specific hands-on tasks. Our goal is to increase your proficiency with the product or technology. You must be able to conduct these tasks in order to pass the exam.

Review Questions: These open-ended, short-answer questions allow you to quickly assess your comprehension of what you just read in the chapter. Instead of asking you to choose from a list of options, these questions require you to state the correct answers in your own words. Although you will not experience these kinds of questions on the exam, they will indeed test your level of comprehension of key concepts.

6. Can a local account be used in a trust relationship? Explain.

7. In a complete trust domain model that uses 4 different domains, what is the total number of trust relationships required to use a complete trust domain model?

A. Single-domain model

B. Single-master domain model

C. Multiple-master domain model

D. Complete-trust domain model

5. What must be created to allow a user account from one domain to access resources in a different domain?

A. Complete Trust Domain Model

B. One Way Trust Relationship

C. Two Way Trust Relationship

D. Master-Domain Model

Exam Questions

The following questions are similar to those you will face on the Microsoft exam. Answers to these questions can be found in section Answers and Explanations, later in the chapter. At the end of each of those answers, you will be informed of where (that is, in what section of the chapter) to find more information..

1. ABC Corporation has locations in Toronto, New York, and San Francisco. It wants to install Windows NT Server 4 to encompass all its locations in a single WAN environment. The head office is located in New York. What is the best domain model for ABC's directory services implementation?

A. Single-domain model

B. Single-master domain model

C. Multiple-master domain model

D. Complete-trust domain model

2. JPS Printing has a single location with 1,000 users spread across the LAN. It has special printers and applications installed on the servers in its environment. It needs to be able to centrally manage the user accounts and the resources. Which domain model would best fit its needs?

Answers to Review Questions

1. Single domain, master domain, multiple-master domain, complete-trust domain. See section, Windows NT Server 4 Domain Models, in this chapter for more information. (This question deals with objective Planning 1.)

2. One user, one account, centralized administration, universal resource access, synchronization. See section, Windows NT Server 4 Directory Services, in this chapter for more information. (This question deals with objective Planning 1.)

6. Local accounts cannot be given permissions across trusts. See section, Accounts in Trust Relationships, in this chapter for more information. (This question deals with Planning 1.)

Exam Questions: These questions reflect the kinds of multiple-choice questions that appear on the Microsoft exams. Use them to become familiar with the exam question formats and to help you determine what you know and what you need to review or study more.

Answers and Explanations: For each of the Review and Exam questions, you will find thorough explanations located at the end of the section.

Suggested Readings and Resources

The following are some recommended readings on the subject of installing and configuring NT Workstation:

1. Microsoft Official Curriculum course 770: *Installing and Configuring Microsoft Windows NT Workstation 4.0*

   • Module 1: Overview of Windows NT Workstation 4.0

   • Module 2: Installing Windows NT Workstation 4.0

2. Microsoft Official Curriculum course 922: *Supporting Microsoft Windows NT 4.0 Core Technologies*

   • Module 2: Installing Windows NT

   • Module 3: Configuring the Windows NT Environment

3. *Microsoft Windows NT Workstation Resource Kit Version 4.0* (Microsoft Press)

   • Chapter 2: Customizing Setup

   • Chapter 4: Planning for a Mixed Environment

4. Microsoft TechNet CD-ROM

   • *MS Windows NT Workstation Technical Notes*

      • MS Windows NT Workstation Deployment Guide – Automating Windows NT Setup

      • An Unattended Windows NT Workstation Deployment

5. Web Sites

   • www.microsoft.com/train_cert

   • www.prometric.com/testingcandidates/ assessment/chosetest.html (take online

Suggested Readings and Resources: The very last element in every chapter is a list of additional resources you can use if you want to go above and beyond certification-level material or if you need to spend more time on a particular subject that you are having trouble understanding.

Introduction

The second edition of the *MCSE Training Guide: Internet Information Server 4* is designed for advanced end users, service technicians, and network administrators who are pursuing Microsoft certification. The Implementing and Supporting Microsoft Internet Information Server 4.0 (#70-087) exam can be applied to the Microsoft Certified Systems Engineer (MCSE), Microsoft Certified Systems Engineer+Internet (MCSE+Internet), or Microsoft Certified Professional+Internet (MCP+Internet) certifications. The IIS 4 exam measures your ability to implement, administer, and troubleshoot information systems that incorporate components of Internet Information Server, as well as your ability to provide technical support to users of IIS, Index Server, and related services.

WHO SHOULD READ THIS BOOK

This book is designed to help you meet your certification goals by preparing you for the Implementing and Supporting Microsoft Internet Information Server 4.0 exam (#70-087). Today's IIS administrator is part Windows NT administrator, part Web developer, part SQL Server administrator and part Internet Information Server 4 administrator. This exam touches on all of those jobs. However, to cover them all in depth would take a library, not just a single book. So this book fulfills a more modest goal: It prepares you to take the exam and familiarizes you with the different capabilities of Microsoft Internet Information Server 4.

There are facets of running an IIS server that are beyond the scope of the exam and this book. For example, you will not be a SQL administrator when you complete this book. However, each chapter in this book contains a section called "Suggested Readings and Resources" that provides you with what you need to fill in the blanks not covered by this book. So, while you might not be a SQL administrator when you're done, you'll know enough SQL to connect IIS to a SQL server and have a recommendation for some additional reading if you need to expand your SQL expertise.

Another question that comes up a lot is, "Do I need to take a class to pass this test?" Although the information you need to pass the exam is in here, and Microsoft has approved it as study material, there is one thing that is difficult for any book to provide—hands-on experience with the product. If you are able to set up an environment that allows you to perform the exercises outlined in this book, you're going to be in good shape. The simulation engine included on the CD-ROM is another good way to get some hands-on experience. You do not need to take a class in addition to buying this book to pass the exam. However, depending on your personal study habits or learning style, you might benefit from taking a class in conjunction with studying from this book.

One final thing you might consider before taking the IIS exam is what other Microsoft exams would be useful to take first. You may find it helpful to first take the Windows NT Server, Networking Essentials, and TCP/IP exams. They provide plenty of information about the infrastructure in which Microsoft Internet Information Server 4 is deployed.

HOW THIS BOOK HELPS YOU

This book takes you on a self-paced tour of the topics covered by the IIS 4 exam, and teaches you the skills needed to achieve your MCSE or MCP certification. You'll also find helpful hints, tips, real-world examples, exercises, and references to additional study materials. Specifically, it is set up to help you in the following ways:

◆ **Organization**. The material is organized by major exam topics and individual exam objectives. Every objective you need to know for the Implementing and Supporting Microsoft Internet Information Server 4.0 exam is covered in this book. We have also made the information accessible in the following ways:

  • The full list of exam topics and objectives is included in this introduction.

  • Each chapter begins with a list of the objectives to be covered.

  • Each chapter also begins with an outline that provides you with an overview of the material and the page numbers where particular topics can be found.

  • We also repeat objectives in the margin where the most relevant material to that objective is covered (unless the whole chapter addresses a single objective).

  • Information on where the objectives are covered is also conveniently condensed on the tear card at the front of this book.

◆ **Instructional Features**. This book has been designed to provide you with multiple ways to learn and reinforce the exam material. Following are some of the helpful methods:

  • *Objective Explanations*. As previously mentioned, each chapter begins with a list of the objectives covered in the chapter. In addition, immediately following each objective is an explanation in a context that defines it more meaningfully.

  • *Study Strategies*. The beginning of the chapter also includes strategies for approaching the studying and retaining of the material in the chapter, particularly as it is addressed on the exam.

  • *Exam Tips*. Exam tips appear in the margin to provide specific exam-related advice. Such tips might address what material is covered (or not covered) on the exam, how it is covered, mnemonic devices, or particular quirks of that exam.

  • *Review Breaks and Summaries*. Crucial information is summarized at various points in the book in lists or tables. Each chapter ends with a summary as well.

  • *Key Terms*. A list of key terms appears at the end of each chapter.

- *Notes.* These appear in the margin and contain various kinds of useful information, such as tips on technology or administrative practices, historical background on terms and technologies, or side commentaries on industry issues.

- *Warnings.* When using sophisticated information technology, there is always the potential for mistakes, or even catastrophes, that can occur because of improper application of the technology. Warnings appear in the margin to alert you to such potential problems.

- *In-depths.* These more extensive discussions cover material that might not be directly relevant to the exam but are useful as reference material or in everyday practice. In-depths might also provide useful background or contextual information necessary for understanding the larger topic under consideration.

- *Step by Steps.* These are hands-on, tutorial instructions that lead you through a particular task or function relevant to the exam objectives.

- *Exercises.* Found at the end of the chapters in the "Apply Your Knowledge" section, exercises can include additional tutorial material as well as other types of problems and questions.

- *Case Studies.* Each chapter concludes with a review of the chapter and a Case Study. The Case Study is meant to help you understand the practical applications of the information covered in the chapter.

◆ **Extensive practice test options.** The book provides numerous opportunities for you to assess your knowledge and practice for the exam. The practice options include the following:

- *Review Questions.* These open-ended questions appear in the "Apply Your Knowledge" section that appears at the end of each chapter. They allow you to quickly assess your comprehension of what you just read in the chapter. Answers to the questions are provided later in the section.

- *Exam Questions.* These questions also appear in the "Apply your Knowledge" section. They reflect the kinds of multiple-choice questions that may appear on the Microsoft exams. Use them to practice for the exam and to help you determine what you know and what you need to review or study further. Answers and explanations for them are provided.

- *Practice Exam.* A Practice Exam is included in the Final Review section. The Final Review section and the Practice Exam are discussed in a moment.

- *Top Score.* The Top Score software included on the CD-ROM provides further practice questions.

NOTE — For a complete description of the New Riders Top Score test engine, please see Appendix C, "Using the Top Score Software."

◆ **Final Review.** This part of the book provides you with three valuable tools for preparing for the exam:

- *Fast Facts.* This condensed version of the information contained in the book proves extremely useful for last-minute review.

- *Study and Exam Tips.* Read this section early on to help you develop study strategies. It also provides you with valuable exam-day tips and information on new exam question formats, such as adaptive tests and simulation-based questions.

- *Practice Exam.* A full practice test for each of the exams is included. Questions are written in the styles used on the actual exams. Use it to assess your readiness for the "real thing."

The book includes several valuable appendices as well, including a glossary (Appendix A), an overview of the Microsoft certification program (Appendix B), a description of what is on the CD-ROM (Appendix C), how to use the Top Score

software (Appendix D), as well as how to modify IIS through the Registry (Appendix E) and a primer on TCP/IP (Appendix F).

These and all the other book features previously mentioned will provide you with thorough preparation for the exam.

For more information about the exam or the certification process, contact Microsoft:

Microsoft Education: 800-636-7544

Internet: `ftp://ftp.microsoft.com/Services/MSEdCert`

World Wide Web: `http://www.microsoft.com/train_cert`

CompuServe Forum: `GO MSEDCERT`

UNDERSTANDING WHAT THE IIS 4 EXAM (#70-087) COVERS

The Implementing and Supporting Microsoft Internet Information Server 4.0 exam (#70-087) covers the IIS 4 main topic areas represented by the conceptual groupings of the test objectives. Each chapter represents one of these main topic areas. It focuses on determining your skill in seven major categories:

◆ Planning

◆ Installation and Configuration

◆ Configuring and Managing Resource Access

◆ Integration and Interoperability

◆ Running Applications

◆ Monitoring and Optimization

◆ Troubleshooting

The Implementing and Supporting Microsoft Internet Information Server 4.0 certification exam uses these categories to measure your ability. Before taking this exam, you should be proficient in the job skills described in the following sections.

Planning

The Planning section is designed to make sure that you understand the hardware requirements of IIS, capabilities of the product, and its limitations. The knowledge needed here also requires the understanding of general networking concepts. The objectives are detailed in the following:

- Choose a security strategy for various situations. Security considerations include
    - Controlling anonymous access
    - Controlling access to known users and groups
    - Controlling access by host or network
    - Configuring SSL to provide encryption and authentication schemes
    - Identifying the appropriate balance between security requirements and performance requirements
- Choose an implementation strategy for an Internet site or an intranet site for stand-alone servers, single-domain environments, and multiple-domain environments. Tasks include
    - Resolving host header name issues by using a HOSTS file or DNS, or both
    - Choosing the appropriate operating system on which to install IIS

- Choose the appropriate technology to resolve specified problems. Technology options include
    - WWW service
    - FTP service
    - Microsoft Transaction Server
    - Microsoft SMTP Service
    - Microsoft NNTP Service
    - Microsoft Index Server
    - Microsoft Certificate Server

Installation and Configuration

The Installation and Configuration part of the IIS exam is the "meat" of the exam. You are tested on virtually every possible component of the protocol. The objectives are as follows:

- Install IIS. Tasks include
    - Configuring a Microsoft Windows NT Server 4.0 computer for the installation of IIS
    - Identifying differences to a Windows NT Server 4.0 computer made by the installation of IIS
- Configure IIS to support the FTP service. Tasks include
    - Setting bandwidth and user connections
    - Setting user logon requirements and authentication requirements
    - Modifying port settings

- Setting directory listing style
- Configuring virtual directories and servers
- Configure IIS to support the WWW service. Tasks include
  - Setting bandwidth and user connections
  - Setting user logon requirements and authentication requirements
  - Modifying port settings
  - Setting default pages
  - Setting HTTP 1.1 host header names to host multiple Web sites
  - Enabling HTTP Keep-Alives
- Configure and save consoles by using Microsoft Management Console.
- Choose the appropriate administration method.
- Install and configure Certificate Server.
- Install and configure Microsoft SMTP Service.
- Install and configure Microsoft NNTP Service.
- Customize the installation of Microsoft Site Server Express Analysis Content Analyzer.
- Customize the installation of Site Server Express Analysis Report Writer and Usage Import.

Configuring and Managing Resource Access

The Configuring and Managing Resource Access component of the Implementing and Supporting Microsoft Internet Information Server 4.0 certification exam concentrates on how to use the various sharing and authentication components of IIS:

- Create and share directories with appropriate permissions. Tasks include
  - Setting directory-level permissions
  - Setting file-level permissions
- Create and share local and remote virtual directories with appropriate permissions. Tasks include
  - Creating a virtual directory and assigning an alias
  - Setting directory-level permissions
  - Setting file-level permissions
- Create and share virtual servers with appropriate permissions. Tasks include
  - Assigning IP addresses
- Write scripts to manage the FTP service or the WWW service.
- Manage a Web site by using Content Analyzer. Tasks include
  - Creating, customizing, and navigating WebMaps

- Examining a Web site by using the various reports provided by Content Analyzer

- Tracking links by using a WebMap

- Configure Microsoft SMTP Service to host message traffic.

- Configure Microsoft NNTP Service to host a newsgroup.

- Configure Certificate Server to issue certificates.

- Configure Index Server to index a Web site.

- Manage MIME types.

- Manage the FTP service.

- Manage the WWW service.

Integration and Interoperability

The Integration and Interoperability component of the Implementing and Supporting Microsoft Internet Information Server 4.0 certification exam concentrates on configuring IIS to interact with databases:

- Configure IIS to connect to a database. Tasks include

  - Configuring ODBC

- Configure IIS to integrate with Index Server. Tasks include

  - Specifying query parameters by creating the .idq file

- Specifying how the query results are formatted and displayed to the user by creating the .htx file

Running Applications

The Running Applications component of the Implementing and Supporting Microsoft Internet Information Server 4.0 certification exam looks at scripting on IIS and the options available to do so. The objectives are as follows:

- Configure IIS to support server-side scripting.

- Configure IIS to run ISAPI applications.

Monitoring and Optimization

The Monitoring and Optimization component of the IIS exam covers how to monitor your site and optimize it for the greatest performance combination attainable:

- Maintain a log for fine-tuning and auditing purposes. Tasks include

  - Importing log files into a Usage Import and Report Writer Database

  - Configuring the logging features of the WWW service

  - Configuring the logging features of the FTP service

  - Configuring Usage Import and Report Writer to analyze logs created by the WWW service or the FTP service

- Automating the use of Report Writer and Usage Import
- Monitor performance of various functions by using Performance Monitor. Functions include HTTP and FTP sessions.
- Analyze performance. Performance issues include
  - Identifying bottlenecks
  - Identifying network-related performance issues
  - Identifying disk-related performance issues
  - Identifying CPU-related performance issues
- Optimize performance of IIS.
- Optimize performance of Index Server.
- Optimize performance of Microsoft SMTP Service.
- Optimize performance of Microsoft NNTP Service.
- Interpret performance data.
- Optimize a Web site by using Content Analyzer.

Troubleshooting

The Troubleshooting component of the IIS certification exam covers eight components running the entire gamut of troubleshooting. The objectives are as follows:

- Resolve IIS configuration problems.
- Resolve security problems.
- Resolve resource access problems.
- Resolve Index Server query problems.
- Resolve setup issues when installing IIS on a Windows NT Server 4.0 computer.
- Use a WebMap to find and repair broken links, hyperlink texts, headings, and titles.
- Resolve WWW service problems.
- Resolve FTP service problems.

HARDWARE AND SOFTWARE RECOMMENDED FOR PREPARATION

As a self-paced study guide, *MCSE Training Guide: Internet Information Server 4, Second Edition* is meant to help you understand concepts that must be refined through hands-on experience. To make the most of your studying, you need to have as much background and experience as possible. The best way to do this is to combine studying with working on real networks, using the products on which you will be tested. This section gives you a description of the minimum computer requirements you need to build a solid practice environment.

Computers

The minimum computer requirements to ensure
that you can study everything on which you'll be
tested are one or more workstations running
Windows 95 or NT Workstation and two or
more servers running Windows NT Server, all
connected by a network.

Workstations: Windows 95 and Windows NT

- Computer on the Microsoft Hardware
  Compatibility list

- 486DX 33MHz or better

- 16MB RAM

- 200MB hard disk

- 3.5-inch 1.44MB floppy drive

- VGA video adapter

- VGA monitor

- Mouse or equivalent pointing device

- Two-speed CD-ROM drive

- Network Interface Card (NIC)

- Presence on an existing network or use
  of a hub to create a test network

- Microsoft Windows 95 or NT
  Workstation 4.0

Servers: Windows NT Server

- Two computers on the Microsoft Hardware
  Compatibility List

- 486DX2 66MHz or better

- 32MB RAM

- 340MB hard disk

- 3.5-inch 1.44MB floppy drive

- VGA video adapter

- VGA monitor

- Mouse or equivalent pointing device

- Two-speed CD-ROM drive

- Network interface card (NIC)

- Presence on an existing network or use
  of a hub to create a test network

- Microsoft Windows NT Server 4.0

ADVICE ON TAKING THE EXAM

More extensive tips are found in the section
"Study and Exam Prep Tips" in Part II, "Final
Review" of this book, but keep this advice in mind
as you study:

- ◆ **Read all the material.** Microsoft has been
  known to include material not expressly
  specified in the objectives. This book has
  included additional information not reflect-
  ed in the objectives in an effort to give you
  the best possible preparation for the examination—and for the real-world network
  experiences to come.

- ◆ **Work on the Step by Steps and complete
  the Exercises in each chapter.** They will
  help you gain experience using the Microsoft
  product. All Microsoft exams are task-based
  and require you to have experience using
  the Microsoft product in a real networking
  environment.

◆ **Use the questions to assess your knowledge.** Don't just read the chapter content; use the questions to find out what you know and what you don't. Study some more, review, then assess your knowledge again.

◆ **Review the exam objectives.** Develop your own questions and examples for each topic listed. If you can develop and answer several questions for each topic, you should not find it difficult to pass the exam.

> **NOTE** **Exam-Taking Advice** Although this book is designed to prepare you to take and pass the Implementing and Supporting Microsoft Internet Information Server 4 exam (#70-087), there are no guarantees. Read this book, work through the questions and exercises, and when you feel confident, take the practice exam and additional exams using the Top Score test engine. These should tell you whether you are ready for the real thing. When taking the actual certification exam, make sure you answer all the questions before your time limit expires. Do not spend too much time on any one question. If you are unsure, answer it as best you can; then mark it for review when you have finished the rest of the questions.

Remember, the primary object is not to pass the exam—it is to understand the material. After you understand the material, passing the exam should be simple. Knowledge is a pyramid; to build upward, you need a solid foundation. This book and the Microsoft Certified Professional programs are designed to ensure that you have that solid foundation.

Good luck!

NEW RIDERS PUBLISHING

The staff of New Riders Publishing is committed to bringing you the very best in computer reference material. Each New Riders book is the result of months of work by authors and staff members who research and refine the information contained within its covers.

As part of this commitment to you, the NRP reader, New Riders Publishing invites your input. Please let us know if you enjoy this book, if you have trouble with the information or examples presented, or if you have a suggestion for the next edition.

Please note, however, that the New Riders staff cannot serve as a technical resource during your preparation for the Microsoft certification exams or for questions about software- or hardware-related problems. Please refer instead to the documentation that accompanies the Microsoft products or to the applications' Help systems.

If you have a question or comment about any New Riders book, there are several ways to contact New Riders Publishing. We will respond to as many readers as possible. Your name, address, or phone number will never become part of a mailing list or be used for any purpose other than to help us continue to bring you the best books possible. You can write to us at the following address:

New Riders Publishing
Attn: Publisher
201 W. 103rd Street
Indianapolis, IN 46290

If you prefer, you can fax New Riders Publishing at 317-817-7448.

You also can send email to New Riders at the following Internet address:

```
certification@mcp.com
```

NRP is an imprint of Macmillan Computer Publishing. To obtain a catalog or information, or to purchase any Macmillan Computer Publishing book, call 800-428-5331.

Thank you for selecting *MCSE Training Guide: Internet Information Server 4, Second Edition.*

EXAM PREPARATION

This chapter helps you get ready for the Planning section of the exam. Planning is one of the most overlooked facets of an IIS deployment. In many environments, installing IIS is as easy as putting the option pack CD in the machine and running setup. People get into trouble due to lack of planning when they end up without a stable, accessible platform after they finish the installation. Because this is a problem in the "real world," Microsoft considers planning to be an important component of the IIS exam and tests accordingly.

Microsoft defines the following objectives for the Planning section:

Choose a security strategy for various situations. Security considerations include:

- **Controlling anonymous access**
- **Controlling access to known users and groups**
- **Controlling access by host or network**
- **Configuring SSL to provide encryption and authentication**
- **Identifying the appropriate balance between security requirements and performance requirements**

▶ This objective is important because before using Microsoft Internet Information Server to provide access to services and resources, someone certified in IIS needs to understand how to prevent unauthorized users from accessing information they shouldn't.

▶ The last subobjective is necessary because as important as securing an IIS site is, being able to utilize the site successfully is equally important. To successfully answer questions concerning this objective, an understanding of the implications of each security measure and how it impacts performance and usability is required.

CHAPTER 1

Planning

Choose an implementation strategy for an Internet site or intranet site for standalone servers, single-domain environments, and multiple-domain environments. Tasks include:

- **Resolving host header name issues by using a HOSTS file or DNS, or both**

- **Choosing the appropriate operating system on which to install IIS**

▶ This objective is particularly important because for a Microsoft Internet Information Server to be successfully implemented, it must be installed correctly into the existing network infrastructure. This means that the domain infrastructure, name resolution standards, and even the recommended operating system all play a part in a successful IIS implementation.

Choose the appropriate technology to resolve specified problems. Technology options include:

- **WWW service**

- **FTP service**

- **Microsoft Transaction Server**

- **Microsoft SMTP Service**

- **Microsoft NNTP Service**

- **Microsoft Index Server**

- **Microsoft Certificate Server**

▶ This objective is the most obvious and the most important. A person who is certified in Microsoft Internet Information Server needs to understand each of the components of IIS 4 and be able to use them appropriately. Although that seems very straightforward, this is an excellent topic for the scenario-and-simulation-based questions Microsoft tests with.

STUDY STRATEGIES

As you read through this chapter, you should concentrate on the following key concepts:

▶ The different components of Microsoft Internet Information Server and what services they can provide.

▶ The specifics of granting or denying access by host or network address. Pay particular attention to the variable length subnet masks used to identify network addresses.

▶ The differences between implementing on a standalone server, a member server, and a domain controller.

INTRODUCTION

As the Internet continues to explode in popularity and more and more productivity, commerce, and entertainment applications are made available via Internet- and intranet-based servers, the popularity of Microsoft Internet Information Servers will continue to increase. The chances are pretty good that the day you purchased this book, you were browsing a Web server, downloading a file, or maybe even reading a Usenet newsgroup. Microsoft Internet Information Server 4.0 has the capability to provide those services and a number of others.

To gain a solid understanding of the capabilities of IIS 4.0, this chapter starts by deviating a little from the order of the objectives Microsoft provides.

The first thing you should learn about this product is the different components and what services they can provide. The WWW service, FTP service, Microsoft Transaction Server, Microsoft SMTP Service, Microsoft NNTP Service, Microsoft Index Server, and Microsoft Certificate Server each provide a specific service, and they work together to provide a comprehensive suite of Internet services. You will delve deeper into each component in the rest of the book. This chapter provides a solid introduction to each service without going into the specifics of installing and configuring them.

After you have a thorough familiarity with each of the components and where you use them, it's time to discuss access control. Let's say you have been tasked with putting the Human Resources department on your intranet server. It is probably a bad idea for anyone to be able to browse the employee salary information. Does that mean you can't put sensitive information on an internal Web server? Not with IIS's access control mechanisms. This chapter introduces you to the different mechanisms for securing that type of information.

Finally, now that you know what each component does and how to keep your information secure, it's time to talk about the infrastructure in which you will be deploying this server. Should it be part of a domain or is a standalone server adequate? How do you resolve the name of the server? The answers to these questions and others conclude the chapter.

CHOOSING APPROPRIATE TECHNOLOGIES

▶ Choose the appropriate technology to resolve specified problems.

There are a number of components and services that come with the basic Internet Information Server 4.0 product. Many of these have been with IIS since version 2.0 or before, and several are new to this release. Although the title of this section is "Choosing Appropriate Technologies," this can also be considered the introduction to IIS 4.0 services and components. You are introduced to all the new and old features and services of IIS with a discussion of each. The first step towards mastering IIS 4.0 is a thorough understanding of its capabilities. Let's start the discussion with a look at the new management framework for IIS 4.0.

Microsoft Management Console

Although not strictly an IIS service, the Microsoft Management Console (MMC) is an important feature of IIS 4.0. An integral part of the Windows 2000 (formerly Windows NT 5.0) operating system, the MMC is included with the Windows NT 4.0 Option Pack. The MMC provides the next-generation management framework for managing Windows NT servers and services. Through the use of management applications known as *snap-ins,* the MMC provides a single interface for IIS 4.0 today, and for all future releases of Microsoft network operating systems and BackOffice products. Today, Microsoft Transaction Server includes an MMC snap-in for administration of its transaction packages. One additional feature that makes the MMC particularly useful is that it allows an administrator to customize the management interface he works with. A system administrator might only use the operating system and backup snap-ins, whereas the Web manager might use the IIS 4.0 and Transaction Server snap-ins. It is very flexible and powerful. It is also the starting point for all the simulation questions on the exam, so the interface is explored in detail later in the book.

> **EXAM TIP**
>
> **Simulation Questions and the MMC** As Microsoft shifts to more simulation-based questions, being very familiar with the MMC is a good idea. If you cannot navigate through the MMC to make changes to services, you will find simulations hard to complete.

WWW Service

The WWW (World Wide Web) service in IIS 4.0 is the service that allows you to include HTML (Hypertext Markup Language) documents on your site, as illustrated in Figure 1.1, and allows remote clients and browsers to reach them. Although that sounds very simple, and everyone assumes that the use of the WWW service is obvious, let's take a closer look just to be sure it's clear.

FIGURE 1.1
A sample Web site.

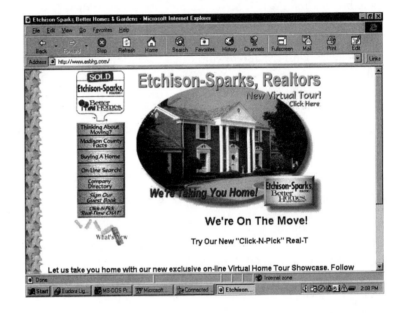

The WWW service allows client machines to access information on the server via a Web browser (like Internet Explorer 4.01) using the Hypertext Transfer Protocol (HTTP). HTTP is the protocol that can be credited with the birth and subsequent explosive growth of the Internet (more specifically, the World Wide Web). It is a generic, stateless, object-oriented protocol that provides a simple, standards-based mechanism for accessing information on the Internet, or in today's business environment, the intranet.

When might you use the WWW service? Let's say you are the network administrator for a company that designs album covers for one of the big recording companies. To ensure the cover designs meet with the company's approval, you need a mechanism for making the designs available to the record executives, band members, and anyone else who has input into the final product.

The WWW service of IIS 4.0 provides the ideal mechanism for this project.

After the designer has completed any cover concepts, a simple HTML page can be developed containing the graphics and any associated text. (Microsoft and others offer a myriad of tools to make this extremely easy.) This page is placed on an IIS 4.0 server, where anyone with the appropriate access can look at the concepts and make a determination as to the cover of choice. If you want to get fancy, you could use some of the other components of IIS to automate a response form, which could be emailed directly to the designer so any changes may be made.

FTP Service

The File Transfer Protocol (FTP) service provides clients attaching to your server the ability to transmit files to and from the server, as illustrated in Figure 1.2.

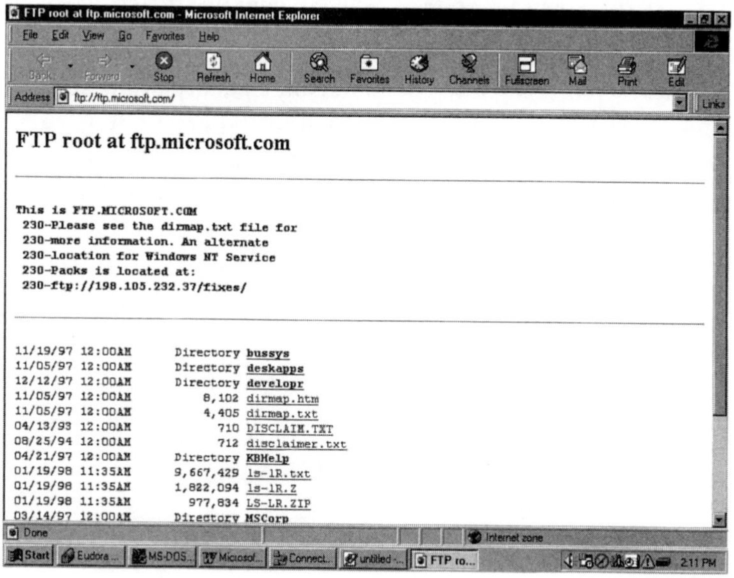

FIGURE 1.2
A sample FTP site.

A veteran protocol for the Internet, FTP has been used as the primary File Transfer Protocol for the Internet since its inception. Today, virtually every operating system bundles an FTP client and there are a number of third-party products available as well. All the

Microsoft operating systems since Windows 95 include a character-based FTP client with their TCP/IP protocol stack.

From the server side of the house, it is rare to find a vendor who does not provide patches and updates via FTP.

In an office environment, you might use an FTP server to make a new database client available to the field or even catalog updates available to a customer.

Microsoft Transaction Server

Microsoft Transaction Server (MTS) is a transaction processing system for developing and managing server applications. It enables you to keep track of transactions that occur on the server. A transaction is an application operation that must be completed before it is considered to have occurred. An example is depositing money in your checking account. You can receive the check, endorse the check, give the check to the teller, and even receive your receipt, but until the amount is posted to your account, the transaction has not occurred.

Transaction processing is critical to the successful deployment of business-critical applications that need to be 100-percent accurate and consistent. There is also a security component to transaction processing that ensures that transactions have not been modified while being processed. These features are critical to successfully deploying business-critical applications like electronic commerce, payroll processing, or even online banking, to name a few.

MTS is particularly useful because it provides a programming model, runtime environment, and graphical administration tool for managing enterprise applications like those mentioned earlier. MTS provides the following capabilities:

◆ Distributed transactions

◆ Automatic management of processes and threads

◆ Object instance management

◆ A distributed security service to control object creation and use

◆ A graphical interface for system administration and component management

Microsoft SMTP Service

Microsoft SMTP Service uses the Simple Mail Transfer Protocol (SMTP) to send and receive email using TCP port 25 for operations. When installed, it can be managed and administered through Internet Service Manager or SMTP Service Manager (HTML). The two functions are almost identical, with the difference being that the latter enables you to administer SMTP through HTML, whereas the former requires administration from the server.

There are a number of clients available for reading SMTP mail, such as Microsoft's Outlook Express, included with Internet Explorer 4.01. These clients allow you to send and receive SMTP mail, which is the primary mail type used on the Internet today. If you want to send e-mail to Cousin Harry at Generic ISP Services Inc., the odds are pretty good you need an SMTP mail server to send it from.

One additional feature of having a bundled SMTP service included with IIS 4.0 is that you can mail-enable Web applications. Let's say you have written a Web-based time card application that requires employees to fill out their time online. With the SMTP service, you can have a copy of each time sheet mailed to the employee, and to the employee's manager for her records, as well as to Accounts Payable so the employee gets paid.

Microsoft NNTP Service

The Microsoft NNTP Service supports the Network News Transport Protocol and enables clients to access newsgroups. Because this feature uses the NNTP protocol, any standard newsreader client can be used to participate in these discussion groups, including Outlook Express. The one important thing to remember is that the NNTP service included with IIS 4.0 only supports local newsgroups. You cannot receive newsfeeds with IIS 4.0.

Microsoft NNTP supports MIME, HTML, GIF, and JPEG. Like SMTP, when installed it can be managed and administered through Internet Service Manager or NNTP Service Manager (HTML).

NOTE

But What If I Want to Read Usenet Newsgroups? It is very easy to say, "Install the NNTP service and you will be able to read local newsgroups," but what do you need to receive the newsgroups from the Internet? First, you need a copy of Exchange server or some other software application that supports newsfeeds. Then, you need a newsfeed from your Internet service provider (ISP). A word of warning, though, if you decide to go this route: There is a huge amount of data available in the Usenet newsgroups and if you fail to take hard drive and memory requirements into account before getting a newsfeed, you can expect to be out of disk space, or even have your server crash, in short order. Check with your ISP for sizing recommendations.

Microsoft Index Server

Microsoft Index Server indexes the full text and properties of documents stored on an Internet or intranet Web site. Users can then query the index by filling in a simple Web form. The Web server forwards the form to the Index Server, which finds any matches and returns the results to the client as a Web page.

Index Server can work with HTML documents as well as Excel and Word documents. This brings you the benefit of being able to add Excel and Word documents to your Web server without converting them to HTML first.

Microsoft Certificate Server

Microsoft Certificate Server enables you to increase the security of your site by issuing certificates (digital identifiers) that use public-key encryption. Certificates enable you to verify that you have secure communication across the network, whether that network is an intranet or the Internet. The server certificates are issued from a third-party organization and contain information about the organization and the public key.

With public-key encryption, there are actually two keys involved, forming a key pair. The first is the public key, which is a known value and the one used to establish a secure HTTP connection. The second key is a private key, known only by the user. The two are mathematical opposites of each other and are used to negotiate a secure TCP/IP connection.

When the connection is established, a session key (typically 40 bits in length) is used between the server and client to encrypt and decrypt the transmissions.

Certificate Server is an integral component of the Microsoft Internet Security Framework (ISF) model. This integration means that Windows NT users and groups can be mapped to certificates and the users still receive the benefit of a single logon to the network.

Requests for certificates come into Microsoft Certificate Server through HTTP, e-mail, or as Remote Procedure Calls. Every request is verified against a policy before a response is issued. Different policies can be in place for different groups of users, and policy modules can be written in Microsoft Visual Basic, C++, or Java.

NOTE

Browser Requirements The browser that requests the certificates must be Microsoft Internet Explorer 3.0 or later, or Netscape Navigator 3.0 or later.

Site Server Express

The Site Server Express component of IIS 4.0 brings site management to IIS. Where earlier versions of IIS allowed you to log usage, Site Server Express provides the ability to analyze that usage. Site Server Express can also graphically map a site, check for broken links, and enable a developer to publish content from a browser directly to the IIS server. No more FTP-ing files to populate a site.

Site Server Express offers a subset of the functionality found in the Microsoft Site Server application. It bundles Content Analyzer, Usage Import and Report Writer, and Microsoft Posting Acceptor:

◆ Content Analyzer contains the management tools you need to view and manage your Web site. With the capability to graphically map a Web site and also manage links, Content Analyzer is an important tool for making IIS 4.0 a competitive server in today's market. You can use Content Analyzer to find broken links, analyze site structure, and even manage remote sites.

◆ Usage Import and Report Writer allows you to import and aggregate log files from multiple servers to a single server. It contains nine predefined reports you can use to identify usage and trends, as well as help you understand the people browsing your site. On an intranet, it might be used to prune unused content and expand on sections browsed heavily; on the Internet, it might be used to tell what products customers are most interested in learning about.

◆ Microsoft Posting Acceptor is a server add-on tool that Web developers can use to publish their content using HTTP POST (Request for Comments (RFC) 1867). Microsoft Posting Acceptor can accept content from any RFC 1867-compliant source, including Microsoft's Web Publishing Wizard and FrontPage applications.

Active Server Pages and Microsoft Script Debugger

Active Server Pages (ASP) can be used to create dynamic HTML pages or build powerful Web applications. ASP pages are files that can contain HTML tags, text, and script commands. The script

> **NOTE**
>
> **What's an RFC?** Request For Comment (RFC) documents are used to make notes about the Internet and Internet technologies. If an RFC can garner enough interest, it might become a standard. There are RFCs on topics ranging from the File Transfer Protocol (RFC 0114, updated by RFC 0141, RFC 0172, RFC 0171) to the Hitchhiker's guide to the Internet (RFC 1118). The first RFC was posted in 1969 by Steve Crocker, and the topic was Host Software. You can find listings of all the RFCs at a number of sites throughout the Internet. One place is http://www.rfc-editor.org/. During the writing of this book, the highest numbered RFC was 2524, but it will be much higher by the time this book is on the shelves. New RFCs are being published all the time.

commands execute on the server and return dynamically built HTML pages to the screen. This allows a developer to literally build a page on-the-fly, customizing the visit for each person browsing it. This is discussed in greater detail in Chapter 5, "Running Applications."

Microsoft Script Debugger is exactly what it sounds like. It is a tool that allows you to test ASP scripts. If you are familiar with software development, you'll understand that this tool can be invaluable for developing ASP applications for a production Web site.

Internet Connection Services for Remote Access Services

Microsoft Internet Connection Services for Remote Access Services provides enhanced Internet connection capabilities, including a dial-up service and Virtual Private Networking (VPN) capabilities. You can also use Internet Connection Services to centrally manage your network's remote access services.

Microsoft Message Queue

Microsoft Message Queue Server (MSMQ) allows applications to communicate with other applications by providing a reliable mechanism for sending and receiving messages. With bundled ActiveX support, security controls, administration tools, and its integration with other Microsoft products, MSMQ adds powerful functionality to distributed application design.

Microsoft Data Access Components

Microsoft Data Access Components are a bundle of components that allow easier access to a variety of data types. Microsoft Data Access Components consist of ActiveX Data Objects (ADO) and Remote Data Service (RDS), the Microsoft OLE DB Provider for ODBC, and Open Database Connectivity (ODBC):

◆ **ActiveX Data Objects (ADO).** ActiveX Data Objects can be used to access and manipulate data in a database server through an OLE DB Provider. Although this is not a new concept, ADO provides this capability bundled with ease of use, high speed, low memory overhead, and a small disk footprint. ADO is considered a key component for developing Web applications that rely on Microsoft technology.

◆ **Remote Data Service (RDS).** The Remote Data Service provides a high-performance data caching technology for connecting databases with Web applications.

◆ **ODBC and the Microsoft OLE DB Provider for ODBC.** The final two components of Microsoft Data Access Components can be used for providing access to ODBC-compatible databases like Microsoft Access or Oracle.

Additional Support for Internet Standards

In addition to new services and components, IIS 4.0 also adds support for a number of Internet standards. This helps IIS 4.0 maintain its industry-leading position as a Web server and can also ease the migration from other Web server platforms to IIS. Let's take a closer look at the additional standards supported.

HTTP 1.1 Support

IIS support for HTTP 1.1 includes the following features:

◆ **Pipelining.** HTTP version 1.0 processes client requests one at a time, waiting until the previous request is completed before servicing the next one. Pipelining can be used to provide improved Web server performance by allowing clients to send many requests before receiving a response from the Web server. This can provide a significant performance boost, depending on the types of requests being made.

◆ **Persistent Connections.** Also known as *Keep-Alives*, persistent connections can be used to reduce the number of connections a client uses to make multiple requests to a Web server. When a browser connects to a Web server and requests a resource, a connection is established with the server. When the request is completed, the connection is dropped. Because this is an expensive process in terms of server processing, persistent connections can be used to reduce or eliminate the need for multiple connections when clients make multiple requests for resources. This is a configurable parameter that is discussed in Chapter 2, "Installation and Configuration."

◆ **HTTP PUT and DELETE.** HTTP PUT and DELETE can be used to post and delete files to and from a Web site using any HTTP 1.1-compliant browser. This is similar to the RFC 1867 support mentioned earlier, but it is not the same.

◆ **Transfer Chunk Encoding.** Transfer Chunk Encoding (also known as *chunked transfers)* allows Active Server Pages (ASP) to transmit variable-length documents more efficiently. Because ASP can be used to build pages on-the-fly, these pages can be a variable length. Transfer Chunk Encoding allows these pages to be broken into "chunks" for more efficient transfers.

RFC 1867 Support

Mentioned earlier, RFC 1867 defines the mechanism for allowing file uploads, such as posting content from a browser directly to a Web server.

HTTP Redirects

Support for HTTP Redirects means that IIS 4.0 site administrators can redirect requests for files to a different Web site, directory, or file. This gives administrators the ability to fulfill resource requests even when content has been removed or moved, or when the name of a virtual directory has changed. When used correctly, this can significantly reduce or even eliminate those pesky "404 File Not Found" errors that inevitably occur when a site is redesigned, or when content is updated or removed.

MICROSOFT INTERNET SECURITY FRAMEWORK

With the introduction of the Microsoft Internet Information Server, Microsoft has introduced the first application that fits into its new security paradigm, the Internet Security Framework. Before discussing the Internet Security Framework, you need to understand the goal of Internet (and intranet) security.

Historically, the purpose of security is to limit access to information to the smallest group of users necessary, while ensuring that people who need access have it. This is a model that works well in an intranet environment, where access can typically be tightly controlled. On the other hand, the Internet is almost diametrically opposed to this theory. Servers on the Internet are usually designed to allow as much access to resources as possible, to the largest population of users. This is a security specialist's nightmare. Yet, despite the problems associated with security and the Internet, companies need more access to the Internet and also need to allow access to the corporate data and even corporate networks from the Internet. Many companies are in a quandary about what to do as the Internet and intranets converge.

Ideally, the convergence of the Internet and intranets should result in an environment where systems can be deployed to meet the new business demands while still preserving investments in existing systems. This environment must also provide a secure network for distributing business-to-business information. It should provide for:

◆ The secure exchange of information

◆ The capability to conduct secure e-commerce

◆ Sophisticated access control mechanisms

◆ A secure authentication technology

Enter the Microsoft Internet Security Framework. The Microsoft Internet Security Framework is the architecture that Microsoft envisions for delivering these capabilities. It plans on accomplishing this by using the best of existing technologies as a platform and extending them using new technologies. The beginnings of this architecture are included in IIS 4.0, with its capabilities as a

Certificate server, bundled Virtual Private Networking, and its ability to use the latest version of Secure Sockets Layer (SSL). The planned release of Windows 2000 will further expand these capabilities by embracing the concept of Public Key Infrastructure and advanced encryption technologies.

Now that you've been introduced to some of the higher-level security issues and Microsoft's Internet Security Framework in particular, let's take a look at the specific security topics surrounding the IIS 4.0 exam.

CHOOSING A SECURITY STRATEGY

▶ Choose a security strategy for various situations.

Microsoft Internet Information Server 4.0 contains a number of security features that are discussed in this section. These are general issues that every IIS administrator needs to consider as he plans to deploy an IIS server into a production environment. These issues include:

◆ Controlling anonymous access

◆ Controlling access to known users and groups

◆ Controlling access by host or network

◆ Configuring SSL to provide encryption and authentication schemes

◆ Identifying the appropriate balance between security requirements and performance requirements

Coincidentally, these five issues are also objectives for the IIS 4.0 exam, which illustrates the importance Microsoft places on them. Each of these objectives is examined in the following sections.

Controlling Anonymous Access

Anonymous access enables clients to access your servers (FTP or WWW) without providing a username, or using the name anonymous. The WWW service is frequently deployed as completely anonymous, although this is changing as more and more e-commerce and sensitive information is moved to the Web. The original FTP service required usernames, but anonymous access was soon added. In fact, for tracking purposes, it is customary to use your e-mail address as a password when using anonymous as a username.

IIS uses the default IUSR_computername account for all anonymous logons. This account, like all other user accounts, appears in the User Manager for Domains utility (see Figure 1.3) and can be administered from there. Under IIS 3.0, this was an issue because the password for this account was not synchronized between IIS and User Manager. If you changed the password in User Manager and neglected to manually synchronize the password in IIS, you were treated to a server that required a user ID and password to access. This has been fixed in IIS 4.0 with an automatic synchronization option.

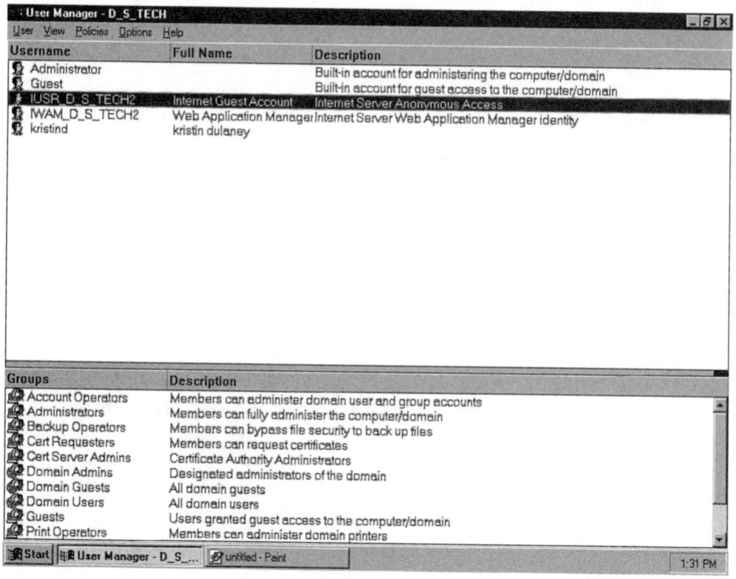

◄FIGURE 1.3
The anonymous user account (IUSR_computername) can be administered from User Manager for Domains.

The permissions granted the IUSR_computername account are used to determine an anonymous user's privileges. The default properties are shown in Figure 1.4, including the fact that the user cannot change the password and that the password does not expire. From a security perspective, it is a good idea to limit the access this account is granted. Making it a member of the Administrators group would be a particularly bad idea.

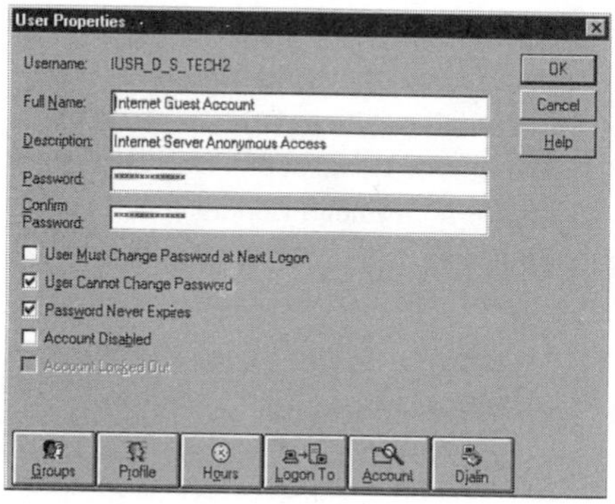

FIGURE 1.4▲
The default account properties for the anonymous user account.

Using Anonymous FTP

Anonymous FTP is one of the most common methods for transferring information on the Internet. Most vendors have FTP sites for distributing patches, fixes, and updates, and most are accessible via anonymous FTP. IIS 4.0 can be used to provide this capability as part of its FTP service.

To configure anonymous access for the FTP service, go to the FTP Accounts Security tab in the Internet Service Manager. From there, you can configure the following options:

◆ **Allow Anonymous Connections.** Select this for anonymous connections. Be sure you want to grant anonymous access before selecting this option.

◆ **Username.** Displays the IUSR_computername name as set up by IIS in Windows NT User Manager for Domains and in Internet Service Manager. This is the default username, and you can change it to a different user ID or rename this ID for extra security.

◆ **Password.** A randomly generated password was created by User Manager for Domains and Internet Service Manager. You must have a password; no blanks are allowed. Under IIS 3.0, if you changed this password, you needed to make sure it matched the one in User Manager for Domains. The Enable Automatic Password Synchronization option was added to eliminate accidental password inconsistencies between IIS 4.0 and User Manager.

◆ **Allow only anonymous connections.** Click this option to limit access to your FTP server to only those who log on as anonymous. This restricts users from possibly logging on with an account that has administrative rights. Because FTP authentication information is passed as clear text, an unscrupulous person with a network analyzer can capture user ID and password information while a user is logging on to the FTP server. Because the user information is the same information used to access the server (or domain if the server is a member server or domain controller), you could inadvertently transmit your NT user ID and password in clear text and enable someone to access your resources without authorization.

NOTE

Using Allow Only Anonymous Connections To use the Allow Only Anonymous Connections, you need to enable Anonymous Connections first. Otherwise, the option is greyed out.

◆ **Administrator.** Select those accounts that are allowed to administer this virtual FTP site. To administer a virtual FTP site, a user should first be a member of the Administrative group under Windows NT. Click the Add button to add a user account to this list. Remove an account by selecting the account and clicking Remove.

> **NOTE**
>
> **FTP Passwords** FTP passwords are *always* transmitted as clear text and, because of that, FTP should be limited to anonymous access only.

Removing Anonymous WWW Access

IIS 4.0 can be set up to verify the identity of clients who access your Web site. On public Web sites on which non-critical or public domain information and applications are available, authentication of users connecting to your Web site might not be important. However, if you have secure data or want to restrict Web access to specific clients, logon and authentication requirements become very important.

Use the following steps to set authentication and logon requirements:

> **NOTE**
>
> **But We Haven't Installed IIS Yet** That is absolutely correct. Due to the organization of the Microsoft Objectives for this exam, some Step by Step examples are included that cannot be completed without completing Chapter 2, "Installation and Configuration" first. To be sure you can complete all the Step by Steps, go to Chapter 2, install IIS, and return to complete the exercises as needed.

STEP BY STEP

1.1 Removing Anonymous Access from a Web Site

1. Open Internet Service Manager.

2. Right-click on a Web site, file (NTFS systems only), or directory you want to configure.

3. Click on Properties. The property sheet for that item is displayed, as shown in Figure 1.5.

4. Click the Directory Security tab (or set File Security, if you want to configure file-specific properties, by selecting the file and choosing its properties).

5. Click the Edit button under Anonymous Access and Authentication Control. The Authentication Methods dialog box appears, as shown in Figure 1.6.

continues

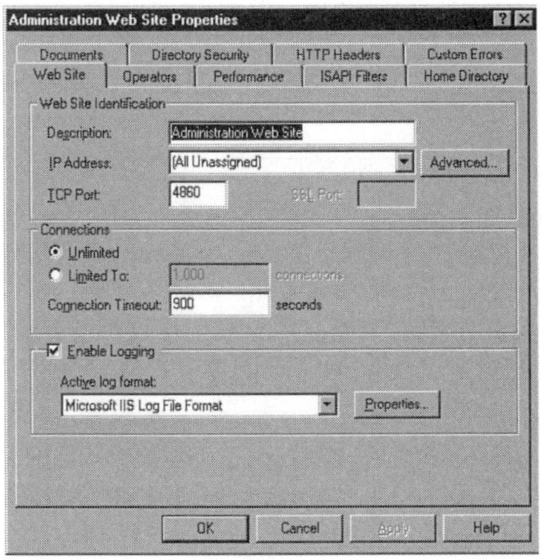

FIGURE 1.5
You can access the properties for a Web site through Internet Service Manager.

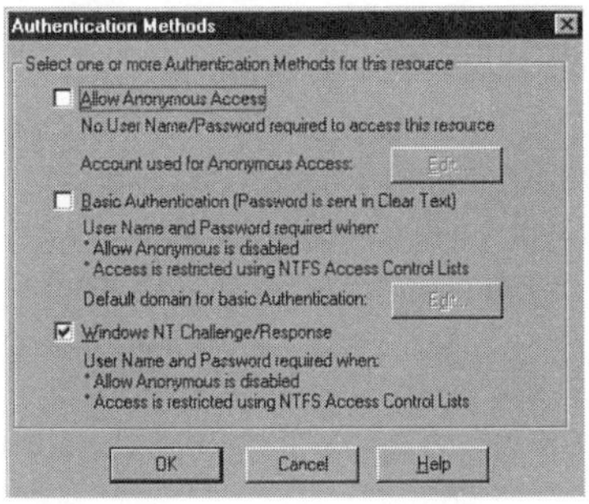

FIGURE 1.6
You can configure different levels of authentication for each Web site.

NOTE — **SSL and Basic Authentication** If you are using the Secure Socket Layer protocol, Basic Authentication transmits the username and password in an encrypted format.

continued

6. Select an authentication method from the following options:

- **Allow Anonymous Access.** This setting enables clients to connect to your Web site without requiring a username or password. Click the Edit button to select the Windows NT user account used to access your computer. By default, the account IUSR_computername is used. This account is granted Log on Locally user rights by default and is necessary for anonymous logon access to your Web site. Click OK to return to the Authentication Methods dialog box.

- **Basic Authentication.** Use this method if you do not specify anonymous access and you want a client connecting to your Web site to enter a valid Windows NT username and password to log on. This sends a password in clear text format (the passwords are transmitted in an unencrypted format). In most circumstances, you should avoid this setting because it exposes your NT user IDs and passwords to anyone with a network analyzer. Click the Edit button to specify a default logon domain for users who do not explicitly name a domain.

- **Windows NT Challenge/Response.** This setting is used if you want to use the Windows NT Challenge/Response mechanism to authenticate the client attempting to connect to your Web site. This capability is only supported in Internet Explorer 2.0 and later. During the challenge/response procedure, encrypted authentication information is exchanged between the client and server to authenticate the user.

7. Click OK.

Preventing Anonymous WWW Access

As a general rule, you want anonymous WWW access at most sites. This isn't the case, however, if you're dealing with sensitive data. In this situation, you can prevent the use of anonymous access by requiring IIS to authenticate users. Authentication can be done using Windows NT users and groups, by host or network, or by Secure Socket Layer authentication.

Authentication of users takes place only if you have disabled anonymous access or anonymous access fails because there isn't an anonymous account with appropriate permissions in NTFS (New Technology File System).

Controlling Access to Known Users and Groups

As opposed to the anonymous model, you can use NTFS permissions to limit access to your site to a defined set of users or groups. In this situation, all users must have a Windows NT account that is valid and they must provide the user ID and password to establish the connection. When connected, the permissions set for the user govern what can and cannot be accessed.

Because the method for securing the resources lies with NTFS permissions, you should be familiar with them. Each NTFS permission is made up of a combination of six rights: (R) Read, (W) Write, (X) Execute, (D) Delete, Change Permissions (P), and Take Ownership (O). The first four rights apply to IIS. You cannot modify permissions or take ownership of a file/directory through IIS. The makeup of each right is listed in the following:

- ◆ **No Access.** No Access overrides all other permissions. It still enables users to connect, but nothing shows up except the following message:

  ```
  You do not have permission to access this directory.
  ```

- ◆ **Read.** Assigns only R and X permissions.

- ◆ **Change.** Assigns R, X, W, and D permissions.

- ◆ **Full Control.** Assigns R, X, W, and D permissions (also includes the capability to change permissions and take ownership).

NOTE

Special Access Permission   There is one additional permission, the Special Access permission, that can be defined as any combination of the six rights. It is not included in the table.

◆ **Special Access.** These permissions are defined by the administrator.

NTFS permissions and capabilities are outlined in Table 1.1.

TABLE 1.1

NTFS FILE AND DIRECTORY PERMISSIONS

	No Access	*Read*	*Change*	*Full Control*
Display subdirectory and file names	O	X	X	X
Display the data and attributes of files	O	X	X	X
Run programs	O	X	X	X
Enter a directory's subdirectories	O	X	X	X
Create subdirectories and add files	O	O	X	X
Modify data in files	O	O	X	X
Change file attributes	O	O	X	X
Delete files and subdirectories	O	O	X	X
Change the permissions of NTFS files and directories	O	O	O	X
Take ownership of NTFS files and directories	O	O	O	X

X indicates an action is permitted; O indicates an action is not permitted.

NOTE

Permissions Accumulate   As with all Windows NT permissions, user and group permissions accumulate, with the exception of No Access, which instantly overrides all other permissions.

Controlling Access by Host or Network

In addition to limiting access to your site on the basis of users or groups, you can limit it based upon the host or network the access is coming from. There are two models you can operate under. The first is where you select a group of networks or hosts and grant them access. In doing so, you are saying that only they can come in, whereas everyone else is denied access.

The other model is to select a group of networks or hosts and deny them access. By this, you are saying that this group is not allowed access, whereas everyone else is. The solution to your situation is dependent upon your individual site and needs.

To grant access to only a few, do the following:

STEP BY STEP

1.2 Granting Access to Only a Few Users

1. Start Internet Service Manager, select the Web site (or file or directory), and open the properties.

2. Choose either Directory Security or File Security, based upon which approach to security you want to take. The Directory Security tab is shown in Figure 1.7. Recall that file security is set through the file properties.

3. Click Edit under IP Address and Domain Name Restrictions.

4. Select Denied Access from the IP Address and Domain Name Restrictions dialog box.

5. Click Add.

6. Select either Single Computer, Group of Computers, or Domain Name from the Grant Access On dialog box, shown in Figure 1.8.

7. Type in the IP address of those to whom you're giving access or click the DNS Lookup button to browse for them by name.

8. Click OK twice.

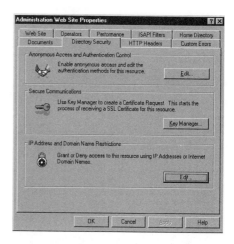

FIGURE 1.7▲
The Directory Security property sheet allows you to configure the security for the Web site.

FIGURE 1.8▲
From this dialog box, you can deny access to the site in one of three ways.

Exercise 1.1 illustrates how to deny access to a select group of hosts or networks. To pass this exam, you must understand the concept of Variable Length Subnet Masks, which allows you to divide a range of addresses to a group smaller than one of the standard address classes.

N O T E **TCP/IP Background**   For more detailed information on TCP/IP, refer to Appendix F, "TCP/IP and Subnetting."

If you don't want to get into the nuts and bolts of subnetting, memorize the subnet mask table shown in Table 1.2. Pay particular attention to the number of hosts available with each subnet. This is a common type of test question on the IIS 4.0 exam.

TABLE 1.2

VALID SUBNET RANGE VALUES FOR A CLASS C ADDRESS RANGE

Last Digits of Subnet Address	Number of Addresses in Range
128	128
192	64
224	32
240	16
248	8
252	4
254	2
255	1 (not used)

Using Secure Socket Layer to Secure IIS 4.0

N O T E   **Public Key Infrastructure**   Will you be tested on Public Key Infrastructure on the Microsoft Internet Information Server 4.0 exam? No, you won't. This section is meant to provide you with a brief introduction to the underlying infrastructure that makes the use of SSL and certificates possible.

There are a number of components you need to understand before looking at using Secure Socket Layer (SSL) as a security mechanism for your IIS Web site. These components include the following:

◆ Public Key Infrastructure (PKI)

◆ Certificates

◆ Certificate Authorities

Public Key Infrastructure

To understand the concept of a Public Key Infrastructure (PKI), you first need to understand a little about cryptography. Before this discussion progresses too far, be aware that to fully understand how cryptography and PKI really works is beyond the scope of this book. In fact, it is an excellent topic for an entire book, and you'll find some recommended reading on the topic at the end of this chapter. That being said, cryptography is the science of protecting data by using mathematical algorithms to take plain text data in conjunction with an encryption key and generate encrypted data. With a good cryptographic algorithm, it is mathematically improbable that a person can decrypt a message starting with only the encrypted text and a fast computer. That is not to say that it cannot be done; more and more encryption algorithms are falling victim to the ever-faster computers available today. Generally, a decryption key is needed to decode the data.

The fundamental property of public key cryptography is that the encryption and decryption keys are different. How does that work, you ask? Encryption with a public key encryption key is a one-way function; plain text is transformed to encrypted text easily but the encryption key is not used in the decryption process. A different (but mathematically related) decryption key is used to decrypt the data. What this means in the context of PKI is that the user has a pair of keys, a public key and a private key. By making the public key available, you enable others to send you encrypted data that can only be decrypted using your private key. In the context of SSL, a certificate is used as a public key for transactions with the SSL server, and the server then decrypts the data using its private key.

Certificates—What Are They and How Do You Use Them?

Think of certificates as an electronic version of an electronic key card. When you want access to a resource, you pull out your electronic key and open the door, using your unique electronic ID. Certificates provide a similar mechanism, but they are used in the context of the relationship between a public encryption key and the person, server, or company owning the corresponding private key. A certificate is a particular type of digitally signed statement concerning a specific public encryption key. The certificate is electronically signed by its issuer, the holder of the private encryption key. Generally, certificates also contain other information, including identity information. This means that when issuing a certificate, the issuer (the holder of the private key) verifies the connection between the issuer's identity and the encryption keys.

The most common form of certificates in use today is based on the X.509 standard. This is a fundamental technology used in the Certificate server included with IIS 4.0.

Certificate Authorities

A certificate authority (CA) is simply a company or service that issues certificates. With a copy of IIS 4.0, anyone can be a certificate authority, using the bundled Certificate server. In the larger context of the Internet, there are companies like Verisign and CyberTrust that act as guarantor of the certificates they issue. That means they act as the ultimate certificate authority, authenticating that you are who your certificate says you are.

Secure Socket Layer

If you have worked on the Internet or with the TCP/IP protocol, you are undoubtedly aware that Web traffic is very susceptible to unauthorized interception. In the case of anonymous access, like FTP downloads or browsing public Web sites, this lack of security really isn't an issue. However, if you want to conduct business transactions over the Web, this casual approach to security really isn't appropriate. Enter the SSL protocol. Although there is no standard way to secure an FTP connection, you can use the SSL protocol in Internet Information Server to encrypt and securely transfer your critical information over the Web. Be prepared to trade some processor cycles in exchange for this added security.

The SSL protocol is used to provide a secure data connection in conjunction with an authentication process. This process creates a secure point-to-point connection between a client's Web browser and a Web server. SSL security is based on a combination of public key and symmetric key cryptography, in addition to digital signature and certificate technology. Any more detail would probably be more confusing than enlightening and is out of scope for this book, so we'll save that topic for another time. The important thing to remember is that although the client browser and the IIS server have never before communicated with each other, they can agree to transmit encrypted data by using a cryptographic key pair. By using digital signatures, as discussed earlier, each party can positively identify the other.

Configuring SSL

Now that you understand some of the underlying infrastructure necessary to effectively use SSL, it's time to look at configuring SSL on your IIS 4.0 server. As an interesting aside, SSL can be used to authenticate not only specific users, but also the anonymous user. If SSL is enabled and a user attempts anonymous access, the Web server looks for a valid certificate on the client and rejects those lacking such.

> **Planning for the Effect of SSL on Performance**   Never use SSL on a server with a processor that cannot afford the extra load. The processor impact of SSL is substantial because everything must be encrypted.

STEP BY STEP

1.3 Enabling SSL

1. Start Internet Service Manager and click the Key Manager icon. The Key Manager utility is displayed, as shown in Figure 1.9.

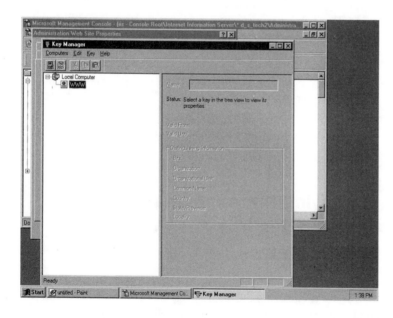

FIGURE 1.9
The Key Manager utility is used to generate certificate requests.

2. Use Key Manager to generate a certificate request file by choosing Key, Create New Key.

continues

continued

3. Submit the request for a certificate to an online authority and obtain their approval (which can take days or months).

4. Save the certificate, which is returned as an ASCII file.

5. Start Internet Service Manager again and click on Key Manager. Select the key from the window and choose Install Key Certificate. You have now completed this part and must assign it to a Web site.

6. Select a Web site in Internet Service Manager and open the properties.

7. Go to Advanced under Web Site Identification.

8. Assign the Web site IP address to port 443 under the Multiple SSL identities of this Web Site dialog box.

9. Click Edit on the Secure Communications option of the property sheet. This opens the Secure Communications dialog box.

10. On the Secure Communications dialog box, set the Web server to require a secure channel and enable the Web server's SSL client certificate authentication.

Identifying the Appropriate Balance Between Security and Performance Requirements

One of the most difficult issues in any server implementation of a Web server is balancing the security requirements with the usability and performance requirements. When there is no security, users can access resources without any difficulties and without sacrificing performance for things like authentication or encryption. Taking security to its extreme, often referred to as absolute security, users cannot access resources at all. This is the equivalent of turning off the server and placing it in a closet. The trick is finding a balance between the two extremes.

Common sense plays a large part in the decision on how much security to implement. For example, security should be tighter at any financial institution or site conducting e-commerce than at a user's home page. Likewise, site security should be tighter at any site involving medical or employment information than one containing sports scores. You also need to be aware of the implications of different technologies. SSL, for example, adds a significant amount of processor overhead to handle the encryption for the data stream. You might also want to consider adding faster or additional processors to compensate for the additional overhead.

Using strict authentication schemes can impact not only performance and usability, but administrative overhead as well. The permissions and access for each user must be set up and checked from time to time to ensure they do not need to be changed. For small user populations, this is not a big deal, but for large groups of users, you might need to add administrators just to handle user creations, modifications, and deletions.

For an intranet, you should consider creating a group of users who need to access your documents and assigning the Log on Locally right to the group. Use Windows NT Challenge Response for authentication and make certain that only the selected group has permission to read and access the documents. An alternate approach is to control access to the network infrastructure through the use of firewalls and remote access authentication and allow anonymous access to the site itself. This can be more practical in large corporations.

For an e-commerce site, or other types of secure Web sites, consider using Microsoft Certificate Server in combination with SSL. Keep in mind there is additional overhead for the SSL encryption algorithms, and you need to administer the creation, distribution, and modification of the certificates.

UNDERSTANDING IMPLEMENTATION STRATEGIES

▶   Choose an implementation strategy for an Internet site or an intranet site for standalone servers, single-domain environments, and multiple-domain environments.

When implementing IIS, there are several factors to consider: the environment, the method of host name resolution, and the operating system. One of the following sections examines the host name issues, whereas another looks at operating system possibilities. The following section concentrates on the issues of environment.

Environments

There are three possibilities for IIS environments in the Windows NT world: a standalone server, a single-domain environment, and a multiple-domain environment.

On a standalone server, it is important that IIS be able to interact with the LAN, WAN, or other network architecture that you're seeking. Confining IIS to a standalone server adds a level of security because anyone who penetrates the security of the server can access only that server and nothing more. As we discussed in the anonymous access section, using Basic Authentication can expose your user ID and password to network analyzers.

In a single-domain environment, IIS is often installed on the Primary Domain Controller (PDC). In so doing, IIS can capitalize on the security of the PDC and user/resource authentication there. However, placing IIS on the PDC can add a considerable (additional) load on an already busy server. The balance must be weighed at each site, and it might be more beneficial to place IIS on a member server instead of a Domain Controller. This would allow the server to be a member of the domain, for security, while not taxing it with authentication duties.

In a multiple-domain environment, it is important that IIS be accessible to all of the domains. If you are using Windows NT users and groups for authentication, domain trust relationships become an important part of your installation planning. Because multiple-domain environments are usually multiple site networks, bandwidth becomes extremely important. As users from multiple sites access the Web server over WAN links, through Virtual Private Networks, and through Remote Access Services, the local network and the physical network interface in the IIS server can become saturated. You might want to consider using the best (fastest) network interface card (NIC) possible, or even multiple NICs. Also ensure your server has an ample amount of RAM and fast processor(s) to service all of the traffic the IIS server will face.

Resolving Host Name Issues with HOSTS or DNS

There are two methods of resolving host names in a Windows NT environment: with static HOSTS files and with the Domain Name System. This section looks at both name resolution methods.

Understanding the HOSTS File

The HOSTS file is an ASCII text file that statically maps local and remote host names to IP addresses. On a Windows NT machine, it is located in the \systemroot\System32\Drivers\etc directory.

In most operating systems (such as UNIX) and prior to Windows NT version 4.0, the HOSTS file is case sensitive. Regardless of operating system, the file is limited to 255 characters per entry. Any TCP/IP utility that needs to resolve a name to an IP address looks in the HOSTS file for the resolution of the name. In the absence of a DNS infrastructure (discussed in the next sections), a HOSTS file must reside on each host that needs to be able to perform name resolution. The file is read from top to bottom at boot and is loaded into memory for faster resolution. This means that to update a HOSTS file, you need to reload it into memory. There are a variety of ways to do this, including rebooting the host. When the host is trying to resolve an address, it checks the HOSTS file entries in sequential order. As soon as a match is found for a host name, the process stops. This means that when there are duplicate entries, anything past the first entry is ignored. For better performance, place the most commonly used names near the top of the file.

The following is a sample HOSTS file:

```
# Copyright (c) 1993-1995 Microsoft Corp.
#
# This is a sample HOSTS file used by Microsoft TCP/IP for
# Windows NT.
#
# This file contains the mappings of IP addresses to host
➥names.
# Each entry should be kept on an individual line. The IP
➥address
# should be placed in the first column followed by the
# corresponding host name. The IP address and the host name
# should be separated by at least one space.
#
```

```
# Additionally, comments (such as these) may be inserted on
# individual lines or following the machine name denoted by
➥a '#'
# symbol.
#
# For example:
#
#     102.54.94.97      rhino.acme.com        # source
server
#     38.25.63.10       x.acme.com            # x client
➥host

127.0.0.1      localhost
```

You might notice that, as with many other types of files, the #
symbol is used to indicate a comment. To improve performance,
keep comments to a minimum. They are read as well, even though
they are comments, so the first 17 lines of the sample are just
overhead. If you must use a large number of comments, try to
place them at the end of the file.

The second thing to note is the following entry:

```
127.0.0.1      localhost
```

This is a loopback address for every host. This is a reserved address
in the TCP/IP protocol that references the host's internal card,
regardless of the actual host address, and can be used for
diagnostics to verify that things are working properly internally,
before testing that they are working properly on the network.

Within the HOSTS file, fields are separated by whitespace that can
be either tabs or spaces. As mentioned earlier, a host can be referred
to by more than one name—to do so, separate the entries on the
same line with whitespace, as shown in the following example:

```
127.0.0.1      me loopback localhost
199.9.200.7    SALES7 victor
199.9.200.4    SALES4 nikki
199.9.200.3    SALES3 cole
199.9.200.2    SALES2 victoria
199.9.200.1    SALES1 nicholas
199.9.200.5    SALES5 jack
199.9.200.11   ACCT1
199.9.200.12   ACCT2
199.9.200.13   ACCT3
199.9.200.14   ACCT4
199.9.200.15   ACCT5
199.9.200.17   ACCT7
```

The aliases are other names by which the system can be referenced.
Here, me and loopback do the same as localhost, whereas nicholas is
the same as SALES1. If an alias is used more than once, the search
stops at the first match because the file is searched sequentially.

One thing to realize about the HOSTS file in today's networks is that it is of little or no value. Today's networks are so large and change so often that there is no practical method for maintaining a HOSTS file on anything but the smallest, most isolated networks. Imagine trying to put all the hosts on the Internet into a text file so you could type in a name instead of an IP address. You'd be at it well into the next century.

Understanding DNS

The Domain Name System (DNS) is a better way to resolve host names in a TCP/IP environment. DNS is the primary system used to resolve host names on the Internet. In fact, DNS had its beginning in the early days of the Internet.

In its early days, the Internet was a small network established by the Department of Defense for research purposes. This network linked computers at several government agencies with a few universities. The host names of the computers in this network were registered in a single HOSTS file located on a centrally administered server. Each site that needed to resolve host names downloaded this file. Few computers were being added to this network, so the HOSTS file wasn't updated too often and the different sites only had to download this file periodically to update their own copies. As the number of hosts on the Internet grew, it became more and more difficult to manage all the names through a central HOSTS file. The number of entries was increasing rapidly, changes were frequently being made, and the different Internet sites trying to download a new copy were crushing the HOSTS file server.

DNS was introduced in 1984 as a way to resolve host names without relying on one central HOSTS file. With DNS, the host names reside in a database that can be distributed among multiple servers, decreasing the load on any one server and also allowing more than one point of administration for this naming system. The name system is based on hierarchical names in a tree-type directory structure. DNS enables more types of registration than the simple host-name-to-TCP/IP-address mapping used in HOSTS files and enables room for future defined types.

Because the database is distributed, it can support a much larger database than can be stored in a single HOSTS file. In fact, the database size is virtually unlimited because more servers can be added to handle additional parts of the database.

History of Microsoft DNS

DNS was first introduced in the Microsoft environment as part of the Resource Kit for Windows NT Server 3.51. It wasn't available as part of the Windows NT 3.51 distribution files. With the release of the 4.0 version of Windows NT, DNS is now an integrated service that ships with the Windows NT 4.0 media. Although DNS is not installed by default when you install Windows NT 4.0, you can add DNS as one of the services to be installed, or you can install DNS later. DNS is implemented as a standard Windows NT service and is installed using the Network applet in the Control Panel. Because this book is not about DNS, but IIS, we do not delve any deeper into the Windows NT DNS service.

Microsoft DNS is based on RFCs (Requests for Comments) 974, 1034, and 1035. Another popular implementation of DNS is called BIND (Berkeley Internet Name Domain), developed at UC Berkeley for its version of UNIX. However, BIND isn't totally compliant with the DNS RFCs. Microsoft's DNS does support some features of BIND, but Microsoft DNS is based on the RFCs, not on BIND.

The Structure of DNS

Some host name systems, like NetBIOS names, use a flat database. With a flat database, all names exist at the same level, so there can't be any duplicate names. These names are like Social Security numbers: Every participant in the Social Security program must have a unique number. The Social Security system is a national system that encompasses all workers in the United States, so it must use an identification system to distinguish between all the individuals in the United States.

DNS names are located in a hierarchical path, like a directory structure. You can have a file called TEST.TXT in C:\ and another file called TEST.TXT in C:\ASCII. In a network using DNS, you can have more than one server with the same name, as long as each is located in a different path.

Because of DNS's hierarchical structure, there can be two hosts with the same name, so long as they're not at the same place in the hierarchy. For instance, there's a server named *www* at microsoft.com, and one at compaq.com, but because they're at different places in the domain tree they're still unique. So when

you try to browse to www.microsoft.com, you do not end up at the
www.compaq.com server.

DNS Domains

The Internet Network Information Center (InterNIC) controls the
top-level domains. These have names like com (for businesses), edu
(for educational institutions like universities), gov (for government
organizations), and org (for non-profit organizations). There are also
domains for countries. You can visit the InterNIC Web site at
http://www.internic.com/. Table 1.3 summarizes common Internet
domains.

TABLE 1.3

COMMON INTERNET DOMAINS

Name	Type of Organization
com	Commercial organizations
edu	Educational institutions
org	Non-profit organizations
net	Networks (the backbone of the Internet)
gov	Non-military government organizations
mil	Military government organizations
num	Phone numbers
arpa	Reverse DNS
xx	Two-letter country code

DNS Host Names

To refer to a host in a domain, use a fully qualified domain name
(FQDN), which completely specifies the location of the host. An
FQDN specifies the host name, the domain or subdomain the
host belongs to, and any domains above that in the hierarchy until
the root domain in the organization is specified. On the Internet,
the root domain in the path is something like com, but on a private
network the top-level domains might be named according to some
internal naming convention. The FQDN is read from left to right,
and each host name or domain name is specified by a period. The
syntax of an FQDN follows:

```
host name.subdomain. ... .domain
```

An example of an FQDN is www.microsoft.com, which refers to a server called www located in the subdomain called Microsoft in the domain called com. Referring to a host by its FQDN is similar to referring to a file by its complete directory path. However, a complete file name goes from general to specific, with the file name at the rightmost part of the path. An FQDN goes from specific to general, with the host name at the leftmost part of the name.

Fully qualified domain names are more like addresses. An address starts with the most specific information: Who is to receive the letter. Then the address specifies the house number in which the recipient lives, the street on which the house is located, the city where the street is located, and finally, the most general location, the state where that city is located.

Reverse Lookup

Looking up an IP address to find the host name is exactly the same as the process of looking up an FQDN using a DNS Server (only backwards). An FQDN starts with the specific host and then the domain; an IP address starts with the network ID and then the host ID. Because you want to use DNS to handle the mapping, both must go the same way, so the octets of the IP address are reversed. That is, 148.53.66.7 in the inverse address resolution is 7.66.53.148.

After the IP address is reversed, it is going the same way as an FQDN. Now you can resolve the address using DNS. Just as you need to do with the resolution of a name to an address, you need to create a zone. The name of this zone needs to follow a precise naming convention. Take the network portion of the address—for example, in the Class B address, 148.53.66.7 has a network address of 148.53; or for the Class C address 204.12.25.3, it is 204.12.25. Now, create a zone in which these numbers are reversed and to which you add in-addr.arpa—that is, 53.148.in-addr.arpa or 25.12.204.in-addr.arpa, respectively.

NOTE

Inverse Address Resolution—The Final Octet In actuality, the final octet of the IP address is rarely reversed into an Inarpa address.

Choosing an Appropriate Operating System

There are three operating systems that Internet Information Server 4.0 runs on: Windows NT Server, Windows NT Workstation, and Windows 95.

Windows 95 should not be considered a practical choice for a production environment because it—in and of itself—is not a server operating system. Windows 95 is limited to only one connection at a time and has no built-in method of true, secure, user authentication. Windows 95, however, is an excellent platform for a mobile development workforce to use on laptops while fine-tuning IIS applications that aren't yet live.

Windows NT Workstation 4.0 includes Peer Web Services, a limited version of IIS 2.0. Windows NT Workstation can be used with IIS for a very small intranet implementation. The number of concurrent connections Workstation can support is limited to 10, and that makes the product less than minimal for an Internet Server service. Like Windows 95, it is ideal for a laptop operating system that a mobile development workforce can use for tuning applications.

Windows NT Server 4.0 supports an unlimited number of concurrent connections, up to 256 phone connections (RAS), and is fine-tuned for a production server environment. As such, there is no better operating system on which to run IIS, and this should be the one used in all production Internet environments.

Now that you've reviewed the chapter, let's look at a quick case study to see how you can apply this information to an IIS installation.

> **NOTE**
>
> **IIS and Platforms** It's a little deceptive to say that there are three operating systems that Microsoft Internet Information Server 4.0 runs on. IIS runs as IIS only on Windows NT Server. On Windows 95 and Windows NT Workstation, it runs as Peer Web Services, a scaled down version of IIS 4.0.

CASE STUDY: PLANNING AN IIS 4 IMPLEMENTATION FOR THE LAW OFFICES OF LEGAL BEAGLES LEAGAL SERVICES, INC.

ESSENCE OF THE CASE

Your customer has asked you to provide an intranet server with the following capabilities:

▶ SMTP mail

▶ Web service

▶ Security controls

▶ Workflow applications

SCENARIO

You are the network administrator for Legal Beagles Legal Services, a 1,000-person law firm. Although you have a local area network and some Windows NT File and Print servers, you have not been asked to deploy any IIS components yet. Until now. The senior partner of the firm has been reading technical magazines between flights and has decided it's time for the firm to get a handle on this Internet/intranet thing. Here's what she wants:

continues

continued

◆ The ability to send and receive Internet e-mail.

◆ An intranet server with the capability to post HTML documents containing information ranging from announcements to directions to the company picnic.

◆ The ability to restrict access to one section of the server to senior partners. This will contain case files and customer strategy documents.

◆ The ability to have users fill out expense forms online and have them mailed to the Accounts Payable department for reimbursement.

The big surprise is she doesn't want to spend a lot of money on different applications for each of these tasks. What do you need to plan for?

Analysis

To specify a solution, you have to assume some things are true of the company.

Assumptions

You can assume that the company is in some way connected to the Internet, so it has the connectivity needed to send and receive Internet e-mail. You can also assume it has a TCP/IP infrastructure, so it can get to the server.

Solution

Well, given the title of this book, it's a safe bet that the first thing you need is Microsoft Internet Information Server 4. This is your base platform.

But what pieces/strategies do you need to handle each of these requirements? Let's look at them one at a time.

The Ability to Send and Receive Internet E-mail

The SMTP service of IIS can send and receive Internet e-mail using the Simple Mail Transport Protocol, TCP/IP port 25. You need to make sure that anyone wanting to send Internet e-mail configures her client to point at the IIS server, and you want to be sure the SMTP server sends any mail destined for your company to the existing mail server(s). The mechanics of this process are discussed later in the book.

An Intranet Server with the Ability to Post HTML Documents

Microsoft Internet Information Server 4.0 comes with a WWW service ready to go. You should expect to plan a directory structure for storing things like HTML documents, graphics, and any other files you think will be on the server. If the senior partner plans on making a monthly pep talk via the intranet server, you might want a Speeches or WAVs subdirectory specifically to store them in. It is critical that you use conventions for the creation and storage of these files on the server. Otherwise, you will find yourself relying on File Finder every time someone asks you to change something.

The Ability to Restrict Access to One Section of the Server to Senior Partners

Put on your Windows NT Administrator hat. This is a matter of correctly configuring the users and

CASE STUDY: PLANNING AN IIS 4 IMPLEMENTATION FOR THE LAW OFFICES OF LEGAL BEAGLES LEAGAL SERVICES, INC.

groups in conjunction with NT NTFS permissions to ensure only the appropriate people have access to the site. If the information is extremely sensitive, you might consider setting up SSL on the server so the traffic is encrypted across the network.

The Ability to Have Users Fill Out Expense Forms Online

This is a little more complex than the other requirements because it involves using multiple Microsoft Internet Information Server 4.0 components to make it work. First, you need the WWW service to make the application available to the end user.

When that's finished, you need to develop the application. This is a great use for Active Server Pages and the Microsoft Script Debugger. To get the information to the Accounts Payable department, you can leverage the SMTP service and send the information in an e-mail message.

Other things you should probably think about are the security requirements for the rest of the site, how you want to do name resolutions, which is dependent on your DNS infrastructure, and, of course, what operating system to use. In this case, given the number of users, Windows NT Server 4.0 is really the only choice.

CHAPTER SUMMARY

Let's recap what we've discussed in this chapter. The first thing to keep in mind while preparing for this section of the exam is the different components of the Microsoft Internet Information Server 4.0. You should remember the different components of IIS 4.0 and their functions:

◆ **Microsoft Management Console (MMC).** The MMC provides the next-generation management framework for managing Windows NT servers and services. Through the use of management applications known as *snap-ins,* the MMC provides a single interface for IIS 4.0 today.

◆ **WWW.** The WWW (World Wide Web) service in IIS 4.0 is the service that allows you to include HTML (Hypertext Markup Language) documents on your site.

◆ **FTP.** The File Transfer Protocol (FTP) service provides clients attaching to your server the ability to transmit files to and from the server.

KEY TERMS

Before taking the Microsoft Internet Information Server 4.0 exam, make sure you are familiar with the following terms and their meanings:

• Active Server Pages (ASP)
• ActiveX Data Objects (ADO)
• Anonymous login
• Certificate Server
• Domain Name System (DNS)
• File Transfer Protocol (FTP)
• HOSTS file

continues

CHAPTER SUMMARY (continued)

KEY TERMS

- HyperText Markup Language (HTML)
- HyperText Transfer Protocol (HTTP)—especially HTTP 1.1
- Index Server
- Internet Explorer
- Internet service provider (ISP)
- Microsoft Management Console
- Microsoft Transaction Server (MTS)
- Network News Transfer Protocol (NNTP)
- Newsfeed
- Open Database Connectivity (ODBC)
- Persistent connections
- Remote Data Services (RDS)
- Secure Sockets Layer (SSL)
- Simple Mail Transfer Protocol (SMTP)
- TCP/IP
- World Wide Web (WWW)

◆ **Microsoft Transaction Server.** Microsoft Transaction Server (MTS) is a transaction processing system for developing and managing server applications.

◆ **Microsoft SMTP Service.** Microsoft SMTP Service uses the Simple Mail Transfer Protocol (SMTP) to send and receive e-mail.

◆ **Microsoft NNTP Service.** The Microsoft NNTP Service supports the Network News Transport Protocol and enables clients to access newsgroups.

◆ **Microsoft Index Server.** Microsoft Index Server indexes the full text and properties of documents stored on an Internet or intranet Web site.

◆ **Microsoft Certificate Server.** Microsoft Certificate Server enables you to increase the security of your site by issuing certificates (digital identifiers) that use public-key encryption. Certificates enable you to verify that you have secure communication across the network, whether that network is an intranet or the Internet.

◆ **Site Server Express.** The Site Server Express component of IIS 4.0 brings site management to IIS. Whereas earlier versions of IIS allowed you to log usage, Site Server Express provides the ability to analyze that usage.

◆ **Active Server Pages and Microsoft Script Debugger.** Active Server Pages (ASP) can be used to create dynamic HTML pages or build powerful Web applications. Microsoft Script Debugger is exactly what it sounds like—a tool that allows you to test ASP scripts.

◆ **Internet Connection Services for Remote Access Services.** Microsoft Internet Connection Services for Remote Access Services provides enhanced Internet connection capabilities, including a dial-up service and Virtual Private Networking (VPN) capabilities.

CHAPTER SUMMARY

◆ **Microsoft Message Queue.** Microsoft Message Queue Server (MSMQ) allows applications to communicate with other applications by providing a reliable mechanism for sending and receiving messages.

◆ **Microsoft Data Access Components.** Microsoft Data Access Components are a bundle of components that allow easier access to a variety of data types. Microsoft Data Access Components consist of ActiveX Data Objects (ADO) and Remote Data Service (RDS), the Microsoft OLE DB Provider for ODBC, and Open Database Connectivity (ODBC).

◆ **Additional Support for Internet Standards.** In addition to new services and components, IIS 4.0 also adds support for a number of Internet standards, including the following:

  • HTTP 1.1 support

  • RFC 1867 support

  • HTTP redirects

After you are familiar with the components of IIS, you need to be able to plan for your security. You should be familiar with Microsoft's Internet Security Framework, as well as the general issues that every IIS administrator needs to consider as he plans to deploy an IIS server into a production environment. These issues include the following:

◆ **Controlling anonymous access.** The WWW and FTP services included with IIS 4 both allow for different levels of anonymous access. Each level has different ramifications from a security password, and there are justifications and pitfalls for the use of each.

◆ **Controlling access to known users and groups.** IIS provides the ability to use Windows NT security to control access to resources. By using Windows NT users and/or groups in conjunction with NTFS file and directory security, it is possible to control access to virtually any level of granularity.

continues

◆ **Controlling access by host or network.** IIS also provides the ability to use IP addresses to control access, whether by specific host address or by using subnetting to either permit or deny access to a certain segment of contiguous IP addresses.

◆ **Configuring SSL to provide encryption and authentication schemes.** Secure Socket Layer can be used in conjunction with certificates to provide secure, encrypted access to an IIS server. Due to the need to encrypt the entire data stream, this does add significant processing overhead, but it provides extremely robust security for critical data.

◆ **Identifying the appropriate balance between security requirements and performance requirements.** The more secure a site is, the less usable it is from a user's perspective, and vice versa. The user's dream environment is one without restrictions: no passwords, encryption overhead, or access control. The security administrator's dream configuration is to take the hard drives and lock the data in a safe, out of harm's way. As an IIS administrator, a large part of your job is to find a balance between the two extremes.

After you have determined how much security you need, it's time to determine how to resolve names in your environment. It is a rare user that can remember that, for example, Macmillan's Web site can be reached by pointing his Web browser at the IP address 204.95.236.226. Nor will he generally remember that the IP address for your IIS server is something equally cryptic. Name resolution is (pardon the pun), the name of the game. In this chapter, we discussed the two methods available to you: using a HOSTS file on each PC or using DNS (Domain Name System.) Given the severe limitations of the HOSTS file, DNS is almost always the answer for any environment over 10 users. In the chapter, we also discussed a bit about where DNS came from and what it can do for your environment.

CHAPTER SUMMARY

Finally, you need to remember how to go about selecting the correct operating system for your Web server. Microsoft Internet Information Server 4.0 runs in its native form on Windows NT Server 4.0 or as a less comprehensive version known as Peer Web Services on Windows NT Workstation 4.0 or Windows 95/98. As a general rule, Windows NT Server 4.0 is the best solution, but you should be familiar with the pros and cons of each solution.

APPLY YOUR KNOWLEDGE

Exercises

NOTE

But We Haven't Installed IIS Yet
That is absolutely correct. Due to the organization of the Microsoft objectives for this exam, some exercises are included that cannot be completed without completing Chapter 2, "Installation and Configuration" first. To be sure you can complete all the exercises, go to Chapter 2, install IIS, and return to complete the exercises as needed.

1.1 Denying Access to a Select Group of Hosts or Networks

To deny access to only a few networks or hosts, do the following.

Estimated time: 15–30 minutes

1. Start Internet Service Manager, select the Web site (or file or directory), and open the properties.

2. Choose either Directory Security or File Security, based on which you want to assign access for.

3. Click Edit under TCP/IP and Domain Name Restrictions.

4. Select Granted Access from the IP Address and Domain Name Restrictions dialog box.

5. Click Add.

6. Select either Single Computer, Group of Computers, or Domain Name from the Deny Access On dialog box.

7. Type in the IP address of those to whom you're denying access, or click the DNS Lookup button to browse for them by name.

8. Click OK twice.

1.2 Find the Local Host Name and Test It

The following exercise steps show you how to find the local host name and verify that you can ping it.

Estimated time: 10 minutes

1. From the Start menu, choose Programs, MS-DOS prompt.

2. Type HOSTNAME to see the local host's name.

3. Type PING {HOSTNAME}. (The {HOSTNAME} is the value returned in step 2).

1.3 Edit the HOSTS File

The following exercise steps show you how to find and edit the HOSTS file on a Windows NT Server machine.

Estimated time: 15 minutes

1. From the Start menu, choose Programs, MS-DOS prompt.

2. Change the directory to the appropriate location by typing the following:

   `cd\systemroot\System32\Drivers\etc`

   (systemroot is your Windows NT directory.)

3. Type PING ME and notice the error that comes back because the host isn't found.

APPLY YOUR KNOWLEDGE

4. Type EDIT HOSTS. The last line of the file should read

```
127.0.0.1 localhost
```

5. Move one space to the right of the last character and enter

```
ME
```

The line now reads

```
127.0.0.1 localhost ME
```

6. Exit the editor and save the changes.

7. Type PING ME and notice the successful results.

1.4 Viewing Internet Explorer Certificates

To view the certificates presently in Internet Explorer 4.0, do the following:

Estimated time: 10 minutes

1. In Internet Explorer, select Internet Options from the View menu.

2. Select the Content tab and click Personal.

3. If any certificates are there, they are displayed in the list box. You can then select one and click the button marked View Certificates.

4. Select each Field to view the details in the Details box.

1.5 Turning on Windows NT Challenge/Response

To turn on the Windows NT Challenge/Response authentication, do the following

Estimated time: 10 minutes

1. Choose a Web site in Internet Service Manager and choose the property sheet.

2. Click Edit under Anonymous Access and Authentication Control.

3. Choose Windows NT Challenge/Response from the Authentication Methods dialog box.

1.6 Reviewing the Different Components of Microsoft Internet Information Server 4

To review each of the components of Microsoft Internet Information Server 4, do the following:

Estimated time: 30 minutes

1. Open Internet Service Manager.

2. Select the Default Web Site, right-click and select properties. Review the different configuration tabs to understand the capabilities and configuration options of the Web Service. Click OK when you are done.

3. Select the Default FTP Site, right-click and select properties. Review the different configuration tabs to understand the capabilities and configuration options of the FTP Service. Click OK when you are done.

APPLY YOUR KNOWLEDGE

4. Select the Default SMTP Site, right-click and select properties. Review the different configuration tabs to understand the capabilities and configuration options of the SMTP Service. Click OK when you are done.

5. Select the Default NNTP Site, right-click and select properties. Review the different configuration tabs to understand the capabilities and configuration options of the NNTP Service. Click OK when you are done.

6. Click on the Key Manager icon (Fist holding a key) to open the Key Manager. This application allows you to configure the Microsoft Certificate Server. Click OK when you are done reviewing the application.

7. Open the Transaction Server Explorer. Under the Computers folder, right-click on My Computer and select properties. Review the different tabs to understand the capabilities and configuration options of the Microsoft Transaction Server. Click OK when you are done.

8. Open Index Server Manager. Review the different settings to understand the capabilities and configuration options of the Microsoft Index Server. Close the application when you are done.

1.7   Setting NTFS Permissions

In order to control access to IIS-based resources by users and groups, you need to be able to set NTFS permissions. This exercise walks you through the process. (Note: You need an NTFS volume to complete this exercise.)

Estimated time: 10 minutes

1. Open Windows NT Explorer.

2. Select a directory on your NTFS volume. Right-click and select Properties.

3. Go to the Security tab and select Permissions.

4. Click on Add to add a user or group to access that resource. This will Open the Add Users and Groups dialog box.

5. Select the group you want to add, and select the access to be granted in the Type of Access pull-down box. If you want to add a single user, you will need to click on the Show Users button.

6. Click OK and that user/group will be added with the permission specified.

7. Close Windows NT Explorer.

1.8   Verifying the Server Role Before Installing Microsoft Internet Information Server 4

As discussed in the chapter, it is important from a security perspective to ensure that Microsoft Internet Information Server 4 is not installed on a domain controller. This exercise will guide you through checking the server's role in the domain.

Estimated time: 10 minutes

1. Open Server Administrator from the Administrative Tools menu.

2. In the Computer column, locate the computer you are checking. It should be listed as "Windows NT Workstation or Server." This indicates that it is a member server, and not a domain controller. A Primary Domain Controller will be listed as "Windows NT 4.0

APPLY YOUR KNOWLEDGE

Primary" and a Backup Domain Controller will be listed as "Windows NT Backup."

3. Continue checking servers as needed. Close the application. If your server did not show up in Server Manager, you either had the wrong domain, or the server is configured as a stand-alone server and as such is not a member of a domain.

1.9   Choosing an Operating System

This exercise will assist you in determining the operating system onto which you should load Microsoft Internet Information Server 4.

Estimated time: 10 minutes

1. Analyze the following requirements:

   • Use of the site.

   • Number of concurrent users to be accessing the site.

   • Security level necessary for the site.

2. If the use of the site is for development only, use Windows 95/98, or Windows NT Workstation. You will not need the additional security or over-head of the Windows NT Server for this effort.

   If the use of the server is as an Intranet or Internet Server, see task 3.

3. If the number of concurrent users will exceed 10, you need to use Windows NT Server.

4. If you need to control access by user/group, you will need Windows NT Workstation or Server to support the use of NTFS. If you need any sort of site security, you should run Windows NT Server.

Review Questions

1. You have just installed IIS for Flying High Airlines. The security administrator wants to know if IIS has done anything to compromise the security of the system, like adding any users. You need to tell him about the user IIS adds to the system. What is the name of the user account set up by default for the anonymous account to use?

2. You are a network consultant working for the Little Guy bakery. You know DNS can be used for dynamic resolution of host names to IP addresses, but this bakery only has 10 computers and the owner doesn't want to have to maintain an additional server for just 10 PCs. You decide to use the static address resolution capabilities of the HOSTS file. What is the maximum length of an entry in the HOSTS file?

3. You are a Web consultant working with John Donson Sports Cars, Inc. The dealership has an IIS-based intranet, but is presently only running the Web and FTP services. The owner would like to give his salesmen the ability to chat about different cars on the lot, share sales tips, and so on. What service do you need to install?

4. You are the Web administrator for the Really Green Nurseries chain. You recently set up an intranet Web site to sell trees over the Internet, a radical idea for the nursery industry. You need to check and see if the site is successful or not.

APPLY YOUR KNOWLEDGE

How can you best do that using the components of IIS?

Exam Questions

1. You are the Web administrator at Little Faith Enterprises, and you are considering deploying Microsoft Internet Information Server 4.0. You know that Internet Information Server provides you with the ability to share information with any type of computer that can use the TCP/IP protocol, but you need to know what services you can count on IIS providing.

   Which of the following services are provided as part of IIS?

   A. FTP

   B. SNMP

   C. TCP/IP

   D. WWW

2. You are the IIS administrator for the Garbonzo Beanery, an upscale vegetarian eatery. You need to create a Web site on your IIS server to which the public is not allowed access. Instead, only the internal hosts that fall within a specified IP address range can get to it. You set the IP and Domain Name Restriction specifications to an IP address of 192.2.2.0 and the subnet mask to 255.255.255.240.

   Which host addresses can access the site?

   A. 192.2.2.0 through 192.2.2.3.

   B. 192.2.2.0 through 192.2.2.7.

   C. 192.2.2.0 through 192.2.2.15.

   D. 192.2.2.0 through 192.2.2.31.

   E. 192.2.2.0 through 192.2.2.61.

3. You are the network administrator for Little Faith Enterprises, and you need to be able to dynamically resolve host names to IP addresses because your users keep forgetting all those addresses and can't navigate around your internal Web servers.

   Which service should you install?

   A. DNS

   B. DHCP

   C. WINS

   D. BDC

4. You are the lead systems programmer for Hot Dogs Inc., a pet store chain. You are in the process of writing a Web commerce application for the company's IIS-based Internet server and it is absolutely critical that you maintain accurate status of all the sales being processed by the site.

   What IIS component should you install?

   A. Install the Microsoft Script Debugger.

   B. Install Microsoft Transaction Server.

   C. Enable logging and use the Report Writer to analyze the number of sales transactions.

   D. Install the SMTP Service and have the application send an e-mail every time a sale is processed successfully.

APPLY YOUR KNOWLEDGE

5. Which of the following is not part of a fully qualified domain name? (Choose all options that apply.)

   A. Type of organization

   B. Host name

   C. Company name

   D. CPU type

6. You are a consultant trying to sell the Hot Foot Shoe Company a DNS server to provide name resolution for its internal IIS intranet. To sell the MIS Director, you need to pitch the benefits of installing DNS.

   What are the benefits of DNS? (Select all options that apply.)

   A. It allows a distributed database that can be administered by a number of administrators.

   B. It allows host names that specify where a host is located.

   C. It allows WINS clients to register with the WINS server.

   D. It allows queries to other servers to resolve host names.

7. You are the network administrator for Good Tunes Music Inc. You are about to deploy your first Microsoft-based DNS server into an environment with a variety of DNS servers running a variety of versions and platforms. You need to be sure it will interoperate with the existing infrastructure.

   With what non-Microsoft DNS platforms is Microsoft DNS compatible?

   A. Only UNIX DNS servers that are based on BIND

   B. Only UNIX DNS servers that are based on the DNS RFCs

   C. UNIX DNS servers that are either BIND-based or RFC-based

   D. Only other Microsoft DNS servers

8. In the DNS name `www.microsoft.com`, what does Microsoft represent?

   A. The last name of the host

   B. The domain in which the host is located

   C. The IP address of the building in which the host is located

   D. The directory in which the host name file is located

9. Evan wants to install a service or server on his IIS system that will enable users to upload files to his site. Which server/service should he consider?

   A. WWW

   B. FTP

   C. Microsoft Transaction Server

   D. SMTP

   E. NNTP

10. Kristin wants to install a service or server on her IIS system that will enable users to upload files to newsgroups. Which server/service should she consider?

    A. WWW

    B. FTP

APPLY YOUR KNOWLEDGE

C. Microsoft Transaction Server

D. SMTP

E. NNTP

11. Spencer wants to install a service or server on his IIS system that will enable users to send e-mail to the Internet. Which server/service should he consider?

    A. WWW

    B. FTP

    C. Microsoft Transaction Server

    D. SMTP

    E. NNTP

12. Microsoft NNTP supports which of the following file types?

    A. MIME

    B. UUENCODE

    C. HTML

    D. GIF

    E. PDF

13. You are a consultant for the Really Small Realtors realty office. There are only five employees, but they would like to have an intranet server with house listings on it so clients can view them. They are a small company and don't anticipate growing any time soon. They would like to do this as cheaply as possible.

You recommend Microsoft Internet Information Server 4.0 running on which of the following operating systems?

A. Windows NT Workstation

B. Windows NT Server

C. Windows 98

D. Windows NT Server, Enterprise Edition

Answers to Review Questions

1. IUSR_computername is the name of the anonymous account automatically created during the installation of IIS. See "Controlling Anonymous Access."

2. Each line in the HOSTS file is limited to 255 characters in length. See "Understanding the HOSTS File."

3. The easiest way to enable the sales people to share information as described would be to install and configure the NNTP Service. See "Choosing Appropriate Technologies."

4. To see how much activity a site is getting, you need to do two things. First, you need to enable logging on the site. Then, using the Usage Import and Report Writer components of IIS, you can generate a variety of reports on how much activity the site is generating. See "Choosing Appropriate Technologies."

APPLY YOUR KNOWLEDGE

Answers to Exam Questions

1. **A, D.** IIS includes FTP and WWW servers. B is incorrect; the SNMP service is included as part of Windows NT and, although necessary for gathering TCP/IP statistics with Performance Monitor, is not correct. C is also incorrect; TCP/IP is the protocol you need to communicate with an IIS server, but it is also included with Windows NT. See "Choosing Appropriate Technologies."

2. **C.** Setting an IP address of 192.2.2.0 and subnet mask to 255.255.255.240 makes the valid host range 192.2.2.0 through 192.2.2.15. See "Controlling Access by Host or Network."

3. **A.** The DNS server resolves host names to IP addresses. B, C, and D are incorrect for the following reasons. DHCP (Dynamic Host Control Protocol) is used to dynamically assign IP addresses. WINS (Windows Internet Naming Service,) is a system that used to resolve the IP address of a Windows NT or Windows 9X computer. Although similar in function to DNS, this is used for proprietary name resolution in Microsoft networking. A BDC (Backup Domain Controller) is used for authentication, not name resolution. See "Understanding DNS."

4. **B.** Microsoft Transaction Server is used to ensure transactional integrity and can be used to keep track of any sales transactions on the system. A is incorrect because, although the Microsoft Script Debugger might be useful for writing the application, it cannot be used to track transactions. Checking the logs only shows you the number of transactions, it does not give you a real-time status, so C is incorrect. D is incorrect because sending an e-mail on completions also

eliminates the real time status you need. See "Choosing Appropriate Technologies."

5. **D.** CPU type is not a component of an FQDN. See "Understanding DNS."

6. **A, B, D.** Although DNS on a Windows NT server can be configured to query the WINS server for a name resolution, WINS clients do not register themselves directly with the DNS server. C is incorrect because WINS clients cannot register with a DNS server, only with a WINS server. See "Understanding DNS."

7. **C.** Windows NT DNS is based on the RFCs for DNS, but it is designed to be compatible with DNS servers based on BIND as well. See "Understanding DNS."

8. **B.** The path specifies a host named www in a domain Microsoft. The domain microsoft is located in the top-level domain com. See "Understanding DNS."

9. **B.** FTP is used to enable clients to upload and download files. See "Choosing Appropriate Technologies."

10. **E.** NNTP is used to communicate with newsgroups. See "Choosing Appropriate Technologies."

11. **D.** SMTP is used to send e-mail to the Internet. The WWW service is used to serve Web pages. See "Choosing Appropriate Technologies."

12. **A, C, D.** NNTP accepts HTML, MIME, JPEG, and GIF. B is incorrect; UUENCODE is a method for encoding binary files into ASCII text and then decoding them back into a binary. This is often used by SMTP servers to transfer file attachments. See "Microsoft NNTP Service."

APPLY YOUR KNOWLEDGE

13. **A.** Microsoft Internet Information Server 4.0 on Windows NT Workstation has the same functionality as a Windows NT Server-based implementation, but is limited to 10 connections. It is a less expensive solution than Windows NT Server. B is incorrect; Windows NT Server would work but is more expensive. C is also incorrect; Windows 98 is a client operating system and is not suited for use as a production server. D is also incorrect because the Enterprise version of Windows NT is not correct for the same reason Windows NT Server wasn't…it is more expensive than Windows NT Workstation. See "Choosing an Appropriate Operating System."

Suggested Readings and Resources

1. Comer, Douglas. *Internetworking With TCP/IP: Principles, Protocols, and Architecture, Third Edition.* Prentice Hall: 1998.

2. Heywood, Drew. *Networking With Microsoft TCP/IP, Third Edition.* New Riders Publishing: 1998.

3. *Inside Windows NT Server 4, Certified Administrator's Resource Edition.* New Riders Publishing: 1997.

4. Howell, Nelson and Forta, Ben. *Using Microsoft Internet Information Server 4 (Special Edition Using...),* Que: 1997.

5. Scrimger, Rob and Adam, Kelli. *MCSE Training Guide: TCP/IP.* New Riders Publishing: 1998.

6. Siyan, Karanjit S. *Windows NT TCP/IP.* New Riders Professional Library: 1998.

7. Tulloch, Mitch. *Administering Internet Information Server 4 (Windows NT Technical Expert).* Computing McGraw-Hill: 1998.

In the previous chapter, we discussed how to plan for a successful Microsoft Internet Information Server 4.0 implementation. The next step to successfully deploy IIS 4.0 is to actually install IIS. This chapter covers the Installation and Configuration objectives for the exam. One of the keys to how well your IIS server performs after it has been put into production is how it was installed and configured before it was deployed. In this chapter, we discuss the installation and configuration options for the various components of IIS 4.0.

Microsoft defines the Installation and Configuration objectives as:

Install IIS. Tasks include the following:

- **Configuring a Microsoft Windows NT Server 4.0 computer for the installation of IIS**

- **Identifying differences to a Windows NT Server 4.0 computer made by the installation of IIS**

▶ Installing IIS is a straightforward process, because Microsoft has done such a good job standardizing the installation procedure for any of its applications. The key to an IIS installation, after the planning is complete, is making sure your Windows NT 4.0 computer is prepared properly, and you should also understand what the installation changes.

Configure IIS to support the FTP service. Tasks include the following:

- **Setting bandwidth and user connections**
- **Setting user logon requirements and authentication requirements**
- **Modifying port settings**
- **Setting directory listing style**
- **Configuring virtual directories and servers**

CHAPTER 2

Installation and Configuration

▶ One of the first applications for the TCP/IP protocol, FTP is still used heavily out on the Internet. This objective expects you to understand how to set up the FTP service component of IIS 4.0.

Configure IIS to support the WWW service. Tasks include the following:

- **Setting bandwidth and user connections**

- **Setting user logon requirements and authentication requirements**

- **Modifying port settings**

- **Setting default pages**

- **Setting HTTP 1.1 host header names to host multiple Web sites**

- **Enabling HTTP Keep-Alives**

▶ A newcomer to the TCP/IP protocol, the WWW is the most prevalent application on the Internet, with the possible exception of e-mail. This objective expects you to understand how to set up the WWW service component of IIS 4.0.

Configure and save consoles by using Microsoft Management Console.

▶ As we discussed in Chapter 1, "Planning," the Microsoft Management Console (MMC) is the single point of administration for the next generations of Microsoft applications. To understand IIS administration, you need to know how to use the MMC. From a testing perspective, this is particularly useful knowledge for the new simulation questions showing up on more and more Microsoft certification tests.

Choose the appropriate administration method.

▶ There are different ways you can administer an IIS server. This objective requires you to understand the alternatives.

Install and configure Certificate Server.

▶ To implement IIS 4.0, you need to be familiar with the installation and configuration of all the components. Microsoft Certificate Server enables you to increase the security of your site by issuing certificates (digital identifiers) that use public-key encryption. This objective requires you to understand the installation and configuration of Certificate Server.

Install and configure Microsoft SMTP Service.

▶ Microsoft SMTP Service uses the Simple Mail Transfer Protocol (SMTP) to send and receive e-mail using TCP port 25 for operations. This objective requires you to understand the installation and configuration of the Microsoft SMTP (Simple Mail Transport Protocol) Service.

Install and configure Microsoft NNTP Service.

▶ The Microsoft NNTP Service supports the Network News Transport Protocol and enables clients to access newsgroups. This objective requires you to understand the installation and configuration of the Microsoft NNTP Service.

Customize the installation of Microsoft Site Server Express Content Analyzer.

▶ The Site Server Express Content Analyzer component of IIS 4.0 brings site management to IIS. Where earlier versions of IIS allowed you to log usage, Site Server Express provides the ability to analyze that usage. This objective requires you to understand the installation and configuration of the Microsoft Site Server Express Content Analyzer.

Customize the installation of Microsoft Site Server Express Usage Import and Report Writer.

▶ Microsoft Site Server Express Usage Import and Report Writer allows you to import and aggregate log files from multiple servers to a single server. This objective requires you to understand the installation and configuration of the Microsoft Site Server Express Usage Import and Report Writer.

As you read through this chapter, you should concentrate on the following key concepts:

▶ Understand the setup and use of the Microsoft Management Console (MMC). This is key not only to managing the IIS application, but also to future Microsoft technologies, including the yet to be released Windows 2000 product line.

▶ Be familiar with the subcomponents and functionality of each of the IIS components. If asked, "What service does such and such?", you should be able to identify the component and, if necessary, the subcomponent.

▶ Be familiar with the ports used by each of the applications. Also, be aware of the possible consequences of using a non-standard port for any of these applications.

▶ Pay attention to the methods for creating multiple sites using the same IIS server. This includes using multiple IP addresses or just a single IP address in conjunction with HTTP 1.1 Host Headers.

▶ IIS can be configured to limit bandwidth used, known as *bandwidth throttling*. Pay attention to where and how that is accomplished.

▶ Be familiar with the use of HTTP Keep-Alives and the potential consequences of enabling or disabling them.

▶ Know what the *metabase* is and what information is stored in it.

INTRODUCTION

Microsoft makes it easy to install Internet Information Server (IIS) 4.0 under Windows NT Server 4.0. During installation, setup wizards walk you through the process. Although you don't need to know a whole lot about IIS before jumping into the IIS setup, you should know the requirements of IIS and how your Windows NT Server 4.0 system should be set up. This chapter covers these points.

After you install IIS, you need to know how to configure its World Wide Web and FTP services, along with setting up Microsoft Management Console (MMC) consoles and how to choose the appropriate administration method. You learn how in this chapter. The following topics are covered:

◆ Installing IIS

◆ Configuring IIS to support the FTP service

◆ Configuring IIS to support the WWW service

◆ Configuring and saving consoles by using Microsoft Management Console

◆ Verifying server settings by accessing the metabase

◆ Choosing the appropriate administration method

◆ Customizing the Installation of Microsoft Site Server Express Analysis Content Analyzer

◆ Customizing the Installation of Microsoft Site Server Analysis Report Writer and Usage Import

INSTALLING IIS

▶ Install IIS.

Microsoft Internet Information Server (IIS) 4.0 is the newest version of the Internet and Web server designed to run under Windows NT Server 4.0. Setting up and configuring IIS is the first step in setting up an Internet or intranet site.

IIS 4.0 includes the following features:

- ◆ Authentication Server
- ◆ SMTP Mail Server
- ◆ Microsoft Management Console
- ◆ NNTP News Server
- ◆ Script Debugger
- ◆ Site Analyst
- ◆ Transaction Server
- ◆ Usage Analyst
- ◆ Web Publishing Wizard
- ◆ Windows Scripting Host
- ◆ FrontPage Server Administrator

After you install IIS 4.0, you can add Hypertext Markup Language (HTML) files to your server for users to connect to and view.

Configuring a Microsoft Windows NT Server 4.0 Computer for the Installation of IIS

IIS 4.0 is available only as part of the Windows NT 4.0 Option Pack. Currently, IIS 4.0 is available on CD-ROM from Microsoft or as a large download from Microsoft's Web site. You can download it as part of the Windows NT 4.0 Option Pack from Microsoft at the following address:

```
http://www.microsoft.com/ntserver/nts/downloads/
➥recommended/NT4OptPk/default.asp
```

You also can order an Option Pack CD-ROM from Microsoft from the same site. With this download, you're provided with IIS 4.0, Microsoft Site Server Express 2.0, Transaction Server 2.0, Microsoft Message Queue Server 1.0, Certificate Server 1.0, Index Server Express, Internet Explorer 4.0, remote-access services for virtual networking, and Windows NT Service Pack 3.

Before you set up IIS 4.0, your system must meet or exceed the hardware requirements summarized in Tables 2.1 and 2.2. Table 2.1 shows requirements for a system running an Intel x86 processor. Table 2.2 lists requirements for a system running a DEC Alpha processor.

> **NOTE**
>
> **IIS Versions**   The version of IIS provided with Windows NT 4.0 Server is IIS 2.0. This book covers how to install IIS 4.0.

TABLE 2.1

IIS 4.0 HARDWARE REQUIREMENTS FOR AN INTEL SYSTEM

Hardware Device	Requirements
CPU	Minimum of a 66MHz 486DX processor. For better performance, you need a Pentium 133-or-higher processor.
Hard disk space	Minimum of 30MB, but it is recommended you have at least 120MB. This does not include storage needed for files you plan to distribute via IIS.
Memory	Minimum of 32MB. For Web sites on which you will store multimedia files or expect a great deal of traffic, 48MB is the recommended minimum.
Monitor	Super VGA monitor with 800×600 resolution.

TABLE 2.2

IIS 4.0 HARDWARE REQUIREMENTS FOR AN ALPHA SYSTEM

Hardware Device	Requirements
CPU	Minimum of 150MHz processor.
Hard disk space	Minimum of 120MB, but you should allocate up to 200MB for best performance.
Memory	Minimum of 48MB. For better performance, have at least 64MB.
Monitor	Super VGA monitor with 800×600 resolution.

Before you install IIS 4.0, remove any installations of a previous version of IIS. You also should disable other versions of FTP, Gopher, or World Wide Web services you have installed under Windows NT Server 4.0. This includes the Windows Academic Center (EMWAC) service included with the Windows NT Resource Kit.

> **NOTE**
>
> **Hard Disk Space with Full Install** If you install all the components that ship with IIS 4.0, you need over 355MB of hard disk space.

You also should have the following software installed:

◆ Windows NT Server 4.0

◆ Service Pack 3 (or later) for Windows NT Server 4.0

◆ Internet Explorer 4.01 or later

You also must be logged on to the Windows NT Server computer with Administrator privileges.

For systems in which file-level security is needed, configure Windows NT Server with the NT File System (NTFS). NTFS enables you to limit access to files and directories. Systems running FAT do not allow you to limit access at the file level, only the directory level. You cannot install the SMTP Service without an NTFS partition.

Another pre-installation consideration is the need to have TCP/IP (Transmission Control Protocol/Internet Protocol) on your Windows NT 4.0 computer. TCP/IP is used to provide Internet connectivity to retrieve data from the Internet.

Finally, you should never use DHCP (Dynamic Host Configuration Protocol) to assign addresses for Web servers. DHCP automatically assigns IP (Internet Protocol) addresses to computers configured to use DHCP; this is a terrific benefit for administration or if you have a limited number of addresses. Due to the static nature of a Web server, DHCP is not recommended for assigning server addresses. Imagine trying to call your mother if her telephone number were randomly assigned every morning from a pool of a hundred or so numbers. Finding the address of your Web server when its address is assigned in the same manner is just as difficult.

For systems connecting to the Internet, you need to get at least one registered TCP/IP address from the ARIN (The American Registry of Internet Numbers) or from an Internet Service Provider (ISP). That will make your server addressable from the Internet at large.

> **N O T E**
>
> **More DHCP Information**   You do have the ability to reserve addresses for specific machines using DHCP, but that would defeat the whole ease of administration we just discussed.

SECURING YOUR IIS INSTALLATION

To help secure your IIS installation, you should perform the following tasks in addition to the tasks described previously:

· Turn on auditing (file and directory auditing requires the NTFS file system).

- Limit the Guest account and other accounts to specific directories on the server.

- Limit who has membership to the Administrators group.

- Start only those services and protocols required by your system.

- Use complex password schemes. Actually, using any password scheme is a step in the right direction. Make it as complex as your users will tolerate.

- Review network share permissions.

- Disable NetBIOS over TCP/IP for additional security.

Installing IIS 4.0

After you get Windows NT Server 4.0 set up to receive IIS 4.0, you're ready to start the IIS 4.0 setup program. Make sure you are connected to the Internet or to your intranet before installing IIS.

To start IIS 4.0 setup, insert the Option Pack CD-ROM and locate the Setup icon in Internet Explorer. Double-click the Setup icon. If you downloaded IIS 4.0 from the Internet, you can double-click the setup file.

Next, perform the following steps:

NOTE

Finish Install After Starting If you decide you don't want to install IIS 4.0 and you've already started the IIS 4.0 setup program, don't cancel it. This leaves files on your system that the uninstall program cannot remove. Finish the entire installation process and then uninstall IIS 4.0 if you don't want it on your system.

STEP BY STEP

2.1 Installing Microsoft Internet Information Server 4.0

1. Click Next on the Welcome to the Windows NT 4.0 Option dialog box. The End User License Agreement screen appears.

2. Click Accept.

3. Click Custom. A dialog box with components appears.

continues

continued

> **N O T E**
>
> **IE 4.0 with IIS 4.0** IIS 4.0 relies on Internet Explorer 4.0 for many of its management and configuration tasks. If you do not already have IE 4.0 installed, you are prompted to install it when you start the IIS 4.0 setup. Be sure to click Yes if prompted to install IE 4.01. Windows NT needs to shut down and restart before continuing with the IIS installation.

You also can click Minimum or Typical, but these steps assume you want to have control over the components that are installed.

4. Click the component you want to install. If you want to change the specific options (called subcomponents) that install with the components, click the Show Subcomponents button. This displays a dialog box with the specific options that fall under a component heading. Selected components and subcomponents have check marks next to them.

Specific components and their subcomponents are listed in Table 2.3.

TABLE 2.3

IIS 4.0 SETUP OPTIONS

Component	Subcomponent	Description
Certificate Server	Certificate Server Certificate Authority	Enables you to create certificate authority on the IIS server to issue digital certificates to users accessing your Web.
	Certificate Server Documentation	Documents to help you install and configure Certificate Authorities.
	Certificate Server Web Client	Enables you to post Web pages on your server to submit requests and retrieve certificates from a certificate authority.
FrontPage 98 Server Extensions	FrontPage Server Extensions Files	Enables you to author Web pages and administer Web sites using Microsoft FrontPage and Visual InterDev.
Visual InterDev RAD	Visual InterDev RAD Remote Deployment Support	Enables you to deploy applications remotely on the Web server.
Internet Information Server (IIS)	Common Program Files	Files used by several IIS components.
	Documentation	Product documentation for IIS.
Internet Information	File Transfer	Provides FTP support to set up

Component	Subcomponent	Description
Files	Protocol (FTP) Server	an FTP site to allow users to upload and download files from your site.
	Internet News Server	Installs the Microsoft Internet News Server for NNTP news.
	Internet Service Manager	Provides a snap-in for the Microsoft Management Console (MMC) to administer IIS.
	Internet Service Manager (HTML)	Provides an HTML-based administrative tool for IIS. You use IE 4.0 with this manager to administer IIS.
	SMTP Server	Installs the SMTP (Simple Mail Transfer Protocol) Server for e-mail.
	World Wide Web Samples	Installs sample IIS Web sites and other samples.
	World Wide Web Server	Installs the Web server so clients can access your Web site.
Microsoft Data Access Components (MDAC, ADO, ODBC, and OLE)	ActiveX Data Objects (ADO) 1.5	Installs the ActiveX Data Objects and other 1.5 OLE DB and ODBC files.
	Data Sources	Installs the drivers and providers to access common data sources, including Jet and Access (ODBC), Oracle, and SQL Server data sources.
	Remote Data Service 1.5	Installs Remote Data Service. Click the Show Subcomponents (RDS/ADC)button to see options for this subcomponent.
Microsoft Index Server	Index Server System Files	Installs the files for the Index Server system.
	Language Resources	Installs Index Server language resources. Click the Show Subcomponents button to see a list of these languages. US English Language is the default setting.
Microsoft Index	Online	Installs Index Server

continues

TABLE 2.3	*continued*	

IIS 4.0 SETUP OPTIONS

Component	*Subcomponent*	*Description*
Server	Documentation	documentation.
	Sample Files	Installs sample files on how to use the Index Server.
Microsoft Message Queue (MSMQ)	Administration Guide	Installs the MSMQ Administration Guide.
	Administration Tools	Enables you to control and monitor your message queuing enterprise.
	Microsoft Message	Installs the required Queue Server MSMQ files.
	Software Development Kit	Installs the MSMQ SDK for creating MSMQ applications with C or C++ APIs, or with ActiveX components.
Microsoft Script	Microsoft Script Debugger	Installs the Microsoft Debugger Script Debugger to debug Active Server Pages scripts and applications.
Microsoft Site Server Express 2.0	Analysis—Content	Enables you to analyze your site with content, site visualization, link management, and reporting tool.
	Analysis—Usage	Enables you to analyze your site usage.
	Publishing— Posting Acceptor 1.01	Enables IIS to receive files uploaded to it using the HTTP POST protocol.
	Publishing— Web Publishing Wizard 1.52	Automatically uploads new or revised content to Web servers.
Internet Connection Services for RAS (Remote Services)	Connection Manager Administration Kit	Sets up dial-up profiles in Access Connection Manager.
	Connection Point Services	Provides administration and services to phonebooks.
Internt Connection	Internet	Installs the Internet

Component	Subcomponent	Description
Services for RAS (Remote Services)	Authentication Services	Authentication Service.
	Product Documentation	Installs documentation for Remote Access Services.
Transaction Server	Microsoft Management	Installs MMC, which is an interface for Console (MMC) systems management applications.
	Transaction Server (MTS) Core Components	Installs MTS files.
	Transaction Server Core Documentation	Installs MTS product documentation.
	Transaction Server	Installs headers, libraries, and samples Deployment to help you create transaction components.
Windows Scripting Host	Windows Scripting Host Files	Installs executable files for the Windows Scripting Host.
	Windows Scripting Host Sample Scripts	Provides sample scripts.

The following steps assume all components and subcomponents are selected. Depending on your choices, you might not see all the dialog boxes shown in these steps.

5. Click Next. A dialog box showing the default publishing folders appears. The following list summarizes these folders:

   • Web services are installed in the C:\Inetpub\wwwroot folder.

   • FTP services are installed in the C:\Inetpub\ftproot folder.

   • Applications are installed in the C:\Program Files folder.

   You can change any of these default folders by typing over them or clicking the Browse button next to them.

6. Click Next. The Transaction Server dialog box displays.

continues

continued

The MTS Install Folder field shows where Transaction Server is installed. By default, this folder is named C:\Program Files\Mts. You can change this folder if you'd like.

7. Click Next. A dialog box to set remote administration features displays. You can choose to administer IIS from a Local account, in which no other account information is needed, or from a Remote account on another machine, which requires the Administrator Account name and its password. You can click the Browse button to locate the Administrator account.

8. Click Next. The Index Server dialog box displays the default folder for the index. This default directory is C:\Inetpub. You can change this folder if you'd like.

9. Click Next. The Mail Server dialog box displays the default folder for the mailroot directory. Other folders (mail queue, mailbox, and badmail) are created under this folder. The default for this folder is C:\Inetpub\Mailroot.

10. Click Next. The News Server dialog box displays the default folder for the nntpfile directory. Articles and data files used by the news server are stored under this folder. The default for this folder is C:\Inetpub\nntpfile.

11. Click Next. Select from one of the following types of MSMQ servers:

- **Primary Enterprise Controller (PEC).** Installs only one PEC on the network and contains the master copy of the MSMQ Information Store. This PEC acts as the Primary Site Controller for one site. You must have SQL Server installed to choose this option.

- **Primary Site Controller (PSC).** Installs one PSC for each site, which is a physical set of computers communicating with each other, usually paralleling the physical location of the computers. You must have SQL Server installed to choose this option.

N O T E

Why Install the MSMQ (Microsoft Message Queuing Server) Server?
You would use this service if you want to build a large-scale, distributed application that relies on a reliable messaging infrastructure. MSMQ provides reliable communications between applications that can continue to operate reliably even when networked systems are unavailable. You would probably not use MSMQ if you want to host your company's Web site using IIS; but you would absolutely want to use it if you were developing a distributed e-commerce application.

- **Backup Site Controller (BSC).** BSCs provide a backup of the PSC in case the PSC fails. You must have SQL Server installed to choose this option.

- **Routing Server.** Provides routing services, remote message store, and store-and-forward services. These servers are spread across the network to enable messages to reach a target queue via different paths. Each PEC, PSC, and BSC also acts as a Routing Server.

12. Click Next. The Microsoft Certificate Server Setup— Introduction dialog box displays. This wizard shows how to create a new certificate authority.

13. Click Next. In the Certificate Server, choose Storage Location dialog box, enter the location to store configuration files and certificate files. Unless the Windows NT domain controller is available for use, enter a shared folder.

14. Click Next. Fill in your identification information, including name, state, country, locality, and other items.

15. Click Next. In the Choose Key Storage Location dialog box, enter the names you want for the System Store and Container for your keys.

16. Click Next. In the Choose Database Location dialog box, you are shown the default folder in which the certificate information is stored.

17. Click Next. The Choose CSP and Hashing dialog box shows the Cryptographic Services Providers (CSP) you can select. You also can choose the hash algorithms from the Hash list.

18. Click Next. The Choose Certificate Output File Names dialog box shows the signature and key exchange certificate names. You can change these if necessary; however, the default names should suffice for most installations.

19. Click Next. You can enter a comment to identify the certificate later.

20. Click Next. Setup now completes the installation process and installs the IIS files on your hard disk. This process may take a long time to complete.

NOTE

This Isn't the Kind of Hash You Have with Your Eggs To create a digital signature, you first create a hash value from the message. A hash value is a number generated from a string of text. The hash is substantially smaller than the text itself and is generated by an algorithm that makes it extremely unlikely that some other text will produce the same hash value. This hash value is then encrypted by a public-key encryption algorithm, using the private key of the signer.

continues

continued

21. Click Finish when all the files are installed to your system.

22. Click Yes when prompted to restart your computer.

Identifying Changes to a Windows NT Server 4.0 Computer Made by the Installation of IIS

When you install IIS 4.0, your Windows NT Server 4.0 computer includes some new components, as follows:

◆ **Microsoft Management Console (MMC).** The host for the Internet Service Manager. Internet Service Manager is IIS's administrative program.

◆ **Registry changes.** Viewed by selecting Start, Programs, Windows NT 4.0 Option Pack, Microsoft Site Server Express 2.0, Documentation. Expand the Microsoft Internet Information Server option, click Administrator's Reference in the left pane (see Figure 2.1), and click Registry. Click the topic you want to read, such as WWW Service Registry Entries.

FIGURE 2.1
The Windows NT 4.0 Option Pack Documentation allows you to view the different Registry changes made by the installation of Microsoft Internet Information Server 4.0.

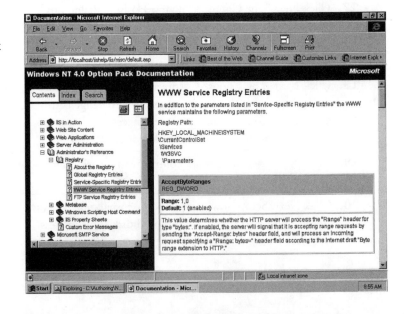

◆ **New services.** Include the FTP Publishing Service, IIS Administration Service, Content Index, and World Wide Web Publishing Service.

◆ **User Manager for Domains.** Lists a new username in the list of user accounts. This username is IUSR_computername and allows anonymous access to Internet services on your computer.

◆ **Performance Monitor.** Used to track several IIS services, including Content Index, Content Index Filter, FTP Service, HTTP Content Index, HTTP Service, and Internet Information Services Global. Some of the over 75 counters added to Performance Monitor enable you to track connections, bytes transferred, and cache information.

> **NOTE**
>
> **Service Defaults** The three services added during IIS 4.0 installation—FTP Publishing Service, IIS Administration Service, and World Wide Web Publishing Service—are set to start when you start Windows NT Server. You can change the default settings for each service from the Services dialog box.

INSTALL AND CONFIGURE CERTIFICATE SERVER

▶ Install and configure Certificate Server.

Although the installation of the Certificate Server is just part of the entire IIS installation, we need to discuss a little about what it is and how you configure it.

Microsoft Certificate Server enables you to increase the security of your site by issuing certificates (digital identifiers) that use public-key encryption. Certificates enable you to verify that you have secure communication across the network, whether that network is an intranet or the Internet. The server certificates are issued from a third-party organization and contain information about the organization and the public key.

There are three subcomponents to the Certificate Server that can be installed. They are the following:

◆ **The Certificate Server Certificate Authority.** This allows you to create a certificate authority on your Microsoft Internet Information Server 4.0 server.

◆ **The Certificate Server Documentation.** This component provides just what it sounds like—documentation for the Certificate Server.

◆ **The Certificate Server Web Client.** This allows you to submit certificate requests from a Web form and retrieve certificates after they have been issued.

When you install the Certificate Server, you are prompted for several pieces of information before you can complete the installation. These include the following:

◆ **A configuration data storage location.** This location is used to store certificates and configuration files. Because these certificates are essentially the digital keys to your information, be sure this is a secure location.

◆ **The location of the Certificate Server's database.** By default, this is located in the \Winnt\Server32\CertLog.

◆ **A location to store the server log file.** This is also \Winnt\ Server32\CertLog by default.

◆ **Location for your server in the Certificate Authority Hierarchy.** Your Certificate Server can either be the Root CA or a non-Root CA.

◆ **A Cryptographic Service Provider and Hash Algorithm.** These determine how the information contained in the certificates are encrypted.

◆ **Identity.** You need to supply information about the identity of the CA you are configuring. This includes the name of the CA, organization, department, city, state, and country. You can also include a comment.

Before you can start issuing certificates with Certificate Server, you must create a Certificate Request File. This file is then sent to a certificate authority (CA).

After you have gotten your key, you're ready to start issuing certificates.

NOTE

What Is a Certificate Authority?
A certificate authority is nothing more than a trusted third-party organization or company that issues digital certificates used to create digital signatures and public-private key pairs. In the case of the IIS Certificate Server, the CA issues the first certificate, allowing the IIS Certificate Server to generate certificates using the first certificate. The CA is used to guarantee that the owner of a certificate is who he claims to be. CAs are growing more and more important as e-commerce becomes more prevalent because they guarantee that the two parties exchanging information are really who they claim to be.

INTRODUCTION TO PUBLIC KEY INFRASTRUCTURE (PKI) AND CERTIFICATES

Although this is not tested in depth, this is an excellent opportunity to talk a little bit more about what you are actually deploying when you set up Certificate Server and start issuing certificates to secure your data.

When you talk about using a Public Key Infrastructure, certificates, and digital signatures, you are talking about encryption. Each of these topics deals with taking your data, encrypting it at one end, and providing a mechanism for decrypting it at the other end. The first technique used for encrypting data was a technique called symmetric key cryptography. This involves encrypting and decrypting a message using the same key, which must be known to the user who is encrypting the data and the user who needs to decrypt the data. The major drawback to this method is the fact that both parties must share the key. That means the key is vulnerable to being stolen because it must be passed from one user to the other.

The latest method for sharing secure data is public-key cryptography. Public-key cryptography uses separate keys to encrypt or decrypt a message. This means the message is the only thing that needs to be shared. Each party in a transaction has a key pair, which consists of two keys with a particular relationship that allows one to encrypt a message that the other can decrypt. One of these keys is made publicly available (possibly through a certificate authority, discussed shortly), and the other is a private key. A message encrypted with a person's public key can't be decrypted with that same key, but can be decrypted with the private key that corresponds to it. Using your private key to encrypt a document is the equivalent of signing your name to a contract and is known as a digital signature. So if I want to send you a secure message, I would take your public key, encrypt the message, and only you would be able to decrypt it because only you have your private key.

The Public Key Infrastructure (PKI) provides the infrastructure for maintaining the public and private key pairs used to encrypt and decrypt these messages. The purpose of this infrastructure is to establish a level of trust between the keys, which are stored as digital certificates. A digital certificate is nothing more than a file that contains the certificate owner's public key and name and the certificate signer's name. This file is digitally signed with the signer's private key. This certificate starts a chain of trust from the certificate authority, a trusted third-party agency tasked with maintaining

continues

continued

secure certificates through the sending user to the receiving user's digital certificate. This certificate chain is called a trust map.

All PKIs start with a root certificate. The root certificate is trusted because the owner of it claims to be trustworthy. Examples of this include CyberTrust and VeriSign. The owner of a root certificate establishes this trust by protecting the signing root private key; if it is stolen, it can be used to falsely sign certificates. The root certificate is then used to sign other certificates, verifying that the public key of those certificates is the equivalent of the owner name. This means that anything done with the matching private key is performed for that named entity, which can be a user or a corporation.

The bottom line is these are all pieces of a public-key encryption infrastructure that allow electronic transactions to take place as securely as paper signature-based transactions occur today.

INSTALL AND CONFIGURE MICROSOFT SMTP SERVICE

▶ Install and configure Microsoft SMTP Service.

Although the installation of the SMTP is just part of the entire IIS installation (much like Certificate Server, discussed in the previous section), we need to discuss a little about what it is and how you configure it.

Microsoft SMTP Service uses the Simple Mail Transfer Protocol (SMTP) to send and receive e-mail using TCP port 25 for operations. After it is installed, it can be managed and administered through Internet Service Manager or the SMTP Service Manager(HTML). The two function almost identically, with the difference being that the latter enables you to administer SMTP through HTML, whereas the former requires administration from the server.

To configure the SMTP Service, do the following:

STEP BY STEP

2.2 Configuring the SMTP Service

1. Select Start, Programs, Windows NT 4.0 Option Pack, Microsoft Internet Information Server, Internet Service Manager.

2. Expand the Internet Information Server folder.

3. Expand the SMTP server that you want to modify.

4. Right-click the Default SMTP Site entry. (Your SMTP site might be named something different.)

5. Click Properties. The SMTP Site Properties sheet appears. Some of the key parameters you might need to modify include the following:

- The inbound and outbound TCP connection ports. The default is port 25.

- The Identity and IP address of this SMTP site.

- The number of inbound and outbound connections. If you decide to enable the limits, the default is 1,000 connections for both inbound and an additional 1,000 for outbound connections.

- You can enable logging.

- You can limit message size. The default, if you apply limits, is 2,048KB.

- You can also configure local storage of message queues and site security.

For more information on SMTP Service configuration, check the "Optimizing the Performance of the SMTP Service" section of Chapter 6.

6. Set the appropriate parameters and click Apply.

7. Click OK to close the Properties window.

> **NOTE**
>
> **How Does It Know?** A common question when working with SMTP servers is, "How does it know where to send the mail?" It's a great question, and it has a surprisingly simple answer. Let's say you want to send Bill Gates a note to tell him how much you like the latest beta release of Windows 2000. You would address the message to billg@microsoft.com. When the SMTP server receives this message, it makes a DNS query to the Microsoft DNS server and asks for the domain's MX (Mail eXchange) records. These are the DNS entries for Microsoft's SMTP mail servers. After the SMTP server at your end has that information, it knows where to send your e-mail.

Optimizing the SMTP Service is covered in depth in Chapter 6, "Monitoring and Optimization."

INSTALL AND CONFIGURE MICROSOFT NNTP SERVICE

▶ Install and configure Microsoft NNTP Service.

The NNTP service is another service that is just part of the entire IIS installation (much like Certificate Server and the SMTP Service, discussed in the previous sections). We need to discuss a little about what it is and how you configure it.

The Microsoft NNTP Service supports the Network News Transport Protocol and enables clients to access newsgroups. Because this feature uses the NNTP protocol, any standard newsreader client can be used to participate in these discussion groups, including Outlook Express, included with Internet Explorer 4.01. The one important thing to remember is that the NNTP Service included with IIS 4.0 only supports local newsgroups. You cannot receive newsfeeds with IIS 4.0. To manage the NNTP Service, you can use either the Internet Service Manager or the NNTP Service Manager (HTML).

To configure the NNTP Service, do the following:

STEP BY STEP

2.3 Configuring the NNTP Service

1. Select Start, Programs, Windows NT 4.0 Option Pack, Microsoft Internet Information Server, Internet Service Manager.

2. Expand the Internet Information Server folder.

3. Expand the NNTP server that you want to modify.

4. Right-click the Default NNTP Site entry. (Your NNTP site might be named something different.)

5. Click Properties. The NNTP Site Properties sheet appears. At installation, you might need to configure the following items:

   • The standard and SSL ports for newsreader access. Port 119 is default for an unencrypted connection, and port 563 is the default for the SSL connection.

- The Identity and IP address of this NNTP site.

- The number of connections. Default is 5,000.

- The connection timeout. Default is 600 seconds.

- You can enable logging.

- You can configure the posting rules. This is where you determine if your users will be able to post or not.

- You can set the Home Directory.

- You can set up the newsgroups the server will host.

- You can also configure the Expiration policy and see who is connected to the server.

For more information on NNTP Service configuration, check the "Optimizing the Performance of the NNTP Service" section of Chapter 6.

6. Set the appropriate parameters and click Apply.

7. Click OK to close the Properties window.

Optimizing the NNTP Service is covered in depth in Chapter 6, "Monitoring and Optimization."

CONFIGURING IIS TO SUPPORT THE FTP SERVICE

▶ Configure the FTP Service.

An FTP (File Transport Protocol) server provides clients attaching to your server the capability of transmitting files to and from the server. Although FTP is one of the oldest Internet services, it is still one of the most popular ways to transfer files over the Internet.

Before you go live with your IIS 4.0 server, you might want to configure some of the settings related to FTP. These include the following:

◆ Setting bandwidth and user connections

◆ Setting user logon requirements and authentication requirements

◆ Modifying port settings

◆ Setting directory listing style

◆ Configuring virtual directories and servers

Setting User Connections

To conserve bandwidth for other clients accessing your FTP site, consider limiting the number of connections that can be made to your FTP server. When connection limits are maxed out, those attempting to connect to your server are rejected and must try again later. Another task you should consider for your FTP site is to limit the bandwidth used by the WWW server. You are shown how to do this in the "Setting Bandwidth and User Connections" section later in this chapter. This provides more bandwidth for your FTP service.

To set user connections, perform the following steps:

STEP BY STEP

2.4 Setting User Connection Limits for the FTP Service

1. Select Start, Programs, Windows NT 4.0 Option Pack, Microsoft Internet Information Server, Internet Service Manager.

2. Expand the Internet Information Server folder.

3. Expand the FTP server that you want to modify.

4. Right-click the Default FTP Site entry. Your Web site might be named something different.

5. Click Properties. The FTP Site Properties sheet appears.

6. On the FTP Site tab, click the Limited To option (see Figure 2.2).

7. Enter a value in the connections field. The default is 100,000, but you might want to lower this if your resources are limited.

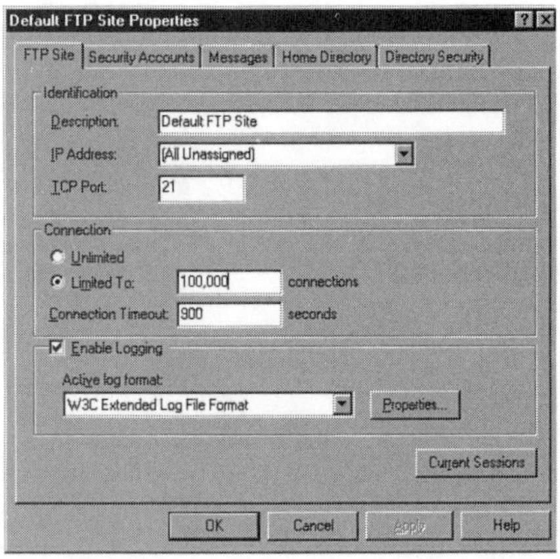

FIGURE 2.2
The FTP Site tab allows you to identify the site, limit the number of concurrent connections, and enable logging.

8. In the Connection Timeout field, enter a value for the amount of time when your server should automatically disconnect an idle session. The default is 15 minutes (900 seconds), but an average setting is 5 minutes (300 seconds). For an infinite amount of time, enter all 9s in this field.

9. Click OK, or keep this open if you want to continue changing FTP site settings.

> **NOTE**
>
> **Timeout Value**   Even if a connection is lost or a client stops working, your site continues to process data until the timeout value is reached. Setting an appropriate timeout value limits the loss of resources due to these lost connections.

Setting User Logon Requirements and Authentication Requirements

To enable clients to access your FTP server, you need to set up user logon and authentication requirements. If you want to allow all users access to your FTP server, you must allow anonymous connections. Users with the name anonymous can then log on to your site by using their e-mail address as their password.

IIS uses the default IUSR_computername account for all anonymous logons. Permissions set up for this account determine an anonymous user's privileges.

On the FTP Site Properties sheet, Security Accounts tab, you can configure the following options:

◆ **Allow Anonymous Connections.** Select this for anonymous connections.

◆ **Username.** Displays the IUSR_computername name as set up by IIS in the Windows NT User Manager for Domains and in the Internet Service Manager.

◆ **Password.** A randomly generated password was created by User Manager for Domains and Internet Service Manager. You must have a password here; no blanks are allowed. If you change this password, make sure it matches the one in the User Manager for Domains and Internet Service Manager for this user.

◆ **Allow only Anonymous Connections.** Click this option to limit access to your FTP server to only those who log on as anonymous. This restricts users from logging on with an account that has administrative rights.

> **WARNING**
>
> **Secure FTP?**   Actually, not with Internet Information Server 4.0. Back when the FTP protocol was written, security was not really a concern. There were so few users on what would become the Internet that passing clear text user IDs and passwords was common. In today's slightly more dangerous environment, it is important to remember that all user IDs and passwords sent to IIS's FTP Service (or any other standard FTP service) are sent as clear text and can be read by any network packet sniffer. Be careful about using your administrative accounts to FTP to your server. You never know who could be picking up your password.

◆ **Administrator.** Select those accounts who are allowed to administer this virtual FTP site. Click the Add button to add a user account to this list. Remove an account by selecting the account and clicking Remove.

◆ **Enable Automatic Password Synchronization.** Select this option to automatically synchronize the IUSR_Computername account password seen here with the IUSR_computername account password contained in the Windows NT User Account database.

Modifying Port Settings

Port settings are used by clients to connect to your FTP site. By default, the FTP server is set up with a port setting of 21. You can change this setting to a unique TCP port number, but you must announce this setting to all clients who want to access your server.

Perform the following steps to change the port number:

STEP BY STEP

2.5 Changing the Port for the FTP Service

1. Choose the following: Start, Programs, Windows NT 4.0 Option Pack, Microsoft Internet Information Server, Internet Service Manager.

2. Expand the Internet Information Server folder.

3. Expand the server in which you want to modify the port value (see Figure 2.3).

4. Right-click the Default FTP Site entry. Your FTP site might be named something different.

5. Click Properties. The FTP Site Properties sheet opens (see Figure 2.4).

NOTE
HTML Version of ISM You can use the HTML version of Internet Service Manager if you want to administer IIS from Internet Explorer 4.0. The procedures shown in this chapter, however, show how to use the Microsoft Management Console (MMC) to run the Internet Service Manager.

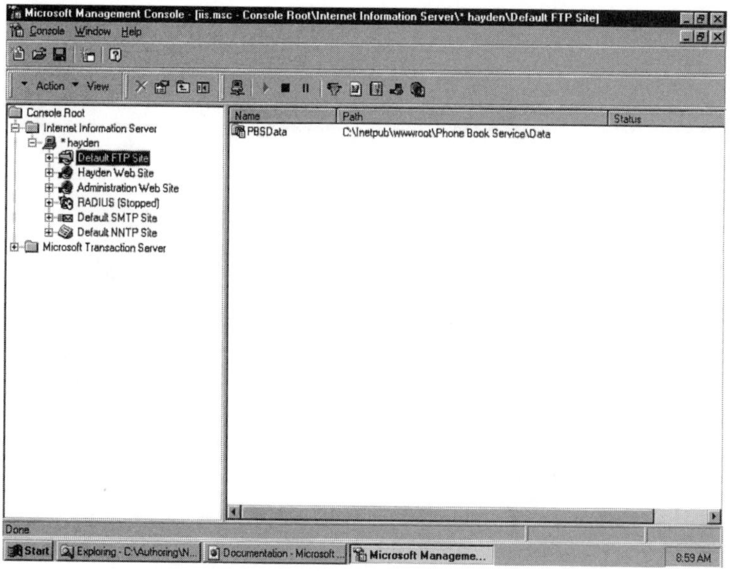

◀**FIGURE 2.3**
The Internet Service Manager is a snap-in to the Microsoft Management Console and is used to administer your FTP site.

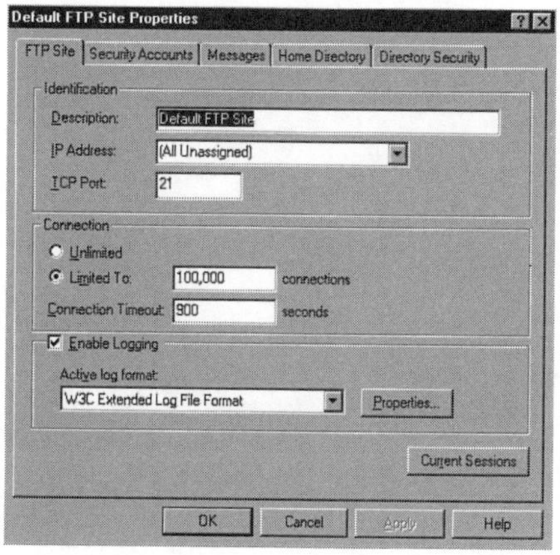

6. Change the Port Value to a new setting.

7. Click OK.

FIGURE 2.4▲
The FTP Site Properties sheet can be used to change the TCP Port setting.

Setting Directory Listing Style

A directory listing style is the way in which your server displays a directory listing. Windows NT Server uses a listing style similar to DOS (such as C:\folder\subfolder). However, you can change this to display in UNIX format. UNIX format (such as /c/directory/subdirectory/) is commonly found on the Internetand is expected by most Web browsers. Use UNIX format for the greatest compatibility with the Internet.

To change your server's directory listing style, perform the following steps:

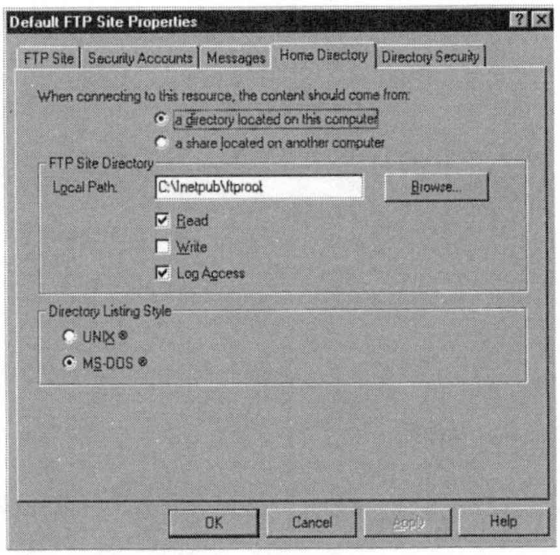

FIGURE 2.5
The Home Directory tab includes settings for changing the directory listing style, as well as other default FTP directory settings.

NOTE

DOS Users If you have DOS users who are unable to read file names in your FTP directory, you might need to change the directory listing style to Microsoft-DOS.

STEP BY STEP

2.6 Changing the Directory Listing Style

1. From the FTP Site Properties sheet (see the preceding section), click the Home Directory tab (see Figure 2.5).

2. Under Directory Listing Style, select UNIX. The default is MS-DOS.

3. Click OK, or keep this open if you want to continue changing FTP settings.

Configuring FTP Home Directory

IIS 4.0 enables you to change the home directory for your virtual server. When you install the FTP service, IIS 4.0 creates a default home directory called \inetpub\ftproot. This directory, which has no name and is indicated by a slash (/) in an URL, is the primary location for FTP files.

You place files in the home directory and its subdirectories to enable clients to access them (the files).

To change your home directories, perform the following steps:

STEP BY STEP

2.7 Changing the FTP Site Home Directory

1. From the FTP Site Properties sheet (see the preceding section), make sure the Home Directory tab appears (refer to Figure 2.5).

2. In the When Connecting to This Resource, the Content Should Come From area, select one of the following paths:

- **A Directory Located on This Computer.** Select this option to specify a local directory.

- **A Share Located on Another Computer.** Select this option to specify a directory on another computer on the network.

3. In the Local Path field (or Network Share if you select the second option from the preceding list), enter the path to the directory you want to specify as the home directory. For local directories, use standard syntax, such as C:\directory\subdirectory. However, network paths must follow the Universal Naming Convention (UNC), such as \\computername\sharename. For shares, enter the username and password to access that computer, if prompted.

4. Set the home directory access controls from the following options:

   - **Read.** Lets clients read and download files you store in the home directory or in virtual directories. You must select Read permissions for FTP directories or every request for a file stored in the home directory results in an error message being returned to the client. By default, this option is selected.

   - **Write.** Lets clients upload files to the home directory on your FTP server. This option should be selected only for FTP servers in which users must upload files. By default, this option is not selected.

   - **Log Access.** Provides a record of visitors to the home directory. By default, this option is selected.

5. Click OK.

> **NOTE**
>
> **NTFS Settings and Home Directories**
> Directory settings for home directories set up on NTFS drives must match NTFS settings. If settings do not match, IIS uses the most restrictive settings.

IIS 4.0 also enables you to create virtual directories, which enable you to set up directories located on other servers for your visitors to access. You set up Virtual Directories from Internet Service Manager. Perform the following steps to create virtual directories for your FTP service:

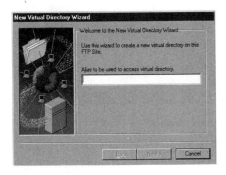

FIGURE 2.6
Assign a name to your new Virtual Directory.

NOTE

You Don't Have Permission to Read, but You Can Write If you ever log on to an FTP server to retrieve a file, but you can't see the file, that's because you don't have Read Access to that directory. It is not unusual to find vendors that allow you to write to a directory, but not read from it. One type of FTP server you see this on is a technical support FTP server, where customers are dropping log files to be reviewed. You don't want people to read other customer's error logs, so you only grant Write Access.

STEP BY STEP

2.8 Creating a Virtual Directory for the FTP Service

1. Right-click on the FTP server and select New, Virtual Directory. The New Virtual Directory Wizard displays (see Figure 2.6).

2. Enter a name for the Virtual Directory. The name you enter here is the name placed in the URL to access this directory.

3. Click Next. Enter the path to the directory to which you want the Virtual Directory to point. Use UNC notation for directories on another system.

4. Click Next. Set the following permissions to the Virtual Directory:

   - **Allow Read Access.** Enables visitors to read files on the Virtual Directory.

   - **Allow Write Access.** Enables visitors to write files to the Virtual Directory.

5. Click Finish.

CONFIGURING IIS TO SUPPORT THE WWW SERVICE

▶ Configure IIS to support the WWW service.

After you install IIS 4.0, you can configure the WWW service for your Web site. The configuration changes you can make include the following:

◆ Setting bandwidth and user connections

◆ Setting user logon requirements and authentication requirements

◆ Modifying port settings

◆ Setting default pages

◆ Setting HTTP 1.1 host header names to host multiple Web sites

◆ Enabling HTTP Keep-Alives

Setting Bandwidth and User Connections

To conserve bandwidth for other clients accessing your Web site, consider limiting the number of connections that can be made to your site. When connection limits have been reached, those attempting to connect to your server are rejected and must try again later. You can limit the number of connections to your Web site, e-mail, or news servers.

Another thing that you should consider for your Web site is limiting the bandwidth used by the Web server. This leaves bandwidth available for other services, such as e-mail or news services. Limiting bandwidth is known as throttling bandwidth, and it limits only the bandwidth used by static HTML files. If you have multiple sites set up, you can throttle the bandwidth used by each site.

Optimization of the WWW Service is covered in depth in Chapter 6, "Monitoring and Optimization."

To set user connections and set bandwidth throttling, follow Exercise 2.2 at the end of the chapter.

NOTE

Viewing Your Web Site's Connection Activity If you want to view your Web site's connection activity, open Windows NT Performance Monitor and set it to view FTP Service or Web Service from the Object list. You then can view Anonymous Users/sec, Bytes Received/sec, and other counters. Use this information to help you set the bandwidth and user connections.

Setting User Logon Requirements and Authentication Requirements

IIS 4.0 can be set up to verify the identity of clients who access your Web site. On public Web sites on which non-critical or public domain information and applications are available, authentication of users connecting to your Web site might not be important. However, if you have secure data or want to restrict Web access to specific clients, logon and authentication requirements become very important.

Perform the following steps to set authentication and logon requirements:

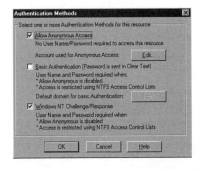

FIGURE 2.7▲
You can set logon and authentication requirements from the Directory Security tab.

FIGURE 2.8▶
Select one or more authentication methods from the Authentication Methods dialog box.

STEP BY STEP

2.9 Configuring Authentication and Logon Settings

1. Open Internet Service Manager.

2. Right-click a Web site, file (the NTFS file system is required to do file level security), or directory you want to configure.

3. Click Properties. The property sheet for that item appears.

4. Click the Directory Security (or File Security if you want to set file-specific properties on an NTFS partition) tab (see Figure 2.7).

5. Click the Edit button under Anonymous Access and Authentication Control. The Authentication Methods dialog box appears (see Figure 2.8).

6. Select an authentication method from the following options:

- **Allow Anonymous Access.** This option enables clients to connect to your Web site without requiring a username or password. Click the Edit button to select the Windows NT user account used to access your coputer. The default account IUSR_computername is used. This account is granted Log on Locally user rights by default and is necessary for anonymous logon access to your Web site. Click OK to return to the Authen-tication Methods dialog box.

- **Basic Authentication.** Use this method if you do not specify anonymous access and you want a client connecting to your Web site to enter a valid Windows NT username and password to log on. This sends a password in clear text format with the passwords being transmitted in an unencrypted format. Click the Edit button to specify a default logon domain for users who do not explicitly name a domain.

- **Windows NT Challenge/Response.** This setting is used if you want the Windows NT Challenge/Response feature to authenticate the client attempting to connect to your Web site. The only Web browsers that support this feature include Internet Explorer 2.0 and later. During the challenge/response procedure, encrypted information is exchanged between the client and server to authenticate the user.

NOTE **Authentication in IIS** IIS 4.0 uses the Basic and Windows NT Challenge/Response to authenticate users if anonymous access is denied either through the dialog box or NTFS permissions.

7. Click OK.

If you have a server certificate installed, you also can use the Secure Sockets Layer (SSL) to authenticate users logging on to your Web site.

Modifying Port Settings

In a process similar to setting the port for FTP sites, you can change the default port setting for your Web site to any unique TCP port number. If you do this, however, you must let all clients know of your port setting before they can connect to your Web site. For a port setting other than the default, which is 80, the user must enter the port value as part of the URL. For example, the Internet Service Manager(HTML) uses a separate port in IIS to keep the admin utility secure. Following is a sample URL to access that tool:

```
http://localhost:2106/iisadmin/
```

NOTE **Why Change the Default Port Setting?** You will find that the default port setting is generally modified for privacy or security reasons. Many applications that offer Web-based management use a custom port setting to keep the administrative Web site out of the view of the average Web surfer. Otherwise, it's generally a good idea to leave the default port alone.

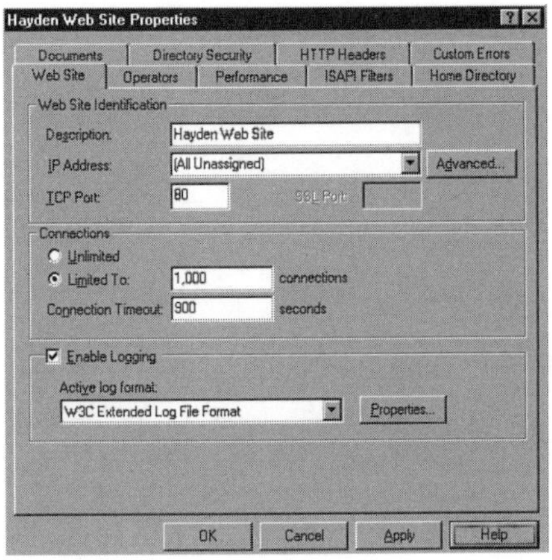

Note the :2106, telling the browser to connect to the site using port 2106.

To set the port setting, perform the following steps:

FIGURE 2.9
The default port setting is usually the best for public Web sites, but you can change it by modifying the TCP Port setting on the Web Site tab.

STEP BY STEP

2.10 Changing the Default Port Setting

1. In the Web Site Properties dialog box, click the Web Site tab (see Figure 2.9).

2. In the TCP Port field, enter a new value for the port address. This must be a unique TCP value for your server.

3. Click OK, or keep this open if you want to continue changing Web site settings.

Setting Default Pages

From your browsing of the Internet, you might have noticed that to reach many sites you do not have to enter a specific document name (such as default.html) when accessing the Web site's home page. You can set IIS 4.0 to display a default page when clients access your site without a specified document in the URL. From this default page (usually your home page or index page), you can direct users to other documents or resources on your site.

IIS 4.0 enables you to specify more than one default document and list the documents in order of preference. When a client connects to your site, IIS searches for the top document and displays it if it is found. If it can't be found—for example, it is being updated or edited—the next default document is displayed.

To set default pages, perform the following:

STEP BY STEP

2.11 Specifying the Default Page for a Web Site

1. From the Web Site Properties sheet, click the Documents tab (see Figure 2.10).

2. Select the Enable Default Document check box. This option is enabled by default.

3. Click the Add button to specify a different default document.

4. In the Add Default Document dialog box, specify a new default document. An example of one that many Web sites use is index.htm.

5. Click OK.

6. Click the up or down arrows on the Documents tab to modify the search order for the default documents.

7. Click the Enable Document Footer option if you want IIS to insert an HTML file (which is really a short HTML document with formatting tags for footer content) to the bottom of your Web documents.

8. Enter the path and file name for the footer file.

9. Click OK, or keep this open if you want to continue changing Web site settings.

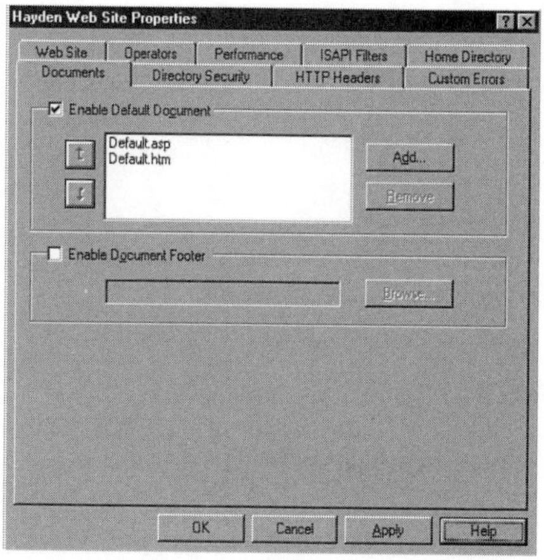

FIGURE 2.10

Setting a default document enables users to connect to your Web site without specifying a document name.

Setting HTTP 1.1 Host Header Names to Host Multiple Web Sites

IIS 4.0 provides support for HTTP 1.1 host headers to allow multiple host names to be associated with one IP address. With this feature, a separate IP address is not needed for every virtual server you support. Microsoft Internet Explorer 3.0 and later and Netscape Navigator 2.0 and later support this feature, but many other browsers do not.

To set host header names for multiple Web sites, perform the following steps:

STEP BY STEP

2.12 Setting up HTTP 1.1 Host Headers

1. From the Web Site Properties sheet, click the Web Site tab. (Host headers only work for Web sites.)

2. Click the Advanced button. The Advanced Multiple Web Site Configuration dialog box displays (see Figure 2.11).

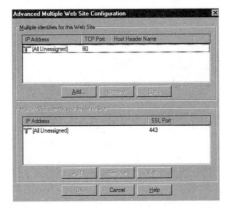

FIGURE 2.11►
Add a host header name for each Web site you are hosting. These sites all share the same IP address.

3. Click the Add button. The Advanced Web Site Identification dialog box displays (see Figure 2.12).

4. Fill in the IP Address, TCP Port, and Host Header Name fields. The IP Address field must include an IP address that has already been configured on the server. The Host Header Name field must include a registered DNS value.

5. Click OK.

6. Click OK to close the Advanced Multiple Web Site Configuration dialog box, or click Add to continue adding new multiple host header names to this site.

7. Click OK to close the Web Site Properties sheet.

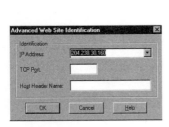

FIGURE 2.12▲
Fill in the TCP/IP Address, Port, and Header information to identify the new host.

Enabling HTTP Keep-Alives

You can enable IIS 4.0's Keep-Alives feature to allow clients to maintain open connections. This way, a client does not need to re-establish connections for each request. By enabling Keep-Alives, you decrease the amount of time a client waits to connect to another document or application on your site. You also increase the amount of resources devoted to this client.

To enable HTTP Keep-Alives, perform the following steps:

STEP BY STEP

2.13 Enabling HTTP Keep-Alives

1. From the Web Site Properties sheet, click the Performance tab (see Figure 2.13).

2. Select the HTTP Keep-Alives Enabled check box. This option is enabled by default. If a check mark already appears in this check box, no changes are needed.

3. Click OK.

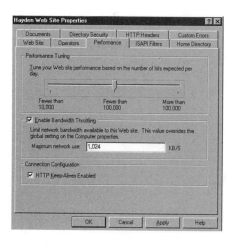

FIGURE 2.13
Enable the HTTP Keep-Alives setting on the Performance tab.

CONFIGURING AND SAVING CONSOLES BY USING MICROSOFT MANAGEMENT CONSOLE

▶ Configure and save consoles by using Microsoft Management Console.

Microsoft Management Console (MMC) is used to organize and perform management tasks for IIS 4.0. MMC does not actually administer any part of IIS or your network; rather, it provides a framework for other applications (called snap-ins) to administer parts of the network. Internet Service Manager, for instance, is a snap-in. When Internet Service Manager starts (not the HTML version), an MMC console (see Figure 2.14) appears with the Internet Service Manager displayed as a snap-in.

FIGURE 2.14
Saving the Microsoft Management Console configuration is as easy as going to Console, Save or Console, Save As.

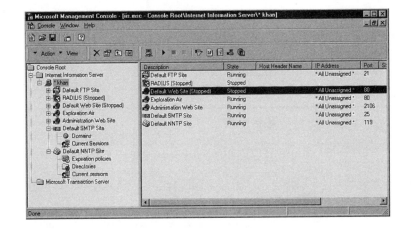

To save a particular MMC configuration for later use, perform the following steps:

STEP BY STEP

2.14 Saving a Microsoft Management Console Configuration

1. Open the Microsoft Management Console (see Figure 2.14) by selecting Start, Programs, Windows NT 4.0 Option Pack, Microsoft Internet Information Server, Internet Service Manager.

2. Make any changes to the MMC configuration you think are appropriate. You can change the listing style, the root view of the server, or display the Description bar, among other things.

3. From the menu, select Console and then Save or Save As. If you select Save, the configuration is saved to the default configuration file. If you select Save As, you open the standard Windows Save As dialog box (see Figure 2.15). The file can be named anything you like, and the extension is

.MSC, of the type Microsoft Management Console Files. The default path for these files is WINNT\SYTEM32\ INETSRV. If you decide to store your MMC configuration files some place other than the default, be sure to remember where you saved them.

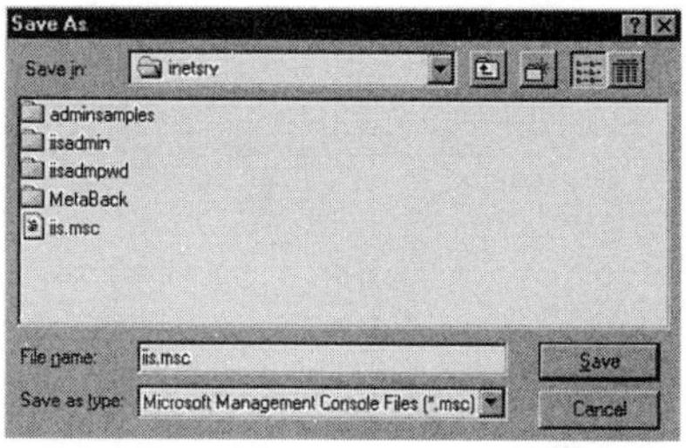

In the future, Microsoft BackOffice and Windows NT will offer MMC snap-in administration tools. Other vendors are expected to provide snap-ins as well. To add a snap-in to the MMC, perform the following steps:

FIGURE 2.15▲
The standard Save As dialog box is used to save console configurations.

STEP BY STEP

2.15 Adding a Snap-In

1. Open the Microsoft Management Console (refer to Figure 2.14) by selecting Start, Programs, Windows NT 4.0 Option Pack, Microsoft Internet Information Server, Internet Service Manager.

2. From the menu, select Console and then Add/Remove Snap-in. This opens the Add/Remove Snap-in dialog box, shown in Figure 2.16.

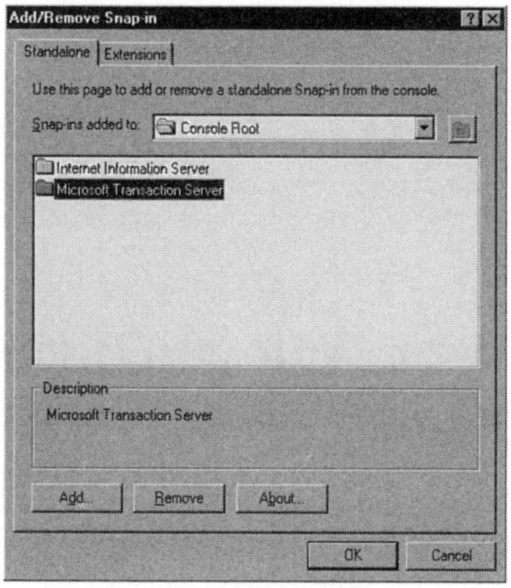

◀FIGURE 2.16
The Add/Remove Snap-in dialog box allows you to see what snap-ins are installed. You can also add, remove, or get more information about the installed snap-ins from this dialog box.

continues

continued

3. Click on Add to open the Add Standalone Snap-in dialog box, shown in Figure 2.17. You can expect the list of available snap-ins to expand as more and more applications fall under the MMC framework. For now, just be aware that this is where you add a snap-in, if it is necessary.

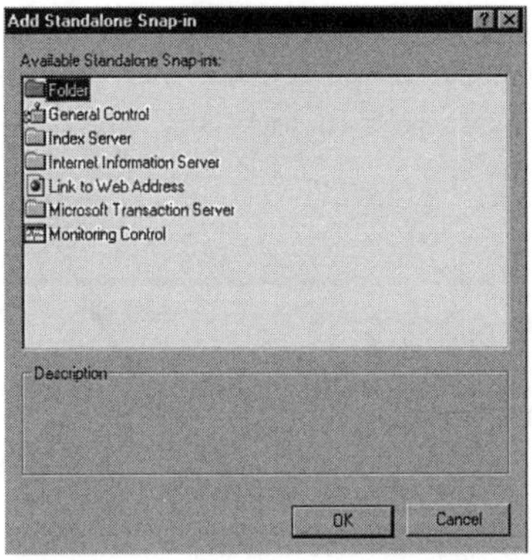

FIGURE 2.17
The Add Standalone Snap-in dialog box allows you to select the type of snap-in to be installed.

Spend Some Time with the MMC
For the exam, make sure you know how to navigate through the MMC interface. Because the MMC is a framework for all the next generation Microsoft administrative tools, it is important to understand it. By the same token, the MMC is not actually part of IIS itself, so it is not generally tested heavily. You might see it in any simulation questions, because it's tough to simulate administering Microsoft Internet Information Server 4.0 without using the MMC.

When you start a snap-in in MMC, a console displays. Consoles have one or more windows. The Internet Service Manager, for instance, includes two windows. On the left side, called the scope pane, a tree view is shown. The right pane, which shows the results of selecting something on the left page, is called the results pane.

You can view multiple windows in a console and then save that view for later. You might, for instance, create one window to show a snap-in for changing settings and another window to display a Web page with program updates. You can then display that window view or share it with other users via e-mail, floppy disk, or network.

VERIFYING SERVER SETTINGS BY ACCESSING THE METABASE

The metabase is a memory-resident data storage area that stores your IIS 4.0 configuration values. The metabase is analogous to, but not identical to, the Windows NT Registry. It is also faster and more flexible than the Registry. The metabase has keys that correspond to IIS elements; each key has properties that affect the configuration of that element. The hierarchy of the NNTP service keys, for example, is shown in Figure 2.18.

If you are looking for the metabase in the file system, it is stored in the \Winnt\System32\Inetsrv subdirectory, in a file named *MetaBase.bin.* This is a binary file, so don't try to edit it with your favorite word processor. Although any changes made to the information in the metabase are recorded in this file, IIS actually uses a copy in memory for faster access to the information. Information contained in the metabase includes the following:

◆ Web site configuration information

◆ IIS logging configuration information

◆ FTP and WWW service configuration information

◆ Virtual directory configuration information

◆ Filter configuration information

◆ Secure Socket Layer (SSL) protocol configuration information

You can use the IIS Administration Objects to configure your IIS 4.0 installation, as well as change settings that affect the operation of your IIS Web server, FTP site, virtual directories, and other components. One application that uses the IIS Administration in Objects is the Internet Service Manager (HTML) that you use in Internet Explorer 4.0 (see Figure 2.19).

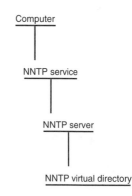

FIGURE 2.18▲
The hierarchy of the NNTP service keys.

EXAM TIP

The Registry Versus the Metabase
Be sure to remember what information is stored in the Registry and what is stored in the metabase.

◀FIGURE 2.19
The HTML version of Internet Service Manager uses IIS Administration Objects to configure IIS components.

NOTE

How Do I Edit the Metabase? In short, you don't. You can't edit the metabase directly like you can the Registry. Any changes made to the metabase must be made through a Microsoft Internet Information Server 4.0 configuration utility.

Choosing the Appropriate Administration Method

▶ Choose the appropriate administration method.

As mentioned previously, IIS 4.0 provides two main ways to administer your IIS installation. You still must use the common Windows NT administration tools to set file and directory rights and user accounts and to view performance measurements. But to administer IIS 4.0, you use Internet Service Manager either as a snap-in to MMC or as an HTML application in Internet Explorer 4.0.

With Internet Service Manager (HTML), you can manage your Web site remotely using a standard Web browser (IE 4.0 is recommended). This makes it convenient for administrators to manage a Web site when physically away from the Web site. An administrator, for instance, can be located in a different building than where the Web server is housed. By using Internet Service Manager (HTML), the administrator can connect to the server and administer it from the remote location.

Internet Service Manager (HTML) can be customized using Active Server Pages and the IIS Administration Objects. By customizing Internet Service Manager (HTML), or by creating new HTML-based administration tools, ISPs and administrators can create pages for customers or users to modify settings on the Web.

For administration tasks on the server, administrators can use familiar Windows NT Server administration tools, including the following:

◆ **User Manager for Domains.** Create a new user or group for your system to access file, print, and Web services.

◆ **Event Viewer.** Monitor system events and log application and security events used by the Web server. Event Viewer also can be used to audit access to secure files, as well as users logging on to the server.

◆ **Performance Monitor.** Monitor the performance of IIS 4.0, including FTP and Web services, including HTTP and indexing counters. Use Performance Monitor to get a view of server load.

NOTE

Directly Editing the Metabase If you have access to the Microsoft Internet Information Server 4.0 Resource Kit, you can edit the metabase directly using the MetaEdit utility. MetaEdit is similar to the Windows NT Registry Editor (RegEdt/RegEdt32), but operates on the metabase instead.

Monitoring of Microsoft Internet Information Server 4.0 is covered in depth in Chapter 6, "Monitoring and Optimization."

CUSTOMIZING THE INSTALLATION OF MICROSOFT SITE SERVER EXPRESS ANALYSIS CONTENT ANALYZER

▶ Customize the installation of Microsoft Site Server Express Content Analyzer.

The Site Server Express Content Analyzer (Content Analyzer, for short) enables you to create WebMaps to give you a view of your Web site, helping you to manage your Web site. WebMaps are graphical representations of resources on your site. These resources can include HTML documents, audio and video files, Java applets, FTP resources, and applications. Content Analyzer also enables you to manage your links. You can ensure that links are included in the resources and that they all work correctly.

When you install IIS 4.0, you have the option of installing all or part of the Microsoft Site Server Express 2.0 tool. If you choose the Content Analyzer option (refer to Table 2.3) and want to install the Content Analyzer, the Analysis-Content subcomponent should be selected.

The system requirements and recommendations for installing Content Analyzer are shown in Table 2.4.

TABLE 2.4

CONTENT ANALYZER SYSTEM REQUIREMENTS

Component	Requirement	Recommendation
CPU	Intel 486 66MHz	120MHz Pentium
RAM	16MB	32MB
Hard disk space	14MB	—
Internet connection	Modem	Direct

continues

TABLE 2.4   *continued*

CONTENT ANALYZER SYSTEM REQUIREMENTS

Component	Requirement	Recommendation
Browser	IE 3.0 or later Netscape Navigator 3.0 or later	IE 4.0
Authoring tools	Not required	Recommended
Multimedia applications	Not required	Recommended

After IIS 4.0 is installed, you start Content Analyzer by selecting Start, Programs, Windows NT 4.0 Option Pack, Site Server Express 2.0, Content Analyzer. Click the Open WebMap button to display WebMaps in Content Analyzer. A sample IS WebMap is included, named SAMPLE.WMP. The Content Analyzer displayed, as shown in Figure 2.20. This screen shows an example of a WebMap created by Content Analyzer and displayed in Tree and Cyberbolic views.

FIGURE 2.20

Most Web site administrators find it easier to use the tree and Cyberbolic views to view WebMaps.

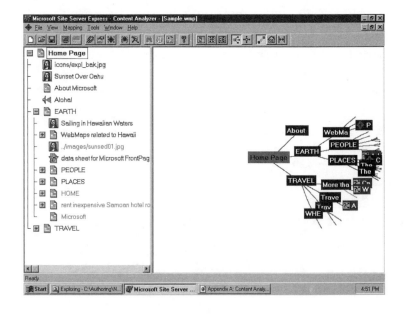

CUSTOMIZING THE INSTALLATION OF MICROSOFT SITE SERVER ANALYSIS REPORT WRITER AND USAGE IMPORT

▶ Customize the installation of Microsoft Site Server Express Usage Import and Report Writer.

Site Server Express includes two types of usage components: the Usage Import (see Figure 2.21) and Report Writer (see Figure 2.22). These tools enable you to gather and review IIS 4.0 log files from a server. With the data you collect from nine different reports, you can chart and identify trends on the usage of your IIS server.

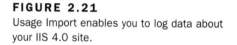

FIGURE 2.21
Usage Import enables you to log data about your IIS 4.0 site.

The Usage Import and Report Writer tools are covered in depth in Chapter 6, "Monitoring and Optimization."

FIGURE 2.22
Report Writer is used to create reports from data logged by IIS and then imported into a database by Usage Import.

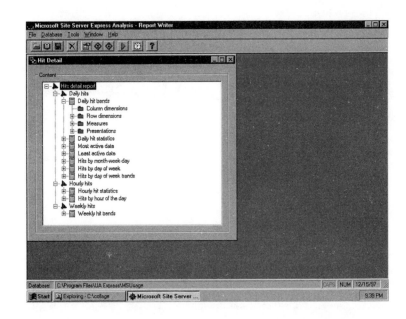

When you plan to use Usage Import and Report Writer, you should also install a relational database. The database is used to store imported log file data so each of the Site Server Express components can interact with the database to process, organize, and analyze the data. Usage Import is used to filter and configure the data in the database. Report Writer then uses that information to create reports based on the activity on your IIS site.

You can install Report Writer if you select to install the Site Server Analysis Usage Import component. The system requirements and recommendations for installing Usage Import and Report Writer are shown in Table 2.5.

TABLE 2.5

USAGE IMPORT AND REPORT WRITER SYSTEM REQUIREMENTS

Component	Requirement	Recommendation
CPU	90MHz Pentium	133MHz Pentium
RAM	16MB	32MB
Hard disk space	15MB	Additional space for log files needed

Component	*Requirement*	*Recommendation*
Internet connection	Modem	Direct
Browser	HTML 2-compatible browser that supports tables	IE 4.0

You might be wondering, "What is Whois?" Whois is an Internet utility that returns information about a domain name or IP address. For example, the command

```
'WHOIS MCP.COM'
```

returns the following:

```
Registrant:
Macmillan Computer Publishing (MCP-DOM)
   201 W. 103rd St.
   Indianapolis, IN 46290

   Domain Name: MCP.COM

   Administrative Contact:
      Armonaitis, Keith  (KA1987)
➥keith_armonaitis@PRENHALL.COM
      201-909-6318 (FAX) 201-909-6350
   Technical Contact, Zone Contact:
      Hoquim, Robert  (RH159)  robert@IQUEST.NET
      317-259-5050 ext. 505
   Billing Contact:
      Quinlan, Joseph  (JQ253)
➥joseph_quinlan@PRENHALL.COM
      201-909-6269 (FAX) 201-909-6350

   Record last updated on 25-Jun-98.
   Database last updated on 24-Jan-99 06:52:55 EST.

   Domain servers in listed order:

   NS1.IQUEST.NET            198.70.36.70
   NS2.IQUEST.NET            198.70.36.95
   NS2.MCP.COM               204.95.224.200


The InterNIC Registration Services database contains ONLY
non-military and non-US Government Domains and contacts.
Other associated whois servers:
   American Registry for Internet Numbers - whois.arin.net
   European IP Address Allocations         - whois.ripe.net
   Asia Pacific IP Address Allocations     - whois.apnic.net
   US Military                             - whois.nic.mil
   US Government                           - whois.nic.gov
```

NOTE

Uses of the Internet Connection
You can use the Internet connection to resolve IP addresses, run Whois inquiries, and conduct HTML title lookups.

This is probably more information than you wanted, but you did ask. This tool is more frequently used on UNIX systems and is not

NOTE **Access and Usage Import and Report Writer** When Access is used with Usage Import and Report Writer, a default database by the name of ANALYST.MDB is created by the installation program. A compressed copy of ANALYST.MDB in its original format (no Internet sites or log file data are contained in this file) is created in a ZIP file called TEMPLATE.ZIP. Use this file if you need to create a new database.

included in the Windows NT installation software. It is in the Windows NT Resource Kit as part of the POSIX compatibility software. IIS has the capability to make Whois queries, but does not add the explicit command to the operating system.

You also might want to install the following optional reporting applications:

◆ Microsoft Word version 7 (or later) to create Word reports

◆ Microsoft Excel version 7 (or later) to create spreadsheet reports

◆ Microsoft Access or the Access runtime version

◆ Microsoft SQL Server if the total size of your databases are more than 75MB per month

◆ Precompiled DLL for Microsoft ISAPI

◆ Source code for Apache and Netscape NSAPI server extensions

You should now be prepared to apply all your installation and configuration expertise to the following case study.

CASE STUDY: INSTALLING MICROSOFT INTERNET INFORMATION 4.0 FOR LEGAL BEAGLES

ESSENCE OF THE CASE

The following are the components you need:

▶ The WWW service to serve Web pages

▶ The FTP service for file uploading and downloading

▶ The SMTP service for e-mail services

▶ Microsoft NNTP Service for hosting discussion groups

▶ Site Server Express Content Analyzer

SCENARIO

In this scenario, you return to the case study from the previous chapter. In that scenario, you planned your installation. In this chapter, you complete the installation. You are the network administrator for Legal Beagles, a 1,000-person law firm. You have just finished planning for the installation of an Internet/intranet server. Now, you need to install Microsoft Internet Information Server 4.0. The components that you have decided you need to install are listed in "Essence of the Case."

CASE STUDY: INSTALLING MICROSOFT INTERNET INFORMATION 4.0 FOR LEGAL BEAGLES

ANALYSIS

Your analysis reveals the following:

ASSUMPTIONS

You can assume that the company is in some way connected to the Internet, so they have the connectivity needed to send and receive Internet e-mail. You can also assume they have a TCP/IP infrastructure, so they will be able to get to the server.

SOLUTION

The solution is both simple and complex. The short answer is to install IIS. Actually, there is a bit more to it than that. There are certain items you need to remember not only during installation, but for the production configuration of each of the services after installation. Let's look at each of the services you are installing and some of the things you should keep in mind for each.

THE WWW SERVICE

Quite possibly, WWW is the most common of all the services that you need to install. WWW provides the functionality of serving Web pages. Following are some things to keep in mind when configuring this service: Will you be using TCP/IP port 80, the standard port? Will you be hosting multiple sites on the server? If so, how will you be differentiating the site? Finally, how much traffic will this site need to support? There are a

number of limitations you can set on the WWW service that can affect performance.

THE FTP SERVICE

Used for file uploads and downloads, FTP is one of the core IIS services. Some things to keep in mind when configuring the FTP service is the directory listing style, whether to use the standard port, how secure the access needs to be, and how much traffic the site will be handling.

THE SMTP SERVICE

The SMTP service sends and receives Internet mail. A couple parameters of particular interest here are the number of concurrent connections and the message size limitations. It is also crucial that the server has access to DNS to ensure correct message delivery.

MICROSOFT NNTP SERVICE

The NNTP service allows your IIS server to host newsgroups in the same fashion as the now infamous Usenet newsgroups. Because this service does not accept newsfeeds, the groups you can host all need to be local. One of the most important things to consider when setting this service up is what newsgroups do you plan to host? If this server will be servicing a large number of newsgroups, you should also look into the concurrent connections and expiration parameters for this service.

continues

CASE STUDY: INSTALLING MICROSOFT INTERNET INFORMATION 4.0 FOR LEGAL BEAGLES

continued

SITE SERVER EXPRESS CONTENT ANALYZER

Last but not least, the Site Server Express Content Analyzer ties it all together, by allowing the logs of the other services to be imported and reported on. This is what allows you to find broken links on your site, check the amount of data transferred to and from your FTP site, and see who has been using what resources on your site. Being able to report these types of things to management is critical to a successful IIS deployment in many corporate environments.

CHAPTER SUMMARY

KEY TERMS

Before you take the exam, make sure you are comfortable with the definitions and concepts for eacj of the following key terms:

- Anonymous login
- Certificate authority
- Certificate Server
- Domain Name System (DNS)
- File Transfer Protocol (FTP)
- HyperText Markup Language (HTML)
- HyperText Transfer Protocol (HTTP), especially HTTP 1.1
- Index Server
- Internet Explorer
- Microsoft Management Console

In this chapter, we discussed a number of the facets of installing Microsoft Internet Information Server 4.0. Topics of special interest include the following:

- ◆ Installing Microsoft Internet Information Server 4.0
- ◆ IIS 4.0 includes the following components:
  - Authentication Server
  - SMTP Mail Server
  - Microsoft Management Console
  - NNTP News Server
  - Script Debugger
  - Site Analyst
  - Transaction Server
  - Usage Analyst
  - Web Publishing Wizard
  - Windows Scripting Host
  - FrontPage Server Administrator

CHAPTER SUMMARY

Before you install Microsoft Internet Information Server 4.0, you should make sure your server meets the minimum requirements.

You also should have the following software installed:

◆ Windows NT Server 4.0

◆ Service Pack 3 (or later) for Windows NT Server 4.0

◆ Internet Explorer 4.01 or later

For improved security, you should use NTFS for any volumes hosting IIS files.

◆ Identifying Changes Made by the Installation of IIS

Installing Microsoft Internet Information Server 4.0 adds a number of components to the Windows NT Server, including the following:

• Microsoft Management Console (MMC)

• New services including FTP Publishing Service, IIS Administration Service, Content Index, and World Wide Web Publishing Service

• The IUSR_computername user

◆ Installing and Configuring Certificate Server

There are three subcomponents to the Certificate Server that can be installed, as follows:

• The Certificate Server Certificate Authority

• The Certificate Server Documentation

• The Certificate Server Web Client

◆ Installing and Configuring Microsoft SMTP Service

Some of the more important parameters for the Microsoft SMTP Service include the following:

• The inbound and outbound TCP connection ports. The default is port 25.

continues

KEY TERMS
• Network News Transfer Protocol (NNTP)
• Newsfeed
• Persistent connections
• Secure Sockets Layer (SSL)
• Simple Mail Transfer Protocol (SMTP)
• TCP/IP
• WebMap
• Whois
• World Wide Web (WWW)

CHAPTER SUMMARY (continued)

- The identity and IP address of this SMTP site.

- The number of inbound and outbound connections.

- Logging.

- Message size.

◆ Installing and Configuring the Microsoft NNTP Service

Some of the more important parameters for the NNTP service include the following:

- The standard and SSL ports for newsreader access. Port 119 is default for an unencrypted connection and port 563 is the default for the SSL connection.

- The identity and IP address of this NNTP site.

- The number of connections.

- The connection timeout.

- Logging.

- Posting rules.

- Home Directory.

- You can set up the newsgroups the server will host.

- The Expiration policy.

◆ Configuring IIS to Support the FTP Service

Some of the more important parameters to configure for the FTP Service include the following:

- User logon requirements.

- Port settings.

- Directory listing style.

- FTP Home Directory.

- Virtual directories and servers.

CHAPTER SUMMARY

◆ Configuring IIS to Support the WWW Service

Much like the other services discussed in the chapter, the WWW service has a number of options you can configure, including the following:

- Bandwidth and user connections.

- User logon requirements and authentication requirements.

- Port settings.

- Setting HTTP 1.1 host header names to host multiple Web sites.

- Enabling HTTP Keep-Alives.

◆ Configuring and Saving Consoles by Using Microsoft Management Console

Microsoft Management Console (MMC) is used to organize and perform management tasks for IIS 4.0. MMC does not actually administer any part of IIS or your network; rather, it provides a framework for other applications (called snap-ins) to administer parts of the network. Internet Service Manager, for instance, is a snap-in.

◆ Verifying Server Settings by Accessing the Metabase

The metabase is a memory-resident data storage area that stores your IIS 4.0 configuration values. The metabase is analogous to, but not identical to, the Windows NT Registry and is used to store IIS-specific information, including the following:

- Web site configuration information.

- IIS logging configuration information.

- FTP and WWW service configuration information.

- Virtual directory configuration information.

- Filter configuration information.

- Secure Socket Layer (SSL) protocol configuration information.

continues

CHAPTER SUMMARY (continued)

◆ Choosing the Appropriate Administration Method

IIS 4.0 provides two main ways to administer your IIS installation. To administer IIS 4.0, you use Internet Service Manager, either as a snap-in to MMC or as an HTML application in Internet Explorer 4.0.

◆ Customizing the Installation of Microsoft Site Server Express Content Analyzer

The Site Server Express Content Analyzer (Content Analyzer for short) enables you to create WebMaps to give you a view of your Web site, helping you to manage your Web site.

◆ Customizing the Installation of Microsoft Site Server Analysis Report Writer and Usage Import Site Server Express includes two types of usage components: the Usage Import and Report Writer. These tools enable you to gather and review IIS 4.0 log files from a server.

APPLY YOUR KNOWLEDGE

This section allows you to assess how well you understand the material in the chapter. Review and Exam questions test your knowledge of the tasks and concepts specified in the objectives. The excercises provide you with opport unities to engage in the sorts of tasks that comprise the skill sets the objectives reflect.

Exercises

2.1   Installing IIS

The following exercise walks you through a simple installation of IIS.

Estimated time: 30–45 minutes

1. Insert the Option Pack CD-ROM and locate the Setup icon in Internet Explorer. Double-click on the Setup icon. If you downloaded IIS 4.0 from the Internet, double-click on the setup file.

2. Click Next on the Welcome to the Windows NT 4.0 Option dialog box. The End User License Agreement screen appears.

3. Click Accept.

4. Click Custom.

5. Click the components you want to install. Click Next. A dialog box showing the default publishing folders appears. A list summarizing folder locations appears.

6. Click Next. Walk through the dialog boxes adding the components you selected in step 5.

7. After installing the components, click Next. Setup now completes the installation process and installs the IIS files on your hard disk.

8. Click Finish when all the files are installed to your system.

9. Click Yes when prompted to restart your computer.

2.2   Setting User Connections and Bandwidth Throttling

The following exercise walks you through setting user connections and setting bandwidth throttling.

Estimated time: 15–30 minutes

1. Select Start, Programs, Windows NT 4.0 Option Pack, Microsoft Internet Information Server, Internet Service Manager.

2. Expand the Internet Information Server folder.

3. Expand the server that you want to modify.

4. Right-click the Default Web Site entry. Your Web site might be named something different.

5. Click Properties. The Web Site Properties sheet appears.

6. On the Web Site tab, click the Limited To option (see Figure 2.23).

FIGURE 2.23
Use the Web Site tab to set the number of simultaneous connections to your site.

APPLY YOUR KNOWLEDGE

7. Enter a value in the connections field. The default is 1,000, but you might want to lower this if your resources are limited.

8. In the Connection Timeout field, enter a value for the amount of time when your server should automatically disconnect an idle session. The default is 15 minutes (900 seconds), but an average setting is 5 minutes (300 seconds). For an infinite amount of time, enter all 9s in this field.

9. Click the Performance tab (see Figure 2.24).

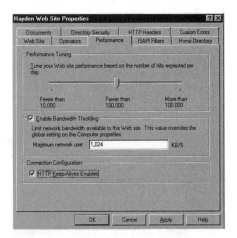

FIGURE 2.24▲
Set the bandwidth throttling value to limit the bandwidth available to your Web site.

10. Click the Enable Bandwidth Throttling option.

11. In the Maximum Network Use field, enter a value for the amount of bandwidth (measured in KB/S) you want IIS to use.

12. Click OK, or keep this open if you want to continue changing Web site settings.

2.3   Configuring Views

The following exercise shows you how to copy a Window view, create a view with a different root, and close the scope pane.

Estimated time: 15 minutes

1. Select Start, Programs, Windows NT 4.0 Option Pack, Microsoft Internet Information Server, Internet Service Manager. MMC displays with Internet Service Manager (see Figure 2.25).

FIGURE 2.25▲
MMC with Internet Service Manager snap-in displayed.

2. Select Window, New Window. A copy of the window displays.

3. To create a view with a different root, click the node you want to view as the root.

4. Click the Action menu.

5. Click New window from here. A new window appears with the node you select as the root node (see Figure 2.26).

APPLY YOUR KNOWLEDGE

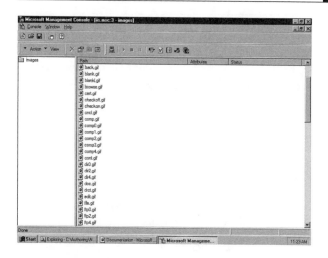

FIGURE 2.26
A node selected as the root node.

6. To view only the results pane, click the Action menu.

7. Click the Scope Pane option. The scope pane (the left pane) is removed so only the results pane shows.

8. To save this console, select Console, Save As.

9. Fill out the Save As dialog box. Consoles have an MSC extension.

10. Click Save.

2.4   Configuring Windows NT for Installation of Internet Information Server 4

The following exercise shows you how to prepare your Windows NT 4.0 server for installing IIS 4.0. This exercise presupposes the installation of Windows NT Server 4.0.

Estimated time: 45 minutes

1. Opening a Web browser on the server, go to the Microsoft Web Site and download the latest Service Pack for Windows NT Server 4.0.

2. Uncompress the file and run Update.exe. Read the License Agreement and select "I agree." When asked if you want to create an uninstall directory, say "Yes." Reboot the server when the Service Pack installation is complete.

3. Once the server has booted, log on and open your Web browser again. Go out to Microsoft's Web page and download the latest version of Internet Explorer. This will be a file called "IESETUP.EXE"

4. Execute the IESETUP.EXE file, and follow the prompts to install and configure Internet Explorer. The version should be IE 4.01 or greater in order to work with IIS 4.0.

5. Reboot the server when the browser is installed. You are now ready to install IIS 4.0.

2.5   Reviewing The Registry Changes Made Microsoft Internet Information Server 4

The following exercise shows you how to review the Registry changes made by an IIS 4.0 installation.

Estimated time: 15 minutes

1. Open the Registry Editor (REGEDT32.EXE).

2. Go to Start, Programs, Windows NT 4.0 Option Pack, Microsoft Site Server Express 2.0, Documentation. Click on Administrator's Reference in the left pane and click Registry. Click on the topic you want to read, such as WWW Service Registry Entries.

APPLY YOUR KNOWLEDGE

3. Use the Registry Editor to review the Registry changes described in the documentation.

4. Close both applications when you are done.

2.6 Setting User Logon Requirements and Authentication Requirements for the FTP Service

The following exercise shows you how to set user logon requirements and authentication requirements for the FTP Service

Estimated time: 15 minutes

1. Open Internet Service Manager.

2. Select the FTP Site you wish to modify. Right-click and select Properties.

3. Select the Security Accounts tab.

4. Change the setting to establish the required configuration. Select OK and close the Internet Service Manager application.

2.7 Enabling the HTML Service Manager

The following exercise shows you how run the HTML Service Manager to manage your Microsoft Internet Information Server 4 server.

Estimated time: 15 minutes

1. Open Internet Service Manager(HTML).

2. This will start Internet Explorer and open the URL http://localhost:<random port>/iisadmin/iisnew.asp

3. Select the Font Size by clicking on it. (Large or Small)

4. You now have access to the Internet Service Manager from an HTML interface.

2.8 Customizing the Installation of Microsoft Certificate Server

The following exercise shows you how to Customize the installation of Microsoft Certificate Server

Estimated time: 25 minutes

1. Run the Windows NT 4.0 Option Pack Setup program.

2. Select Microsoft Certificate Server and click on Show Subcomponents.

3. Select the subcomponents you want to install.

4. Click OK. Click Next.

5. Follow the setup wizard to complete the installation of Internet Information Server 4. Click Finish when you are done.

2.9 Customizing the Installation of Microsoft Site Server Express Content Analyzer

The following exercise shows you how to customize the installation of Microsoft Site Server Express Content Analyzer.

Estimated time: 25 minutes

1. Run the Windows NT 4.0 Option Pack Setup program.

2. Select Microsoft Site Server Express 2.0 and click on Show Subcomponents.

3. Select the subcomponents you want to install.

4. Click OK. Click Next.

5. Follow the setup wizard to complete the installation of Internet Information Server 4. Click Finish when you are done.

APPLY YOUR KNOWLEDGE

2.10 Customizing the Installation of Microsoft Site Server Express Usage Import and Report Writer

The following exercise shows you how to customize the installation of Microsoft Site Server Express Usage Import and Report Writer.

Estimated time: 25 minutes

1. Run the Windows NT 4.0 Option Pack Setup program.

2. Select Microsoft Site Server Express 2.0 and click on Show Subcomponents.

3. Select the subcomponents you want to install.

4. Click OK. Click Next.

5. Follow the setup wizard to complete the installation of Microsoft Internet Information Server 4. Click Finish when you are done.

Review Questions

1. You are an IIS consultant and your customer, Little Faith Enterprises, has asked you to design an IIS solution for their Internet server. The client asks you to outline the features of IIS 4.0 that should be installed to search documents, provide digital certificates, and provide newsgroup capabilities. What features would you list?

2. You are the Web administrator for the Got Bux Bank. You are setting up an IIS server to act as the bank's internal Web server. You need to have Basic Authentication enabled for the site. What two conditions must be met for Basic Authentication to work?

3. You are an IIS consultant for Little Faith Enterprises. As part of your consulting service, the client has asked you to provide some training on the administration of his site. What applications does the client potentially need to be familiar with to administer the IIS server?

4. You are the Web administrator at the Get Stuffed Taxidermy Company. You are using Microsoft Internet Information Server 4.0 to host your company's intranet site. You notice that inactive or slow connections seem to be consuming an inordinate amount of network resources. Describe the technique you should use to resolve this resource problem.

5. You've set up the FTP Service on a client's IIS server. What is the default authentication method used by the FTP service?

6. What is the metabase and why is it used by IIS?

7. You're asked by another administrator in your office to provide a copy of your MMC console of your Web site. Can you do this? If so, how?

Exam Questions

1. You are an IIS consultant working for the House of Pain Dental Clinic. They have asked you to install IIS 4.0 on a server to act as their intranet, where they will store patient records and an appointment calendar.

   What two changes to Windows NT should you make before installing IIS?

   A. Install TCP/IP and WINS

   B. Install TCP/IP and use NTFS

APPLY YOUR KNOWLEDGE

C. Install WINS and use FAT32

D. None of the above

2. You are a brand new network administrator at the Too Bright Lighting Company. As you are starting your training on IIS 4.0, you are introduced to the Microsoft Management Console (MMC), used for managing and administering IIS tasks and resources. What types of applications can you run in MMC?

A. DHTML pages

B. Plug-ins

C. Snap-ins

D. All of the above

3. You are the administrator for an Internet site at You Are Write Publishing. You are hosting the company's Internet Web site using Microsoft Internet Information Server 4.0. The president of the company wants people to be able to access the site's home page without needing to enter a file name. She feels that entering the domain name (www.urwrite.com) is easier to remember.

What must you enable in IIS to allow this?

A. A default page

B. An index page

C. home.html

D. A virtual server with index.html

4. You are the administrator of the Adventures in Accounting Payroll Specialists' IIS-based Internet and intranet sites. Because the company has locations throughout the country, you are away from the office often. You still need to be able to administer the IIS servers.

What is the best administration method for this situation?

A. Connect to your FTP server as administrator

B. Use Internet Explorer 4.0 to access the default page

C. Use Internet Service Manager (HTML) to connect to the server via the Internet

D. All of the above

5. You are a Web consultant and Exponent Mathematics has hired you to install IIS to support e-mail, Web and FTP services, and database access for their planned Internet Web site. What are the minimum components you must install?

A. SMTP service, WWW service, FTP service, Site Server Express, Index Server

B. Full install

C. NNTP service, Web and FTP services, ODBC support

D. SMTP service, WWW service, FTP service, Microsoft Data Access Components 1.5 with Data Sources

6. You're hired by a client to install IIS. The client wants to ensure that the WWW service is as secure as possible. Pick three choices from the following that help provide a secure environment for IIS:

A. Limit the Guest account and other accounts to specific directories on the server

B. Turn off auditing

C. Review network share permissions

D. Limit who has membership to the Administrators group

APPLY YOUR KNOWLEDGE

7. As the administrator of your company's intranet site, you need to connect to the server remotely for administration concerns. You plan to use Internet Service Manager (HTML). What privileges are required to do this?

   A. Guest rights

   B. Local user rights

   C. Administrator rights

   D. None of the above

8. You are an IIS administrator in an accounting firm. You are asked to install IIS on a server and you start the installation process. During the IIS Setup routine, you decide to end the installation to start it again the following day. What is your best course of action?

   A. Click the Cancel button to stop setup.

   B. Finish setup and then uninstall IIS.

   C. Shut down and restart Windows NT Server 4.0 and edit the Metabase.

   D. None of the above.

9. You are the Web administrator for Honest Abe's Used Car Sales. You are maintaining an IIS-based intranet server used to store the features and pricing of all the cars on the lot, as well as the anticipated profit margin on each vehicle. You are using Internet Service Manager to manage the site and want to hide the scope pane for easier administration.

   Select the correct sequence of steps from the following answers to complete this task:

   A. Select Console, Hide Scope Pane

   B. Select Window, Panes, Hide Scope Pane

   C. Select View, List

   D. Select Action, Scope Pane

10. As a Web consultant, you've been asked to set up IIS at Wonderful Widgets Manufacturing. The company wants IIS to be set up so that Internet users must log on using a user name and password. The firm wants the Windows NT Challenge/Response authentication feature to be used to authenticate these users.

    Which of the following is required to do that?

    A. The user must use an HTML 3.2–compatible browser.

    B. The user must use Internet Explorer 2.0 or later.

    C. The user must invoke Challenge/Response authentication on his/her client.

    D. None of the above.

11. You are the Windows NT administrator for Wild Weasel Pets. You have been asked to add the FTP service to your Microsoft Internet Information Server 4.0 server, so that customers are enabled for the anonymous uploading of files to the FTP server.

    What permission(s) is(are) needed to do this?

    A. Write-Only

    B. Execute

    C. Read

    D. Both A and C

12. You are an IIS administrator, and your manager has asked you to install IIS on a new server to be used for a departmental intranet server. During

APPLY YOUR KNOWLEDGE

IIS installation, what services can be installed? (Choose three.)

A. Certificate Server

B. Transaction Server

C. Message Queue

D. Gopher

13. In question 12, you installed IIS on a Windows NT Server 4.0 server. What are two changes that have been made to this server after IIS has been installed?

   A. You no longer can use IE 4.0 as a client application.

   B. Performance Monitor has Web Service objects available.

   C. User Manager for Domains lists a new user name in the list of user accounts.

   D. The metabase replaces the Windows NT Registry.

14. You are an Internet administrator in a small foam packaging firm. You've set up IIS to run an Internet site. What is the name of the new user created by IIS during installation? (computername is the computer name on which IIS is installed.)

   A. IISR_computername

   B. anon_computername

   C. IWAM_computername

   D. IUSR_computername

15. You use Performance Monitor to monitor activity on your IIS server. Pick three counters that you

can add to Performance Monitor to track the Web Service object:

A. Anonymous Users/sec

B. Bytes Created/sec

C. Files/sec

D. Total Head Requests

16. You are the administrator of the Yummy Fruits and Vegetables produce company's Internet servers, running Microsoft Internet Information Server 4.0. Management has decided it wants to add an additional Web site for the Fruits division of the company.

What steps do you need to follow to creates this new Web site?

   A. Open Internet Service Manager, select the server the site will be created on, and go to Create, New, Web Site. Follow the wizard to complete the site.

   B. Open Internet Service Manager, select the server the site will be created on, and go to Action, New, WWW Site. Follow the wizard to complete the site.

   C. Open Internet Service Manager, select the server the site will be created on, and go to Action, New, Web Site. Follow the wizard to complete the site.

   D. Open Internet Service Manager, select the New Web Site Wizard, and follow the wizard to complete the site.

Answers to Review Questions

1. Microsoft Index Server 3.0 is used for searching capabilities, Microsoft Certificate Server to provide certificates for authentication, and the NNTP service to provide hosting for the newsgroups. See "Installing IIS 4.0." There is also an unspoken need for the WWW service because you cannot initiate an Index Server search without entering your search criteria into a Web form.

2. Anonymous access must be disabled, and anonymous access is denied because Windows NT permissions are set requiring the user to log on with a user name and password. See "Setting User Logon Requirements and Authentication Requirements" in the section "Configuring IIS to Support the WWW Service."

3. The client can use standard Windows NT Server administration tools, including Performance Monitor and User Manager for Domains for managing the server component of the equation. In addition, Internet Service Manager can be used as a snap-in to the Microsoft Management Console (MMC) for managing the IIS application. For remote administration, Internet Service Manager (HTML) can be used in Internet Explorer 4.0. See "Choosing the Appropriate Administration Method."

4. Set the connection timeout period to a reasonable amount. See "Setting Bandwidth and User Connections."

5. Anonymous authentication. This allows any user to access the FTP site using the access permissions assigned to the IUSR_*servername* user account. See "Setting User Logon Requirements and Authentication Requirements" in the section " Configuring IIS to Support the FTP Service."

6. The metabase is a hierarchical database that stores IIS 4.0 settings. The metabase has keys that correspond to IIS elements; each key has properties that affect the configuration of that element. It is analogous to the Windows NT Registry, but it is much faster and more flexible then the Registry. See "Verifying Server Settings by Accessing the Metabase."

7. Yes, you can. Create a console view of the Web server you want to share and select Action, New Window From Here. When the new window displays, select Console, Save As and save the console with an MSC extension. Send the file to the other administrator. See "Configuring and Saving Consoles by Using Microsoft Management Console."

Answers to Exam Questions

1. **B.** For systems in which file-level security is needed, use NTFS so you can limit access to files and directories. Also, you need TCP/IP if you plan to have users access the system. IIS 4.0 is a TCP/IP-only application. Regarding A, this is half right. You need TCP/IP, but WINS isn't required. C is incorrect, especially because Windows NT can't read the FAT32 file system. See "Configuring a Microsoft Windows NT Server 4.0 Computer for the Installation of IIS."

2. **C.** MMC does not actually administer any part of IIS or your network; rather, it provides a framework for other applications (called snap-ins) to administer parts of the network. Internet Service Manager, for instance, is a snap-in. When Internet Service Manager starts (not the HTML version), an MMC console appears with the Internet Service Manager displayed as a snap-in.

APPLY YOUR KNOWLEDGE

A is incorrect; dynamic HTML pages are actually served by the WWW service. B is also incorrect; plug-ins are components you add to your Web browser to view custom data on the Web. See "Configuring and Saving Consoles by Using Microsoft Management Console."

3. **A.** You can set IIS 4.0 to display a default page when clients access your site without a specified document in the URL. From this default page (usually your home page or index page), you can direct users to other documents or resources on your site. Answer B sounds plausible, because many early Web sites used index.html as the name of the default page. C is incorrect; it provides you a possible name for your default page, but it is not correct. D is also incorrect; this sounds impressive, but you don't need a virtual server to set the default page. See "Setting Default Pages."

4. **C.** With Internet Service Manager (HTML), you can manage your Web site remotely using a standard Web browser, such as IE 4.0. This makes it convenient for administrators to manage a Web site when physically away from the Web site. An administrator, for instance, can be located in a different building than where the Web server is housed. A is incorrect; connecting using FTP does not allow you to do anything other than transfer files. B is closer, but the administrative application resides on TCP/IP port 2106 by default. Accessing the default page does not give you that access. See "Choosing the Appropriate Administration Method."

5. **D.** Table 2.3 describes the different services and components you can install with IIS 4.0. See "Installing IIS 4.0."

6. **A, C, D.** To help secure your IIS installation, you should perform the following tasks:

   - Turn on auditing.
   - Limit the Guest account and other accounts to specific directories on the server.
   - Limit who has membership to the Administrators Group.
   - Start only those services and protocols required by your system.
   - Use complex password schemes.
   - Review network share permissions.

   Turning off auditing is actually a bad idea because it removes your ability to see who is accessing your system. See "Configuring a Microsoft Windows NT Server 4.0 Computer for the Installation of IIS."

7. **C.** By using Internet Service Manager (HTML), the administrator can connect to the server and administer it from the remote location. See "Choosing the Appropriate Administration Method."

8. **B.** If you decide you don't want to install IIS 4.0 and you've already started the IIS 4.0 setup program, don't cancel it. This leaves files on your system that the uninstall program cannot remove. Finish the entire installation process, then uninstall IIS 4.0 if you don't want it on your system. See "Installing IIS 4.0."

9. **D.** To view only the results pane, click the Action menu and click the Scope Pane option. The scope pane (the left pane) is removed, so only the results pane shows. See "Configuring and Saving Consoles by Using Microsoft Management Console."

APPLY YOUR KNOWLEDGE

10. **B.** The Windows NT Challenge/Response feature authenticates the client attempting to connect to your Web site. The only Web browsers that support this feature include Internet Explorer 2.0 and later. During the challenge/response procedure, encrypted information is exchanged between the client and server to authenticate the user. A is incorrect; the version of HTML has nothing to do with authentication capabilities. C is incorrect because you cannot invoke authentication from the client. Authentication is started by the server when you request access to a resource that is secured. See "Setting User Logon Requirements and Authentication Requirements."

11. **A.** Write enables clients to upload files to the home directory on your FTP server. This option should be selected only for FTP servers in which users must upload files. By default, this option is not selected. See "Configuring IIS to Support the FTP Service."

12. **A, B, C.** Table 2.3 describes the different services and components you can install with IIS 4.0. See "Installing IIS 4.0."

13. **B, C.** When you install IIS 4.0, your Windows NT Server 4.0 computer changes. The following are the changes that occur:

    - Microsoft Management Console (MMC) is the host for the Internet Service Manager. Internet Service Manager is IIS's administrative program.

    - Registry changes can be viewed by selecting Start, Programs, Windows NT 4.0 Option Pack, Microsoft Site Server Express 2.0, Documentation. Click on Administrator's Reference in the left pane and click Registry.

Click on the topic you want to read, such as WWW Service Registry Entries.

    - New services include the FTP Publishing Service, IIS Administration Service, Content Index, and World Wide Web Publishing Service.

    - User Manager for Domains lists a new user name in the list of user accounts. This user name is IUSR_computername and allows anonymous access to Internet services on your computer.

    - Performance Monitor can now be used to track several IIS services including Content Index, Content Index Filter, FTP Service, HTTP Content Index, HTTP Service, and Internet Information Services Global. Some of the over 75 counters added to Performance Monitor enable you to track connections, bytes transferred, and cache information.

See "Identifying Changes to a Windows NT Server 4.0 Computer Made by the Installation of IIS."

14. **D.** User Manager for Domains lists a new user name in the list of user accounts. This user name is IUSR_computername and allows anonymous access to Internet services on your computer. See "Identifying Changes to a Windows NT Server 4.0 Computer Made by the Installation of IIS."

15. **A, C, D.** Performance Monitor can now be used to track HTTP services. Some of the over 75 counters added to Performance Monitor enable you to track connections, bytes transferred, and cache information. See "Identifying Changes to a Windows NT Server 4.0 Computer Made by the Installation of IIS." Chapter 6, "Monitoring and

APPLY YOUR KNOWLEDGE

Optimization," discusses Performance Monitor in more detail.

16. **C.** The correct steps are: Open Internet Service Manager, select the server the site will be created on, and go to Action, New, Web Site. Follow the wizard to complete the site. See "Configuring IIS to Support the WWW Service."

Suggested Readings and Resources

1. Howell, Nelson and Forta, Ben. *Using Microsoft Internet Information Server 4 (Special Edition Using)*. Que Education & Training: 1997.

In this chapter, we discuss the Microsoft Internet Information Server 4.0 topics relating to Configuring and Managing Resource Access. After planning and installing Internet Information Server 4.0, the next logical step is to discuss making it all work. This chapter covers configuring the components of IIS to move your IIS server from installed status to real world, production status.

For the exam, Microsoft defines the Configuring and Managing Resource Access objectives as the following:

Create and share directories with appropriate permissions. Tasks include the following:

- **Setting directory-level permissions**

- **Setting file-level permissions**

▶ These directories should not be confused with the files and directories you are familiar with in Windows NT Explorer. This objective expects you to understand how to create and assign permissions to files and directories being served to the Web as part of a home directory, either through the WWW service or the FTP service of IIS.

Create and share local and remote virtual directories with appropriate permissions. Tasks include the following:

- **Creating a virtual directory and assigning an alias**

- **Setting directory-level permissions**

- **Setting file-level permissions**

▶ Whereas the previous objective dealt with the files and directories that make up the home directory, a virtual directory is any directory that is not the home directory. To master this objective, you should know how to create and assign permissions to virtual directories.

CHAPTER 3

Configuring and Managing Resource Access

Create and share virtual servers with appropriate permissions. Tasks include the following:

- **Assigning IP addresses**

▶ If you are going to manage an IIS server hosting multiple Web sites, you need to know how to create virtual servers and assign each a unique IP address. The same goes for mastering this objective for the exam.

Write scripts to manage the FTP service or the WWW service.

▶ As described in Chapter 1, "Planning," Internet Information Server 4.0 includes the Microsoft Script Debugger. This utility can be used to debug a variety of scripting languages and can assist you in writing scripts to handle some of the day-to-day tasks associated with managing an IIS service.

Manage a Web site by using Content Analyzer. Tasks include the following:

- **Creating, customizing, and navigating WebMaps**

- **Examining a Web site by using the various reports provided by Content Analyzer**

- **Tracking links by using a WebMap**

▶ The heart and soul of managing your IIS installation is the Content Analyzer application. This application helps you to understand how your Web site is set up, precisely what sort of content the site includes (GIFs, JPGs, and so on), and where problems may exist.

Configure Microsoft SMTP Service to host message traffic.

▶ A mail server is only useful when it can send mail. This objective conveys the expectation that you should be able to configure the SMTP service to handle message traffic.

Configure Microsoft NNTP Service to host a newsgroup.

▶ Much like the previous objective for the SMTP service, this objective states that you should be able to set up the NNTP service to host a newsgroup.

Configure Certificate Server to issue certificates.

▶ You need to understand how to use the Certificate Server to create and distribute certificates for authentication.

Configure Index Server to index a Web site.

▶ You need to understand how Index Server can be used to index a Web site.

Manage MIME types.

▶ MIME (Multipurpose Internet Mail Extensions) is a specification for formatting non-ASCII e-mail messages so that they can be sent over the Internet. MIME can be configured to allow the sending and receiving of graphics files, audio files, or full-motion video files, to name a few. For this objective, you need to understand how to manage the MIME types an IIS server can support.

Manage the FTP service.

▶ FTP is one of the oldest TCP/IP applications still in use, and you need to understand how to manage the FTP server component of Internet Information Server 4.0.

Manage the WWW service.

▶ If FTP is one of the oldest applications, WWW is the most popular. If you are going to be supporting an IIS 4.0 server, you need to have a thorough understanding of the WWW service. You need the same understanding for the IIS 4.0 exam.

As you read through this chapter, you should concentrate on the following key concepts:

▶ Configuring different components of Microsoft Internet Information Server to put them into production and then support them.

▶ Creating and assigning permissions to files and directories. Pay particularly close attention to where directories can reside. Also, pay attention to how NTFS and IIS permissions interact.

▶ Content Analyzer is used to gather and help analyze a variety of facts about your Web site. You need to understand the information it can gather and how to use that information.

▶ Know both methods for configuring MIME types, as well as where the MIME type information is stored.

▶ Finally, be familiar with the management aspects of the WWW and FTP services.

▶ The most important part of this chapter is the fact that it covers the day-to-day tasks of maintaining a production IIS server. If you come across something in this chapter that looks like what you would do on a fairly regular basis as an IIS administrator, expect to see it on the test.

▶ Be sure you know what TCP/IP port each of these services use. Even if you don't see it on the exam, you will find it useful if you ever work on a server that uses custom ports or with a firewall where you are specifying which ports and services are allowed and how they work.

INTRODUCTION

So far, we have discussed planning and installing Internet Information Server 4.0 applications. Later in the book, we discuss troubleshooting the same applications. This chapter covers the topics that fall in between those areas. After you install your applications, it's time to look at the day-to-day activities that go into supporting production IIS implementations. As an administrator in the real world, you'll find that as much as 90 percent of what you do with an IIS server is maintenance work. Maintenance includes the creation, deletion, and access control over potentially multiple sites, checking to make sure that the layout and content of the server is functional and ensuring that each of the applications is configured to function. You need to know how to create and support newsgroups for discussions, make sure that SMTP mail is flowing, and use WebMaps to check for broken links on your site. This chapter addresses the broader topics associated with these activities. Many of these applications are addressed elsewhere in this book, but not in the context of configuration and management. Much of the configuration and management of services can be done during the initial planning, installation, or troubleshooting phases. There are a number of topics in this chapter that can help you put the other chapters into perspective. This chapter should clarify much of the information presented in the rest of the book.

CREATING AND SHARING DIRECTORIES

▶ Create and share directories with appropriate permissions.

One of the first things you are asked to do with your IIS server is create a home directory for a Web site. To create and share a new WWW directory, do the following:

STEP BY STEP

3.1 Create a New WWW Directory

1. Select Start, Programs, Windows NT 4.0 Option Pack, Microsoft Internet Information Server, Internet Service Manager.

2. Expand the Internet Information Server folder.

3. Select the IIS server you want to add a WWW site to, as shown in Figure 3.1. (If you are only managing one server, you should only have one choice.)

FIGURE 3.1▶
Select the server to add a Web site to.

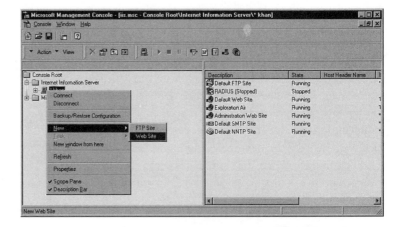

4. Right-click and select New. This brings up the choice of creating a Web site or FTP site. Choose Web Site.

5. Enter the Web site description, as shown in Figure 3.2, and select Next.

6. Select or verify the IP address to use (see Figure 3.3). If you are creating a new site, make certain you use an address that is not currently being used or it will create a conflict with the current one. If you use the same IP address for multiple sites, you can differentiate them by using different TCP port addresses for each site.

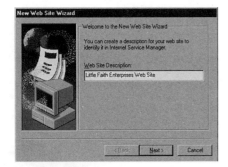

FIGURE 3.2▲
Enter a description for the Web site you are creating.

7. The TCP port defaults to 80. This is the default used for all WWW services. If you want to offer the service but hide it from most browsers, choose another port.

8. If SSL is to be used, enter the appropriate port for it (default is 443) and click Next.

9. Enter the path (see Figure 3.4) for what will appear as the home directory (you also can use the Browse button to specify).

10. By default, the check box appears, allowing anonymous access to the Web site. If you do not want anonymous access, remove the check. Choose Next.

11. Select the access permissions for the directory (see Figure 3.5). Choices include the following:

   • **Allow Read Access—Assigned by default.** This allows users to connect to the site and read the information stored in the home directory. This does not include the capability to list files.

   • **Allow Script Access—Assigned by default.** Users connecting to the site with this permission can execute scripts stored in the home directory.

   • **Allow Execute Access—Includes Script access.** Users granted this access permission can not only execute scripts stored in the home directory, but other applications as well.

   • **Allow Write Access.** This permission allows a user to connect to the site and write to files stored in the home directory.

   • **Allow Directory Browsing**. This permission allows a user to connect to the site and read the list of files stored in the home directory.

12. Choose Finish. Figure 3.6 shows the newly created Web site. Notice that it is created in the *Stopped* mode. You need to manually start the site. To do this, you can either right-click the site and select Start, or click on the Start icon.

FIGURE 3.3▲
Set the Web site port and IP address.

FIGURE 3.4▲
Select the site home directory and enabling anonymous access.

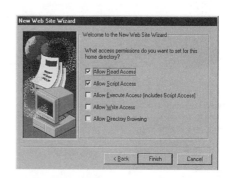

FIGURE 3.5▲
Set the directory permissions.

continues

continued

FIGURE 3.6▶
The Little Faith Enterprises site has been
created, but is in Stopped mode.

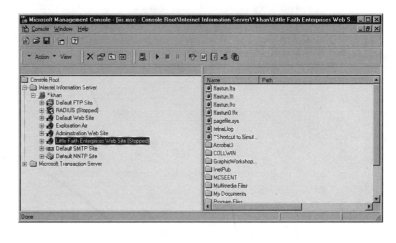

You might also be asked to create an FTP site. To create and share a
new FTP directory, do the following:

STEP BY STEP

3.2 Creating a New FTP Directory

1. Select Start, Programs, Windows NT 4.0 Option Pack,
   Microsoft Internet Information Server, Internet Service
   Manager.

2. Expand the Internet Information Server folder.

3. Select the IIS server you want to add the FTP site to, as
   shown earlier in Figure 3.1. (If you are only managing one
   server, you should only have one choice.)

4. Right-click and select New. This brings up the choice
   of creating a Web site or FTP site. Choose FTP Site.

5. Enter the FTP Site description (see Figure 3.7) and select
   Next.

6. Select or verify the IP address to use (see Figure 3.8).

7. The TCP port defaults to 21. This is the default used
   for the FTP service.

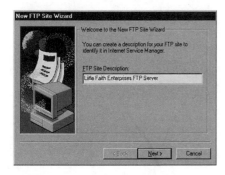

FIGURE 3.7▲
Enter a description for the new FTP site.

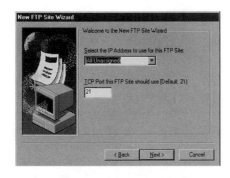

Set the IP Address and TCP Port for the FTP site.

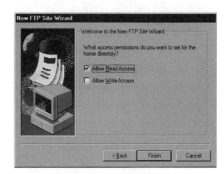

FIGURE 3.9▲
Set the home directory for the new FTP site.

8. Enter the path (see Figure 3.9) for what will appear as the home directory (you also can use the Browse button to specify).

9. Select the access permissions for the directory (see Figure 3.10). Choices include the following:

    • **Allow Read Access—Assigned by default.** This allows users to download files using the FTP protocol.

    • **Allow Write Access.** Write access allows users to upload (or write) files to the site using the FTP protocol.

10. Choose Finish. Notice in Figure 3.11, the new FTP site is stopped. To start the site, you can right-click it and select start, or click on the Start icon.

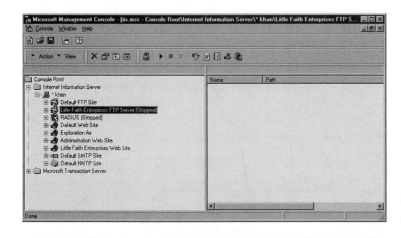

FIGURE 3.10▲
Set the permissions for the new FTP site.

◀FIGURE 3.11
The new FTP site is created and in Stopped status after creation.

NOTE

Execute Versus Script Access
The Execute permission allows for CGI and ISAPI scripts to execute, whereas Script is sufficient for IDC, IDQ, and ASP. These topics are explored further in Chapters 4, "Integration and Interoperability," and 5, "Running Applications."

Choosing the Access Rights

The five rights that you can select for IIS access work in conjunction with all other rights. Like share rights, the IIS rights are *in addition to* NTFS rights and of greatest value when you are using anonymous access. Allowing Read access lets a user view a file if her NTFS permissions also allow it. Taking away Read, however, prevents the user from viewing the file regardless of what NTFS permissions are set.

As listed previously, the names of the rights are pretty self-explanatory. The only caveats to note are that Read and Script access are assigned by default, and Execute is a superset of Script access.

Changing Permissions and Access for Directories

After the wizard has run and the directory is configured for site access, you can change permissions and access for individual directories by selecting the directory in Internet Service Manager, right-clicking, and choosing Properties.

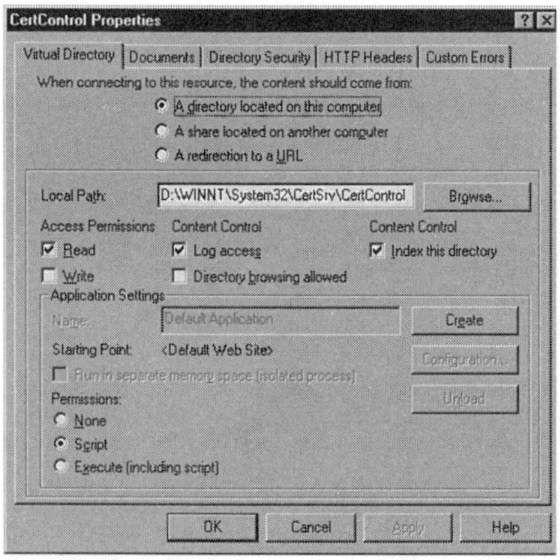

Figure 3.12 shows the properties for a directory. Notice that access permissions have now been set to Read and Write, or any combination thereof, and permissions are now None, Script, or Execute (which includes script).

Click the Directory Security (see Figure 3.13) tab of the directory's properties and you see that you have the following three items you can configure:

FIGURE 3.12
The properties for a WWW directory.

◆ Anonymous Access and Authentication Control

◆ Secure Communications

◆ IP Address and Domain Name restrictions

The bottom two options are discussed later in this chapter. Selecting Edit on the Enabling Anonymous Access section brings up the dialog box shown in Figure 3.14. From here, you can choose to allow or disallow anonymous access and (by choosing Edit) the name of the anonymous access account (which defaults to IUSR_{computername}). You can also enable password synchronization from this screen.

◀**FIGURE 3.13**
The Directory Security tab allows you configure the different security features of IIS 4.0.

If you disable anonymous access, you have the ability to select one (or both).

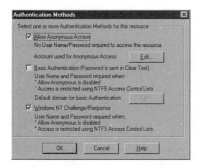

◀**FIGURE 3.14**
The Enabling Anonymous Access dialog box allows you to configure the three methods of controlling authentication to the site.

Changing Permissions and Access for Files

You also can control the permissions for specific files in a similar manner. First, select the file and choose its properties. A screen similar to Figure 3.15 is displayed. By choosing the File Security tab, you can set the same file options that were illustrated in Figure 3.14 for the directory.

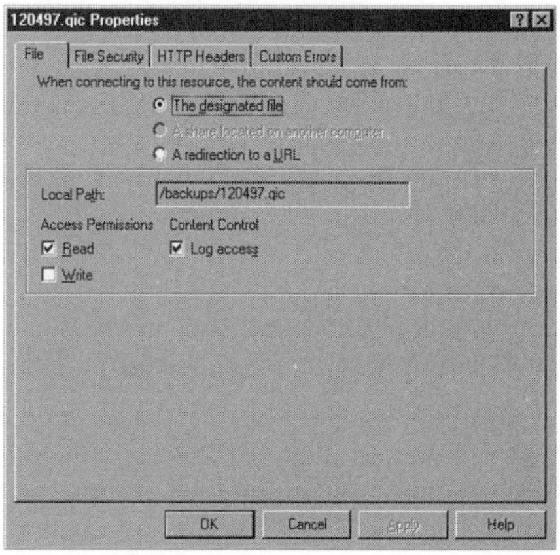

FIGURE 3.15▲
Properties for a file shared through the WWW service.

NOTE

Why Would You Use a Virtual Directory? If you are uncertain why you would want to create an additional shared directory, think of the example of an Internet service provider giving its clients the ability to have their own Web pages. A client's personal Web site, in some cases, is added to the host's domain name (for example, http://www. flash.net/~andrew).

NOTE

Seeing Virtual Directories Where are all virtual directories when you list the home directory contents via a Web browser? (You need the Allow Directory Browsing permission to see the files and subdirectories.) They are not visible in a directory list. They need to be explicitly pointed to in the HTML code of the Web site; otherwise, they cannot be accessed.

NOTE

NetWare Servers and Virtual Directories Can a NetWare server host a virtual directory? The short answer is no. But there is a work-around. If you take an NT machine (server or workstation) in the IIS authentication domain and map a drive to the NetWare server, you can configure that mapped drive as a virtual directory. In the real world, avoid doing this if possible. If you ever have a problem with that virtual directory, you not only have to troubleshoot the IIS virtual directory, but also the drive mapped to the NetWare server and the NetWare server itself. In the end, it's probably cheaper to buy another drive to host NetWare-based data and place a copy of the data on it.

CREATING AND SHARING VIRTUAL DIRECTORIES

▶ Create and share local and remote virtual directories with appropriate permissions.

As the name implies, virtual directories are entities that do not exist, but give you the ability to reference relative file locations to make it appear as if they are in a directory. This can allow you to work around issues such as disk space and determining where best to store files.

The disadvantage to using virtual directories is a slight decrease in performance if the directories reside on different servers because files must be retrieved from across the network. This can also affect the performance of your network, if the amount of data being retrieved is significant. Be sure to consider this during the planning phase of your IIS implementation. The only other downside is that virtual directories are not visible in directory listings and must be accessed through explicit links within HTML files.

To host virtual directories, the server must be in the same Windows NT authentication domain as the IIS server. A file share to a NetWare server can even be used if it is mapped to an NT machine in the authentication domain. Aside from this restriction, the directories can be either local or remote.

Creating a Virtual Directory

If you choose to create the virtual directory on a local computer, the Internet Service Manager can be used to assign an alias to it. To create a virtual directory, do the following:

STEP BY STEP

3.3 Creating a Virtual Directory

1. Start the Internet Service Manager from the Programs portion of the Start menu.

---

2. Open a Web site, right-click the left pane and choose New.

3. Select Virtual Directory, as shown in Figure 3.16. This starts the New Virtual Directory Wizard.

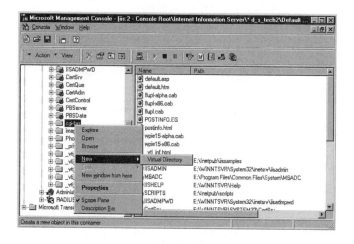

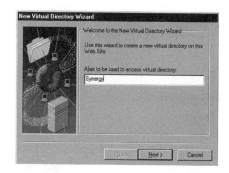

◀**FIGURE 3.16**
Select Virtual Directory from the New menu.

4. Enter an alias to be used for the virtual directory name and click Next, as shown in Figure 3.17.

FIGURE 3.17▲
Enter the alias to be used for the virtual directory.

5. Enter the physical path to the virtual directory, as shown in Figure 3.18 (you also can select the Browse button), and click Next.

6. Select the access permissions for the virtual directory. You might notice that these look familiar. These same permissions can be set for the Web site home directory. Choices include the following:

- Allow Read Access
- Allow Script Access
- Allow Execute Access
- Allow Write Access
- Allow Directory Browsing

The choices and defaults are shown in Figure 3.19.

7. Select Finish.

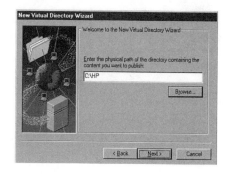

FIGURE 3.18▲
Enter the physical path for the virtual directory.

continues

continued

FIGURE 3.19►
Available access rights for the virtual directory.

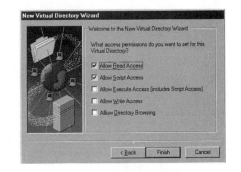

Properties tabs for a virtual directory.

Making Changes After Setup

After the wizard has run and the virtual directory is configured for site access, you can change permissions and access for individual directories or files by selecting the directory\file in Internet Service Manager, right-clicking, and choosing Properties. This opens the Properties dialog box for the Virtual Directory, shown in Figure 3.20. Notice that the available tabs are the same as those for any physical directories in the site's home directory.

CREATING AND SHARING VIRTUAL SERVERS

▶ Create and share virtual servers with appropriate permissions.

The major benefit of virtual servers is that they enable you to expand your site beyond the limitations of a single site per server. You can combine a number of different sites (domain names) on a single server through the implementation of virtual servers.

Also known as multihomed hosts, multihomed servers, or multihoming, virtual servers enable one host to respond to requests for the following three totally different sites:

```
http://www.synergy.com
http://www.synergy_technology.com
http://www.st.com
```

All of the previous domain names are fully qualified domain names (FQDNs). An FQDN completely specifies the location of the host. An FQDN specifies the host name, the domain or subdomain the host belongs to, and any domains above in the hierarchy until the root domain in the organization is specified. On the Internet, the root domain in the path is something like com, but on a private network the top-level domains can be named according to some internal naming convention. The FQDN is read from left to right, with each host name or domain name specified by a period. The syntax of an FQDN follows:

```
host name.subdomain. ... .domain
```

An example of an FQDN is www.microsoft.com, which refers to a server called www located in the subdomain called Microsoft in the domain called com. Referring to a host by its FQDN is similar to referring to a file by its complete directory path. However, a complete file name goes from general to specific, with the file name at the rightmost part of the path.

An FQDN goes from specific to general, with the host name at the leftmost part of the name. FQDNs are more like addresses. An address starts with the most specific information: Who is to receive the letter. The address specifies the house number in which the recipient lives, the street on which the house is located, the city where the street is located, and finally the most general location, the state where that city is located.

Assigning an IP Address

Each site is specified by a unique IP address. If you do not specify a unique IP address, the site will be visible on all the IP addresses on the server. Although you should be familiar with assigning IP addresses, let's take a quick look at how you assign multiple addresses to a single card:

STEP BY STEP

3.4 Assigning Multiple IP Addresses

1. Open the Network Applet in the Control Panel. This opens the Network properties for the server.

continues

continued

2. Click on the Protocols tab, as shown in Figure 3.21.

FIGURE 3.21▶
The Protocols tab of the Network applet.

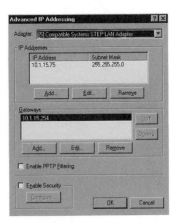

FIGURE 3.22▲
The Microsoft TCP/IP Properties dialog box.

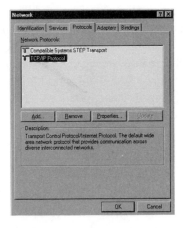

3. Select TCP/IP and click the Properties button. This opens the Microsoft TCP/IP Properties dialog box, shown in Figure 3.22.

4. Because you should already have TCP/IP configured, we'll jump right to adding multiple addresses. Click on Advanced to open the dialog box shown in Figure 3.23.

5. From here, adding additional IP addresses is as easy as clicking the Add button and filling in the appropriate IP address and subnet mask. Click OK when you are done, OK again, and OK to exit.

FIGURE 3.23▲
The Advanced dialog box for TCP/IP properties.

> **NOTE**
>
> **Setting Permissions for a Virtual Server** This should look familiar. Permissions for directories and sites on virtual servers can be configured the same as in the previous sections.

Creating a Virtual Server

To create a virtual server, you must first have created a directory to publish (local or virtual). Then, do the following:

STEP BY STEP

3.5 Creating a Virtual Server

1. Start Internet Service Manager.

---

2. From the Action menu, select New, Web Site (see Figure 3.24).

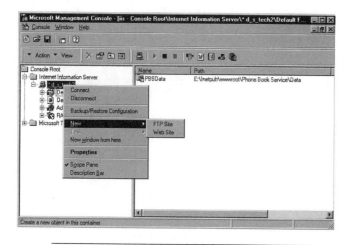

◀**FIGURE 3.24**
Creating a virtual server begins with choosing New, Web Site from the Action menu.

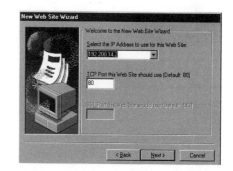

3. Enter an IP address to use for the site and the TCP port, as shown in Figure 3.25. Click Next.

4. Enter the path for the home directory and whether or not anonymous access is allowed. Click Next.

5. Configure the appropriate rights and click Finish.

FIGURE 3.25▲
Enter the IP address and port for the virtual server.

WRITING SCRIPTS FOR SERVICE MANAGEMENT

▶ Write scripts to manage the FTP service or the WWW service.

New to IIS 4.0 is the Microsoft Script Debugger. It can be used to debug scripts written in JavaScript, Visual Basic Scripting Edition (VBScript), and a number of other languages. If you know one of these languages, you can manage administrative tasks simply by writing scripts to manage your services (FTP or WWW).

Management tasks to automate should include the inspection of log files (described in the sections "Managing the FTP Service" and "Managing the WWW Service" later in this chapter). The log files can be examined for statistical information such as the number of hits, errors, and so on.

One way of exploring the log files is with the large number of UNIX-type utilities (all POSIX-compliant) found in the Windows NT Resource Kit. These utilities also can be useful in creating scripts to examine the log files. The utilities include the following:

◆ **find.** Enables you to find a file according to specified criteria, such as date, size, and so on.

◆ **grep.** Enables you to locate an entry within a file. Possibly the most powerful search tool ever written; parameters enable you to search according to case (default is yes), count the entries, find only those that do not match, and more.

◆ **touch.** Enables you to change the extended attributes of a file, such as the date and time associated with the file, without ever opening it.

◆ **wc.** Enables you to count the entries in a file in terms of lines, words, or characters. This is most useful when trying to determine the number of entries in a file.

USING CONTENT ANALYZER

▶ Manage a Web site by using Content Analyzer.

Content Analyzer is a new application for managing your Web site. Using WebMaps, as shown in Figure 3.26, Content Analyzer can show you what is and isn't working on your Web site.

FIGURE 3.26
A sample WebMap created with Content Analyzer.

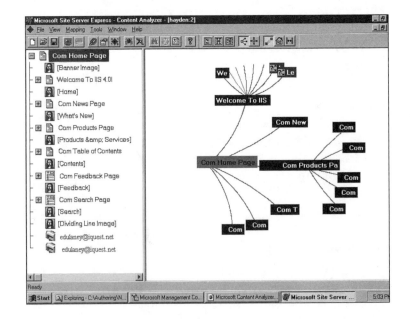

For example, let's say you want to direct all your friends to this great *IIS Training Guide*, so you link your site to mcp.com. Suddenly, New Riders decides it is time for a third edition, so they take the page for this book down. Usually, the way you find out about this is either by getting a note from a visitor letting you know you have a broken link or you manually verify the site from time to time. Content Analyzer automates that task. When you have Content Analyzer create a WebMap of your site, it goes out, follows every link from your site, and tells you where the broken links are. There are three important features of Content Analyzer to remember:

◆ **WebMaps.** A WebMap is a high-level representation of an entire Web site. Content Analyzer gives you two ways to analyze this information. The tree view presents the site in a hierarchical format, allowing you to view the site in a very structured format. The cyberbolic view presents the site in free-form format that concentrates on the site interconnections.

◆ **Content Analyzer Reports.** Content Analyzer can also be used to generate a variety of reports about the Web site. This feature is discussed in the later chapters.

◆ **Link Management.** Content Analyzer includes a number of tools to help you manage your Web site's links.

The graphical representation (WebMap) includes all HTML pages, audio and video files, as well as graphic images and links to other services. The left side of the WebMap display (as shown in Figure 3.25) is a Tree view of the site, whereas the right pane shows Cyberbolic view. You can choose to see either of the two or both—whichever is most convenient for you.

In addition to the graphical representation, Content Analyzer can be used to create a set of links to your site in a report that you can use for troubleshooting. You also can save the maps of your site (to a database, spreadsheet, or HTML file) for comparison at later points in time to see what has changed as time has progressed.

Let's look at how you generate a WebMap for a site:

STEP BY STEP

3.6 Creating a WebMap

1. Open Content Analyzer by going to Start, Programs, Windows NT 4.0 Option Pack, Microsoft Site Server Express 2.0, Content Analyzer. The Content Analyzer Welcome screen opens, as shown in Figure 3.27.

FIGURE 3.27▶
The Content Analyzer Welcome screen.

FIGURE 3.28▲
The New Map dialog box.

FIGURE 3.29▲
Enter the URL of the site you want to map.

2. Click the New WebMap button. The New Map dialog box opens (see Figure 3.28). You can create your WebMap from an URL (universal resource locator) or from a file. This example creates the site from an URL.

3. Select URL and click OK. Figure 3.29 shows the New Map from URL dialog box. Enter the URL to create the map from. You can tell it whether to map the entire site and whether to create reports. Clicking Options opens the Mapping from URL Options dialog box (see Figure 3.30). These options allow you to control the behavior of Content Analyzer as it maps the site. Click OK to close the Options dialog box and click OK to start creating the WebMap.

◀**FIGURE 3.30**
The Options dialog box allows you to control how Content Analyzer maps the site.

4. If you select the Create Reports option, you are prompted for a location for those files, as shown in Figure 3.31. Clicking OK opens a Web browser and displays the report shown in Figure 3.32.

FIGURE 3.31▲
Configure the report location.

Site Summary Report for 10.1.15.75/

Microsoft Site Server offers additional content analysis reports not available in the Express Edition. Click here for Upgrade Information or here for Reports Help

◆ WebMap for 10.1.15.75

Object Statistics			Status Summary			Map Statistics	
Type	Count	Size		Objects	Links	Map Date	Feb 03 00:37 1999
Pages	14	9566	Onsite	16	37	Levels	3
Images	9	34292	OK	12	27	Avg Links/Page	6

◀**FIGURE 3.32**
The resulting site report.

5. Figure 3.33 gives you a closer look at the generated report. Note that this gives all kinds of good information for maintaining your site, as well as for impressing management. Things like the number of pages and average size can help you with your capacity planning. Objects not

continues

continued

found and broken links can be used to report on the
integrity of the site, and you can see how many levels
deep your site is. Close the report and you are returned
to Content Analyzer and your completed WebMap, as
shown in Figure 3.34.

FIGURE 3.33▶
The final report on your Web site.

FIGURE 3.34▶
The final WebMap. Good links are shown
in blue, whereas broken links appear red.

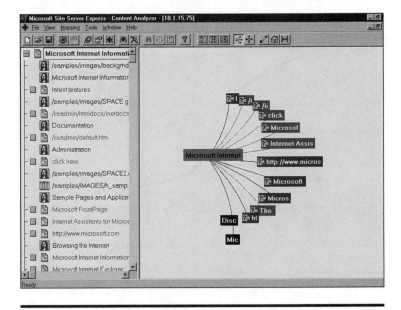

CONFIGURING **SMTP**

▶ Configure Microsoft SMTP Service to host message traffic.

SMTP, an acronym for Simple Mail Transfer Protocol, enables you to send mail to others on your network as well as to the Internet. The SMTP Site property sheet is used to set the basic connection parameters, such as the port to use (default port is 25), number of simultaneous connections (default is 1,000), and length of inactivity before disconnect (default is 600 seconds).

Regardless of its size, each site has only one Microsoft SMTP site for the service. You cannot create additional sites or delete existing ones. To display the SMTP property sheets, do the following:

NOTE

SMTP, Web Pages, and E-Mail
Another great use for the SMTP service is to link its capabilities to a Web page. In other words, if you have a Web site that requires some type of response by the visitor, then you can provide a resource for the visitor to use to send you e-mail, without him needing a mail client on his end. This way, you give the visitor the power to e-mail you something without requiring him to have an e-mail client, such as Outlook, installed on his machine.

STEP BY STEP

3.7 Viewing the SMTP Properties

1. Expand the SMTP tree in Internet Service Manager.

2. Highlight and right-click the SMTP site and choose Properties.

3. The following five tabs are displayed (see Figure 3.35):

   • The SMTP Site tab enables you to determine how this server connects to, sends, and receives messages with other servers.

   • The Operators tab enables you to determine which groups have operator status.

   • The Messages tab lets you configure limits on message size and decide what to do with undeliverable mail; you also can specify a maximum number of recipients who can receive a single message (the default is 100).

   • The Delivery tab specifies how many messages should be sent per connections, the route to use, and so on.

   •The Directory Security tab enables you to specify other servers to accept only or restrict only.

FIGURE 3.35
The SMTP service properties.

CONFIGURING **NNTP**

▶ Configure Microsoft NNTP Service to host a newsgroup.

NNTP, an acronym for Network News Transport Protocol, enables you to configure a server for clients to read newsgroups. The Microsoft NNTP Service included with IIS 4.0 is the server side of the operation, whereas Microsoft Internet Mail and News is a common client (now being replaced in the market by Outlook Express).

The default port for NNTP is 119, although this changes to 563 if SSL is used. When the client connects to the service, it requests a list of available newsgroups. The NNTP service authenticates the user and then sends the list of newsgroups. To view the NNTP Service properties, do the following:

STEP BY STEP

3.8 Viewing the NNTP Properties

1. Expand the NNTP tree in Internet Service Manager.

2. Highlight and right-click the NNTP site and then choose Properties.

3. The following six tabs are displayed (see Figure 3.36):

- The News Site tab identifies the site, allows you to configure how the site handles connections, and allows you to enable and configure logging.

- The Security Accounts tab enables you to configure the account used for anonymous access (much like the WWW and FTP services) and set the administrator for the service.

- The NNTP Settings tab lets you configure the actual news group parameters, including posting parameters and moderated group settings.

- The Home Directory tab allows you to set the location of the home directory, the access controls on that directory, and the Secure Connection settings.

FIGURE 3.36
The NNTP service properties.

- The Directory Security tab enables you to specify other servers to accept only or restrict only.

- The Groups tab allows you to set up and manage the newsgroups configured on your server.

The client picks a newsgroup to view and requests the list of articles. Authentication takes place again by the NNTP service and the list of articles is sent. The client then picks articles she wants to see and the NNTP service sends them.

Posting Articles

The posting of articles works in a similar fashion: NNTP verifies that the client is allowed to post to the newsgroup and takes the article, adds it to the newsgroup, and updates the index.

Every newsgroup has its own directory (with the same name as the newsgroup) and every article is stored as a separate file within that directory (with an .NWS extension). By default, %SystemRoot%\Inetpub\nntproot is the main directory.

Creating a New Newsgroup

When you create a new newsgroup (through the Groups property sheet of Internet Service Manager), NNTP automatically creates the new directory. Within the newsgroup directory, indexes are also stored. Indexes have an extension of .XIX and one is created for every 128 articles.

The NNTP service automatically starts when the Windows NT Server starts but can be paused, stopped, or started from the Services icon of the Control Panel (where it appears as Microsoft NNTP Service). It, like other IIS-related services, also can be paused, stopped, or started from the Microsoft Management Console.

CONFIGURING CERTIFICATE SERVER

▶ Configure Microsoft Certificate Server to issue certificates.

NOTE

Generating Certificates Without Certification   You can generate a certificate with Certificate Server without being certified by an agency, but they generally aren't considered valid outside of your organization.

Microsoft Certificate Server enables you to generate, create, and use keys for digital authentication. To use Certificate Server, you must first obtain a valid server certificate (generated with Key Manager) from a certificate authority (CA). The following table lists the Web sites of several certificate authorities within the United States.

BankGate	http://www.bankgate.com
GTE CyberTrust	http://www.cybertrust.com
Thawte Consulting	http://www.thawte.com
Verisign	http://www.verisign.com

After you create a certificate or a certificate authority has issued you a valid certificate, use Key Manager to activate the certificate.

After you have the certificate activated, you can use Key Manager to generate the certificates for your users. To generate a certificate, do the following:

STEP BY STEP

3.9 Creating a Certificate Using Key Manager

1. Open Internet Service Manager. Clicking the Key Manager icon (the hand holding a key) opens the Key Manager application, as shown in Figure 3.37. Notice that you can create certificates for SMTP, NNTP, or WWW. FTP does not support certificates at this time.

2. Right-click the WWW icon and select Create New Key. This opens the Create New Key dialog box, shown in Figure 3.38. You can choose to immediately send the creation request, or you can have the requests stored in a file for later submittal. Notice that you can select which Certificate Server the request is made to. Click Next.

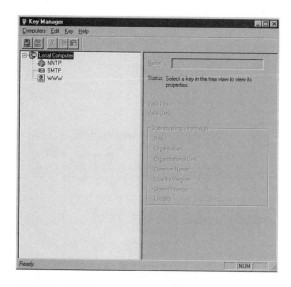

◀ FIGURE 3.37
The Key Manager application.

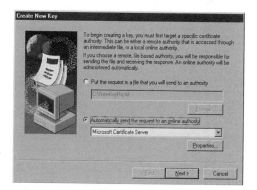

FIGURE 3.38▲
The New Key Request dialog box determines
how your certificate is requested.

3. Next, you are asked to name the certificate, as shown in
Figure 3.39, and determine the size (in bits) of the encryption key. The longer the key, the greater the security, but
the more overhead encryption and decryption is added to
the system. Click Next.

◀ FIGURE 3.39
The New Key Request dialog box determines
how your certificate is requested.

4. Next, you need to identify the organization, organizational
unit, and fully qualified domain name for the authenticating server, shown in Figure 3.40. Fill in the blanks and
click Next.

continues

FIGURE 3.40▲
Identifying your organization and server.

continued

5. Finally, you need to provide a location. This is country, state, and city, as shown in Figure 3.41. Click Finish to complete the key. Figure 3.42 shows the key that has been created. It is ready for distribution.

FIGURE 3.41▶
Adding the location information
to the certificate.

CONFIGURING INDEX SERVER

▶ Configure Index Server to index a Web site.

Index Server is configured based upon the size of the site and the number of documents it contains. The following four items should be taken into consideration when configuring Index Server:

◆ Number of documents in the corpus

◆ Size of the corpus

◆ Rate of search requests arriving at the server

◆ Complexity of queries

Increasing the amount of memory and going with the fastest CPU available increases Index Server performance. The disk space needed for the data is always roughly 40 percent the size of the corpus.

Index Server can be used to index multiple servers by sharing a folder on the remote volume and creating a virtual directory on the indexing server. The biggest difficulty in doing this is maintaining link integrity.

MANAGING MIME TYPES

▶ Manage MIME types.

MIME is an acronym for Multipurpose Internet Mail Extension and is used to define the type of file sent to the browser based upon the extension. If your server is supplying files in multiple formats, it must have a MIME mapping for each file type or browsers will be most likely unable to retrieve the file.

MIME mappings for IIS 4.0 are different than they were in previous versions. The mappings are kept in the Registry under KEY_LOCAL_MACHINE\SOFTWARE\Classes\MIME\Databases\ Content Type and can be viewed, edited, or have new ones added by using Regedit or Regedt32. Figure 3.43 shows an example of the MIME mapping for text files in REGEDT32.EXE.

If you aren't comfortable with editing the Registry directly (and you probably should not be), you also can add entries to the Registry through the HTTP Headers tab of any directory or virtual directory. The File Types button at the bottom of the properties page enables you to enter MIME maps in a much simpler way than editing the Registry. The button is shown in Figure 3.44.

FIGURE 3.43▶
The MIME mapping for text files.

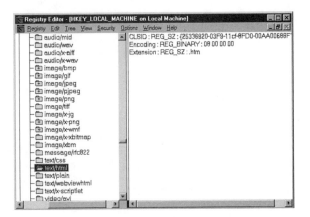

FIGURE 3.44▶
The MIME Map option appears on the HTTP
Headers tab.

FIGURE 3.45▲
The MIME Map enables you to specify the type
extensions and content type.

Selecting this button enables you to specify new MIME types by
giving the associated extension and the content type, as shown in
Figure 3.45.

MANAGING THE FTP SERVICE

▶ Manage the FTP Service.

After installing and running the FTP service, it can be managed
through the following two main utilities:

◆ The Services icon of the Control Panel

◆ Internet Service Manager

Using the Control Panel Method

The first utility of note is the Services icon in the Control Panel. From here, you can start, pause, or stop the FTP Service, as well as configure it for startup in the following three ways:

◆ **Automatic.** The service is started when all of IIS starts (the default).

◆ **Manual.** Requires interaction from the administrator to actively start the service.

◆ **Disabled.** The service does not start at all.

After it is started, the service can be stopped or paused (and started again after being stopped or paused). When the service is stopped, it is unloaded; however, when it is paused, it remains loaded with the intention of being restarted again. Pausing allows connected users to remain connected, but does not allow new users to connect.

FTP Site Options with Internet Service Manager

From the Internet Service Manager, you can select your FTP site and choose to stop, pause, or start the site by right-clicking it. You also can manage all properties of the site from here, as shown in Figure 3.46.

There are five tabs to the properties, each containing specific information on the Web site. Each tab is discussed in the paragraphs that follow in the order in which they appear by default.

FTP Site Tab

The FTP Site tab enables you to change the description (name) of the FTP site, the IP address, and the TCP port. As it has been pointed out before, port 21 is the default TCP port, but changing it to another value enables the site to become hidden. Additional settings on this tab enable you to specify a number of seconds for a connection timeout, limit the number of connections allowed (if bandwidth is an issue; the default is limited to 100,000 connections), and enable logging. By default, the logs are written to %SystemRoot%\System32\Logfiles.

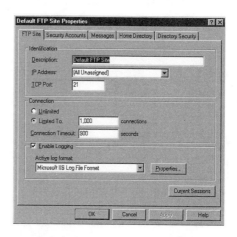

FIGURE 3.46
The Properties sheet for the FTP service.

You can choose for the log files to be created in a number of different time periods. The way you choose for them to be created governs the name of the log files created (which always consists of some combination of variables). The following table summarizes the log files:

Log Time Period	Log File Name
Daily	inyymmdd.log
Weekly	inyymmww.log
Monthly	inyymm.log
Unlimited file size	inetsv#.log
When file size reaches 19MB (19MB is the default, but another MB value can be specified)	inetsv#.log

EXAM TIP

Anonymous Access and Anonymous Access Only   When studying for the exam, remember this two-step approach: You cannot configure only anonymous access until you have first enabled anonymous access.

Security Accounts Tab

The Security Accounts tab enables you to allow or disallow anonymous access and define which Windows NT user accounts have operator privileges. You also can choose to allow only anonymous connections and enable automatic password synchronization.

Messages Tab

The Messages tab enables you to specify a message to be displayed when users access the site. The following are the three messages you can configure:

◆ **Welcome message.** Displays when a user first logs on.

◆ **Exit message.** The last message displayed after the user logs off.

◆ **System Busy.** Displays when there are no user connections left.

NOTE

You Can Be Too Friendly   Be careful about being too inviting in your welcome message. Saying something like "Welcome to my FTP server, glad you could stop by" is very friendly, but if your site is hacked, it could be a handicap in a trial. A common excuse is "I was invited…check out the welcome message." Something along the lines of "Trespassers will be shot" might be a little safer.

Home Directory Tab

The Home Directory tab enables you to specify a home directory in either of the following two ways:

◆ On this computer (the default)

◆ As a share on another computer

If you are specifying a directory on this computer, you must give the path. If you are specifying a share on another computer, you must give the UNC path (\\server\share). In either scenario, you then assign permissions for that directory of Read and/or Write and choose whether or not you want to log access. You also must specify whether directory listings should appear in UNIX style or MS-DOS style. MS-DOS is the default and should be left as such in most implementations for maximum compatibility.

Directory Security Tab

The Directory Security tab enables you to configure IP address and Domain Name restrictions. When configuring, you have the following two choices:

◆ Specify all addresses that are prohibited

◆ Specify all addresses that are allowed access

You might recall that the three ways to enter addresses are as a single computer (by IP address), a group of computers (by IP address), or by domain name. Refer to Chapter 1, "Planning," for more information about entering addresses.

MANAGING THE WWW SERVICE

▶ Manage the WWW service.

After the WWW service is installed and running, it can be managed through the following two main utilities:

◆ The Services icon of the Control Panel

◆ Internet Service Manager

Using the Control Panel Method

The first utility of note is the Services icon in the Control Panel. From here, you can start, pause, or stop the World Wide Web service or configure it for startup in the following three ways:

◆ **Automatic.** The service is started when all of IIS starts (the default).

◆ **Manual.** Starts the service.

◆ **Disabled.** The service does not start at all.

WWW Site Options with Internet Service Manager

From the Internet Service Manager, you can select your Web site (or any Web site if you have multiple ones) and choose to stop, pause, or start the site by right-clicking it.

You also can manage all properties of the site from here, as shown in Figure 3.47.

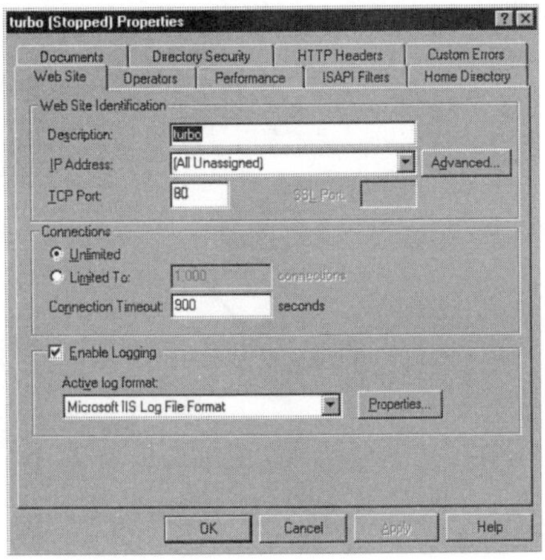

There are nine tabs to the properties, each containing specific information about the Web site. In the order that they appear by default, each tab is discussed in the paragraphs that follow.

FIGURE 3.47
The property sheets for the WWW service.

Web Site Tab

The Web Site tab enables you to change the description (name) of the Web site, the IP address, and the TCP port. As has been pointed out before, port 80 is the default TCP port, but changing it to another value allows the site to become hidden. This is useful in a situation where you want to create an intranet and avoid traffic from the Internet. The Advanced tab enables you to assign multiple identities for the Web site. Additional settings on this tab enable you to configure the SSL port, limit the number of connections allowed (if bandwidth is an issue; the default is unlimited), and enable logging. By default, the logs are written to the following directory:

%SystemRoot%\System32\Logfiles

You can choose for the log files to be created in a number of different time periods. The way you choose for them to be created governs the name of the log files created (which always consist of some combination of variables). The following table summarizes this process:

Log Time Period	Log File Name
Daily	inyymmdd.log
Weekly	inyymmww.log
Monthly	inyymm.log
Unlimited file size	inetsv#.log
When file size reaches 19MB (19MB is the default, but another MB can be specified)	inetsv#.log

NOTE

Changing a Port Number Versus Host Security Settings What is presented here is an example. There's no good reason for changing a port number, unless you want to use blind security. The best way to handle filtering Internet traffic is to change the host security settings for the site, rather than changing the port. Host security settings include any user access settings, IP address restrictions, or file access permissions.

Operators Tab

The Operators tab simply enables you to define which Windows NT user accounts have operator privileges.

Performance Tab

The Performance tab enables you to tune the Web site according to the number of hits you expect each day. Following are the three settings:

◆ Fewer than 10,000

◆ Fewer than 100,000 (the default)

◆ More than 100,000

You also can enable bandwidth throttling from the Performance tab to prevent the entire network from being slow to service the Web site. By default, bandwidth throttling is not enabled. Finally, on the Performance tab, you can enable HTTP Keep-Alives. This maintains the open connection for the duration of the session, allowing the user's browser to make multiple requests without having to break and re-establish the connection for each request.

ISAPI Filters Tab

The ISAPI Filters tab enables you to add or remove filters for the site. ISAPI filters are discussed in great detail in Chapter 5, "Running Applications."

Home Directory Tab

The Home Directory tab enables you to specify a home directory in the following three ways:

◆ On this computer (the default)

◆ As a share on another computer

◆ As an URL to be redirected to

If you are specifying a directory on this computer, you must give the path. If you are specifying a share on another computer, you must give the UNC path (\\server\share). In either scenario, you then assign permissions for that directory. If you go with the third option and redirect the home directory to an URL, you must specify the URL and choose how the client will be sent. You can send the client as one of the following:

◆ The exact URL you enter

◆ A directory below the URL you enter

◆ A permanent redirection for the resource

Documents Tab

The Documents tab enables you to define the default documents to display if a specific document is not specified in the URL request. Multiple files can be listed, and the first one in the list is always used unless it is unavailable. If it is unavailable (or cannot be found), then the next one in the list is used.

Directory Security Tab

The Directory Security tab enables you to configure anonymous access and authentication, as well as secure communications and IP address and domain name restrictions. When configuring the latter, you have the following two choices:

- ◆ Specify all addresses that are prohibited
- ◆ Specify all addresses that are allowed access

The three ways to enter addresses are as a single computer (by IP address), a group of computers (by IP address), or by domain name.

HTTP Headers Tab

The HTTP Headers tab enables you to specify an expiration time for your content (the default is none), set custom headers, assign a rating to your content (to alert parents of pornography and so on) and configure MIME maps (see the section "Managing MIME Types," earlier in this chapter).

Custom Errors Tab

The last tab, Custom Errors, enables you to configure the error message returned to the user when an event occurs. For example, error 400 is, by default, a Bad Request, the file 400.htm is used to return the message 404 is Not Found, and so on.

You should now be prepared to apply this information to the following case study.

CASE STUDY: MANAGING A MICROSOFT INTERNET INFORMATION 4.0 WEB SERVER

ESSENCE OF THE CASE

You need to configure the following services to meet your objectives:

- ▶ Set up a Web site
- ▶ Set up an FTP site
- ▶ Configure the NNTP service

SCENARIO

You are the Web administrator for Little Faith Enterprises, a 50-person consulting firm. You have just installed IIS on a Windows NT Server, and you have been tasked with setting up a Web site, an FTP site, and a discussion group for the company. What do you need to do?

ANALYSIS

Start by approaching each problem one at a time.

continues

CASE STUDY: MANAGING A MICROSOFT INTERNET INFORMATION 4.0 WEB SERVER

continued

Problem 1: Setting Up a Web Site

To set up a Web site, do the following:

1. Select Start, Programs, Windows NT 4.0 Option Pack, Microsoft Internet Information Server, Internet Service Manager.

2. Expand the Internet Information Server folder.

3. Select the IIS server where you want to add a WWW site.

4. Right-click and select New. This brings up the choice of creating a Web site or FTP site. Choose Web Site.

5. Enter the Web site description and select Next.

6. Select or verify the IP address to use.

7. The TCP port defaults to 80. This is the default used for all WWW services. If you want to offer the service but hide it from most browsers, choose another port.

8. Enter the path for what will appear as the home directory (you also can use the Browse button to specify).

9. By default, the check box appears, allowing anonymous access to the Web site. If you do not want anonymous access, remove the check. Choose Next.

10. Select the access permissions for the directory.

11. Click Finish.

Problem 2: Setting Up an FTP Site

To set up the FTP site, do the following:

1. Select Start, Programs, Windows NT 4.0 Option Pack, Microsoft Internet Information Server, Internet Service Manager.

2. Expand the Internet Information Server folder.

3. Select the IIS Server where you want to add the FTP site.

4. Right-click and select New. This brings up the choice of creating a Web site or FTP site. Choose FTP Site.

5. Enter the FTP Site description and select Next (refer to Figure 3.7).

6. Select or verify the IP address to use (refer to Figure 3.8).

7. The TCP port defaults to 21. This is the default used for the FTP service.

8. Enter the path for what will appear as the home directory (you also can use the Browse button to specify).

9. Select the access permissions for the directory.

10. Choose Finish. Notice that back in Figure 3.11, the new FTP site is stopped. To start the site, you can right-click it and select start, or click on the Start icon.

CASE STUDY: MANAGING A MICROSOFT INTERNET INFORMATION 4.0 WEB SERVER

Problem 3: Creating a Discussion Group
To create a discussion group, you need to modify the NNTP service as follows:

1. Expand the NNTP tree in Internet Service Manager.

2. Highlight and right-click the NNTP site, then choose Properties.

3. Select the Groups tab and click Create a Newsgroup.

4. Enter the Newsgroup, the Description, and the Newgroup "prettyname." You can also make the group Read Only and determine if it will be moderated or not.

5. Click OK. You have created a newsgroup.

In three sets of steps, you have configured the services your company needs.

CHAPTER SUMMARY

Let's recap what we've discussed in this chapter. We have looked at a number of different areas of resource management within Internet Information Server 4.0, including the following:

◆ **Creating and Sharing Directories.** The first step in hosting a site with IIS is actually creating the site. We walked through this process earlier in the chapter. Some important things to remember with creating a new Web or FTP site are the default ports for each service and the access controls for the site. Access permissions for a Web site include the following:

- **Allow Read Access—Assigned by default.** This allows users to connect to the site and read the information stored in the home directory. This does not include the ability to list files.

- **Allow Script Access—Assigned by default.** Users connecting to the site with this permission can execute scripts stored in the home directory.

KEY TERMS

- Certificate Server
- File Transfer Protocol (FTP)
- HyperText Markup Language (HTML)
- HyperText Transfer Protocol (HTTP)
- Index Server
- Microsoft Management Console
- Multipurpose Internet Mail Extensions (MIME)
- Network News Transport Protocol (NNTP)
- Secure Sockets Layer (SSL)

continues

CHAPTER SUMMARY (continued)

KEY TERMS

- Simple Mail Transport Protocol (SMTP)
- TCP/IP
- World Wide Web (WWW)

- **Allow Execute Access—Includes Script access.** Users granted this access permission not only can execute scripts stored in the home directory, but other applications as well.

- **Allow Write Access.** This permission allows a user to connect to the site and write to files stored in the home directory.

- **Allow Directory Browsing.** This permission allows a user to connect to the site and read the list of files stored in the home directory.

For an FTP site, the permissions are a little bit different, as follows:

- ◆ **Allow Read Access—Assigned by default.** This allows users to download files using the FTP protocol.

- ◆ **Allow Write Access.** Write access allows users to upload (or write) files to the site using the FTP protocol.

- ◆ **Changing Permissions.** We discussed how to locate a file or directory in Internet Service Manager and open the properties for the item.

- ◆ **Creating and Sharing Virtual Directories.** As the name implies, virtual directories are entities that do not exist, but give you the ability to reference relative file locations to make it appear as if they are in a directory. This can allow you to work around issues, such as disk space, and determine where best to store files. These directories only differ from the home directory in their location. Permissions and controls are the same as the physical directories.

  There are two things to remember. First, a virtual directory does not appear in a directory listing. It must be referred to explicitly in an HTML link. Second, a virtual directory can only be hosted on a machine that is in the same authentication domain as the IIS server.

- ◆ **Creating and Sharing Virtual Servers.** The major benefit of virtual servers is that they enable you to expand your site beyond the limitations of a single site per server. You can

CHAPTER SUMMARY

combine a number of different sites (domain names) on a single server through the implementation of virtual servers.

◆ **Writing Scripts for Service Management.** New to IIS 4.0 is the Microsoft Script Debugger. It can be used to debug scripts written in JavaScript, Visual Basic Scripting Edition (VBScript), and a number of other languages. If you know one of these languages, you can manage administrative tasks simply by writing scripts to manage your services (FTP or WWW).

◆ **Using Content Analyzer.** Content Analyzer is a new application for managing your Web site. Using WebMaps, Content Analyzer can show you what is and isn't working on your Web site. The following are the three main components to Content Analyzer:

• **WebMaps.** A WebMap is a high-level representation of an entire Web site. Content Analyzer gives you two ways to analyze this information. The tree view presents the site in a hierarchical format, allowing you to view the site in a very structured format. The cyberbolic view presents the site in free-form format that concentrates on the site's interconnections.

• **Content Analyzer Reports.** Content Analyzer can also be used to generate a variety of reports about the Web site.

• **Link Management.** Content Analyzer includes a number of tools to help you manage your Web site's links.

◆ **Configuring SMTP.** SMTP, an acronym for Simple Mail Transfer Protocol, enables you to send mail to others on your network as well as to the Internet. Important configuration items include the following:

• Default port—25

• Number of Simultaneous Connections (default is 1,000)

• Length of inactivity before disconnect (default is 600 seconds)

continues

CHAPTER SUMMARY (continued)

◆ **Configuring NNTP.** The NNTP service enables you to configure a server to host newsgroups.

Some important parameters for the NNTP service include the following:

- The Default Port— 119 (563 if SSL is used.)

- The Moderated Groups settings

- The Directory Security settings

◆ **Configuring Certificate Server.** Microsoft Certificate Server enables you to generate, create, and use keys for digital authentication. To use, you must first obtain a valid server certificate (generated with Key Manager) from a certificate authority. Keys (certificates) are created using Key Manager, which is part of Internet Service Manager.

◆ **Configuring Index Server.** Index Server is configured based upon the size of the site and the number of documents it contains. The following four items should be taken into consideration when configuring Index Server:

- Number of documents in the corpus

- Size of the corpus

- Rate of search requests arriving at the server

- Complexity of queries

Note that the disk space needed for the data is always roughly 40 percent the size of the corpus. Also, Index Server can be used to index multiple servers by sharing a folder on the remote volume and creating a virtual directory on the indexing server.

◆ **Managing MIME Types.** MIME is an acronym for Multipurpose Internet Mail Extension and is used to define the type of file sent to the browser based upon the extension. If your server is supplying files in multiple formats, it must have a MIME mapping for each file type or browsers will most likely be unable to retrieve the file.

CHAPTER SUMMARY

MIME types can be configured in the following two ways:

- Registry Editor
- MIME Map option button on the HTTP Headers tab of the Web Site Properties sheet

◆ **Managing the FTP Service and WWW Service.** These actual services can be managed in one of two ways:

- The Services icon of the Control Panel
- Internet Service Manager

The specific property tabs for these services are discussed at length in the chapter and throughout the book.

APPLY YOUR KNOWLEDGE

Exercises

3.1   Changing Permissions for a File

The following exercise illustrates how to add Write permissions to a file.

Estimated time: 15 minutes

1. Start Internet Service Manager.

2. Select a file, right-click it, and choose Properties.

3. Beneath Access Permissions, check the Write check box.

4. Click OK.

3.2   Creating a Virtual Directory

The following exercise walks you through the steps of creating a virtual directory named Scott.

Estimated time: 10 minutes

1. Start Internet Service Manager.

2. Double-click the Internet Information Server until servers are displayed.

3. Double-click a server.

4. Highlight Default Web Site and right-click it.

5. Choose New, Virtual Directory.

6. For a directory alias, enter Scott. Press Next.

7. Click the Browse button for a physical path and find My Briefcase. Select it and then click Next.

8. Change the permissions for the virtual directory so that only Read access is allowed.

9. Select Finish.

10. Double-click the Default Web Site. Scott should now appear as a directory.

3.3   Preventing a Host from Accessing Your Site

The following exercise walks you through the steps of denying access to a host based upon its IP address.

Estimated time: 20–30 minutes

1. Start Internet Service Manager.

2. Double-click the Internet Information Server until servers are displayed.

3. Double-click a server.

4. Highlight Default Web Site and right-click.

5. Choose Properties and select the Directory Security tab.

6. Beneath the IP Address and Domain Name Restrictions frame, click the Edit button.

7. Make certain the active radio button on the IP Address and Domain Name Restrictions screen is Granted Access and click Add.

8. With the active option button on the Deny Access On screen being on Single Computer, enter the IP address 195.200.200.001 and click OK.

9. The word Deny should appear on the IP Address and Domain Name Restrictions screen beside the IP address entered. Click OK.

10. Back at the Directory Security tab, click either OK or Apply, and if you have any child nodes on the Web site, you get the Inheritance Overrides dialog box. For this exercise, just click OK.

11. You have now restricted host 195.200.200.001 from accessing your site.

APPLY YOUR KNOWLEDGE

3.4   Allow Only a Set of Hosts to Access Your Site

The following exercise walks you through the steps of permitting access to your site for only 126 hosts based upon their IP address.

Estimated time: 20–30 minutes

1. Start Internet Service Manager.

2. Double-click the Internet Information Server until servers are displayed.

3. Double-click a server.

4. Highlight Default Web Site and right-click it.

5. Choose Properties and select the Directory Security tab.

6. Beneath the IP Address and Domain Name Restrictions frame, click the Edit button.

7. Make certain the active radio button on the IP Address and Domain Name Restrictions screen is Denied Access and click Add.

8. With the active option button on the Grant Access On screen being on Group of Computers, enter the IP address 195.200.200.001 and the subnet value 255.255.255.128.

9. Click OK.

10. The word Grant should now appear on the IP Address and Domain Name Restrictions screen beside the IP address entered, with the subnet value in parentheses beside it.

11. Click OK.

12. Back at the Directory Security tab, click either OK or Apply. You have now restricted access to your site to 128 hosts only, beginning with 195.200.200.001 and progressing incrementally.

3.5   Set a Default Document

The following exercise walks you through the steps of enabling a default document to be displayed when someone accesses your site without specifying a file name.

Estimated time: 10 minutes

1. Start Internet Service Manager.

2. Double-click the Internet Information Server until servers are displayed.

3. Double-click a server.

4. Highlight Default Web Site and right-click it.

5. Choose Properties and select the Documents tab.

6. Click the Enable Default Document check box.

7. Click the Add button.

8. Enter the name of your default document (such as DEAULT.HTM or DEFAULT.ASP) in the Default Document Name field and click OK.

9. The document now appears in the text field. Following steps 7 and 8, you can enter multiple documents to be displayed in successive order if the first document is unavailable. (The first one in the list is always displayed if it is available.)

3.6   Disable HTTP Keep-Alives

The following exercise walks you through the steps of disabling HTTP Keep-Alives.

Estimated time: 10 minutes

1. Start Internet Service Manager.

2. Double-click the Internet Information Server until servers are displayed.

APPLY YOUR KNOWLEDGE

3. Double-click a server.

4. Highlight Default Web Site and right-click it.

5. Choose Properties and select the Performance tab.

6. Beneath the Connection Configuration frame, click the HTTP Keep-Alives Enabled check box to remove the default check mark.

7. Click the OK or Apply buttons.

3.7 Change the Web Service TCP Port

This exercise walks you through the steps of changing the TCP port of the Web service to hide it from browsers not specifically pointed to it.

Estimated time: 10 minutes

1. Start Internet Service Manager.

2. Double-click the Internet Information Server until servers are displayed.

3. Double-click a server.

4. Highlight the Web site you want to hide and right-click it.

5. Choose Properties and select the Web Site tab.

6. At the TCP Port field, change the default value of 80 to the new port number (such as 7,500).

7. Click the OK or Apply buttons.

3.8 Indexing a Web Site With Index Server

The following exercise shows you how to index a Web Site With Index Server.

Estimated time: 25 minutes

1. Open Index Server Manager.

2. Click on the Action button, and Select New -> Catalog.

3. Name the new catalog and select a location for it. Click OK.

4. Select the newly created catalog, right-click, and select Properties.

5. Configure the Index appropriately. Restart the Index server to begin indexing the site.

3.9 Managing MIME Types

The following exercise shows you how to manage MIME types.

Estimated time: 25 minutes

1. Open Internet Server Manager.

2. Right-click on the Default Web Site and select Properties.

3. Select the HTTP Headers tab.

4. Click on the File Types in the MIME Map section of the tab.

5. Click on New Type to create a new MIME type. You will need a file extension and a MIME Type to complete the new entry.

3.10 Managing the FTP Service

The following exercise shows you how to manage the FTP Service.

Estimated time: 15 minutes

1. Open Internet Server Manager.

2. Right-click on the FTP Site you want to manage and select Properties.

3. Review the FTP Property tabs and manage appropriately, based on your requirements. Common areas for managing include: logging,

APPLY YOUR KNOWLEDGE

access control, directory security and connection limits.

4. Click OK when you are done.

3.11 Using Microsoft Script Debugger

If you are planning on writing scripts for managing your WWW or FTP Services, you need to be familiar with the Microsoft Script Debugger.

Estimated time: 15 minutes

1. Open the Microsoft Script Debugger.

2. Open Internet Explorer Version 4.01 (This is required to run the script)

3. In Internet Explorer, load the file C:\INETPUB\ IISSAMPLES\ISSAMPLES\QUERY.HTM

4. In Microsoft Script Debugger, go to View -> Running Documents. Select query.htm. You will see this script load in the Microsoft Script Debugger in Debug Mode. Look at the available options, including setting and resetting break-points. Close the applications when you are finished.

Review Questions

1. What is the default port used for the WWW service?

2. Where should virtual directories always be stored?

3. Virtual servers allow one server to alias multiple what?

4. What utility included with the Windows NT Resource Kit can be used to count the number of lines in a log file?

5. What are two views that can be seen of a Web site with WebMaps?

6. What is the default port used for the SMTP service?

7. By default, and in the absence of SSL, what is the TCP port that the NNTP service uses?

8. After using Key Manager to generate a digital certificate request file for use with SSL, what must you do next?

9. With Index Server, what percentage of disk space does the data require?

10. MIME is an acronym for what?

11. In terms of increments of time, FTP log files can be created on what basis?

12. You are the IIS administrator for Running Dogs Pet Food. You have been tasked with setting up Microsoft Index Server to index the corporate intranet server. What factors should you keep in mind for maximizing performance and ensuring adequate capacity for the Index Server?

Exam Questions

1. TCP port 80 is the default for which service?

   A. NNTP

   B. SMTP

   C. WWW

   D. FTP

APPLY YOUR KNOWLEDGE

2. By default, anonymous access is enabled for which of the following services after installation?

    A. WWW

    B. FTP

    C. SMTP

    D. NNTP

3. What permissions are assigned to a WWW directory by default during the site creation by the wizard?

    A. Allow Read Access

    B. Allow Write Access

    C. Allow Directory Browsing

    D. Allow Script Access

4. Rob is having difficulty with users properly accessing resources on an intranet Web site that he created. For the directory in question, NTFS permissions allow Read for everyone, but he has removed the Read permission for IIS. What is the effect of this action?

    A. No one can read the files in the directory.

    B. Only those users recognized by NT are allowed to read the files in the directory.

    C. All users can read the files because NTFS overrides IIS permissions.

    D. Only users coming from NT Workstation or NT Server can read the files in the directory.

5. The default user name for the anonymous account on a computer named SPENCER for the WWW service is which of the following?

    A. SPENCER

    B. IUSR

    C. IUSR_SPENCER

    D. SPENCER_IUSR

6. When creating virtual directories, they should reside where?

    A. On the server

    B. In the same authentication domain

    C. On the WAN

    D. Anywhere

7. Karen has created a number of virtual directories at her site, but cannot get them to appear in directory listings. This is most likely caused by which of the following?

    A. Inappropriate permissions

    B. A port other than 80 being used

    C. Virtual directories beyond the server

    D. A failure to use links in HTML files

8. Multihoming is also known as creating which of the following?

    A. Virtual files

    B. Virtual directories

    C. Virtual servers

    D. Virtual private networks

9. TCP port 25 is the default for which service?

    A. NNTP

    B. SMTP

APPLY YOUR KNOWLEDGE

C. WWW

D. FTP

10. How many SMTP sites are allowed for the SMTP service?

    A. 0

    B. 1

    C. 2

    D. Unlimited

11. By default in SMTP, how many users can receive a single message?

    A. 1

    B. 100

    C. 256

    D. 512

12. Allan, a new administrator, notices traffic on TCP port 563. SSL is in use. What service is using port 563, by default?

    A. NNTP

    B. SMTP

    C. WWW

    D. FTP

13. By default, into what directory are FTP log files written to?

    A. %SystemRoot%

    B. %SystemRoot%\Inetpub

    C. %SystemRoot%\Inetpub\Logfiles

    D. %SystemRoot%\System32\Logfiles

Answers to Review Questions

1. The default TCP port used for the WWW service is 80. See "Creating and Sharing Directories."

2. Virtual directories should always be stored on servers within the same NT domain as the IIS server resides. See "Creating and Sharing Virtual Directories."

3. Virtual servers allow one server to alias multiple domain names. See "Creating and Sharing Virtual Servers."

4. The wc utility can be used to count the number of lines in a log file, as well as the number of words or characters. See "Writing Scripts for Service Management."

5. WebMaps enable you to view your site with Tree view, Cyberbolic view, or both. See "Using Content Analyzer."

6. The default TCP port for the SMTP service is port 25. See "Configuring SMTP."

7. By default, and in the absence of SSL, NNTP uses TCP port 119. See "Configuring NNTP."

8. After generating the digital certificate, it must be registered with a certificate authority. See "Configuring Certificate Server."

9. The Index Server data, in all cases, is approximately 40 percent of the size of the corpus. See "Configuring Index Server."

10. MIME is an acronym for Multipurpose Internet Mail Extension. See "Managing MIME Types."

11. FTP logs can be created on a daily, weekly, or monthly basis. See "Managing the FTP Service."

12. Increasing the amount of memory and going with the fastest CPU available increases Index

APPLY YOUR KNOWLEDGE

Server performance. The disk space needed for the data is always roughly 40 percent the size of the corpus. See "Configuring Index Server."

Answers to Exam Questions

1. **C.** The default TCP port for the WWW Service is 80. See "Managing the WWW Service."

2. **A, B.** By default, anonymous access is enabled for WWW and FTP during installation. See "Managing the WWW Service" and "Managing the FTP Service."

3. **A, D.** Allow Read Access and Allow Script access are selected by default. See "Managing the WWW Service."

4. **A.** Taking away the Allow Read Access permission in IIS prevents users from viewing files in the directory. See "Managing the WWW Service."

5. **C.** The default anonymous account user name is always IUSR_computername. See "Managing the WWW Service."

6. **B.** Virtual directories should always be stored on servers within the same NT authentication domain as the IIS server resides. See "Creating and Sharing Virtual Directories."

7. **D.** Virtual directories do not appear in directory listings and must be accessed through explicit links within HTML files. See "Creating and Sharing Virtual Directories."

8. **C.** Multihoming is another word for using virtual servers. See "Creating and Sharing Virtual Servers."

9. **B.** The default TCP port for the SMTP Service is 25. See "Configuring SMTP."

10. **B.** Regardless of the size of the site, only one SMTP service is allowed. See "Configuring SMTP."

11. **B.** By default, in SMTP 100 users can receive a single message. See "Configuring SMTP."

12. **A.** By default, NNTP operates at TCP port 563 with SSL. See "Configuring NNTP."

13. **D.** By default, FTP log files are written to the %SystemRoot%\System32\Logfiles directory. See "Managing the FTP Service."

Suggested Readings and Resources

1. Comer, Douglas. *Internetworking With TCP/IP: Principles, Protocols, and Architecture, Third Edition.* Prentice Hall: 1998.

2. Halabi, Bassam. *Internet Routing Architectures.* Cisco Press: 1997.

3. Heywood, Drew. *Networking With Microsoft TCP/IP, Third Edition.* New Riders Publishing: 1998.

4. Howell, Nelson and Forta, Ben. *Special Edition Using Microsoft Internet Information Server 4.* Que Education and Training: 1997.

5. Siyan, Karanjit S. *Windows NT TCP/IP.* New Riders Professional Library: 1998.

6. Tulloch, Mitch. *Administering Internet Information Server 4 (Windows NT Technical Expert).* Computing McGraw-Hill: 1998.

This chapter helps you get ready for the Integration and Interoperability questions on the exam. Integration and interoperability are two of the most critical components of Microsoft's strategy for deploying applications using IIS. There is a tremendous amount of legacy data stored in databases of all kinds, many with very expensive, high-maintenance front-end clients. By using IIS and a Web browser, it is possible to create applications that leverage that data and use a Web browser as a client. This allows you to deploy fast, inexpensive applications in place of the existing clients.

The other objective for this chapter is understanding how to get information from Microsoft Index Server and present it to a client.

For the exam, Microsoft defines the Integration and Interoperability objectives as the following:

Configure IIS to connect to a database, including configuring ODBC. Tasks include the following:

- **Configuring ODBC**

▶ Microsoft's strategy for deploying Internet applications rests heavily on the capability to serve database information through Web applications. This is a key technology for delivering legacy data through a Web browser interface. You should be familiar with the mechanics of how this is done, as well as have some knowledge of what ODBC is.

Configure IIS to integrate with Index Server. Tasks include the following:

- **Specifying query parameters by creating the .IDQ file**

- **Specifying how the query results are formatted and displayed to the user by creating the .HTX file**

C H A P T E R 4

Integration and Interoperability

▶ If you have been using the Internet even slightly over the last couple of years, you are probably familiar with search engines. The Internet was once described as the world's largest library, but without a card catalog. Companies like Yahoo!, Snap.com, Excite, and AltaVista have brought that card catalog to the Web, making it usable for the average person. Index Server brings the same capabilities to Microsoft Internet Information Server 4.0 by indexing the HTML, Word, and Excel files on the server and making them searchable. For the test, you should be familiar with how to build an .IDQ file to perform a query of the Index Server and how to format the results of that query using an .HTX file.

▶ Microsoft considers this information important enough to make it an objective, so even if you are not a programmer, be familiar with what these files do and some of the basic commands used in the files. The odds are pretty good that you will see at least one question on these files on the exam.

As you read through this chapter, you should concentrate on the following key concepts:

► The uses of the .IDQ and .HTX files in queries of Index Server

► What Open Database Connectivity (ODBC) is and why it is important that your IIS server connect to it

Another important study tip for this chapter is, "Don't get lost in the details!" This chapter looks at the specifics of linking IIS to an ODBC database and then takes an in-depth look at the files needed to create an Index Server query. On the exam, Microsoft does not look for you to write an .IDQ application. Instead, they might ask something like how to pull all the instances of Widget from the departmental Web server. If you know that it's through a combination of the .IDQ and .HTX files, you will get the answer correct.

INTRODUCTION

This chapter examines integration between the WWW service of IIS and other servers and services. The other servers and services discussed fall into one of two categories: databases or Index Server. Connecting IIS to a database enables you to pull or update information from a server dedicated to such a task—such as SQL. Integrating with Index Server enables you to make the available data visible and searchable by those accessing your site. The chapter is organized as follows:

- ◆ Configuring IIS to Connect to a Database, including a look at ODBC
- ◆ Configuring Integration with Index Server

CONFIGURING IIS TO CONNECT TO A DATABASE

▶ Configure IIS to connect to a database, including configuring ODBC.

With the expansion of the World Wide Web into homes around the United States came the expectation that Web browsers would allow users to retrieve data specific to a need. Users grew frustrated at looking at static screen pages and wanted to be able to pull up data and forms based on their requests. From an HTML coding standpoint, creating a Web page for every conceivable request is impractical. The sheer volume of pages would be incomprehensible, and the action of updating the pages each time a piece of data changed would be more than any one person could handle.

To solve the problem, databases such as Microsoft SQL (Structured Query Language) Server or Oracle can be used with Microsoft IIS 4.0. The databases can supply the information to fulfill a query, update information, and add new data through the Web almost as easily as if a user were sitting at a PC on a local area network.

Databases have been around since the early days of computing, and Web servers have been around for a number of years. What is new is the integration of the two to create the dynamic Web sites expected today.

Because Windows NT Server is growing in popularity and it is the platform on which Internet Information Server runs, it is not uncommon to expect the database to which you connect to be Microsoft SQL Server. This is the expectation for the exam and the thrust of the discussion that follows.

Why Put a Database on the Web?

Almost as important as the above question is why use Microsoft Internet Information Server 4.0 to do it with? Before we look at the mechanics of connecting IIS to your favorite database, we should discuss why you would want to do that. Microsoft obviously considers it important because they dedicate an entire section of their objectives for this exam to it. Let's look at some reasons for using IIS to make your database data available on the Web.

◆ **Low Cost.** If you use Windows NT Server, you can't find a much lower cost solution for deploying Web applications than Microsoft Internet Information Server 4.0. In addition, it's a great way to make data available, when measured against the cost of traditional, client-server applications. Even better, you have immediate cross-platform support on the client side. Any machine, be it Windows, Macintosh, or UNIX, has equal access to the data. Even better still, implementing a Web-based database solution can be done relatively quickly and doesn't require a large team of developers. These days, every technician with a keyboard is experimenting with Web development in one form or another. And with IIS, Microsoft provides a number of tools to make it even easier.

◆ **Information Security.** If you are involved with information security, the first question that possibly runs through your mind is "Are you crazy? How can I trust my mission-critical information to a Web server?" The answer is simple: By using IIS, you can leverage the robust security included with Windows NT. In addition, Microsoft Transaction Server (MTS) (discussed in Chapter 1, "Planning") provides the data protection and integrity provided by a transactional data processing server.

◆ **Standards-based.** As we discuss in the rest of this chapter, IIS provides database access using proven standards. ODBC was around long before IIS had the capability to interface with databases. All you are doing is moving your ODBC calls from a customized client application to a Web server and browser.

◆ **Dynamic content.** A final feature that needs to be discussed is Microsoft Internet Information Server 4.0's capability to dynamically build HTML pages based on content stored in a database. If you have attended any of the Microsoft demonstrations of this capability, it is very impressive. Not only can you remove the onus of writing HTML code from the content provider and place it on the server itself, you can also use information provided by the user to personalize his visit to your site. However, because this is not a programming book, we do not delve much deeper into the mechanics of dynamic content.

Now you're convinced that this is the greatest idea since the invention of the Internet. But before you rush off to move all your database information to the Web, let's look at a few things you need to watch out for as you plan your deployment:

◆ **Server Capacity.** Be sure your server has the horsepower to handle the increased overhead associated with database access. You should look at memory, processor number and speed, disk subsystems and controllers, and connectivity. You might want to separate your IIS server and database server onto multiple servers. We discuss performance tuning of IIS in Chapter 6, "Monitoring and Optimization."

◆ **Scalability.** If you have ever worked as a database administrator, you'll recognize this as a common issue with any database applications. Try to plan for growth as you start deploying databases. Setting up a 3GB employee database on a server that has 4GB of available space is probably not a good idea if you expect the size of the company to triple in the next year. When in doubt, make it as big as your budget allows. When the day comes to add another database and you can tell your manager that he doesn't need to buy another database server, you will be a hero.

◆ **Reliability.** The flip side of scalability is reliability. As you move more and more data access to Web-based applications, it becomes significantly more important to make sure the data is always available. You should try to build as much redundancy into your implementation as possible, including RAID arrays, multiple CPUs, hot spare servers, and a variety of other hardware and software solutions available. You need to research specific solutions as your situation dictates.

◆ **Data Security.** We just finished discussing how terrific the data security using IIS could be. However, could is the operative phrase. You need to ensure that you configure the database server, IIS server, and Windows NT security correctly to protect the security and integrity of your data. For applications where transactional processing would be a benefit, MTS is an excellent transaction tracking application.

Now that you are familiar with why you might want to consider taking your databases to the Web and some of the things to consider before you start writing code, let's look at the nuts and bolts of connecting IIS to a database.

Understanding ODBC

ODBC standard defines a method of accessing data in a variety of relational databases. ODBC provides a simple way to connect toan existing database (whether that database is SQL or any ODBC-compliant database). It was designed by Microsoft to address the issue of any number of applications needing to interface with SQL Server. ODBC has the benefit of being fast, lightweight, and vendor independent. Applications written in a variety of languages, including C, C++, Visual Basic, or even Java, can call data using ODBC.

The greatest advantage ODBC offers is that it defines a clear distinction between the application and the database, and thus does not require any specific programming. To use it, you create a query and template for how the output will look.

There are three major components to IIS's implementation of ODBC:

◆ **.HTM (.HTML).** A standard HTML document (like most Web pages on the Internet), this file contains the hyperlink for a query. The request comes from the browser and merely specifies the URL for the .IDC (Internet Database Connector) file on IIS. The user submits her query of the ODBC database through this file.

NOTE **Windows NT Paths** When you start implementing these files, you need to reference the Windows NT path. You should keep in mind that there is a limit of 260 characters on any Windows NT-based pathname.

◆ **.IDC. The** file containing the data source file information and SQL statements for the query. The IDC is an ISAPI DLL (HTTPODBC.DLL) and provides the link for connecting IIS to a variety of ODBC-compliant databases.

◆ **.HTX.** A file of HTML extensions containing the template document with placeholders for the result. This file contains the information for formatting the results of the query in an HTML document that can be read by the user's browser.

Figure 4.1 illustrates the processes involved in answering a query request.

FIGURE 4.1
The process for resolving a database query using Microsoft Internet Information Server 4.0.

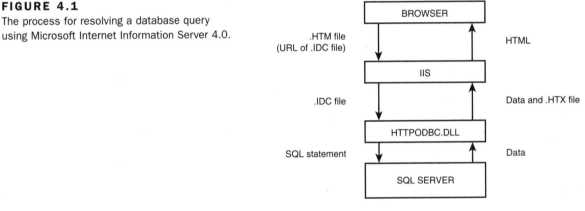

Implementing ODBC

Implementing ODBC is extremely easy and can be broken into the following steps:

<table>
<tr><td rowspan="7" style="writing-mode: vertical-lr;">N O T E</td></tr>
</table>

But Where's the SQL Database?
This section assumes the SQL database already exists. Because this is not a SQL administration book, we do not cover creating a SQL database. Check the "Suggested Readings and Resources" section at the end of the chapter for some SQL administration recommended reading and resources.

STEP BY STEP

4.1 Implementing ODBC

1. Double-click the ODBC icon in the Control Panel.

2. Select the System DSN tab from the ODBC Data Source Administrator dialog box (shown in Figure 4.2).

3. Choose Add and select the driver (SQL, Access, and Oracle appear as choices). This is illustrated in Figure 4.3.

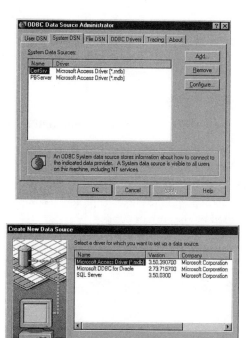

◄**FIGURE 4.2**
The System DSN tab enables you to configure data sources that are available to IIS.

◄**FIGURE 4.3**
Select the new data source(s).

4. Specify the name and description of the data source on the Create a New Data Source dialog box, shown in Figure 4.4.

5. Specify the server to connect to and click Next.

6. If you are using a data source that can perform authentication, such as SQL Server, then specify how authentication is to be done (shown in Figure 4.5).

FIGURE 4.4▲
You must specify a name, description, and server for the data source.

Windows NT or the SQL Server can be used for client authentication. If the SQL Server is used, it uses standard logon security and a SQL Server user ID and password must be given for all connections. If you choose to use Windows NT authentication, the Windows NT user account is associated with a SQL Server user account and integrated security is used to establish the connection.

Figure 4.5 also shows a Client Configuration button. This can be used to customize the configuration if you are using nonstandard pipes.

FIGURE 4.5▲
This dialog box allows you to configure the authentication mechanism to be used from IIS to the ODBC-compliant database.

> **N O T E**
>
> **Configuring Authentication** In real-ity, to get Windows NT logons to work, you need to ensure that three things are correctly configured. First, SQL Server security must be set to Integrated (NT only) or Mixed (NT & SQL). Next, the connection type must be named Pipes or Multiprotocol. NT does not use a different connection type because it does not send your password as clear text. Finally, you must use SQL Security Manager to assign NT users to SQL users.

The Login ID and Password boxes at the bottom of Figure 4.5 are only used if you have selected SQL Server authentication and become grayed out if you are using Windows NT authentication.

Other ODBC Tabs

Other tabs in the ODBC Data Source Administrator dialog box include the following:

◆ **User DSN.** The User DSN tab, shown in Figure 4.6, is used to add, delete, or change the setup of data source names (DSNs). The data sources specified here are local to a computer and can only be used by the current user.

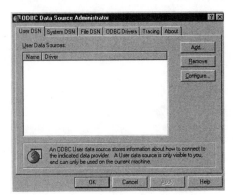

FIGURE 4.6▶
The User DSN tab allows you to configure user specific data sources.

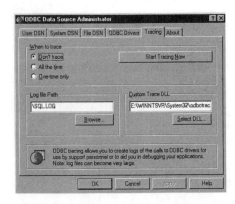

FIGURE 4.7▲
The Tracing tab of the ODBC Data Source Administrator dialog box.

◆ **File DSN.** The File DSN tab is used to add, delete, or change the setup of data sources with file data source names. File-based data sources can be shared between all users that are using the same drivers and are not dedicated to individual users or local machines.

◆ **ODBC Drivers.** The ODBC Drivers tab shows information about the ODBC drivers that are currently installed. The information given includes the name, version, file name, and created date of every ODBC driver (and the name of the company responsible for it).

◆ **Tracing.** The Tracing tab, shown in Figure 4.7, enables you to configure how the ODBC Driver Manager traces ODBC calls to functions. Choices include all of the time, dynamically (by a custom DLL), or for one connection only (as well as not at all).

◆ **About.** The About tab lists the ODBC core components, the actual files they consist of, and the versions. An example of the information it provides is shown in Figure 4.8.

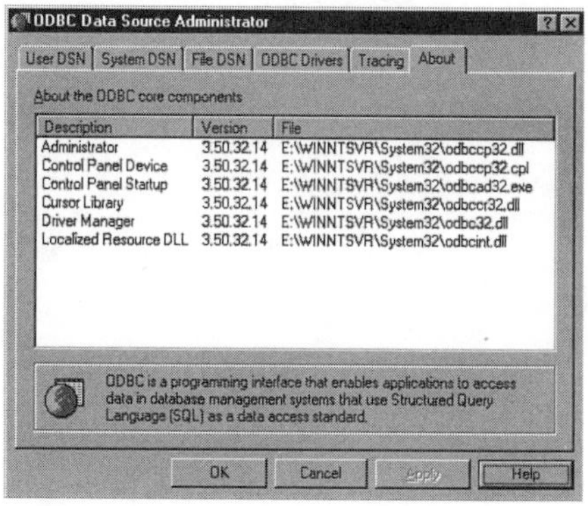

Creating and Developing Applications

After the registration is completed and ODBC is configured, the remaining steps involve creating and developing the files to be used.

Creating an .IDC Application

The .IDC file is actually a server extension that contains the SQL command used to interface between IIS and the HTTPODBC.DLL (an ISAPI DLL) library. There are four required parameters to the file:

◆ Datasource

◆ Username

◆ Template

◆ SQLStatement

Datasource is simply the name of the ODBC data source that has been defined in the ODBC Data Source Administrator dialog box available from the Control Panel.

Username is the user name required to access the data source and can be any valid logon name for the SQL Server database. This (as well as the Password field, if used) is ignored if you use integrated security or if the database doesn't have security installed.

Template specifies the name of the file (.HTX) that will be used as a template to display (and do any necessary interpretation of) the SQL results.

SQLStatement is the list of commands you want to execute. Parameter values can be used if they are enclosed in percent signs (%). If multiple lines are required, a plus sign (+) must be the first character on each line.

FIGURE 4.8
The About tab of the ODBC Data Source Administrator dialog box.

NOTE

ISAPI ISAPI is discussed in Chapter 5, "Running Applications."

An example of an .IDC file follows:

```
Datasource: Synergy
Username:   sa
Template:   syn_temp.HTX
SQLStatement:
+SELECT employeeno, dob, doh
+FROM pubs.dbo.synergy
+WHERE salary>50000
```

The preceding code pulls the employee number, date of birth, and date of hire information from the pubs.dbo.synergy database for every employee exceeding $50,000 in salary. After the data is extracted, it is combined with an .HTX file (in this case, SYN_TEMP.HTX) for formatting.

Optional fields that can be used in the .IDC file include the following:

◆ **DefaultParameters.** To specify default values in the event, nothing is specified by the client.

◆ **Expires.** This is the number of seconds the system waits before requesting a non-cached version of the query results.

◆ **MaxFieldSize.** The maximum buffer space per field (beyond this, truncation takes place). If no value is specified, the value 8192 bytes is used by default.

◆ **MaxRecords.** The maximum number of records to return per query.

◆ **ODBCConnection.** Can either be set to POOL to add the connection to the connection pool (keeping open for future requests) or NONPOOL to not do so.

◆ **Password.** The password for the user name given.

◆ **RequiredParameters.** Parameters that have to be filled in by the client before you can do the query. A comma must separate these parameters or the HTTPODBC.DLL library returns an error message.

◆ **Translationfile.** The path for non-English characters to be found before being returned to the browser.

◆ **Content-type.** A valid MIME type describing what goes back to the client. If the .HTX file has HTML, then this usually is text/html.

The .HTX File

The .HTX file is an HTML template that fills in its blanks with information returned from a query. It accepts SQL information in and returns HTML information out. A quick look at an .HTX file shows that it looks very much like an HTML file and contains many of the same fields.

Database fields that it receives are known as containers and are identified by field names surrounded by percent signs (%) and angle brackets (<>). Thus, the employeeno field that comes from the SQL database is known as <%employeeno%> in an .HTX file.

All processing is done in loops that start with <%begindetail%> and end with <%enddetail%>. Logic can be included with <%if%> and <%endif%>, as well as <%else%> statements. You also can use the following four standard programming operators:

◆ **EQ.** Equal to. If value1 equals value2, return *TRUE.*

◆ **GT**. Greater than. If value1 is greater than value2, return *TRUE.*

◆ **LT**. Less than. If value1 is less than value2, return *TRUE.*

◆ **CONTAINS**. If any part of value1 is contained within value2, return *TRUE.*

Following is an example of an .HTX file:

```
<HTML>
<HEAD>
<TITLE>Welcome to Synergy</TITLE>
</HEAD>
<H2>Employees with Salaries greater than $50,000</H2>
<%begindetail%>
<b>Employee number:</b><%employeeno%> <b>Date of birth and
hire:
➡</b><%dob%>, <%doh%><P>
<%enddetail%>
</HTML>
```

Some useful samples of .HTX files can be found on your system and located by using the NT Find utility from the Start menu to look for files ending in that extension. Three useful ones for working with Index Server are located in the %systemroot%\system32\inetsrv\ iisadmin\isadmin directory of your system, and an example of one is given at the end of this chapter.

Development Tools: Visual InterDev

You might have noticed a few references to tools for developing these applications without all the pain of actually hand-coding the applications. Before we move on to our discussions of Microsoft Index Server, it's a good idea to mention Microsoft's leading tool for developers building dynamic Web applications. Visual InterDev, which is available as version 6.0 during the writing of this book, is an excellent tool for building dynamic, database-driven Web sites. Visual InterDev supports access to virtually any database using Universal Data Access, including ADO, ODBC, and OLE DB. It also includes support for Active Server Pages, middle-tier components written in any language, Dynamic HTML, and includes integrated database design and programming tools to make creating database-driven applications an order of magnitude easier. Please note: This isn't a sales pitch for Microsoft's Web development tools. There are a variety of tools available to ease the pain of writing Web-based applications. Microsoft recommends Visual InterDev for this application.

CONFIGURING INTEGRATION WITH INDEX SERVER

▶ Configure IIS to integrate with Index Server.

Index Server has already been examined several times in this book, including the explanation of it in Chapter 1, "Planning," and details about how to configure it in Chapter 3, "Configuring and Managing Resource Access." This section covers how it handles queries and returns results.

Before we get into making queries, let's take a quick look at the Index Server architecture. This brings some of the different pieces discussed throughout the book into perspective. In this chapter, we discuss the querying of the indexed information we covered in the previous chapters.

Index Server Architecture

As we discussed in Chapters 1 and 3, Index Server is included with Microsoft Internet Information Server 4.0 to provide content indexing for Web sites. When installed and configured properly, Index Server can be used to provide up-to-date indexes of Web server content with little or no administration. Index Server indexes HTML, Microsoft Word, Microsoft Excel, Microsoft PowerPoint, and ASCII text documents with equal ease. You can even write custom filters to handle additional data types. But how does it do it?

When Index Server is initially installed, it indexes every document on the server. This is a function of the installation and configuration. This is a manual process and is straightforward. Maintaining that initial index is the tricky part. The process of indexing begins when a document is added to a Web site that has been indexed. A *scanning* process is constantly running on the Index Server, looking for new documents. When it recognizes that a new document has been added, the *CiDaemon* process is invoked. This process analyzes the new document by filtering it through a series of filter and word breaker DLLs. These filters identify keywords in the document that are added to word lists, which are stored in random access memory until they can be incorporated into the master index.

After the document has been analyzed and the keywords added to the master index, the document is available in the Index Server's database and can be found by using a query.

Writing Index Server Queries

For most intents and purposes, this discussion is very much like the earlier discussion of .HTX files (used to format and return the query results to the user). The difference exists in the files used to hold the queries. Rather than using the .IDC file previously discussed, Index Server uses an .IDQ (Internet Data Query) file. The .IDQ file should always be placed in the Scripts directory and it requires Execute or Script permission to properly function.

There are two sections to the file, which begins with a tag of <Query> (the first section) and is followed by the <Names> section. The Names section is purely optional and not used most of the time. If it is used, it defines nonstandard column names that are referred to in a query. The Query section of the file is all that is required, and it can contain parameters, variables, and conditional expressions.

The restrictions are as follows: Lines must start with the variable you are trying to set, and only one variable can be set per line. Additionally, percent signs (%) are used to identify the variables and references.

> **NOTE**
>
> **Asking Permission** After you create an .IDQ file, it should always be placed in the Scripts directory. More importantly, it requires Execute or Script permission to properly function. Microsoft is notorious for asking permissions questions on almost all their exams, so keep an eye out.

EXAM TIP

Do I Have to Memorize All These Variables? Don't panic. These variables are included as a reference to you when you start working with Index Server. You should not see any of these variables in a "What variable do you use…" type of question on this exam.

Using Variables in .IDQ Files

The variables that can be used in .IDQ files are as follows:

◆ **CiCatalog.** Sets the location for the catalog. If the value is already set, the value here overrides that one.

◆ **CiCodepage.** Sets the server's code page. Again, if the value is already set, the entry here overrides the previous one.

◆ **CiColumns.** Defines a list of columns that is used in the .HTX file.

◆ **CiDeferNonIndexedTrimming.** Is not used by default, but can be set if the scope of the query must be limited.

◆ **CiFlags.** Query flags can be set to DEEP or SHALLOW to determine if only the directory listed in CiScope is searched.

◆ **CiForceUseCi.** By setting to True, you can force the query to use the content index even if it is out of date.

◆ **CiLocale.** Specifies the locale used to issue the query.

◆ **CiMaxRecordsInResultSet.** Specifies the maximum number of results that can be returned from the query.

◆ **CiMaxRecordsPerPage.** Specifies the maximum number of records that can appear on a display page.

◆ **CiRestriction.** A restriction that you are placing on the query.

◆ **CiScope.** Specifies the starting directory for the search.

◆ **CiSort.** Specifies whether the results should be sorted in ascending or descending order.

◆ **CiTemplate.** Specifies the full path of the .HTX file from the root. Index Server is bound by the Windows NT shell limit of 260 characters per path.

As with most script files, a pound sign (#) can be used to specify a comment. At whatever point the # sign is in the line, from there on the line is ignored.

Using Conditional Expressions in .IDQ Files

The following conditional expressions can be used in .IDQ files:

- ◆ **CONTAINS.** If any part of value1 is contained within value2, return *TRUE.*

- ◆ **EQ.** Equal to. If value1 equals value2, return *TRUE.*

- ◆ **GE.** Greater than or equal to. If value1 is greater than or equal to value2, return *TRUE.*

- ◆ **GT.** Greater than. If value1 is greater than value2, return *TRUE.*

- ◆ **ISEMPTY.** If value1 is null, return *TRUE.*

- ◆ **LE.** Less than or equal to. If value1 is less than or equal to value2, return *TRUE.*

- ◆ **LT.** Less than. If value1 is less than value2, return *TRUE.*

- ◆ **NE.** Not equal to. If value1 does not equal value2, return *TRUE.*

An Example of the .IDQ File

The following is an example of an .IDQ file:

```
[Query]
CiColumns=employeeno,dob,doh
CiMaxRecordsInResultSet=50
CiMaxRecordsPerPage=20
#20 used for compatibility with most browsers
CiScope=/
CiFlags=DEEP
CiTemplate=/scripts/synergy.HTX
```

In the example, three columns are queried in the database: employeeno, dob, and doh. The maximum number of records that is returned is 50, with up to 20 on each page of display. The fifth line is a comment line added by the person who created the file. It has no effect on operation whatsoever. The CiScope is set to the root directory with the search (CiFlags) set to go through all subdirectories. The template to use is then specified by the CiTemplate variable.

Some Sample Files

Included with IIS 4.0 are some sample files for each of these applications. Following are the files and their locations:

◆ **Scan .IDQ File.** One of the best examples of an efficient .IDQ file is SCAN.IDQ, located in the %systemroot%/system32\inetsrv\iisadmin\isadmin folder of your system.

◆ **Scan .HTX File.** After SCAN.IDQ has performed its function, results are returned to SCAN.HTX, also located in the %systemroot%/system32\inetsrv\iisadmin\isadmin folder of your system.

◆ **Query .HTM File.** The two preceding items discussed the .IDQ file that gathers results and the .HTX file that formats those results. Missing from the equation is the .HTM file, which first queries for the results. One of the best examples of this file is QUERY.HTM, located in %systemroot$\InetPub\iissamples\ISSamples. It is this file which sends the query to the IDQ file.

CASE STUDY: WEB-ENABLING THE HUMAN RESOURCES EMPLOYEE INFORMATION DATABASE

ESSENCE OF THE CASE

The salient points of the case are as follows:

▶ You have an existing IIS-based intranet.

▶ The Human Resources department has a legacy Microsoft Access database they want to share through the intranet.

▶ The Human Resources department wants each user to be able to access his own benefits information and only his own information.

▶ Due to the projected cost savings, you have a budget for the project.

SCENARIO

You are the Web manager for the Bearly Legal Teddy Bear Company, a 1,500 employee teddy bear manufacturing company. You manage an intranet site consisting of several Microsoft Internet Information Server 4.0 servers that are configured to serve department intranet sites. The Human Resources department has an Microsoft Access database that contains all the employee information, and they want to make it securely available to employees so they can update their benefits information, 401K enrollment, and so on. Human Resources has the following requirements:

CASE STUDY: WEB-ENABLING THE HUMAN RESOURCES EMPLOYEE INFORMATION DATABASE

▶ Making the information in the Microsoft Access database available to the employees.

▶ Each employee should be able to only access his own records and he should be able to update them as needed.

Because this project saves several hundred thousand dollars in human resources costs, you have a healthy budget. How do you go about providing this information on the Web?

ANALYSIS

Your analysis reveals the following:

Assumptions: Because you already administer a number of departments' IIS servers, you can assume you have the necessary infrastructure to support this application.

Solution: Obviously, we will use the ODBC capabilities of Microsoft Internet Information Server 4.0 to accomplish this. Let's look at the steps to get from an IIS server and an Access Database to a database-driven application. We do not discuss the actual code necessary, but instead we look at the big picture. It should go something like the following:

1. First, given your security requirements, you need to migrate your database from MS Access to a full SQL database. This allows you to take advantage of the security features of IIS and SQL.

2. You need to configure the ODBC connection to the SQL database. This procedure is detailed earlier.

3. Next, using a tool like Visual InterDev (or any of the other tools available), you need to code the application that will access the data. This application will consist of an .HTM file containing a query for the database, an .IDC file that contains the information about the data source (the SQL database) and the actual SQL statements, and the .HTX file, which formats the results and presents them to the user.

This case study makes creating this application look simpler than it is in reality, although the trickiest part is getting the security correct. You might even want to investigate integrating Certificate Server into the application and issue each user a certificate to secure her personal data. For more information on Certificate Server, see Chapter 2, "Installation and Configuration."

CHAPTER SUMMARY

KEY TERMS

Before you take the exam, make sure you are comfortable with the definitions and concepts for each of the following key terms:

- Internet Database Connector (IDC)
- .IDQ file
- .HTX file
- Index Server
- Open Database Connectivity (ODBC)

Let's briefly recap this chapter before we move on to the "Apply Your Knowledge" section. The following should put some of this information into perspective for you.

We started the chapter by discussing some of the reasons for moving database applications to the Web. They include the following:

- ◆ **Low Cost.** It's tough to find a lower cost solution for deploying Web applications than Microsoft Internet Information Server 4.0.
- ◆ **Information Security.** By using IIS, you can leverage the robust security included with Windows NT.
- ◆ **Standards Based.** IIS provides database access using proven standards.
- ◆ **Dynamic Content.** IIS can dynamically build HTML pages based on content stored in a database.

We also discussed some considerations before you deploy a database-driven application. They include the following:

- ◆ **Server Capacity.** Be sure your server has the horsepower to handle the increased overhead associated with database access.
- ◆ **Scalability.** Try to plan for growth as you start deploying databases.
- ◆ **Reliability.** It is very important to make sure the data is always available.
- ◆ **Data Security.** You need to ensure that you configure the database server, IIS server, and Windows NT security correctly to protect the security and integrity of your data.

Following this, we got right into the nuts and bolts of ODBC connectivity. Connecting IIS to an ODBC-compliant database is very simple if you follow the steps we covered. After you have connected to the database and made sure security is set up to your liking, the following are three files necessary to access the data:

CHAPTER SUMMARY

◆ **.HTM.** The file containing the hyperlink for a query. The request comes from the browser and merely specifies the URL for the .IDC (Internet Database Connector) file on IIS.

◆ **.IDC.** The file containing the data source file information and SQL statement.

◆ **.HTX.** A file of HTML extensions containing the template document with placeholders for the result.

We finished up the chapter with an in-depth look at creating the .IDQ and .HTX files for an Index Server query. The .IDQ file is used to query the Index Server, whereas the .HTX file formats the response from the server for the client's browser.

That's enough review; let's look at how you might apply some of this knowledge.

APPLY YOUR KNOWLEDGE

Exercises

4.1   Examine the ODBC Core Components

To see which ODBC core components are installed on your system, follow these steps.

Estimated time: 10 minutes

1. Double-click the ODBC icon in the Control Panel.

2. Select the About tab from the ODBC Data Source Administrator dialog box.

3. Note the core components installed and the version number of each.

4.2   Edit the QUERY.HTM File

To modify the QUERY.HTM file to perform a query based upon your database, follow these steps.

Estimated time: 15–30 minutes

1. Start a word processing application such as Microsoft Word 97.

2. Select File, Open menu, switch to All Files, and find the existing copy of QUERY.HTM (by default, in InetPub\iissamples\ISSamples).

3. What appears is the HTML result. Select View, HTML Source, and the code is displayed.

4. Make the changes to reflect your system and database.

5. Choose File, Save, and then Exit. Lastly, confirm that it is saved as an .HTM file.

4.3   Examine the Sample Files on Your System

To examine the sample .HTM, .IDQ, and .HTX files on your system, follow these steps.

Estimated time: 15–30 minutes

1. Start a word processing application such as Microsoft Word 97.

2. Select File, Open menu and go to InetPub\iissamples\ISSamples. To see the listings, you might need to change the file type to All Files.

3. What appears is a number of sample files to use in creating your own scripts. Bring each one up and you can see the HTML result. Select View, HTML Source, and the code is displayed.

Review Questions

1. What would a file with an .HTX extension be used for on a Microsoft Internet Information Server 4.0 server?

2. What are three of the components of IIS's implementation of ODBC, and what are they used for?

3. Give three reasons why you should use Microsoft Internet Information Server 4.0 to put your ODBC-compliant database on the Web.

4. Differentiate between a query to an ODBC-compliant database and a query made using Index Server.

Exam Questions

1. You are the IIS administrator for Little Faith Enterprises. One of the application developers in your company has placed a template file on your IIS Web server and you need to specify the path for the file. How many characters can be used in the path specification?

   A. 8

   B. 255

   C. 256

   D. 260

2. You are a freelance application developer, working for CIC Consulting. They have asked you to develop an IIS application for the Human Resources department that queries an ODBC-compliant employee database. Which of the following file types can contain queries?

   A. HTM

   B. IDC

   C. IDQ

   D. HTX

3. Working on the same application, you need to reference the template. Which of the following files can contain templates?

   A. HTM

   B. IDC

   C. IDQ

   D. HTX

4. You are the Web manager for a small publishing company and you are in the process of developing an application for the Sales department. Sales wants their data to remain secure. Where can Login Authentication to a SQL Server accessed through IIS be done?

   A. On the NT Server

   B. On the SQL Server

   C. On the IIS Server

   D. On the Index Server

5. You are an application developer interviewing for a position with an international food distributor. The manager interviewing you is testing your familiarity with Web-based applications and wants to know in which file the <Query> tag is found. You answer:

   A. SAMPLE.HTM

   B. SAMPLE.IDC

   C. SAMPLE.IDQ

   D. SAMPLE.HTX

6. The manager's next question is, "In which file can the SQL statement parameter be found?"

   A. SAMPLE.HTM

   B. SAMPLE.IDC

   C. SAMPLE.IDQ

   D. SAMPLE.HTX

7. You are an application developer with the We Are Freezing Frozen Fish Consortium. You have been tasked with the development of the first Web

APPLY YOUR KNOWLEDGE

application in your department, but your manager wants to make sure it is heavily commented so he can see what you've done and why. What is the comment character used as the first character in script files to prevent the line from being processed?

A. %

B. <

C. [

D. #

8. You are the lead Web administrator for the Dog Eat Dog Pet Food Company and one of your coworkers is trying to clean up some space on one of your Microsoft Internet Information Server 4.0 Web servers. He has come across a file called HTTPODBC.DLL and wants to know if he can delete it. You want to educate your coworker before he inadvertently deletes a file you need. What do you tell him this file is used for?

A. It is the dynamic link library providing ODBC support on the server.

B. It is the file used to install ODBC support on the server.

C. It is needed for HTTP operations.

D. It should be deleted after installation.

9. You are developing a Web application and get an error message that indicates you have exceeded the maximum number of records accessible. In which file would the `MaxRecords` parameter be found?

A. SAMPLE.HTM

B. SAMPLE.IDC

C. SAMPLE.IDQ

D. SAMPLE.HTX

10. In which file would the `CiCodePage` variable be found?

A. SAMPLE.HTM

B. SAMPLE.IDC

C. SAMPLE.IDQ

D. SAMPLE.HTX

Answers to Review Questions

1. The .HTX file is an HTML template that fills in its blanks with information returned from a query. In other words, it takes the results of a query against a SQL Server and returns it in an HTML format. The resulting file can then be viewed with a standard browser. See "Understanding ODBC."

2. The .HTM file is the HTML file used to submit the query to the database. It specifies the location for the .IDC file on the IIS server.

   The .IDC file contains the data source information for the database being queried as well as the SQL statement(s) used to make the query.

   The .HTX file takes the results of the query and returns them in a browser-readable format. See "Understanding ODBC."

3. Low Cost. Microsoft Internet Information Server 4.0 is the most cost-effective solution if you're using Windows NT Server as your Web server platform. And delivering legacy data via a Web server and browser is very inexpensive when measured against the cost of traditional, client-server applications.

APPLY YOUR KNOWLEDGE

Information Security. By using IIS, you can leverage the robust security included with Windows NT.

Standards based. IIS provides database access using proven standards.

Dynamic content. Microsoft Internet Information Server 4.0 has the capability to dynamically build HTML pages based on content stored in a database. See "Why Put A Database on the Web?"

4. An ODBC query uses an .IDC file to define where its data source is located. The Index Server uses an .IDC file that contains variables defining the search criteria. See "Understanding ODBC."

Answers to Exam Questions

1. **D.** The limit is 260 characters on any Windows NT-based pathname. This is sort of a trick question. You need to be familiar with the Windows NT path limitations. See "Understanding ODBC."

2. **B, C.** Queries can be in either .IDC or .IDQ files. A is incorrect because .HTM files are used to take user information that is then fed into the query files; it cannot make direct queries against a database. D is incorrect because .HTX files are used to format the results of a query. These are also known as templates. See "Understanding ODBC."

3. **D.** .HTX files signify templates. See "Understanding ODBC."

4. **A, B.** SQL Server Login Authentication can be done by SQL Server or NT Server. C is incorrect; the IIS server can only authenticate users connecting to the IIS application. It cannot be used to authenticate users connecting to a SQL

Server. D is also incorrect because the Index Server is not applicable to this question. See "Implementing ODBC."

5. **C.** The `<Query>` tag is used in .IDQ files. See "Writing Index Server Queries."

6. **B.** `SQLStatement` is one of the required parameters of the .IDC file. See "Creating an .IDC Application."

7. **D.** As with many other programming languages, the pound sign (#) is used to signify comments. See "Using Variables in .IDQ Files."

8. **A.** HTTPODBC.DLL is the dynamic link library providing ODBC support on the server. B is incorrect; this file is installed during installation, but is not used to install ODBC support. C is incorrect; you can run HTTP without this .DLL. D is also incorrect, because if you anticipate needing ODBC support, you cannot delete this file at any time. See "Understanding ODBC."

9. **D.** `MaxRecords` is a parameter that can be used in .HTX files. See "Creating an .IDC Application."

10. **C.** `CiCodePage` is one variable that can be used in .IDQ files. See "Using Variables in .IDQ Files."

Microsoft recommends the following sites for more information on the topics discussed in this chapter.

- ActiveX Data Objects: http://www.microsoft.com/ado
- ODBC: http://www.microsoft.com/odbc
- OLE-DB: http://www.microsoft.com/oledb
- Using ODBC in Web applications: http://www.microsoft.com/iis
- Developing Web applications with ODBC: http://www.microsoft.com/vinterdev

Suggested Readings and Resources

1. Amundsen, Michael, *Using Visual InterDev 6.* Que: 1999.

2. Baird, Sean. *SQL Server System Administration.* New Riders Publishing: 1998.

3. Hazelhurst, Peter. *Microsoft SQL Server 6.5 On The Web.* Que Education and Training: 1999.

4. McGehee, Brad. *Using Microsoft SQL Server 7.0.* Que: 1998.

One of the things that it is easy to overlook as you implement Microsoft Internet Information Server 4.0 is its capability to run Web-based applications. This chapter covers the Running Applications objectives for the exam. This area is of particular importance because it can take a while for an IIS administrator to get into application development, which the objectives in this section cover.

Microsoft defines the Running Applications objectives as the following:

Configure IIS to support server-side scripting.

▶ Server-side scripting is another word for Active Server Pages (ASP). ASP was introduced in IIS 3.0 and has been greatly enhanced for this release. ASP allows you to create powerful Web-based applications and is at the center of Microsoft's Web development tools.

Configure IIS to run ISAPI applications.

▶ Internet Server Application Programming Interface (ISAPI) is another of the cornerstones of Microsoft's Web-based application suites. ISAPI applications are Dynamic Link Libraries (DLLs) that IIS loads when needed. They also can be unloaded if not needed.

CHAPTER 5

Running Applications

STUDY STRATEGIES

There are only two objectives for this chapter, so there are only two key concepts:

▶ Understand the components and mechanics of creating an ASP application.

▶ Understand the function and benefits of using ISAPI applications instead of the alternatives. Also understand where an ISAPI application might be used.

INTRODUCTION

This chapter addresses the scripting side of IIS and other servers and services. The topics discussed are ways that scripts can be created and implemented to automate tasks on the IIS server—primarily in conjunction with the WWW service. It is imperative that you understand the material in Chapter 3, "Configuring and Managing Resource Access," and Chapter 4, "Integration and Interoperability," before attempting to understand scripting.

The sample Web site included with IIS 4.0, "Exploration Air," includes some examples of scripting and Active Server Pages. This material is highly recommended. The files are very useful and can provide you with many insights into IIS 4.0 capabilities.

The specific topics covered in this chapter include the following:

◆ Configuring IIS to support server-side scripting

◆ Configuring IIS to run ISAPI applications

◆ Configuring ADO support

CONFIGURING IIS TO SUPPORT SERVER-SIDE SCRIPTING (ACTIVE SERVER PAGES)

Microsoft Internet Information Server 4.0 enables an administrator or Webmaster to use Active Server Pages (ASP) to do Web application programming. ASP simplifies server-side programming and offers support for ActiveX objects (also known as server-side objects), as well as HTML tags and all Active scripting commands.

ASP scripts can perform the same sorts of tasks as CGI (common gateway interface) and ISAPI applications, but are much easier to write and modify. ASP also manages the application and session states on the server, reducing the amount of information that needs to be transmitted back and forth between the server and the client; hence, the expression *server-side scripting*. ASP also has the capability to control some of the more advanced features of HTML programming, like cookies and security certificates.

NOTE

What Exactly Is CGI?   CGI (common gateway interface) is a specification for transferring data between a Web server and a CGI program (commonly known as a *script*). A CGI program is any program designed to process data that conforms to the CGI specification. CGI programs can be written in any programming language, including Perl, C, Java, or Visual Basic, although Perl is one of the more common languages used. CGI programs are a very common method used to process forms or user requests. If you have ever filled out a request for more information or even a guest book on a Web page, the odds are good that a CGI program processed the input data.

One interesting aspect of ASP is the engine that drives an ASP script is an ISAPI extension, the ASP.DLL. This DLL compiles and caches .ASP files in memory at runtime by using a script interpreter. Because ASP must be compiled before execution, complex scripts can be significantly slower than plain HTML and also slower than an ISAPI application the first time they are requested. When compiled, however, the compiled script is cached in server memory, making subsequent requests significantly faster.

The power of ASP lies in the fact that you can create highly interactive pages that are browser independent. If you are concerned with people "borrowing" your proprietary applications from your Web site, ASP allows you to protect your scripting on the server. It is also important to understand that ASP script isn't limited to a particular language. Microsoft's VBScript and JavaScript, as well as any language for which a third-party ActiveX Scripting Engine is available (PerlScript, for example), can be used to create ASP scripts.

The .ASP extension is assigned to all ASP scripts, and the files include text, HTML tags, and ASP script commands. Whereas HTML tags begin with < and end with >, ASP tags begin with <% and end with %>. The tags also are known as delimiters, and the delimiters are the ones that signal the server that processing is required at that point. Look at the following example:

```
It is now <%= Time %>
```

After the server processes the script command, the following is displayed:

```
It is now 14:52:10
```

The easiest way to create ASP files is to start with standard HTML files and add the script commands to them (as well as rename the file from .HTM to .ASP).

Active Server Pages can be used with VBScript, JavaScript, PerlScript, or any other recognized scripting language. Not only can you use a variety of languages, but you also can use multiple languages within the same script. The syntax for doing so follows:

```
<SCRIPT LANGUAGE="VBScript" RUNAT=SERVER>
routine
</SCRIPT>
<SCRIPT LANGUAGE="PerlScript" RUNAT=SERVER>
routine
</SCRIPT>
```

EXAM TIP

Primary Script Commands   For purposes of passing the exam, also know that primary script commands are those within <%%>.

In addition to defining variables by an operation (such as Date, Time, and so on), you also can set variables and reference them within the scripts. This is done through the use of the SET command, and the variable is then referenced in a manner similar to how the Time variable was referenced. You can also create an array of data to reference through use of the Session variable if you want the value to persist between scripts, which is unique for the life of the session. Look at the following example:

```
Session ("City") = "Anderson"
Set Session ("State") = "IN"
How is the weather in <%= Session("City") %>?
```

This is displayed as the following:

```
How is the weather in Anderson?
```

As previously mentioned, the Session variables are kept for the entire duration of the session and abandoned afterward. To force the purging of the variables, you can use the Session.Abandon call. This loses the variables (and ends the session).

The Use of Cookies

Clients using ASP first establish unique session keys, a process carried by the use of HTTP cookies. No buffering is used by default, so all operations that take place are immediately sent to the browser. This causes a session cookie to be sent for every browser interaction, but you can elect to turn on buffering and prevent the sending of some unnecessary cookies.

> **NOTE**
> **Cookies** Cookies are components of a session or information stored on the client's machine.

A Walkthrough of the Steps Involved in Active Server Pages

The following is a simplified example of how ASPs work:

1. The browser sends an HTTP request for an Active Server Page. The server knows it to be an Active Server Page due to the .ASP extension.

2. The server sends the file to ASP.DLL for execution of all code.

3. Processing is done and the server sends back an HTML page.

4. If there is any client-side code, it is executed on the client and the page is displayed in the browser.

Note that during this process, no server-side scripting is sent to the client, so the client can't view the script.

Scripting Hosts

Scripting hosts are designed to improve Operating System operations and there are two scripting hosts available with IIS:

◆ A command-based scripting host

◆ A Windows-based scripting host

The hosts are very similar in nature. The command-based one is called by CSCRIPT.EXE, and the Windows-based host is called by WSCRIPT.EXE.

Parameters that can be used with CSCRIPT.EXE are as follows:

◆ //?. Shows the command-line parameters.

◆ //B. Places the engine in batch mode.

◆ //C. Causes Cscript to be the default engine used by running scripts.

◆ //I. The opposite of //B, it places the engine in interactive mode.

◆ //logo. Shows a logo at execution time.

◆ //nologo. Does not display a logo at execution time.

◆ //R. Registers known script extensions with the engine. Known script extensions include .js, .vbs, and .tcl. This operation is done by default and you need not use the parameter.

◆ //S. Saves the current command-line options for the user.

◆ //T:nn. The timeout specified in number of seconds. The default is no limit, but you can specify a value to prevent excessive script execution.

Figure 5.1 shows the Wscript configuration screen (available from the Run command or any command line).

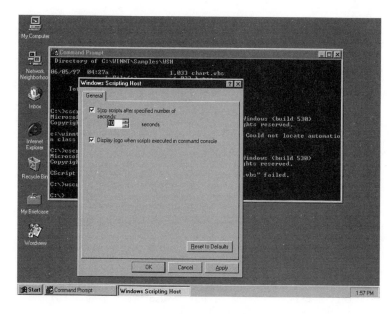

FIGURE 5.1
The Wscript Configuration dialog box.

The options for Wscript configuration enable you to specify a number of seconds after which to stop script execution (equivalent to //T:nn in Cscript) and toggle the banner on and off (//logo and //nologo in Cscript). Wscript does not have the capability for interactive or batch modes.

Adding Conditions

You can add conditional processing to your scripts by using IF..Then..Else logic. The syntax is as follows:

```
If {condition exists} Then
{action to perform}
Else
{another action to perform}
End If
```

You also can run an operation a number of times by using For..Next loops:

```
For Each {variable} in {set}
{action to perform}
Next
```

As with most scripting languages, indentation is not required, but it is used to make it easier to read and debug the script. Additionally, ASP itself is not case-sensitive, but the language used to execute the commands might be.

An Example of Server-Side Scripting

The following is an example based on a script file included with
IIS. The following SHORTCUT.VBS file uses Wscript to create a
NotePad shortcut on the desktop:

```
' Windows Script Host Sample Script
'
' --------------------------------------------------------
'          Copyright (C) 1996 Microsoft Corporation
'
' You have a royalty-free right to use, modify, reproduce
➡and distribute
' the Sample Application Files (and/or any modified version)
➡in any way
' you find useful, provided that you agree that Microsoft
➡has no warranty,
' obligations, or liability for any Sample Application
➡Files.
' --------------------------------------------------------
'
' This sample demonstrates how to use the WshShell object.
' to create a shortcut on the desktop


Dim WshShell, MyShortcut, MyDesktop, DesktopPath

' Initialize WshShell object
  Set WshShell = WScript.CreateObject("WScript.Shell")

' Read desktop path using WshSpecialFolders object
  DesktopPath = WshShell.SpecialFolders("Desktop")

' Create a shortcut object on the desktop
  Set MyShortcut = WshShell.CreateShortcut(DesktopPath &
➡"\Shortcut to notepad.lnk")

' Set shortcut object properties and save it
  MyShortcut.TargetPath =     WshShell.
➡ExpandEnvironmentStrings("%windir%\notepad.exe")
  MyShortcut.WorkingDirectory =     WshShell.
➡ExpandEnvironmentStrings("%windir%")
  MyShortcut.WindowStyle = 4
  MyShortcut.IconLocation = WshShell.
➡ExpandEnvironmentStrings
     ("%windir%\notepad.exe, 0")
  MyShortcut.Save
```

> **NOTE**
>
> **Debugging Your Scripts** One of the components of Microsoft Internet Information Server 4.0 is Microsoft Script Debugger. If you plan to do a lot of ASP scripting, it is a good idea to load Microsoft Script Debugger as one of your IIS components. There is one caveat, however. Microsoft Script Debugger only works with Internet Explorer. You cannot invoke the debugger from a competing browser like Netscape Navigator.

CONFIGURING **IIS** TO RUN **ISAPI** APPLICATIONS

Internet Server Application Programming Interface (ISAPI) applications are an alternative to the common gateway interface (CGI) applications used on other Web servers. As we discussed earlier, the ASP scripting engine is actually an ISAPI DLL. Like ASP, ISAPI can be used to write applications that Web users can activate by filling out an HTML form or clicking a link in an HTML page on your Web server. The user-supplied information can then be responded to and the results returned in an HTML page or posted to a database.

ISAPI is a Microsoft improvement over popular CGI scripting and offers much better performance than CGI because applications are loaded into memory at server runtime. This means they require less overhead and each request does not start a separate process. ISAPI processes are run as part of the same process space as IIS itself. CGI requires a separate process to run the underlying scripts. Additionally, ISAPI applications are created as DLLs on the server and allow pre-processing of requests and post-processing of responses, permitting site-specific handling of HTTP requests and responses.

For administrators who are hosting multiple IIS-based Web servers or Web sites, ISAPI applications can be used to fine tune each site individually, using separate ISAPI filters. This significantly increases the system flexibility, particularly if there are highly interactive applications being hosted on the server.

ISAPI Filters

ISAPI filters and applications are DLLs written to the ISAPI interface. These filters can be used to enhance the functionality of your IIS server. ISAPI filters can intercept specific server events before the server itself handles them. When a filter is loaded, there is a specific set of event notifications it handles, based on its function. If these events occur, the filter has the option of processing the events, passing them on to other filters, or sending them back to the server after it has dealt with them. To see if ISAPI filters have been installed for a Web site, open the properties of the site and click on the ISAPI Filters tab, as shown in Figure 5.2. You can add ISAPI filters to a Web site from this tab.

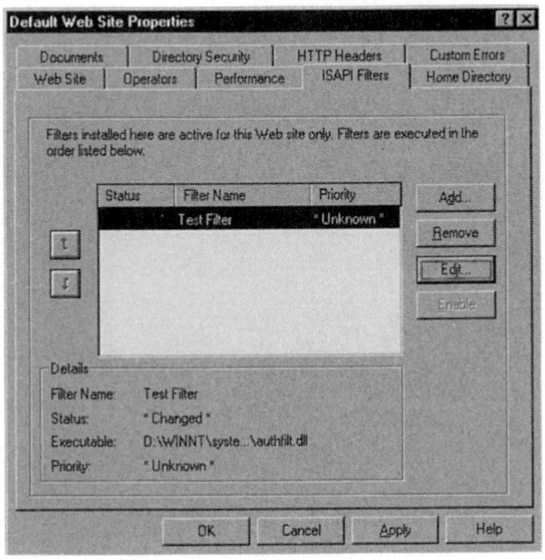

ISAPI filters can be used for applications such as customized authentication, access, or logging. You can create complex sites by combining ISAPI filters and applications.

ISAPI works with OLE connectivity and the Internet Database Connector. This allows ISAPI to be implemented as a DLL (in essence, an executable) or as a filter (translating another executable's output). If ISAPI is used as a filter, then it is not called when the browser accesses an URL, but is summoned by the server in response to an event (which could easily be an URL request). Common uses of ISAPI filters include the following:

◆ Tracking URL usage statistics

◆ Performing authentication

◆ Adding entries to log files

◆ Compression

FIGURE 5.2
The ISAPI Filters tab of the Web Site Properties dialog box.

For the Exam

If you want to become an ISAPI programmer, then you need a book three times the length of this one to learn the language. If you want to pass the exam (which is the purpose of this book), then there are several things you need to know:

◆ ISAPI applications effectively extend server applications to the desktop.

◆ ISAPI is similar to CGI, but offers better performance.

◆ Although created by Microsoft, ISAPI is an open specification that third parties can write to.

◆ ISAPI filters can do pre- or post-processing.

CONFIGURING ADO SUPPORT

The newest enhancement to Microsoft's Web service offering is ADO—ActiveX Data Objects. ADO combines a set of core functions and unique functions for each implementation. ADO was designed to replace all other data access methods and Microsoft recommends migration of all applications to ADO when it is feasible. ADO provides developers with a fast, easy, and productive means for accessing ODBC and OLE DB data sources. Developers can use ADO to easily create data-driven Web-based applications using ASP. In addition, the ADO can be used within an ActiveX component to interact with the data source. Also, because ADO works with OLE DB providers, it can access a variety of data sources.

ADO can access the following:

◆ Text

◆ Relational databases

◆ Any ODBC-compliant data source

ADO grew out of ASP (Active Server Pages) and offers the following benefits:

◆ Low memory overhead

◆ Small disk footprint

◆ Ease of use

◆ De-emphasis on object hierarchy

◆ Capability to use ODBC 3.0 connection pooling

Connection pooling enables you to open database connections and manage sharing across different user requests while reducing the number of idle connections. To use it, you must set a timeout property in the Registry. When a user times out, rather than the connection being totally lost, it is saved in a pool. When the next request comes in, that connection is used, rather than a whole new connection being created each and every time.

Although ADO has a number of benefits, its greatest downside is that it is mostly read-only on the browser. All filtering and processing must be done on the server, and when it reaches the browser, it is in its final state. Although there are ways around this, they are more cumbersome and difficult than other options.

For the Exam

As with ISAPI, if you want to become an ADO programmer, you need to purchase a book specific to that end. If you want to pass the exam, there are only a few things you need to know:

◆ ADO objects are small, compact, and easy to write to.

◆ ADO knows what data to access through DSN (Data Source Name) files.

◆ It is the DSN that contains the user security, database configuration, and location information.

◆ The DSN can be an actual file (text) or merely an entry in the Registry. ODBC enables you to create three types of DSNs: User (in Registry), System (in Registry), or File (text file).

◆ A system DSN applies to all users logged on to the server.

◆ A user DSN applies to a specific user (or set of users).

◆ A file DSN gives access to multiple users and can be transferred between servers by copying the file.

◆ DSN files are created through the ODBC icon of the Control Panel.

◆ ADO connections are written in the files with variable names such as cn. Look at the following example:

```
Set cn = Server.CreateObject("ADODB.Connection")
Cn.Open "FILEDSN=Example.dsn"
```

◆ A RecordSet is a table or query from a subset of the object that you want to retrieve. Rather than retrieving the entire Access or SQL database, you retrieve a component of it, known as a RecordSet object.

◆ ADO commands are written in the files as variables, such
as cm. Look at the following example:

```
Set cm = Server.CreateObject("ADODB.Command")
Cm.CommandText = "APPEND INTO Array (X, Y) VALUES"
```

You should now be prepared to apply all the concepts we have
discussed to a high-level case study. We do not delve into the details
of ASP or ISAPI programming, so this case study looks at some
high-level applications for ASP and ISAPI.

CASE STUDY: IMPLEMENTING A WEB APPLICATION USING ASP AND ISAPI

ESSENCE OF THE CASE

The situation boils down to the following:

▶ You need to create a Catalog Order
Request application to accept catalog
requests.

▶ The application also needs to route
the request to the appropriate regional
inside sales person who calls the
potential customer.

▶ To ensure that users feel comfortable
giving their information, Security wants
a banner displayed upon authentication.

SCENARIO

You are the chief Web developer for the Exponent
Calculator Company. You have an existing IIS-based
Internet Web site, but it consists of static HTML
and graphics. You have been asked by the Sales
department to write an application that allows a
user to input a catalog order request. Sales wants
to follow up each request with a call from the
regional inside sales representative, so the
request should be processed by the application
and forwarded to the appropriate sales person.
You have also been asked by the Security department to add an additional banner telling users that
their information is secure and will not be re-sold
whenever a user authenticates to the Web server.
What should you do?

ANALYSIS

The way to begin here is to approach each part
of the problem a piece at a time.

continues

CASE STUDY: IMPLEMENTING A WEB APPLICATION USING ASP AND ISAPI

continued

Problem 1: Create a Catalog Order Request Form

The answer is to write an ASP script to perform this function. Languages like VBScript and JavaScript allow you to write an ASP application to accept the request, verify the user has completed all the required fields, and pass the data along to another application.

Problem 2: Route the Information Captured to the Appropriate Sales Representative

This can actually be taken care of as part of the application described in Problem 1. What you need to add to the application is a table of all your inside sales representatives, the states they cover, and their e-mail addresses. Then, whenever a request comes in for a catalog, the state code (or you could use the zip code) is cross-referenced with the sales representative table. The request is forwarded to the appropriate person.

Problem 3: Add an Additional Security Banner to the Authentication Process

Remember that ISAPI is used to intercept and handle server events. Authentication is a server event and can be intercepted by an ISAPI application, an additional banner displayed, and then the authentication event can be passed to the server.

CHAPTER SUMMARY

KEY TERMS

- Active Server Pages (ASP)
- ActiveX Data Objects (ADO)
- CGI (common gateway interface)
- HyperText Markup Language (HTML)
- ISAPI (Internet Server Application Programming Interface)

Let's recap what we discussed in this chapter. We looked at the following two different ways to develop applications for Microsoft Internet Information Server 4.0:

- ◆ **Server-side scripting (Active Server Pages).** Microsoft Internet Information Server (IIS) 4.0 enables an administrator or Webmaster to use Active Server Pages (ASP) to do Web application programming. ASP simplifies server-side programming and offers support for ActiveX objects (also known as server-side objects), as well as HTML tags and all Active scripting commands.

CHAPTER SUMMARY

◆ **ISAPI.** The main features of ISAPI include the following:

- ISAPI applications effectively extend server applications to the desktop.

- ISAPI is similar to CGI, but offers better performance.

- Although created by Microsoft, ISAPI is an open specification that third parties can write to.

- ISAPI filters can do pre- or post-processing.

One of the key applications for ISAPI is ISAPI filters. ISAPI filters and applications are DLLs written to the ISAPI interface. These filters can be used to enhance the functionality of your IIS server.

APPLY YOUR KNOWLEDGE

Exercises

5.1 Run the CHART.VBS Program

This exercise illustrates how to run a script program in Cscript and Wscript.

Estimated time: 15 minutes

1. Open a command line.

2. Enter

   ```
   Cscript{system_root}\Samples\Wsh\Chart.VBS
   ```

3. Enter

   ```
   Cscript//logo
   {system_root}\Samples\Wsh\Chart.VBS
   ```

4. Enter

   ```
   Cscript//nologo
   {system_root}\Samples\Wsh\Chart.VBS
   ```

5. From the Run command, enter

   ```
   Wscript {system_root}\Samples\Wsh\Chart.VBS
   ```

5.2 View the FAVLIST.HTM Sample ISAPI Script

This exercise illustrates how to view an ISAPI sample included with Microsoft Internet Information Server 4.0.

Estimated time: 15 minutes

1. Open Internet Explorer.

2. Enter the following in the Address box:

   ```
   IIS Drive Letter:\InetPub\wwwroot\samples\
   ➥isapi\favlist.htm
   ```

3. After the script has loaded, go to View, Source.

4. Review the sample application as needed.

Review Questions

1. What are the three items that can be contained within Active Server Pages?

2. What are the two ways that ISAPI can be implemented?

3. What three types of files can ADO be used to access?

Exam Questions

1. You are applying for a job with Zanzibar Imports to do Web development for their IIS-based Internet Web site. The hiring manager asks you what file extension is used to signify, and is required for, Active Server Pages.

   You respond:

   A. ASP

   B. EXE

   C. COM

   D. HTM

2. The manager's next question is to identify which of the following could not be included as part of an Active Server Page:

   A. HTML

   B. Text

   C. Microsoft Access data

   D. Script commands

3. You are a Web developer for Great Shots Photo Developing and you have written an ASP

APPLY YOUR KNOWLEDGE

application to allow customers to input comments about the service. You are working with a number of ASP variables and you know one of them is cleared after a customer's connection is dropped.

Which variable in Active Server Pages is erased from existence when a connection is no longer there?

A. BROWSER

B. USER

C. USERSESSION

D. SESSION

4. You are a new Web developer with the Just for Cats Pet Clothing retail chain. You have been asked to write a script for the company's IIS-based intranet Web site.

What are the scripting hosts included with IIS?

A. Cscript

B. Wscript

C. Uscript

D. Pscript

5. You have decided to use the Cscript host and are trying to figure out what some of the parameters do. You know the //B parameter is used to place a script in batch mode.

Which Cscript parameter is the opposite of the //B parameter?

A. //T

B. //R

C. //S

D. //I

E. //C

6. As you continue to develop your application, you find you need to use conditional script commands. You know conditional script commands in .ASP files begin with IF, but you're not sure what they need to end with.

A conditional statement that starts with IF must end with:

A. FI

B. END IF

C. ENDIF

D. IF END

7. You are a Web developer with Little Faith Enterprises and you are writing an ISAPI filter for your IIS-based Web site. Before you can write the application, you need to know what type(s) of processing ISAPI filters can do? What type(s) of processing can they do?

A. Pre-processing only

B. Post-processing only

C. Both pre- and post-processing

D. Neither pre- nor post-processing

8. One other piece of information you need is exactly how ISAPI is implemented on an IIS server.

ISAPI is implemented as

A. A TSR

B. A DLL

C. An EXE

D. An ASP

9. You are the lead programmer at Exponent Calculators. You are trying to decide if ActiveX Data Objects (ADO) are a technology you want to use on your Microsoft Internet Information Server 4.0 Web site. Which of the following are benefits of ADO that might convince you to use it?

   A. Small disk footprint

   B. High memory overhead

   C. Improved authentication

   D. Emphasis on object hierarchy

10. You have decided to implement ADO as a technology on your Web site. Now you need to configure Data Source Names to access your data.

   What are the two types of DSNs?

   A. HTML files

   B. Text files

   C. Registry entries

   D. Executables

Answers to Review Questions

1. Active Server Pages can contain text, HTML code, and script commands. See "Configuring IIS to Support Server-Side Scripting (Active Server Pages)."

2. ISAPI can be implemented as a DLL or a filter. See "Configuring IIS to Run ISAPI Applications."

3. ADO can be used to access text files, relational databases, or ODBC-compliant data sources. See "Configuring ADO Support."

Answers to Exam Questions

1. **A.** Active Server Pages must have the .ASP file extension. EXE and COM files are both application file extensions, and HTM is used to indicate an HTML document. See "Configuring IIS to Support Server-Side Scripting (Active Server Pages)."

2. **C.** Access data would not be Active Server Pages. You can include HTML, text, and scripting in an ASP application. See "Configuring IIS to Support Server-Side Scripting (Active Server Pages)."

3. **D.** The SESSION variable goes away when the session (or connection) has been disconnected. See "Configuring IIS to Support Server-Side Scripting (Active Server Pages)."

4. **A, B.** Both Cscript and Wscript are included with IIS. The other applications referenced do not exist. See "Scripting Hosts."

5. **D.** //I places the engine in interactive mode, the opposite of //B, which places it in batch mode. //T:nn specifies the timeout specified in number of seconds. //R registers known script extensions with the engine. //S saves the current command-line options for the user. See "Scripting Hosts."

6. **B.** Conditional script commands in .ASP files that begin with IF must end with END IF. FI is used by C scripts, ENDIF is used by other languages. IF END is not used by any language. See "Scripting Hosts."

APPLY YOUR KNOWLEDGE

7. **C.** ISAPI filters can do both pre- and post-processing. See "Configuring IIS to Run ISAPI Applications."

8. **B.** ISAPI is implemented as a DLL. See "Configuring IIS to Run ISAPI Applications." TSRs (Terminate and Stay Residents) are applications run locally on a system, as are EXEs. ASPs are a type of Web page, not an ISAPI implementation.

9. **A.** A benefit of ADO is its small disk footprint. High overhead is not a benefit for any application. Improved authentication and object hierarchy are not features of ADO. See "Configuring ADO Support."

10. **B, C.** DSNs can be text files or Registry entries. See "Configuring ADO Support."

Suggested Readings and Resources

1. Clements, Kevin, Wuestefeld, Chris, and Trent, Jeffrey. *Inside ISAPI.* New Riders Publishing: 1997.

2. Hettihewa, Sanjaya. *SAMS Teach Yourself Active Server Pages 2.0 in 21 Days.* Sams Publishing: 1999.

In the previous five chapters, we have covered planning, installing, maintaining, and running applications on your IIS server. This chapter covers the Monitoring and Optimization portion of the exam. After your server is up and running, fully configured, and in production, you need to understand how to monitor the server for usage, performance issues, and capacity planning. The objectives for this section of the exam cover the tools and procedures for making sure your Microsoft Internet Information Server 4.0 server is performing at its best, has adequate capacity, and can tell you who is using the server.

Microsoft defines the Monitoring and Optimization objectives as the following:

Maintain a log for fine-tuning and auditing purposes. Tasks include the following:

- **Importing log files into a Usage Import and Report Writer database**

- **Configuring the logging features of the WWW service**

- **Configuring the logging features of the FTP services**

- **Configuring Usage Import and Report Writer to analyze logs created by the WWW service or the FTP service**

- **Automating the use of Usage Import and Report Writer**

▶ To monitor the FTP and WWW services, you have to be able to analyze the usage of those services. How many people downloaded a copy of your catalog using FTP? How many visits has your site had this month? This is the kind of information you need to manage your site. Microsoft expects you to understand how to set up and analyze the WWW and FTP logs on your IIS server using the Usage Import and Report Writer database and application.

CHAPTER 6

Monitoring and Optimization

Monitor performance of various functions by using Performance Monitor. Functions include HTTP and FTP sessions.

▶ If you have not been introduced to Performance Monitor, this is where you can monitor statistics associated with all the components of Windows NT, as well as statistics for Windows NT applications. For this objective, you need to understand the metrics associated with the HTTP (the protocol associated with the WWW service) and FTP protocols.

Analyze performance. Performance issues include the following:

• **Identifying bottlenecks**

• **Identifying network-related performance issues**

• **Identifying disk-related performance issues**

• **Identifying CPU-related performance issues**

▶ The previous objective dealt with two very specific protocols for evaluating IIS performance. This objective takes a look at the big picture. How do the various components of the server interact, and how can you tell where the bottlenecks are? These are the kinds of questions you must be able to answer for this objective.

Optimize performance of IIS.

▶ This objective deals with the specific performance tuning of the IIS server itself. This includes the WWW and FTP services.

Optimize performance of Index Server.

▶ There are ways to optimize the Index Server searching capabilities. You should be familiar with how to optimize Index Server searches based on your requirements.

Optimize performance of Microsoft SMTP Service.

▶ The SMTP (Simple Mail Transport Protocol) service has a number of settings that can impact server performance, from the number of supported connections to the maximum message size. Although this topic is not one that is tested too heavily, you should be familiar with the setup of the SMTP service and what settings impact performance.

Optimize performance of Microsoft NNTP Service.

▶ The main settings affecting the performance of an NNTP server are the number of supported connections and the expiration time for messages. In this chapter, we look at and discuss the capabilities of both.

Interpret performance data.

▶ This objective requires you to be able to take all the information and configurations listed in the previous objectives and figure out what they mean.

Optimize a Web site by using Content Analyzer.

▶ Content Analyzer is Microsoft's preferred method for figuring out the detailed information about a Web site. To handle Content Analyzer questions, you need to be able to interpret the information that is returned by Content Analyzer when it is run against a Web site.

As you read through this chapter, you should concentrate on the following key concepts:

▶ Understand how Performance Monitor is used and what specific parameters can be measured for IIS.

▶ Understand the general guidelines for finding and correcting server bottlenecks. If you have taken the Windows NT Server exam, this should be review, but be sure you can locate a bottleneck on your server.

▶ Be familiar with the performance settings for each of the IIS components. Each component has a couple of key settings or configurations that significantly affect performance. Be aware of what they are, where they are, and what happens when you change them.

▶ Pay attention to any sections that deal with interpreting performance data. You need to understand the results of a Content Analyzer session, how to interpret Performance Monitor information, and understand what the information in log files indicates. These sections are interspersed throughout the chapter as we discuss other objectives for the chapter.

INTRODUCTION

This chapter covers the different ways you can analyze and optimize the performance of your Microsoft Internet Information Server 4.0. We start at the beginning, with the WWW and FTP logs files, and follow-up with importing them into the Report Writer and Usage Import Database. Next, we discuss using the Report Writer and Usage Import Database to analyze those log files, including methods for automating this process. The Performance Monitor and some of the IIS processes that can be monitored with it are examined next. We also discuss the process of finding bottlenecks on your IIS server and some of the ways to remove them. Finally, we look at the performance tuning of each of the IIS components, and the impact of each.

MAINTAINING IIS 4.0 LOGS

▶ Maintain a log for fine-tuning and auditing purposes.

Microsoft gives you a number of tools to monitor and optimize your IIS 4.0 Web site. Each time a user interacts with your Web site and requests resources from it, such as a Web page, image file, or similar item, a hit is recorded in a log file. You can create logs for each IIS 4.0 service to help you fine-tune and optimize your site, plan for future expansion, and review the security of your site. IIS 4.0 also enables you to send log data to a text file or to an Open Database Connectivity (ODBC)-compliant database, such as Microsoft SQL Server or Microsoft Access.

Using IIS 4.0 logs is one of the most important tasks in fine-tuning and auditing an IIS site. In the following sections, you learn how to configure WWW and FTP services logging, configure Report Writer and Usage Import to analyze logs created by these services, and automate the Report Writer and Usage Import.

Configuring the Logging Features of the WWW Service

Probably one of the first things you want to do when administering your IIS 4.0 site is to configure the logging features of the WWW and FTP services. One thing to keep in mind as you look at these logs is, although they provide plenty of information, they cannot provide definitive information on users or their use. Tools for analyzing the traffic and usage patterns of a Web site have gotten better over the last couple years, but you are still subject to the limitations of TCP/IP in determining exactly what people are doing on your site. That's why trending and pattern analysis are usually more useful than trying to track a single user's activity on the site.

Log file data can give you a historical record of who has visited your site (based on visiting IP addresses), content exchanges (client downloads and uploads), which pages are the most popular on your site, and other information. A log file can be studied, for example, to determine the best time for maintenance (tape backups, software upgrades, and so on). Do you want to have a tape backup running at 5:00 A.M. EST if your logs show you have an average of 5,000 European users accessing the site at that time? Perhaps 8:00 P.M. might prove a better time for that type of activity. A careful analysis of the log files can help you make those types of decisions.

See the next section, "Configuring the Logging Features of the FTP Service," for information on configuring logging features for the FTP service.

To configure logging features for your WWW service, perform the following steps:

N O T E

Accessing the Log File   Your log file can be accessed only after you stop your site. You can do this by starting Internet Service Manager, selecting the site, and clicking the Stop button on the Internet Service Manager toolbar. Click the Start button to start the site again.

STEP BY STEP

6.1 Configuring the WWW Service Log

1. Select Start, Programs, Windows NT 4.0 Option Pack, Microsoft Internet Information Server, Internet Service Manager. Internet Service Manager opens in the Microsoft Management Console (MMC) (see Figure 6.1).

2. Right-click the Web site you want to configure.

3. Click Properties. The Web Site Properties dialog box displays (see Figure 6.2). (Alternately, you can select the Web site and go to Action, Properties to open the Site Properties.)

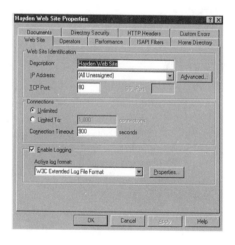

4. Click the Enable Logging option.

5. Click the Active Log Format drop-down list and select the
type of log format you want to create. The following are
the supported log file formats:

- **Microsoft IIS Log Format.** This is a fixed ASCII format that records basic logging items, including username, request date, request time, client IP address,
  number of bytes received, HTTP status code, and other
  items. This is a comma-delimited log file, making it
  easier to parse than other ASCII formats.

- **NCSA Common Log File Format.** This is a fixed
  ASCII format endorsed by the National Center for
  Supercomputing Applications (NCSA). The data it logs
  includes remote host name, username, HTTP status
  code, request type, and the number of bytes received by
  the server. Spaces separate different items logged.

- **ODBC Logging.** This is a fixed format that is logged
  to a database. This log includes client IP address, username, request date, request time, HTTP status code,
  bytes received, bytes sent, action carried out, and the
  target. When you choose this option, you must specify

FIGURE 6.2▲
The Web Site Properties dialog box for the
Hayden Web site.

continues

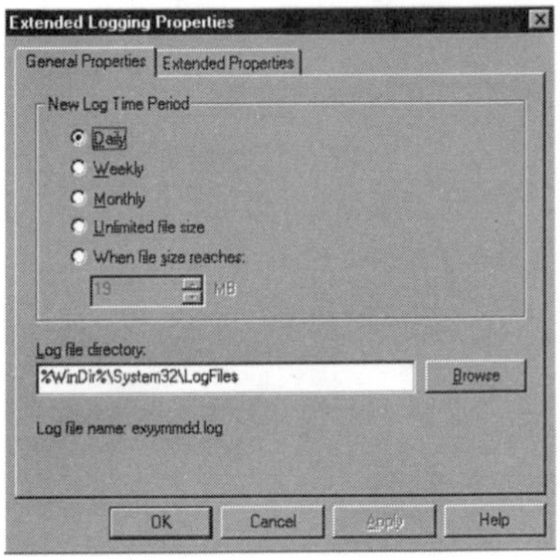

FIGURE 6.3
The Extended Logging Properties dialog box for the W3C Extended Log File Format.

N O T E

WWW Log File Syntax   The log file syntax is shown next to the Log File Name label; an example of the syntax is exymmdd.log. The first two characters in the name, ex, denote the type of log file format you selected *in* step 5. These characters include in for Microsoft IIS Log file Format, *nc* for NCSA Common Log File Format, and ex for W3C Extended Log File Format.

The remaining characters in the log file name syntax correspond to the date the file is created: yy is the year, mm is the month, and dd is the day.

If you select the ODBC Logging format, you must specify a Data Source Name (DSN), which does not follow these naming schemes.

---

continued

the database for the file to be logged to. In addition, you must set up the database to receive that log data.

- **W3C Extended Log File Format.** This is a customizable ASCII format endorsed by the World Wide Web Consortium (W3C). This is the default setting. You can set this log format to record a number of different settings, such as request date, request time, client IP address, server IP address, server port, HTTP status code, and more. Data is separated by spaces in this format.

The following steps show how to configure the W3C Extended Log File Format.

6. Click the Properties button. The Extended Logging Properties dialog box displays (see Figure 6.3). If you select a log format other than W3C Extended Log File Format from the Active Log Format drop-down list, the properties dialog box for that format displays.

7. In the New Log Time Period section, set the period when you want IIS to create a new log file for the selected Web site. The default is Daily, but you can select Weekly, Monthly, Unlimited File Size, or When File Size Reaches. If you select the last option, you need to set a maximum file size the log file can reach before a new file is created. The default here is 19MB. For active Web sites, the log file can reach sizes of over 100MB very quickly.

8. Enter the directory in which you want to store the log file. The default is %WinDir\System32\LogFiles. Click the Browse button to locate a new directory graphically.

9. Click the Extended Properties tab to display the logging options you can set, as shown in Figure 6.4. (This tab is available only when you select the W3C Extended Log File Format option.) On this tab, you can set the options described in Table 6.1.

FIGURE 6.4
The Extended Properties tab.

The default Extended Logging Options for the W3C Extended Log File Format include Time, Client IP Address, Method, URI Stem, and HTTP Status.

10. Click OK to close the Extended Logging Properties dialog box.

11. Click OK to close the Web Site Properties dialog box.

> **NOTE**
>
> **Logging to a File Versus a Database** As you decide on a logging format, one thing to keep in mind is that storing log information in a file is much faster than placing it into an ODBC-compliant database. There is quite a bit less overhead in writing to disk than there is in writing to a remote database.

TABLE 6.1

W3C EXTENDED LOG FILE FORMAT LOGGING OPTIONS

Option	Description
Date	Date the activity occurred
Time	Time the activity occurred
Client IP Address	IP address of the client attaching to your server
User Name	Name of user who accessed your server
Service Name	Client computer's Internet service
Server Name	Server name where the log entry was created
Server IP	Server IP address where the log entry was created
Server Port	Shows the port number to which the client is connected
Method	Shows the action the client was performing
URI Stem	Logs the resource the client was accessing on your server, such as an HTML page, CGI program, and so on

continues

TABLE 6.1 | *continued*

W3C EXTENDED LOG FILE FORMAT LOGGING OPTIONS

Option	*Description*
URI Query	Logs the search string the client was trying to match
HTTP Status	Shows the status (in HTTP terms) of the client action
Win32 Status	Shows the status (in Windows NT terms) of the client action
Bytes Sent	Shows the number of bytes sent by the server
Bytes Received	Shows the number of bytes received by the server
Time Taken	Shows the amount of time to execute the action requested by the client
User Agent	Reports the browser used by the client
Cookie	Shows the content of any cookies sent or received by the server
Protocol Version	Shows the protocol used by the client to access the server (HTTP or FTP)
Referrer	Shows the URL of the site from where the user clicked on to get to your site

N O T E

Restarting Logging   Logging on your Web server has stopped because you have run out of disk space. What do you need to do to restart logging? With IIS 4.0, all you need to do is free some disk space. The logging function automatically restarts after there is enough disk space for additional log file entries.

Log files can grow very large, so be sure the server has plenty of free disk space. Logging shuts down if your server runs out of disk space when trying to add a new log entry to a file. When this happens, you see an event logged in the Windows NT Event Viewer. Another event is logged when IIS is able to continue logging IIS activities (when disk space is freed up, for example).

Configuring the Logging Features of the FTP Service

As with the WWW service, you can configure the logging features of the FTP service in IIS 4.0. To do this, perform the following steps:

STEP BY STEP

6.2 Configuring the FTP Service Log

1. Select Start, Programs, Windows NT 4.0 Option Pack, Microsoft Internet Information Server, Internet Service Manager. Internet Service Manager opens in the Microsoft Management Console (MMC) (refer to Figure 6.1).

2. Right-click on the FTP site you want to configure.

3. Click Properties. The Default FTP Site Properties dialog box displays (see Figure 6.5).

4. Click the Enable Logging option.

5. Click the Active Log Format drop-down list and select the type of log format you want to create. You can choose from Microsoft IIS Log File Format, ODBC Logging, and W3C Extended Log File Format. NCSA Common Log File Format is not supported on FTP sites. Refer to step 5 in the Step by Step 6.1 for an explanation of these formats.

The following steps show how to configure the W3C Extended Log File Format.

6. Click the Properties button. The Extended Logging Properties dialog box displays (see Figure 6.6). If you select a log format other than W3C Extended Log File Format from the Active Log Format drop-down list, the properties dialog box for that format displays.

7. In the New Log Time Period section, set when you want IIS to create a new log file for the selected FTP site. The default is Daily, but you can select Weekly, Monthly, Unlimited File Size, or When File Size Reaches. If you select the last option, you need to set a maximum file size the log file can reach before a new file is created. The default here is 19MB.

8. Enter the directory in which you want to store the log file. The default is %WinDir\System32\LogFiles. Click the Browse button to locate a new directory graphically.

continues

FIGURE 6.5▲
The Default FTP Site Properties dialog box.

FIGURE 6.6▲
The Extended Logging Properties dialog box for the W3C Extended Log File Format.

FIGURE 6.7
The Extended Properties tab.

continued

9. Click the Extended Properties tab to display the logging options you can set, as shown in Figure 6.7. (This tab is available only when you select the W3C Extended Log File Format option.) On this tab, you can set the options described in Table 6.1.

10. Click OK to close the Extended Logging Properties dialog box.

11. Click OK to close the FTP Site Properties dialog box.

Importing Log Files into a Report Writer and Usage Import Database

The Report Writer and Usage Import Database help you analyze and create reports based on logs created by IIS. Usage Import reads the log files and places the data into a relational database. Report Writer is used to create analysis reports based on the log file data.

To begin using these tools, you first import the log file or files you want to analyze into a Report Writer and Usage Import database. The database is dedicated for storing the imported data from a log file.

Both Report Writer and Usage Import connect to this database when they start. You can see the name of the database each tool connects to by looking at the bottom of its screen on the status bar (see Figure 6.8). If Report Writer or Usage Import cannot find the database it is configured to connect to, you are prompted to enter the name of a valid database.

Relational databases are used because of their efficient use of data storage. Relational databases do not require redundant information from your log file to be stored. This results in smaller databases and less required disk space. In some cases, the database can be 10-20 percent smaller than the original log file.

Relational databases are also used because they enable you to analyze your data in a more flexible way. You can cross-reference over 200 different Internet server usage data properties.

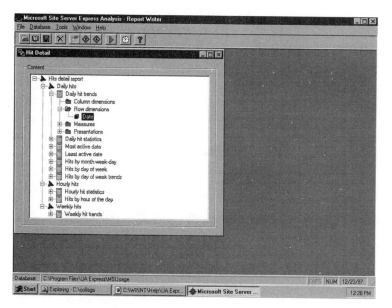

◀**FIGURE 6.8**
The Report Writer status bar (at the bottom left of the screen) shows you the database being accessed.

To import log files into Usage Import so that you can analyze your site's data in Report Writer, perform the following steps:

STEP BY STEP

6.3 Importing a Log File Using Usage Import

1. Make sure you can access the IIS log file on the local computer.

2. Select Start, Programs, Windows NT 4.0 Option Pack, Microsoft Site Server Express 2.0, Usage Import. Usage Import starts. The first time you start Usage Import, you need to configure an Internet site in the database before you can start importing logs. Usage Import displays the Microsoft Site Server Express Analysis dialog box (see Figure 6.9), which informs you that you must use the Server Manager to configure your Internet site.

NOTE **Creating a New Site** If the Microsoft Site Server Express Analysis dialog box does not display, you've already configured a site under Usage Import. You can start Server Manager again by selecting File, Server Manager after Usage Import starts. Right-click on the Log Data Source item in the Server Manager and click on New Server. The Server Properties dialog box displays, which is explained in step 5.

◀**FIGURE 6.9**
The Microsoft Site Server Express Analysis dialog box.

continues

continued

3. Click OK. The Log Data Source Properties dialog box
displays (see Figure 6.10).

FIGURE 6.10
The Log Data Source Properties dialog box.

4. From the Log Data Source Properties dialog box, click the
log file format for your log data source. Some of the file formats include NCSA Common Log File Format, Microsoft
IIS Log File Format, Microsoft IIS Extended Log File
Format, W3C Extended Log File Format, and others. The
options available here correspond to the type of server you
are analyzing. You can read more about the log file types
supported in the "Configuring the Logging Features of the
WWW Service" and "Configuring the Logging Features of
the FTP Service" sections, earlier in this chapter.

5. Click OK. The Server Properties dialog box displays (see
Figure 6.11). Set the following items on this dialog box:

- **Server Type.** Sets the type of server for which your log
file is configured. You can select World Wide Web, FTP,
Gopher, or RealAudio servers.

- **Directory Index Files.** Enter your server's index file,
such as DEFAULT.ASP, INDEX.HTML,
HOME.HTM, or other name. This is the name
of the file that is displayed in the client when the URL
ends in a slash (/).

- **IP Address.** Enter the IP address of the server. This
field is optional.

NOTE

Creating Custom Log Files To create customizable log files, use the
W3C Extended Log File Format.
Compared to other log file formats,
such as NCSA Common Log File
Format and Microsoft IIS Log Format,
the W3C Extended Log File Format
also records the greatest amount of
information about your Web site,
including referring URL and cookie
information.

- **IP Port.** Enter the server's IP port number. The default is 80.

- **Local Timezone.** Enter the local time zone where your content is stored.

- **Local Domain.** Enter the domain name for the local network that is hosting your content. This setting is used to distinguish hits from internal and external clients. If you use a hosting service or host at an Internet service provider's network (such as One.Net), enter the domain of that service, such as one.net.

6. Click OK. The Site Properties dialog box displays (see Figure 6.12).

7. Enter the URL of the home page in the Home Page URLs field on the Basic tab. This information is required. As an optional entry, fill in the Server Filesystem Paths for This Site field. If you have multiple URLs, list them all in this field.

8. Click the Excludes tab (see Figure 6.13). Here, you can set log file information that should be excluded from the database. These settings are optional. You can enter the name of hosts you want to exclude in the Hosts to Exclude from Import field. To exclude log file information based on inline image requests, enter the image file types in the Inline Images to Exclude from Import field. Some common file types you might enter here include gif, jpg, jpeg, and png. You can opt to exclude these entries to decrease the time it takes to import the log file and make the database smaller.

FIGURE 6.11▲
The Server Properties dialog box.

◄FIGURE 6.12
The Site Properties dialog box.

FIGURE 6.13▲
The Excludes tab of the Site Properties dialog box.

continues

continued

> **NOTE**
>
> **Calculating Bandwidth**   Even if you
> have excluded inline images, you still
> get accurate bandwidth calculations.

9. Click OK. The Usage Import window displays with the Log File Manager and Server Manager windows (see Figure 6.14). The Log File Manager organizes, filters, and imports log files for analysis. The Server Manager, on the other hand, sets up the site structure for which the logs are imported. Before any data can be imported into a database, the servers and sites that created the log data must be configured in the Service Manager.

FIGURE 6.14▶
The Usage Import window controls the importing of the log file into the Usage Import Database.

10. In the Log File Manager window, enter the complete path for your log file in the Log Location field. Click Browse to locate the file graphically.

11. Click the Start Import button on the Usage Import window toolbar (this tool is a green right-facing arrow). After Usage Import finishes importing the log file, the Microsoft Site Server Express Analysis dialog box displays, telling you the import is complete and how long the import process took (see Figure 6.15).

FIGURE 6.15▲
The Microsoft Site Server Express Analysis dialog box tells you when the import is complete and how long it took to complete.

12. Click OK. The Usage Import Statistics dialog box displays (see Figure 6.16).

13. Click Close.

Now that you have a log imported into the database, the next step is to generate a report with it. When you are ready to create a report of a log file in Report Writer, perform the following steps:

FIGURE 6.16▲
The Usage Import Statistics dialog box.

STEP BY STEP

6.4 Creating a Report from an Imported Log File

1. Select Start, Programs, Windows NT 4.0 Option Pack, Microsoft Site Server Express 2.0, Report Writer. Report Writer starts and displays the Report Writer opening dialog box (see Figure 6.17).

2. Select the From the Report Writer Catalog option on the Report Writer dialog box. You can create your own report using the From Scratch option. However, it's a good idea to use the Report Writer Catalog option the first few times you run Report Writer to see how the tool works.

FIGURE 6.17▲
The Report Writer opening dialog box allows you to create a new report or open an existing report.

3. Click OK. The Report Writer dialog box with the Report Writer Catalog field displays (see Figure 6.18).

4. Select the plus sign next to the Detail Reports or Summary Reports folders, depending on the type of summary you want to create.

5. Click a report type, such as Hits Detail report. To read about each type of report, click on it and view a description in the Report Description area at the bottom of the Report Writer dialog box.

6. Click Next. The Report Writer dialog box shown in Figure 6.19 displays. From this dialog box, you set the date range of the data to analyze. The default is Every Request You've Imported. You also can narrow the date ranges, such as This Week, This Year, or a specific range (Before 12/25/98, for example).

FIGURE 6.18▲
The Report Writer Catalog field displays the available reports.

continues

continued

FIGURE 6.19▶
This Report Writer dialog box is used to set the date range of the log file data to analyze.

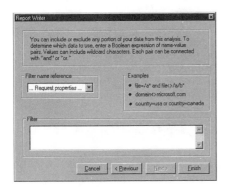

FIGURE 6.20▲
Use this Report Writer dialog box to filter log file data.

FIGURE 6.21▶
The Hit Detail window is used to show the results of the hit analysis.

7. Click Next. The Report Writer dialog box shown in Figure 6.20 displays. From this dialog box, you can filter log file data using Boolean expressions and items included in the Filter Name Reference drop-down list. To use an item in the drop-down list, select the down arrow, click on the item, and drag the item to the Filter field. This enables you to create expressions and drag-and-drop filter name reference items into your expressions.

8. Click Finish. The Hit Detail window for the report you want to generate displays (see Figure 6.21). From this window, you can see the types of information that will be included in your new report. You can delete items from this window by selecting the item and pressing Delete.

FIGURE 6.22▲
The Report Document dialog box allows you to name your report.

9. Click the Create Report Document toolbar button on the Report Writer toolbar. The Report Document dialog box displays (see Figure 6.22).

10. Enter a file name and select the format of the report. The default report format is HTML, which automatically displays in your Web browser. You also can select Microsoft Word and Microsoft Excel, which you can display in those applications. Click the Template button if you want to specify a report template that you have created.

11. Click OK. The report document is created. The Report Writer Statistics dialog box displays as well. Click Close to close this dialog box. If you specified the HTML format in step 10, your registered Web browser launches with the report displayed (see Figure 6.23).

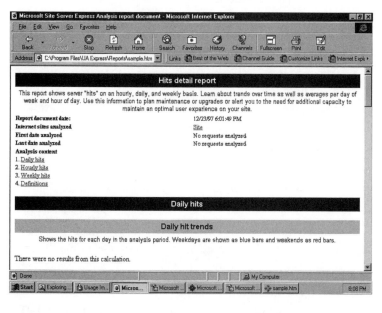

FIGURE 6.23

A Report Writer document displayed in Internet Explorer 4.0.

Configuring Report Writer and Usage Import to Analyze Logs Created by the WWW Service or the FTP Service

You learned earlier how to import a log file into Usage Import and how to create a report in Report Writer. You learn here how to configure Report Writer and Usage Import to analyze logs that are created by your WWW or FTP service.

FIGURE 6.24▲
The Usage Import Options dialog box.

N O T E

Getting Your Changes Saved On any
of the Usage Import Options tabs,
click the Save As Default Options
button if you want your changes to be
saved.

FIGURE 6.25▲
The IP Resolution tab.

The Usage Import Options

In Usage Import, you can access the Usage Import Options dialog
box by selecting Tools, Options. This dialog box (see Figure 6.24)
enables you to configure several settings and save them as your
default settings or use them only during the current Usage Import
session. If you opt not to save them as default settings, the next
time you start Usage Import, the previous settings are used. Click on
each tab to open the configuration options referenced for each of the
following figures.

On the Import tab, you can set the following options:

◆ **Drop Database Indexes.** For analysis purposes, database
indexes must be created. After you have a large amount of data
in a database, however, you can enable this option and drop
indexes during the import process.

◆ **Adjust Requests Timestamps to.** Turn on this option if you
want all time stamps in log files to adjust to the time zone
shown in the drop-down list. This is handy if you have Web
sites in servers in multiple time zones.

◆ **Exclude Spiders.** By selecting this option, you tell IIS to
disregard hits from Internet search engines (which use spiders
to search the Internet) and other agents shown on the Spider
List tab.

◆ **Lookup Unknown HTML File Titles.** Performs HTML title
lookups on HTML files added to the database during the log
file import.

◆ **Resolve IP Addresses.** Uses DNS to resolve IP addresses
found in log files during the import process. This can be very
useful for log analysis because microsoft.com is certainly more
easily interpreted in a report then 207.46.130.x.

◆ **Whois Query for Unknown Domains.** Tells Usage Import
to perform a Whois query for unknown organization names.

The IP Resolution tab (see Figure 6.25) includes the following
options:

◆ **Cache IP Resolutions for *n* Days.** Enables you to set the
number of days between IP lookups.

◆ **Timeout a Resolution Attempt after *n* Seconds.** Enables you to set the number of seconds for Usage Import to attempt to resolve an IP address. After this time, Usage Import stops attempting to resolve the IP address. Higher values mean better results, but slow down the import process.

◆ **Use a Resolution Batch Size of *n* IPs.** Specifies the batch size Usage Import uses for IP resolution.

The Log File Overlaps tab (see Figure 6.26) includes the following two options:

◆ **To Be Considered an Overlap, Records Must Overlap by at Least *n* Minutes.** Overlap periods are redundancies introduced in your log file database because of log files being accidentally re-imported, resuming interrupted logging actions, concatenating two log files, and running logs on separate servers. This setting allows you to configure the period of time the import module uses to evaluate an overlap condition. If you specify shorter periods, overlaps can be reduced, but later analysis can be adversely affected.

◆ **If an Overlap Is Detected.** This setting enables you to choose what an action Usage Import should do when an overlap is detected. You can choose from these options: Import All Records, Stop the Import, Stop All Imports, and Discard Records and Proceed.

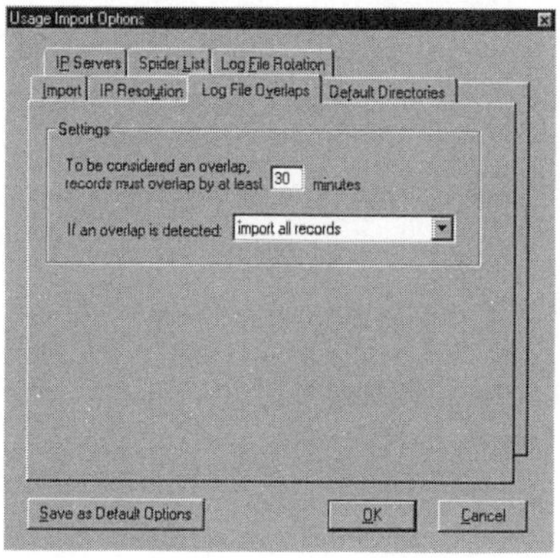

The Default Directories tab (see Figure 6.27) includes one option, the Log Files field. Use this field to specify the default directory for log files and import files.

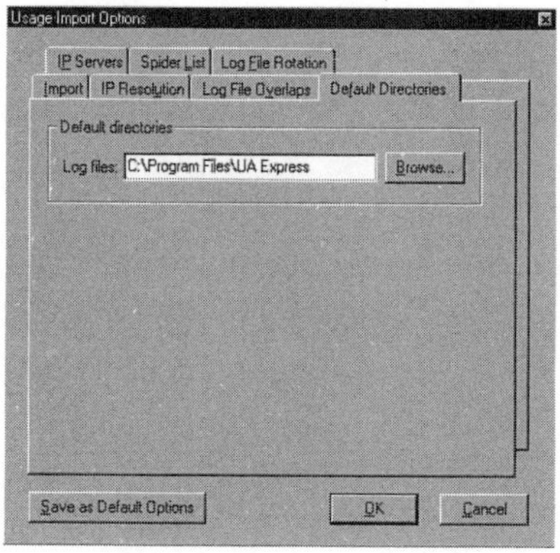

WARNING

Effects of a Large Resolution Batch Size A large number setting in the Use a Resolution Batch Size of *n* IPs option can cause your DNS server to crash. Report Writer might also show a large number of unresolved addresses, which might not be correct.

FIGURE 6.26▲
The Log File Overlaps tab.

◀FIGURE 6.27
The Default Directories tab.

FIGURE 6.28▲
The IP Servers tab.

The IP Servers tab (see Figure 6.28) includes the following two options:

◆ **HTTP Proxy.** Import uses the proxy server host name (if specified) and port number for all HTML title lookups.

◆ **Local Domain of DNS Server.** This setting clarifies hosts returned from IP resolutions. Enter your DNS server here, or, if an ISP maintains your DNS server, enter your ISP's setting here.

The Spider List tab (see Figure 6.29) includes common spider agents you want to exclude if the Exclude Spiders option is selected on the Import tab. You can delete any agent here by selecting it and pressing Delete. On the other hand, you can add to the list by placing an asterisk (*) after the Freeloader item and then entering the word and, followed by the name of the agent. No spaces are allowed between words.

FIGURE 6.29▶
The Spider List tab.

> **N O T E**
> **Proxy Servers** For proxy servers that require user names and passwords, use the syntax username: password@hostname.

Finally, the Log File Rotation tab includes the item at the end of an import (see Figure 6.30). This option enables you to control the treatment of data that is cut off due to file rotation. This is data that is divided at the end of one file and begins again at the start of a new log. You can select from these options: Commit Open Visits to Database, Discard Open Visits, and Store Open Visits for Next Import.

Click OK on the Usage Import Options dialog box to close it and use the settings you've configured.

FIGURE 6.30▲
The Log File Rotation tab.

The Report Writer Options

You can configure Report access Writer options by opening Report Writer and selecting Tools, Options. The Report Writer Options dialog box displays (see Figure 6.31).

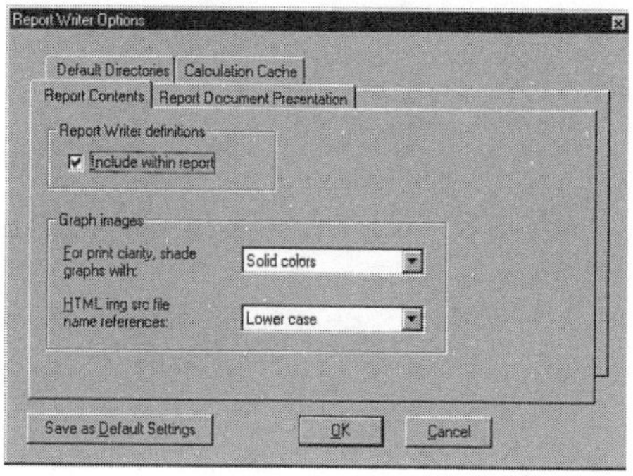

FIGURE 6.31▲
The Report Writer Options dialog box.

On the Report Contents tab (refer to Figure 6.31), you can set the following options:

- **Include Within Report.** Use this option to have Report Writer include usage definitions at the bottom of every report. After you become more familiar with Report Writer documents, you might want to disable this option so your reports don't have these definitions.
- **For Print Clarity, Shade Graphs with.** Use this option to specify solid colors and pattern lines for graph shading. For printed reports on noncolor printers, select the Pattern Lines option.
- **HTML img src File Name References.** Select which case to use when naming image and source files. For UNIX systems, use the correct case option for your system. In most situations, lowercase is the best choice.

NOTE

Getting Changes Saved On any of the Report Writer Options tabs, click the Save As Default Settings button if you want your changes to be permanently saved.

On the Report Document Presentation tab (see Figure 6.32), you can set the following options on how the report is styled:

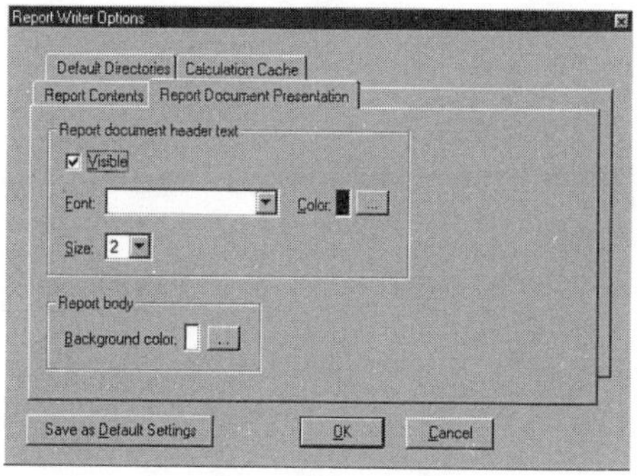

FIGURE 6.32▲
The Report Document Presentation tab.

- **Visible.** Specify this option so Report Writer displays header information, including analysis time period, site analyzed, and report sections.
- **Font, Color, and Size options.** Use these options to specify the font, color, and size of the header information text.
- **Background Color.** Click the ellipsis button (...) to display the Color dialog box in which to specify a background color for your report.

The Default Directories tab (see Figure 6.33) includes these two options:

- **Report Documents.** Set the path for your completed reports in this field.
- **Analysis Files.** Set the path for your completed analysis files in this field.

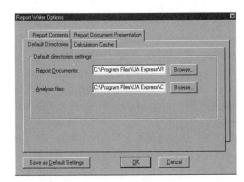

FIGURE 6.33▲
The Default Directories tab.

FIGURE 6.34▲
The Calculations Cache tab.

Finally, the Calculation Cache tab (see Figure 6.34) includes these options:

◆ **Cache All Calculations.** Enables you to cache report calculations in the Cache folder for future use. By using cache calculations, you can speed up report generations.

◆ **Don't Cache Anything.** Turns off the calculations cache feature.

◆ **Cache Directory.** Sets the directory in which calculations are cached.

◆ **Maximum Cache Size.** Sets the maximum amount of cached material the Cache directory can hold. This setting is in kilobytes.

◆ **Clear Cache Now.** Click this button when you want to clear the calculations cache.

Click OK in the Report Writer Options dialog box to close it and use the settings you've configured.

Automating the Use of Report Writer and Usage Import

A handy feature of the Report Writer and Usage Import is the automation capability. To automate Report Writer and Usage Import activities, use the Scheduler tool. You can set up Scheduler so that a report is generated every day when you arrive at work or a report is created at the end of the week to be dispersed to your Internet site administration team.

When you use Scheduler, you create jobs that have tasks scheduled to begin at specific times and days. Tasks are simply activities, such as importing a log or creating a report. After you set up a job, Scheduler creates a batch file that runs to execute the specific tasks.

To create a new job in Usage Import, perform the following steps:

STEP BY STEP

6.5 Creating a Job to Automate Report Writer and Usage Import

1. Open Usage Import and click on the Scheduler toolbar button (or select Tools, Scheduler). The Scheduler window displays (see Figure 6.35).

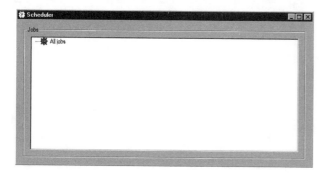

◄**FIGURE 6.35**
The Scheduler window.

FIGURE 6.36▲
The Job Properties dialog box.

2. Double-click the All Jobs item. The Job Properties dialog box displays (see Figure 6.36).

3. Click the Active (NT Only) check box. If this is cleared, the Scheduler does not run the specified job. This is handy if you want to disable a specific job without deleting it entirely. This way, you have the option of enabling it again without going through the process of setting up the job again.

4. In the Occurs area, select when you want the job to start.

5. If you chose Every or Next in the preceding step, select the day(s) you want the job to run in the Days area. Press Ctrl to select multiple days.

6. Enter the time you want the job to run in the Time field.

7. Click the Message Log tab (see Figure 6.37). You can save messages about the results of each task in a log file by entering the path and file name for the log file in the Message Log field. From the drop-down list, you can

continues

NOTE

Time Format   Times are entered in 24-hour format, so 3:00 P.M. is denoted as 15:00 hours.

FIGURE 6.37▲
The Message Log tab.

continued

> **N O T E**
>
> **Renaming the Job**   You can click on the New Job name twice (do not double-click it) to rename the job.

select variables to be added to the file name. When the file is created, the variables, such as $d(23)$, are replaced by actual values.

8. Click OK to save your new job to the Scheduler window (see Figure 6.38).

FIGURE 6.38▶
Your new job is added to the Scheduler window.

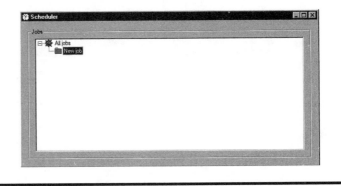

You now need to add tasks to your new job. Perform the following steps:

STEP BY STEP

6.6 Adding Tasks to a Job

1. Right-click your new job and select New Task. The Task Properties dialog box displays (see Figure 6.39).

2. Select the type of task you want to add to your job by clicking on the Task Type drop-down list. If you want to automate the database compacting tasks, for instance, select Compact Database. The options available on the Task Properties dialog box change when you pick a different task.

3. Fill out the fields (if any are shown) for the task you select.

4. Click OK to save your new task. The Scheduler window shows the new task under your new job (see Figure 6.40). Again, you can rename the new task by clicking it twice.

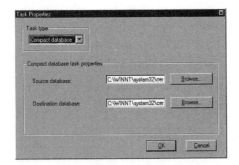

FIGURE 6.39▲
The Task Properties dialog box.

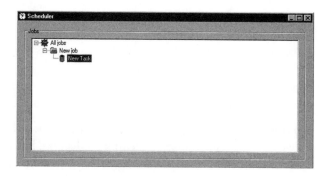

FIGURE 6.40
A new task added to your new job.

5. Continue adding tasks to your job by repeating steps 1 through 4.

6. When finished, close the Scheduler window and click Yes when prompted to start the job.

INTRODUCTION TO PERFORMANCE MONITORING

▶ Monitor performance of various functions by using performance monitor.

If you are familiar with the Performance Monitor, please skip this introduction. If, by some chance, you have not used this utility before, you need to understand the fundamentals of its use. Be sure to check the "Suggested Readings and Resources" section for references to more in-depth information on Performance Monitor.

Performance Monitor can be found in the Administrative Tools program group. Performance Monitor collects data about systems resources and then presents them in a graphical format for interpretation by an administrator. Performance Monitor can be used for a number of tasks including the following:

◆ **Establishing System Baselines.** Establishing baselines is a critical capability to master if you truly want to be able to monitor the system. If you don't know how the system performs when things are running normally, you are at a severe disadvantage when you start looking for bottlenecks on a misbehaving system.

NOTE

Doesn't This Look Familiar? If you have passed the Windows NT 4 Server and/or the Windows NT 4 Server Enterprise exams, you have undoubtedly studied Performance Monitor before. Having passed the Windows NT Server exam is an excellent preparation tool for this exam. It will make it much easier to follow some of the NT-specific questions that are included on this exam, particularly the questions surrounding Performance Monitor.

◆ **Identifying Bottlenecks.** After you establish your system base-line, you can monitor it periodically to find out whether you are approaching bottlenecks on any of the system's components. This is particularly useful when you are trying to justify upgrades to the system. Management loves to see facts when justifying spending several thousand dollars on upgrades.

◆ **Monitoring Resource Usage over a Period of Time.** Not only can you do spot checks to identify bottlenecks, but you also can run Performance Monitor to see how resources are utilized over a period of time. For example, let's say you are monitoring memory usage. If you watch the monitor, you can see the amount of available RAM gets lower as you install more applications. Before this becomes an issue, you can see the trend and upgrade the server memory before it becomes an emergency.

◆ **Perform Capacity Planning.** With Performance Monitor, you can collect information with set parameters, and by altering the parameters, you can determine future resource requirements. For example, if you have ten typical users connecting to a Web server, you can take the data related to their system usage and determine the requirements (approximately, of course) for 1,000 users. This type of proactive capacity planning is something that many organizations lack these days and is a very useful skill for any administrator.

◆ **Troubleshooting.** Performance Monitor can provide valuable information if you are having problems with the system. Performance Monitor can quickly identify abnormal resource utilization and can help reduce the time needed to track down problems with a system that is having problems.

All of these things are critical to your ability to effectively administer a Windows NT server, and any applications running on that server, including Microsoft Internet Information Server 4.0.

Monitoring Performance of Various Functions Using Performance Monitor

IIS 4.0 provides several powerful tools to monitor and administer your Internet server, but you can still use common Windows NT administration tools to monitor IIS 4.0's performance. One such tool that is indispensable for IIS 4.0 monitoring is Performance Monitor. With Performance Monitor, you can monitor functions related to HTTP and FTP sessions. Performance Monitor is used when you want to see trends and patterns in your site's usage. When you install IIS 4.0, new objects related to Web and FTP services are added to Performance Monitor along with specific counters for those services. Objects are individual occurrences of a system resource, such as Web service, FTP service, Active Server Pages, Browser, and other items. Counters, on the other hand, are statistics relating to the objects, such as Debugging Requests, Memory Allocated, and Request Wait Time (all of which relate to the Active Server Pages object).

Performance Monitor can be started from the Administrative Tools (Common) folder. To specify the object and counter(s) you want to track, select Edit, Add to Chart. The Add to Chart dialog box displays (see Figure 6.41).

> **NOTE**
>
> **One Other Useful Metric**   In addition to the statistics added with the installation of IIS 4.0, there is one other set of statistics you should monitor on an IIS 4.0 server. It is frequently useful to be able to see what is happening with the TCP/IP protocol. You've installed the TCP/IP protocol in preparation for installing the IIS application, so you should have the TCP/IP metrics available, right? Unfortunately, it's not that easy. To add the TCP/IP metrics to Performance Monitor, you need to install the SNMP (Simple Network Management Protocol) service. After the SNMP Service has been installed, you can get a handle on what TCP/IP is doing on your server, including monitoring TCP/IP packets in and out of the server.

FIGURE 6.41
Add objects and counters to Performance Monitor from the Add to Chart dialog box.

The Performance Monitor screen shown in Figure 6.42 is monitoring functions relating to Web and FTP service. The following objects and counters are used:

◆ Web Services object with Anonymous User/sec, Bytes Sent/sec, and Maximum NonAnonymous Users counters selected

◆ FTP Server object with Bytes Total/sec, Current Anonymous Users, and Maximum Connections counters selected

FIGURE 6.42
An example of monitoring Web and FTP services in Performance Monitor.

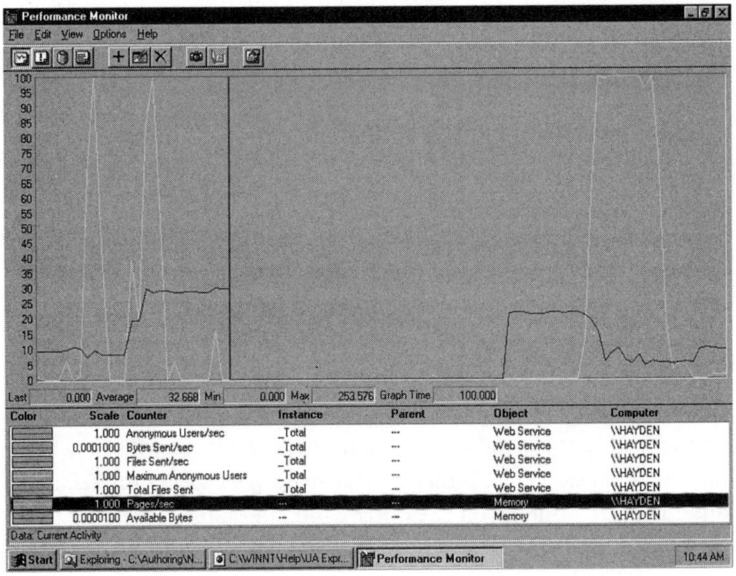

Table 6.2 lists the objects and counters available in Performance Monitor to help you monitor IIS 4.0.

TABLE 6.2

IIS 4.0-RELATED OBJECTS AND COUNTERS IN PERFORMANCE MONITOR

Object	Counter
Active Server Pages	Debugging Requests
	Errors During Script Runtime
	Errors From ASP Preprocessor
	Errors From Script Compilers
	Errors/Sec
	Memory Allocated
	Request Bytes In Total
	Request Bytes Out Total
	Request Execution Time
	Request Wait Time
	Requests Disconnected
	Requests Executing

Object	*Counter*
Active Server Pages	Requests Failed Total
	Requests Not Authorized
	Requests Not Found
	Requests Queued
	Requests Rejected
	Requests Succeeded
	Requests Timed Out
	Requests Total
	Requests/Sec
	Script Engines Cached
	Session Duration
	Sessions Current
	Sessions Timed Out
	Sessions Total
	Template Cache Hit Rate
	Template Notifications
	Templates Cached
	Transactions Aborted
	Transactions Committed
	Transactions Pending
	Transactions Total
	Transactions/Sec
FTP Service	Bytes Received/Sec
	Bytes Sent/Sec
	Bytes Total/Sec
	Current Anonymous Users
	Current Connections
	Current NonAnonymous Users
	Maximum Anonymous Users
	Total Anonymous Users

continues

TABLE 6.2 *continued*

IIS 4.0-RELATED OBJECTS AND COUNTERS IN
PERFORMANCE MONITOR

Object	*Counter*
FTP Service	Total Connection Attempts
	Total Files Received
	Total Files Sent
	Total Files Transferred
	Total Logon Attempts
	Total NonAnonymous Users
Internet Information Services Global	Cache Flushes
	Cache Hits
	Cache Hits %
	Cache Misses
	Cached File Handles
	Current Blocked Async I/O Requests
	Directory Listings
	Measured Async I/O Bandwidth Usage
	Objects
	Total Allowed Async I/O Requests
	Total Blocked Async I/O Requests
	Total Rejected Async I/O Requests
NNTP Server	Article Map Entries
	Article Map Entries/Sec
	Articles Deleted
	Articles Deleted/Sec
	Articles Posted
	Articles Posted/Sec
	Articles Received
	Articles Received/Sec

Object	*Counter*
NNTP Server	Articles Sent
	Articles Sent/Sec
	Articles Total
	Bytes Received/Sec
	Bytes Sent/Sec
	Bytes Total/Sec
	Control Messages Failed
	Control Messages Received
	Current Anonymous Users
	Current Connections
	Current NonAnonymous Users
	Current Outbound Connections
	Failed Outbound Logons
	History Map Entries
	History Map Entries/Sec
	Maximum Anonymous Users
	Maximum Connections
	Maximum NonAnonymous Users
	Moderated Postings Failed
	Moderated Postings Sent
	Sessions Flow Controlled
	Total Anonymous Users
	Total Connections
	Total NonAnonymous Users
	Total Outbound Connections
	Total Outbound Connections Failed
	Total Passive Feeds
	Total Pull Feeds
	Total Push Feeds
	Total SSL Connections

continues

TABLE 6.2	*continued*

IIS 4.0-RELATED OBJECTS AND COUNTERS IN PERFORMANCE MONITOR

Object	*Counter*
NNTP Server	Xover Entries
	Xover Entries/Sec
SMTP Server	% Recipients Local
	% Recipients Remote
	Avg Recipients/Msg Received
	Avg Recipients/Msg Sent
	Avg Retries/Msg Delivered
	Avg Retries/Msg Sent
	Bytes Received Total
	Bytes Received/Sec
	Bytes Sent Total
	Bytes Sent/Sec
	Bytes Total
	Bytes Total/Sec
	Connection Errors/Sec
	Directory Drops Total
	Directory Drops/Sec
	Directory Pickup Queue Length
	DNS Queries Total
	DNS Queries/Sec
	ETRN Messages Total
	ETRN Messages/Sec
	Inbound Connections Current
	Inbound Connections Total
	Local Queue Length
	Local Retry Queue Length
	Message Bytes Received Total
	Message Bytes Received/Sec

Object	*Counter*
SMTP Server	Message Bytes Sent Total
	Message Bytes Sent/Sec
Message Bytes Total	Message Bytes Total/Sec
	Message Delivery Retries
	Message Received/Sec
	Message Send Retries
	Messages Delivered Total
	Messages Delivered/Sec
	Messages Received Total
	Messages Refused for Address Objects
	Messages Refused for Mail Objects
	Messages Refused For Size
	Messages Retrieved Total
	Messages Retrieved/Sec
	Messages Sent Total
	Messages Sent/Sec
	NDRs Generated
	Number of MailFiles Open
	Number of QueueFiles Open
	Outbound Connections Current
	Outbound Connections Refused
	Outbound Connections Total
	Remote Queue Length
	Remote Retry Queue Length
	Routing Table Lookups Total
	Routing Table Lookups/Sec
	Total Connection Errors
Web Service	Anonymous Users/Sec
	Bytes Received/Sec
	Bytes Sent/Sec

continues

| TABLE 6.2 | *continued* |

IIS 4.0-RELATED OBJECTS AND COUNTERS IN PERFORMANCE MONITOR

Object	*Counter*
Web Service	Bytes Total/Sec
	CGI Requests/Sec
	Connection Attempts/Sec
	Current Anonymous Users
	Current Blocked Asyn I/O Requests
	Current CGI Requests
	Current Connections
	Current ISAPI Extension Requests
	Current NonAnonymous Users
	Delete Requests/Sec
	Files Received/Sec
	Files Sent/Sec
	Files/Sec
	Get Requests/Sec
	Head Requests/Sec
	ISAPI Extension Requests/Sec
	Logon Attempts/Sec
	Maximum Anonymous Users
	Maximum CGI Requests
	Maximum Connections
	Maximum ISAPI Extension Requests
	Maximum NonAnonymous Users
	Measured Async I/O Bandwidth Usage
	NonAnonymous Users/Sec
	Not Found Errors/Sec
	Other Request Methods/Sec
	Post Requests/Sec

Object	*Counter*
Web Service	Put Requests/Sec
	System Code Resident Bytes
	Total Allowed Async I/O Requests
	Total Anonymous Users
	Total Blocked Async I/O Requests
	Total CGI Requests
	Total Connection Attempts
	Total Delete Requests
	Total Files Received
	Total Files Sent
	Total Files Transferred
	Total Get Requests
	Total Head Requests
	Total ISAPI Extension Requests
	Total Logon Attempts
	Total Method Requests
	Total Method Requests/Sec
	Total NonAnonymous Users
	Total Not Found Errors
	Total Other Request Methods
	Total Post Requests
	Total Put Requests
	Total Rejected Async I/O Requests
	Total Trace Requests

Any of the counters in Table 6.2 could be important to you while monitoring your server. It is very dependent on the issue you are having or the process you are trying to evaluate. A few of the more commonly used counters are explained next.

FTP Service

FTP-related counters include the following:

◆ **Bytes Received/Sec.** This counter allows you to see how much traffic is being sent to your FTP server. If your server is being used as an upload server, this tells you what your peak uploading times are and how much data is being sent to the server.

◆ **Bytes Sent/Sec.** This is similar to the preceding counter but is more useful on a download server. This counter tells you how quickly data is being copied from the server.

◆ **Bytes Total/Sec.** An aggregate of the previous two numbers, total bytes per second can be used to track down a network adapter that has reached capacity.

◆ **Current Connections.** A good number to keep track of so you know how many users are accessing your site. This also can be used to ensure you are within Microsoft's licensing standards.

NNTP Server

NNTP counters include the following:

◆ **Articles Posted.** This counter tells you that your NNTP server is still posting messages to your newsgroups. It is a good way to keep track of how many messages are being added to your server.

◆ **Articles Posted/Sec.** Whereas the previous metric gives you overall numbers, this counter tells you the rate at which traffic is being sent to the NNTP server, which is very good information if you are on a congested network segment and suspect NNTP to be the culprit.

Usage

Some useful usage counters include the following:

◆ **Not Found Errors/Sec.** This is a great way to tell how many errors are being generated by your site without analyzing your logs. If this number gets too high, it indicates that it's time to run Content Analyzer.

◆ **Total CGI Requests.** If you are running CGI scripts, this counter tells you how often they are being requested.

◆ **Total Connection Attempts.** Want to know how many people are accessing your site without doing a full log analysis? This counter tracks that information for you.

Web Service

Some useful Web service counters include the following:

◆ **Anonymous Users/Sec.** This can give you a rough order of magnitude estimate on your site usage.

◆ **Bytes Total/Sec.** This is another good counter to monitor if you suspect your Web server is saturating your network. If this number gets too high, you might consider enabling some bandwidth throttling.

ANALYZING PERFORMANCE

▶ Analyze Performance.

As the IIS 4.0 administrator, you are responsible for analyzing the performance of the Internet site. But you also need to pay close attention to other server performance issues. These performance issues include the following:

◆ Identifying Bottlenecks

◆ Identifying Network-Related Performance Issues

◆ Identifying Disk-Related Performance Issues

◆ Identifying CPU-Related Performance Issues

◆ Identifying Memory-Related Performance Issues

Identifying Bottlenecks

Bottlenecks occur when one or more hardware resources is running at capacity while the rest of the system is capable of processing more data. The result is a performance reduction over the entire system.

A bottleneck can occur as a result of insufficient server memory or because of too little bandwidth available to the connected users. Disk subsystems are frequently an issue due to relatively slow disk access to retrieve data. You need to know how to recognize bottlenecks on your system before you can attempt to remedy them.

Finding a bottleneck is a matter of methodical detective work, with a dash of experience. Before you start diagnosing a bottleneck, you need information. Fully document the issue so you understand the symptom and start collecting Performance Monitor data to analyze the system's performance. You should have run a baseline on the system when it was running well, so you have something to which you can compare the present condition of the system.

You also can use Event Viewer to record events and audit situations on your computer that might require your attention. Another useful tool to use to locate bottlenecks is the Task Manager. Task Manager shows you all the ongoing tasks and threads on your computer.

The following sections explore some common bottlenecks that you should become familiar with when administering IIS 4.0.

Identifying Network-Related Performance Issues

Because IIS 4.0 might reside on your local area network server, you should become aware of some of the network-related performance issues that can affect the performance of your Internet site.

According to Microsoft, for medium-to-very-busy sites, you can expect IIS to saturate a 10Mbps Ethernet network adapter. If this happens, it will certainly cause network bottlenecks to occur that will impact site performance. In many instances, the Web server shares the segment with a number of other servers. To add insult to injury, without the proper test equipment, network utilization is a tricky thing to measure. For example, if you have a very high Frames/sec counter, is that good? It does indicate that you are processing many frames through the system. For a hard drive, a high amount of processing I/O is a good thing. But what if the reason the Frames/sec counter is high is that there is a network adapter on the network that is flooding the network with invalid broadcast traffic? Then, that high I/O is a bad thing because it indicates the network is broken.

NOTE

Why IIS Logs Can Create Performance Bottlenecks   As mentioned previously, one performance bottleneck you should be aware of is logging on to a database. As IIS 4.0 logs activities to a database, an ODBC connection must be established. This connection process can take a relatively long time, causing a performance bottleneck to occur. If you cannot speed up the ODBC connection time, consider switching to file-based logging. File-based logging is faster than database logging.

The best way to find this type of an issue is to use a network monitor of some kind (Microsoft's SMS product ships with an excellent one) and look at the network.

If you identify a network bottleneck on the system, there are a couple things you can do. You can buy a faster network adapter or install additional network adapters. You can also look into upgrading your network infrastructure. Going from a shared 10Mbps Ethernet network to a switched 10 or even switched 100 will go a long way towards easing network congestion. Removing unused services and protocols also contributes to your network efficiency, due to the lower system overhead.

What Good Does an Extra Ethernet Adapter Do? Many people think that if you install an additional Ethernet adapter in your server, you are just creating a router, because that card must reside on a different segment. With Windows NT 4.0, you can add multiple cards to a server and have them all reside on the same network segment. With proper configuration of DNS and IIS, you can share the network load across multiple adapters on the same segment.

Identifying Disk-Related Performance Issues

You might encounter hard disk bottlenecks if you have a very large file set, such as an application in the range of 5MB or larger, that is being accessed by clients in a random pattern. Two different Performance Monitor objects relate to monitoring disk activity. Let's take them one at a time.

The *PhysicalDisk* object counters track the activities related to the actual disk drive as a whole. If you are trying to load balance disk activity, the PhysicalDisk counters can be used to see how the hardware drives in the system are being used. If you have one disk with very high usage and another drive which is barely being used, you might want to look at moving an application or the pagefile to the underused disk. The *LogicalDisk* object deals with the partitions on the physical hard drive. These counters are useful for determining which partition is generating all the usage of the PhysicalDisk. One difference you might notice between the PhysicalDisk and the LogicalDisk objects is that even with a single physical disk in the system, you can have multiple LogicalDisk object occurrences. This happens when you have multiple partitions on a single segment. Be careful to select the proper LogicalDisk instance if you want to monitor a specific partition. Instances start numbering from 0, where 0 would be your C: partition, 1 would be the D: partition, and so on.

To identify a bottleneck of this sort, perform the following steps:

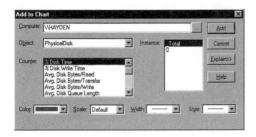

FIGURE 6.43
Select the PhysicalDisk object and %Disk Time counter from the Add to Chart dialog box.

NOTE

Go to a DOS Prompt for Results
Remember, if you want to get results for the disk counters, you need to go to a DOS Prompt and type diskperf -y. This enables performance tracking for the hard drives and can be used with an 'e' parameter as well. Diskperf -ye enables disk performance monitoring for drives in a stripe set. Diskperf -n disables the performance tracking.

STEP BY STEP

6.7 Identifying a Disk-Related Bottleneck

1. Start Performance Monitor.

2. Select Edit, Add To Chart.

3. From the Add to Chart dialog box, select the PhysicalDisk (or LogicalDisk) item from the Object drop-down list (see Figure 6.43).

4. From the Counter list, select % Disk Time.

5. Click Add.

6. Click Done.

The following four counters are particularly useful for determining how well your drives are performing:

◆ **%Disk Time.** This counter tracks the percentage of time the disk spent performing I/O processes. Consistently high values here indicate a heavily used drive. Moving files/applications that generate plenty of disk I/O to a different physical disk can help address this issue. The pagefile is a frequent candidate to be moved to a different physical disk, due to the amount of disk activity it can generate. Remember, it needs to reside on a different physical disk to move the overhead. Putting it on a different partition located on the same physical disk defeats the purpose.

◆ **Current Disk Queue Length.** This counter tracks the number of pending I/O write requests. If this number is consistently more than 2 or 3, you have a heavily utilized disk, and you should look into a faster drive or offloading some of the load.

◆ **Disk Bytes/sec.** This counter shows you the data transfer rate for data on to and off of the drive. The higher the number, the more efficient the drive's performance. Consistently low numbers can indicate a need for an upgrade. Degradation of this number over time can indicate a future drive failure.

◆ **Avg. Disk Bytes/Transfer.** This is very similar to the previous counter. The higher the number, the more efficient the data transfers are to and from the drive.

If you have concerns about drive performance, you should do a couple things. First, move high-use applications (like the pagefile) to less utilized drives. Next, you can look into implementing a striped array instead of single drives. Finally, you can upgrade to faster drives. You should also remember that the drive controller can be a bottleneck and might need to be upgraded.

Identifying CPU-Related Performance Issues

You can identify CPU bottlenecks by measuring the amount of the server CPU that is being utilized. Perform the following steps to measure this value:

STEP BY STEP

6.8 Identifying CPU Bottlenecks

1. Start Performance Monitor.

2. Select Edit, Add To Chart.

3. From the Add To Chart dialog box, select the Processor item from the Object drop-down list object.

4. From the Counter list, select % Processor Time (the other important Processor counters are listed shortly).

5. From the Instance list, select the number of the processor(s) you want to monitor. These numbers start at zero (zero signifies the first CPU in the system).

6. Click Add.

7. Click Done.

Under the Processor object, there are the following four important counters to keep an eye on:

◆ **%Processor Time.** This counter tracks the total processor utilization. It's a bit too general to tell you precisely where the problem is, but it can give you a good idea that you're having utilization problems.

◆ **%User Time.** This tells you the amount of processor time being used by applications. These are User Processes, that is, applications being run by users, not system applications. If you have an application that is using a large amount of processing resources, it shows up here.

◆ **%Privileged Time.** This is the amount of utilization the Windows NT operating system (the Kernel) is using. If you have a system service that is using too much processor, this counter tells you.

◆ **Interrupts/Sec.** This counter keeps track of the number of hardware interrupts the CPU is servicing. Your baseline is very useful if you think this is where the problem lies. It's difficult to tell what's a good number for your processor to deal with. If you go back to your baseline, you can see if the number has risen significantly.

If you identify a processor issue, the best course of action is to upgrade the processor, or in the case of systems that support symmetric multiprocessing, you can add additional CPUs. You can also move other applications (such as database applications) you run on the Web server to another computer or add more computers on which you replicate your site and then distribute processing across them.

Identifying Memory-Related Performance Issues

You can identify memory bottlenecks by measuring the amount of memory that is being utilized. Perform the following steps to measure this value:

STEP BY STEP

6.9 Identifying Memory Bottlenecks

1. Start Performance Monitor.

2. Select Edit, Add To Chart.

3. From the Add To Chart dialog box, select the Memory item from the Object drop-down list object.

4. From the Counter list, select Pages/Sec (the other important Memory counters are listed shortly).

5. Click Add.

6. Click Done.

Under the Memory Object, the following three counters are useful for monitoring memory:

◆ **Pages/Sec.** This counter tracks the number of page faults on the system. A page fault occurs when an application requests information from RAM that isn't in RAM and must be retrieved from the pagefile, or information needed to be written to the pagefile to free up RAM for application information. This number should be extremely low. If it's too high, you need to add more RAM because it indicates there is not enough RAM to support the applications.

◆ **Committed Bytes.** This is the total amount of information stored in RAM and in the pagefile. If this number is constantly greater than the amount of installed RAM, you need more memory. The pagefile should only be written to as a last resort for the application. Any disk I/0 is significantly slower than retrieving information from RAM and can seriously affect performance.

◆ **Commit Limit.** This counter can be used to fine-tune the size of your pagefile. This counter tracks the amount of space remaining in the pagefile before it needs to be extended. When Windows NT is forced to automatically extend the size of the pagefile, it affects the performance of the system. Disk I/O, as mentioned in the preceding paragraph, is very slow. By keeping track of this counter, you can make sure your pagefile is the correct size.

In many cases, the answer to memory issues is to add more RAM. The other piece of the memory puzzle is the pagefile. Microsoft's general rule for the pagefile is to take the amount of RAM in the system and make the pagefile that number plus 12 megabytes. That gives you the minimum for the pagefile. Set the maximum based on your requirements or as a percentage of available disk space.

OPTIMIZING THE PERFORMANCE OF IIS

▶ Optimize the performance of IIS.

One of the greatest improvements to IIS 4.0 is the inclusion of the Microsoft Management Console (MMC) to help you manage and administer IIS. With MMC, you can make global performance changes (such as limiting bandwidth usage), set service master properties, and configure other IIS properties to help optimize its performance.

To change global performance properties under IIS, perform the following steps:

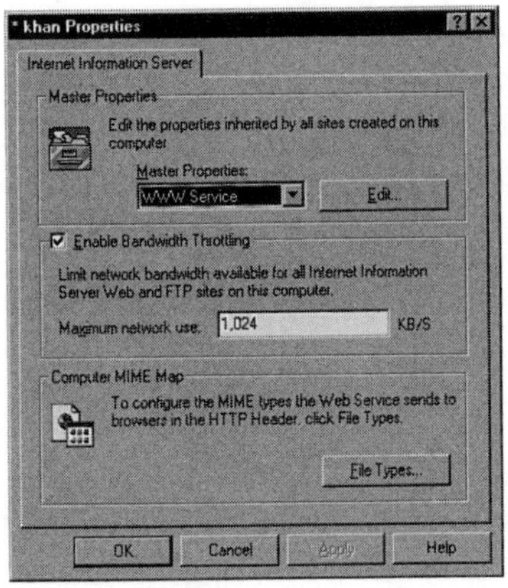

STEP BY STEP

6.10 Changing Global Performance Properties

1. Open Internet Service Manager in MMC.

2. Right-click the server you want to modify.

3. Select Properties to display the Server Properties dialog box for that server (see Figure 6.44).

4. Click the Enable Bandwidth Throttling option to control the amount of bandwidth consumption by all IIS services. You might want to do this if your network card is set up to handle multiple services, such as e-mail and Web services. In the Maximum Network Use field, enter a bandwidth value in KB/S (kilobytes/second).

   To get a bandwidth value for your server, begin with a value that is 50 percent of your connection bandwidth. You can then increase or decrease this value to tweak your system requirements.

5. Click the Master Properties drop-down list. This displays the services (WWW and/or FTP) you have installed and those for which you can customize default master properties. Master properties are standard settings for all the Web sites or FTP sites hosted on your server. After you set

FIGURE 6.44
The Server Properties dialog box.

master properties for all your sites, you can still modify
settings for individual sites. Master Properties provides you
with an easy and quick way to set common parameters for
all your sites.

6. Select the service you want to modify.

7. Click Edit. The Service Master Properties dialog box
   for your site displays (see Figure 6.45).

From this dialog box, you can set the following performance
parameters:

◆ Connections

◆ Performance Tuning

◆ Enable Bandwidth Throttling

◆ HTTP Keep-Alives

These parameters are discussed in more detail in the following
sections.

FIGURE 6.45
The Service Master Properties dialog box.

Connections

You find the Connections area on the Web Site tab of the Service
Master Properties dialog box. This area includes the Unlimited
and Limited To options that control the number of simultaneous
connections your Web or FTP sites allow. Click the Limited To
option to specify the number of simultaneous connections to your
sites. Then enter a value in the connection field (the default is
1,000). If you do not want to limit the number of connections,
select the Unlimited option (which is the default setting).

You also can set the timeout value for each inactive connection. This
value is set in seconds and automatically disconnects a client after
that client has been inactive on your site for the set number of seconds. In the Connection Timeout field, enter a value for the amount
of time your server should automatically disconnect an idle session.
The default is 15 minutes (900 seconds), but an average setting is
five minutes (300 seconds). For an infinite amount of time, enter all
9s in this field.

NOTE

Setting Timeout Values Even if a
connection is lost or a browser stops
working, your site continues to
process data until the timeout value is
reached. Setting an appropriate timeout value limits the loss of resources
due to these lost connections.

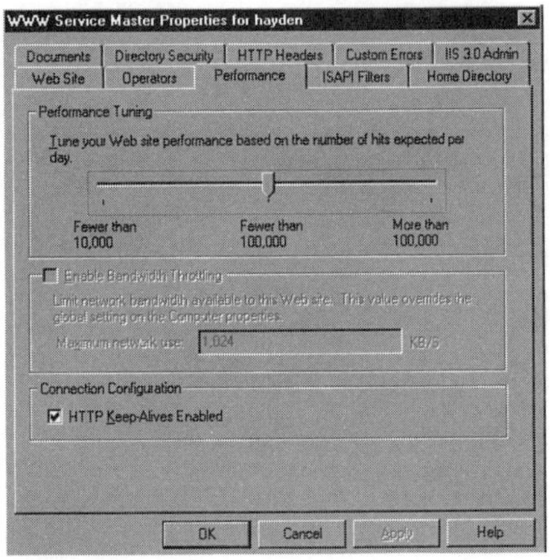

FIGURE 6.46
The Performance tab on the Service Master
Properties dialog box.

NOTE

Performance Tab Versus Properties
The value you set on the Performance
tab overrides settings for bandwidth
throttling set on the Computer
Properties sheet. This is true even if
the value on the Performance tab is
set higher than that on the Computer
Properties sheet.

Performance Tuning

The Performance tab (see Figure 6.46) on the Service Master
Properties dialog box includes the Performance Tuning option. This
option is set to the estimated number of connections you anticipate
for your site. Move the slider to the appropriate value. If you anticipate fewer than 10,000 visitors each day, move the slider to the far
left; for a site with fewer than 100,000 visitors, keep the slider in the
middle; and for a busy site that has over 100,000 visitors, move the
slider to the far right.

When you move the slider to a setting, IIS 4.0 alters the resources
allocated to the service. Settings that are higher than the actual
number of connections result in faster connections and improve
Web server performance. This is because more resources are allocated
to fewer connections. On the other hand, if you set the Performance
Tuning slider to a number that is much higher than the actual
number of connections, you will notice a decrease in overall server
performance, because server memory is being wasted (basically it is
not being utilized). This setting devotes more resources to your Web
service and fewer resources to other server applications. You should
compare your daily hit logs with the Performance Tuning setting to
ensure this setting closely matches the actual connections to your site.

Enable Bandwidth Throttling

Another performance option you can set is also on the Performance
tab. The Enable Bandwidth Throttling option, which you were shown
how to set at the server level in the "Optimizing the Performance of
IIS" section, sets the global bandwidth used by your Web site.

Click the Enable Bandwidth Throttling option and set a bandwidth
setting based on kilobytes per second (KB/S).

HTTP Keep-Alives

The final performance optimization setting you can modify on the
Performance tab is the Connection Configuration option. This
includes the HTTP Keep-Alives Enabled option. You can enable IIS
4.0's Keep-Alive feature to enable clients to maintain open connections. This way, a client does not need to re-establish connections for

each request, such as for each request for an image, document, or other resource. By enabling Keep-Alive, you not only decrease the amount of time a client waits to connect to another document or application on your site, but also increase the amount of resources devoted to this client.

Click the HTTP Keep-Alives Enabled option to turn on this feature to ensure that clients with slower connections are not prematurely closed. You should enable this feature for better server performance so that repeated requests from an individual client are not necessary when a page containing multiple elements is accessed.

Inheritance Overrides

If you make any changes to the Service Master Properties options, you also affect all individual sites under that service. When you click OK to save settings on the Service Master Properties dialog box, the Inheritance Overrides dialog box appears if a value you've changed will be overridden based on values of an individual site or child node (see Figure 6.47). You can select a site or sites that should be changed to use the new settings. Any existing sites that you do not manually select retain their old settings. New sites use the new properties.

Select the child node(s) from the Descendants with Overridden Defaults for the Current Property that you want to change to match the new value you set on the Service Master Properties dialog box. Click OK.

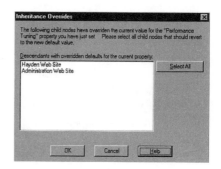

FIGURE 6.47
The Inheritance Overrides dialog box.

OPTIMIZING THE PERFORMANCE OF INDEX SERVER

▶ Optimize performance of Index Server.

Microsoft Index Server is used to index the contents and properties of Internet or intranet documents stored on an IIS server. You are shown how to install Index Server in earlier chapters, but one way to optimize its performance is to run it on a system with an optimum configuration. By and large, the basic Windows NT Server configuration provides adequate Index Server performance. This situation is probably best suited, however, for a small organization or an Internet site that does not expect a large amount of daily traffic.

To optimize the performance of Index Server, you should start by looking at the configuration of the computer on which it resides. The following are the factors you need to measure to set this configuration:

◆ Number of documents in the corpus, which is the collection of documents and HTML pages indexed by Index Server

◆ Corpus size

◆ Rate of search requests

◆ Kind of queries

You'll find that the amount of memory you have installed greatly affects the performance of Index Server. For sites that have fewer than 100,000 documents stored in the corpus, a minimum of 32MB is required and recommended. However, if you have 100,000 to 250,000 documents, the recommended amount of memory jumps from 64 to 128MB, whereas the minimum required still is 32MB. For sites with 250,000 to 500,000 documents, you need a minimum of 64MB of RAM, but it is recommended that you have 128 to 256MB. Finally, if you have over 500,000 documents, you must have 128MB of RAM installed, but at least 256MB is recommended.

Another system configuration setting you should pay attention to is the amount of free hard disk space where the Index Server catalog is stored. If less than 3MB of free space is available on the index disk, indexing and filtering are temporarily paused until additional disk space is made available. The event log records a message like the following:

```
Very low disk space was detected on drive "x". Please free
➡up at least "xMB" of space for content index to continue.
```

NOTE **If You Want It Fast, Get a Fast CPU and Lots of RAM** Keep in mind that complex search queries run faster when Index Server is installed on a computer with a faster CPU. Also, a faster CPU and additional memory improve indexing performance.

NOTE **Minimum Amount of Disk Space** The minimum amount of available disk space should be at least 30 percent of the corpus. However, during a master merge (which deletes redundant data and enables queries to run faster), you might need up to 40 percent of the corpus.

OPTIMIZING THE PERFORMANCE OF THE SMTP SERVICE

▶ Optimize performance of Microsoft SMTP Service.

The Microsoft SMTP service enables IIS 4.0 to deliver messages over the Internet. Microsoft SMTP supports basic SMTP (Simple Mail

Transfer Protocol) delivery functions and is compatible with SMTP mail clients.

When you install IIS 4.0, you also can install Microsoft SMTP. The default settings for Microsoft SMTP can be used, but you also can customize your SMTP service to optimize it for your system. The following are some of the ways you can optimize Microsoft SMTP:

◆ Set connection limits

◆ Set message limits

◆ Specify a smart host

Setting Connection Limits

You can set the number of simultaneous connections for incoming and outgoing connections. To set this number, open Microsoft Management Console (MMC), right-click on the SMTP site you want to modify, and select Properties. The SMTP Site Properties dialog box displays (see Figure 6.48).

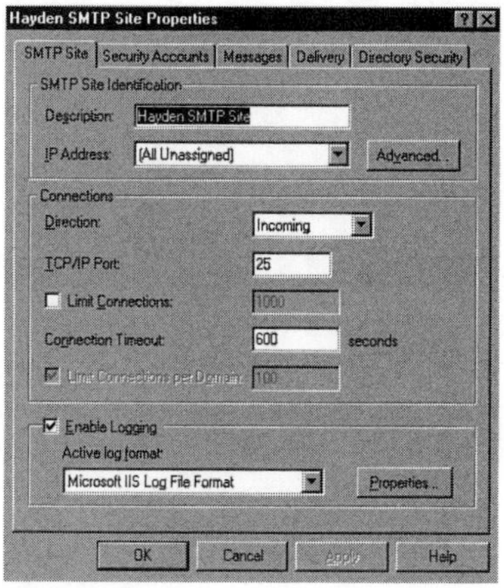

On the SMTP Site tab, perform the following steps to set the connection limit:

FIGURE 6.48
The SMTP Site Properties dialog box.

STEP BY STEP

6.11 Setting SMTP Connection Limits

1. Click the Limit Connections option.

---

2. In the Limit Connections option field, enter the number of simultaneous connections for your SMTP service. For incoming messages, the default is 1,000 and the minimum is 1. For outgoing messages, the default is 500 and the minimum is 1. Outgoing messages refers to the number of concurrent outbound connections to all remote domains.

---

3. In the Connection Timeout field, enter the period of time before an inactive connection is disconnected. The default is 600 seconds for both incoming and outgoing messages.

---

4. In the Limit Connections per Domain field, enter the number of outgoing connections to a single remote

continues

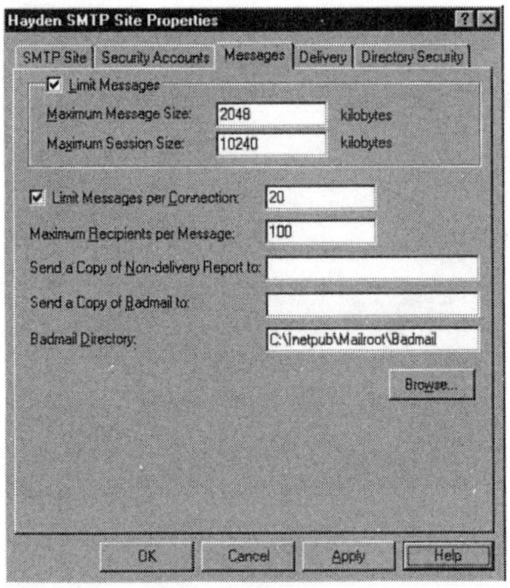

continued

domain. This option is available only with outgoing connections. The default is 1,000 connections and should be less than or equal to the value set in the Limit Connections field.

5. Click Apply.

FIGURE 6.49
The Messages tab of the SMTP Site Properties dialog box.

> **NOTE**
> **Maximum Message Size Versus Maximum Session Size**   If a single message exceeds the Maximum Message Size, it can still be processed by SMTP Server if it does not exceed the Maximum Session Size.

> **NOTE**
> **Determining a Value for the Limit Message per Connections Option**
> To determine a value for the Limit Messages per Connections Option limit, run Performance Monitor and select the SMTP Server object. In the Counter list, select Messages Sent/Sec. The Limit Messages per Connection value should be less than the value indicated by the performance counter.

Message Limits

You can set limits on the size and number of messages each connection can have. To do this, click the Messages tab of the SMTP Site Properties dialog box (see Figure 6.49) and perform the following steps:

STEP BY STEP

6.12 Limiting Message Size

1. Click the Limit Messages option.

2. In the Maximum Message Size field, enter the value for the maximum size of a message (in kilobytes). The minimum size is 1KB; the default is 2,048KB (2MB).

3. In the Maximum Session Size field, enter the value for the maximum size of a message before the connection is closed. Set this value to the same or higher than the Maximum Message Size. The default is 10MB.

4. Click the Limit Messages per Connections option to specify the number of messages that can be sent in one connection. You can use this value to increase system performance by enabling SMTP Server to use multiple connections to deliver messages to a remote domain. When the limit is reached, a new connection is opened and the transmission continues until all messages are delivered.

5. Click Apply.

Specifying a Smart Host

Instead of sending all outgoing messages directly to a remote domain, you can route all messages through a smart host. A smart host enables you to route messages over a more direct or less costly connection than other routes.

To set up a smart host, do the following:

STEP BY STEP

6.13 Setting an SMTP Smart Host

1. Select the Delivery tab (see Figure 6.50) on the SMTP Site Properties dialog box.

2. In the Smart Host field, enter the name of the smart host server. You can enter a string or an IP address in this field. To increase system performance when using an IP address here, enclose the address in brackets. Microsoft SMTP then looks at the IP address as an actual IP address without looking at it as a string value first.

3. Select the Attempt Direct Delivery Before Sending to Smart Host option. This option is used if you want SMTP service to attempt to deliver remote messages locally before forwarding them to the smart host server. The default is to send all remote messages to the smart host, not to attempt direct delivery.

4. Click OK.

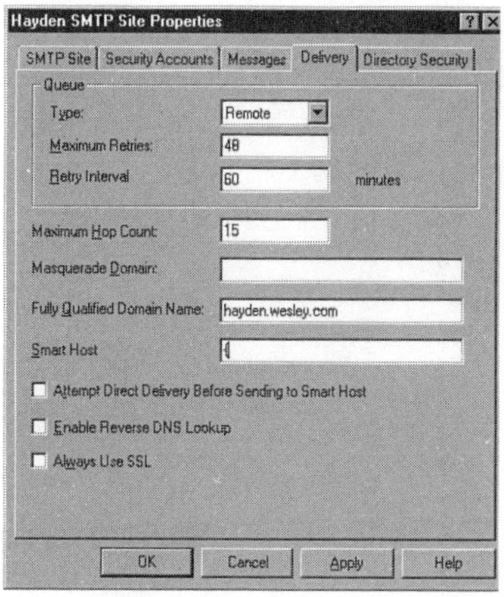

NOTE

Smart Hosts   Smart hosts are similar to the route domain option for remote domains. With a remote domain, however, only messages for that remote domain are routed to a specific server. On the other hand, with smart hosts, all outgoing messages are routed to that server. If you set up a smart host, you can still designate a different route for a remote domain. The route domain setting overrides the smart host setting.

FIGURE 6.50
The Delivery tab of the SMTP Site Properties dialog box.

OPTIMIZING THE PERFORMANCE OF THE NNTP SERVICE

▶ Optimize performance of Microsoft NNTP Service.

The Microsoft NNTP Service is used to let users exchange communications via the Internet Network News Transport Protocol

(NNTP). Users can post and view articles, much like they can when attached to the Usenet news service available on the Internet.

Similarly to the Microsoft SMTP Server, you can run Microsoft NNTP Service without modifying its default settings. However, you might want to tweak some of its properties to get better performance out of it. Two optimization tasks you can perform are changing connection settings and modifying client postings.

Changing Connection Settings

You can limit the number of simultaneous news client connections to a virtual server. You can set a value up to two billion—in other words, a relatively unlimited number of connections. To do this, open the Microsoft Management Console and right-click the NNTP site you want to modify. Select Properties to display the NNTP Site Properties dialog box (see Figure 6.51).

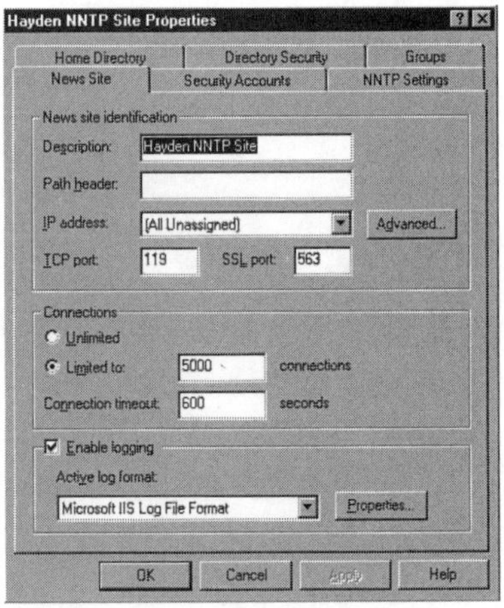

On the News Site tab, perform the following steps:

FIGURE 6.51
The NNTP Site Properties dialog box.

STEP BY STEP

6.14 Limiting NNTP Client Connections

1. Click the Unlimited option if you want to specify that there is no limit to the number of simultaneous connections.

2. Click the Limited to option and fill in the connections field with the number of simultaneous connections you want to limit NNTP to handling. The default is 5,000. Increase or decrease this value depending on your server size and needs.

3. In the Connection Timeout field, enter a value for NNTP Server to automatically disconnect inactive clients. The default is 600 seconds.

4. Click Apply.

Modifying Client Postings

The NNTP Settings tab includes options for modifying client posting parameters (see Figure 6.52). This tab enables you to set the maximum size of news articles posted to your NNTP Server.

To modify client postings, perform the following steps:

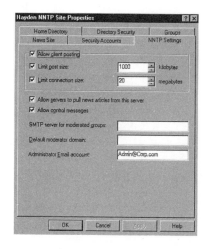

FIGURE 6.52
The NNTP Settings tab.

STEP BY STEP

6.15 Modifying NNTP Client Settings

1. Select the Limit Post Size option.

2. Enter a value to indicate the maximum size of a news article that a client can post to your NNTP Server. The default is 1,000KB. However, you might want to decrease this value if you want your news server to be set up to handle smaller articles. Increase this value, on the other hand, to allow larger articles to be posted. If an article exceeds this value, it still is posted if the article does not surpass the Limit Connection Size value.

3. Click the Limit Connection Size option.

4. Enter a value to indicate the maximum size for articles that a news client can post to your news server. The default is 20MB.

5. Click OK.

INTERPRETING PERFORMANCE DATA

▶ Interpret performance data.

The following are two tools primarily used for monitoring TCP/IP traffic, and they are the primary tools for gathering data for interpretation:

◆ Performance Monitor

◆ Network Monitor

Performance Monitor

Performance Monitor has been covered earlier in the chapter. Be sure to keep in mind that for TCP/IP statistics you need to install the SNMP service.

Network Monitor

Network Monitor is a Windows tool that enables you to see network traffic that is sent or received by a Windows NT computer. Network Monitor is included with Windows NT 4.0, but it must be installed to be active.

To install Network Monitor, open Control Panel, Network and then add the Network Monitor Tools and Agent from the Services tab. The version of Network Monitor that comes with Windows NT 4.0 is a simple version; it captures traffic only for the local machines (incoming and outgoing traffic).

Microsoft's System Management Server (SMS), a network management product, comes with a more complete version of Network Monitor that enables you to capture packets on the local machine for the entire local network segment. Both versions enable you to capture the packets that are flowing in and out of your computer. The Full version that comes with SMS also gives you extra functionality, such as the ability to capture all packets on the local network or on remote networks, edit those packets, and derive statistics about protocols and users on the network.

There are two pieces to the Network Monitor. The Agent captures the data. The Monitor Tool can be used to view the data. You also can filter out traffic that isn't important to the troubleshooting process.

The Network Monitor can be used to diagnose more complex issues with connectivity by enabling you to see the actual packets that are flowing on the network, verifying which steps are being used to resolve names or which port numbers are being used to connect.

NOTE

Limitations of Network Monitor
As with ISAPI, filters enable you to limit what you are viewing and keep the data from being overwhelming. The most commonly used filters are INCLUDE and EXCLUDE, which capture, or avoid capturing, specific data. The Network Monitor included with Windows NT Server can monitor only the specific system on which it is installed, unlike the Network Monitor in SMS, which can monitor other systems on the network.

OPTIMIZING A WEB SITE USING CONTENT ANALYZER

▶ Optimize a Web site by using Content Analyzer.

The Site Server Express Content Analyzer (Content Analyzer for short) enables you to create WebMaps to give you a view of your Web site, helping you manage your Web site. WebMaps are graphical representations of resources on your site. These resources can include HTML documents, audio and video files, Java applets, FTP resources, and applications. Content Analyzer also enables you to manage your links. You can ensure that links are included in the resources and that they all work correctly.

You can use Content Analyzer to optimize your Web site. Following are some of the ways you can do this:

◆ Import usage data to review how users are using your site (see Figure 6.53).

Important data you can view here includes how many hits a page receives, which pages are being hit the most, and from which URLs those hits are coming.

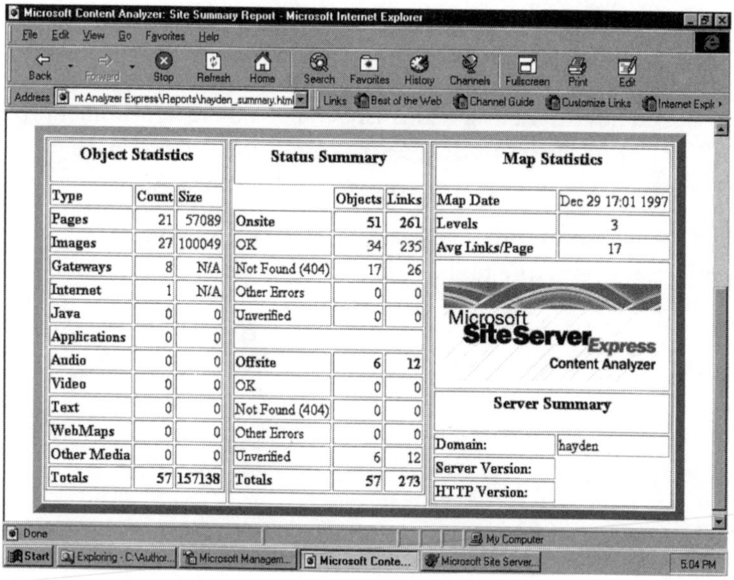

FIGURE 6.53
Content Analyzer provides a report of your site.

◆ Export the tree view of your site's WebMap to be an HTML index or table of contents for your site.

You also can use the index report from the Content Analyzer site report to serve as an HTML index of your site's contents.

◆ Assign helper applications to file types to edit source files.

From Content Analyzer, you can set helper applications to create and view site resources. This enables you quickly to check a broken link and fix it in an HTML editor, such as Microsoft FrontPage.

◆ View resource properties from within Content Analyzer.

You can view name, size, load size, modification date, URL, MIME type, HTTP status, and other properties.

◆ View a resource's links in Content Analyzer.

When viewing links within a resource, you can see the hyperlink text, MIME type, size, order, HTTP status, number of links, location of the linked document, hits, and other link information. Use this information to fine-tune or fix link-related problems in your documents.

◆ Verify onsite and offsite links. Links that are unavailable are shown in red.

These links might be broken, or an offsite link might not have been available when you attempted to verify it. This chapter does not teach you how to use Content Analyzer. For a more in depth look at Content Analyzer, see Chapter 3, "Configuring and Managing Resource Access" for more information and a Step by Step.

You should now be prepared to apply all the monitoring and optimization expertise to the following case study.

CASE STUDY: TRACKING DOWN AN IIS PERFORMANCE ISSUE

ESSENCE OF THE CASE

The essence of the case is as follows:

▶ Your employer, a computer manufacturing company, has just rolled out an electronic commerce site to sell its products on the Web.

▶ The site is running Microsoft Internet Information Server 4.0.

▶ Users are complaining that Web pages load very slowly. This is particularly true for users connecting to the Internet via dial-up modem.

SCENARIO

You are the Webmaster for the Wild Widgets Inc., a computer manufacturing company. In an attempt to emulate some of your successful competitors, you are trying to bring your products to the Web through an electronic commerce site running Microsoft Internet Information Server 4.0. Your site has just gone live and you are running into problems. Users are complaining that the pages load very slowly, particularly over a modem connection. You need to find the performance problem and correct it so people can use the site effectively.

ANALYSIS

Your Web server is suffering a fairly significant performance problem. To find the problem, you need to perform a thorough analysis of the server usage, hardware performance, and content.

The first thing to look at is the usage of the site. You need to configure logging for the WWW service to try to figure out if users are flooding the server. Because this is a daily issue, you set up the log to roll over once a day. After logging has been set up, you need to use the Usage Import and Report Writer utilities to generate some reports on usage. After reviewing the reports from the first couple days, you don't notice any unusual traffic patterns or usage that could be causing the performance issue described.

Because you've ruled out usage issues, it's time to dig into Performance Monitor and take a look to see what the hardware is doing. You set up a chart to look at the Processor, Memory, and Disk

continues

CASE STUDY: TRACKING DOWN AN IIS PERFORMANCE ISSUE

continued

counters discussed in the chapter. After allowing Performance Monitor to collect data for a couple days, you examine the results. By comparing some of the off-peak times with peak times, you find that all the parameters look fine. There doesn't appear to be any hardware performance problems. You also set up a network monitoring program to keep an eye on network traffic, but after taking a look at TCP/IP statistics and checking the network for errors, you can't find any network issues.

The next area to look at is the performance settings of the IIS server itself. You check to make sure network applications are favored over local, make sure there is no bandwidth throttling

configured, and look at the other settings we discussed in this chapter on optimizing IIS. Everything looks fine here.

The last thing to do is to take a look at the makeup of the site itself, using the Content Analyzer application. You set it up to analyze your site, and you find that the average size of a page is 1.2MB. That doesn't make any sense, because most of this is just HTML. Upon further discovery, you find that the Web designer included a high resolution, very intricate background as the default page for the site. It is a 1MB file and is causing the problem.

You replace the background file with a scanned copy of the corporate logo at a whopping 24KB, and the problem is solved.

CHAPTER SUMMARY

KEY TERMS

- Active Server Pages (ASP)
- ActiveX Data Objects (ADO)
- Domain Name System (DNS)
- Dynamic Host Control Protocol (DHCP)
- File Transfer Protocol (FTP)

Let's recap what we've discussed in the "Monitoring and Optimization" chapter. We have looked at a number of different areas to consider while optimizing your IIS server:

◆ **Analyzing Logs.** Log file data can give you a historical record of who has visited your site (based on visiting IP addresses), content exchanges (client downloads and uploads), which pages are the most popular ones on your site, and other information. A log file can be studied—for example, to see what parts of your Web site are the most and least popular. After you've got your log files configured, you can analyze the information they contain using the Report Writer and Usage Import Database.

To begin using these tools, you first import the log file or files you want to analyze into a Report Writer and Usage Import database. The database is dedicated for storing the imported data from a log file.

CHAPTER SUMMARY

After you have the log in the database, it's time to generate some reports. Report Writer includes report templates to ease your first attempts to create usable reports, as well as the capability to customize reports as needed.

To automate Report Writer and Usage Import activities, use the Scheduler tool. You can set up Scheduler so that a report is generated every day when you arrive at work or a report is created at the end of the week to be dispersed to your Internet site administration team.

◆ **Using Performance Monitor to Identify Bottlenecks.**
Performance Monitor can be found in the Administrative Tools program group. Performance Monitor collects data about systems resources and then presents them in a graphical format for interpretation by an administrator. Performance Monitor can be used for a number of tasks, including the following:

- **Establishing System Baselines.** Establishing baselines is critical to monitoring the system. If you don't know how the system performs when things are running normally, you will have a tough time finding bottlenecks when they occur.

- **Identify Bottlenecks.** After you establish your system baseline, you can monitor it periodically to find out whether you are approaching bottlenecks on any of the system's components.

- **Monitoring Resource Usage over a Period of Time.** Not only can you do spot checks to identify bottlenecks, but you also can run Performance Monitor to see how resources are utilized over a period of time.

- **Perform Capacity Planning.** With Performance Monitor, you can collect information with set parameters, and by altering the parameters, you can determine future resource requirements.

- **Troubleshooting.** Performance Monitor can provide valuable information if you are having problems with the system.

continues

KEY TERMS
- Hypertext Markup Language (HTML)
- Hypertext Transfer Protocol (HTTP)
- HTTP Keep-Alives
- Index Server
- Microsoft Management Console
- Performance Monitor
- Secure Sockets Layer (SSL)
- Simple Mail Transport Protocol (SMTP)
- TCP/IP
- Usage Import and Report Writer
- World Wide Web (WWW)

CHAPTER SUMMARY (continued)

◆ There are four categories of bottlenecks to be aware of, each with their own set of critical parameters to monitor:

- **Identifying Network-Related Performance Issues.** If you identify a network bottleneck on the system, there are a couple things you can do. You can buy a faster network adapter or install additional network adapters. You can also look into upgrading you network infrastructure. Going from a shared 10Mbps Ethernet network to a switched 10 or even switched 100 goes a long way towards easing network congestion. Due to the lower system overhead, removing unused services and protocols also contributes to your network efficiency.

- **Identifying Disk-Related Performance.** If you have concerns about drive performance, you should do a couple of things. First, move high-use applications (like the pagefile) to less utilized drives. Next, you can look into implementing a striped array instead of single drives. Finally, you can upgrade to faster drives. You should also remember that the drive controller can be a bottleneck and might need to be upgraded.

- **Identifying CPU-Related Performance.** If you identify a processor issue, the best course of action is to upgrade the processor, or in the case of systems that support symmetric multiprocessing, you can add additional CPUs. You can also move other applications (such as database applications) you run on the Web server to another computer or add more computers on which you replicate your site and then distribute processing across them.

- **Identifying Memory-Related Performance.** In many cases, the answer to memory issues is to add more RAM. The other piece of the memory puzzle is the pagefile. Microsoft's general rule for the pagefile is to take the amount of RAM inthe system and make the pagefile the size of the RAM plus 12. That gives you the minimum for the pagefile. Set the maximum based on your requirements, or as a percentage of available diskspace.

CHAPTER SUMMARY

◆ **Optimizing the various components of IIS.** We discussed the steps required to optimize several of the IIS components, including the Global IIS and Windows NT settings, Index Server, SMTP Server, and NNTP Server.

◆ **Using Content Analyzer.** The Site Server Express Content Analyzer (Content Analyzer for short) enables you to create WebMaps to give you a view of your Web site, helping you manage your Web site. WebMaps are graphical representations of resources on your site. These resources can include HTML documents, audio and video files, Java applets, FTP resources, and applications. Content Analyzer also enables you to manage your links. You can ensure that links are included in the resources and that they all work correctly.

Exercises

6.1 Creating a Report of a Log File

In the following exercise, you use Report Writer to create a report on the contents of a log file.

Estimated time: 30 minutes

1. Select Start, Programs, Windows NT 4.0 Option Pack, Microsoft Site Server Express 2.0, Report Writer. Report Writer starts and displays the Report Writer opening dialog box.

2. Select the From the Report Writer Catalog option on the Report Writer dialog box.

3. Click OK. The Report Writer dialog box with the Report Writer Catalog field appears.

4. Select the plus sign next to Detail Reports.

5. Click Hits Detail report.

6. Click Next. The Report Writer dialog box displays. Set the date range of the data to analyze for a one-month time period.

7. Click Next. The Report Writer dialog box displays.

8. Click Finish. The Detail window for the report you want to generate displays.

9. Click the Create Report Document toolbar button on the Report Writer toolbar. The Report Document dialog box displays.

10. Enter a file name and keep the default report format of HTML.

11. Click OK. The report document is created.

6.2 Configuring FTP Service Logging Features

The following exercise shows you how to configure the logging features of the FTP service in IIS 4.0.

Estimated time: 15 minutes

1. Select Start, Programs, Windows NT 4.0 Option Pack, Microsoft Internet Information Server, Internet Service Manager. Internet Service Manager opens in the MMC.

2. Right-click the FTP site you want to configure.

3. Click Properties. The FTP Site Properties dialog box displays.

4. Click the Enable Logging option.

5. Click the Active Log Format drop-down list and select the type of log format you want to create. The following steps show how to configure the W3C.

6. In the New Log Time Period section, set when you want IIS to create a new log file for the selected FTP site.

7. Enter the directory in which you want to store the log file. The default is %WinDir\System32\LogFiles.

8. Click the Extended Properties tab to display the logging options you can set (this tab is available only when you select the W3C Extended Log File Format option). On this tab, you can set the options described earlier in Table 6.1.

9. Click OK to close the Extended Logging Properties dialog box.

10. Click OK to close the FTP Site Properties dialog box.

6.3 Creating Automatic Jobs in Usage Import

This exercise walks you through creation of a new job in Usage Import.

Estimated Time: 20 minutes

1. Open Usage Import and click on the Scheduler toolbar button. The Scheduler window displays.

2. Double-click on the All Jobs item. The Job Properties dialog box displays.

3. Click the Active (NT Only) check box. If this is cleared, the Scheduler does not run the specified job.

4. In the Occurs area, select when you want the job to start.

5. If you chose Every or Next in the preceding step, select the day(s) you want the job to run in the Days area. Press Ctrl to select multiple days.

6. Enter the time you want the job to run in the Time field.

7. Click the Message Log tab. You can save messages about the results of each task in a log file by entering the path and file name for the log file in the Message Log field. From the drop-down list, you can select variables to be added to the file name. When the file is created, the variables, such as $d(23)$, are replaced by actual values.

8. Click OK to save your new job to the Scheduler window.

6.4 Adding an IIS Counter to Performance Monitor

This exercise walks you through adding an IIS Counter to Performance Monitor.

Estimated time: 20 minutes

1. Open Performance Monitor.

2. Go to Edit, Add to Chart. This opens the Add to Chart dialog box. The first field should be the name of your computer. In the Object box, select FTP Service. In the Instance box select the FTP Site you would like to monitor.

3. In the Counter box, select Current Connections.

4. You can configure the characteristics of the counter as it appears in Performance Monitor using the settings at the bottom of the dialog box.

5. Click Add to add the counter. For an explanation of the counter, click on the Explain button.

6.5 Fine Tuning Index Server Performance Using the Registry

This exercise walks you through fine-tuning of Index Server parameters.

Estimated time: 25 minutes

1. Open the Registry Editor (REGEDT32.EXE).

2. Go to the Registry key HKEY_LOCAL_ MACHINE\SYSTEM\CurrentControlSet\ Control\ContentIndex.

3. All the parameters for Index Server can be adjusted within this key. As always, if you are manipulating the Registry, be sure to back it up first, and be careful making changes.

4. Adjust the parameters as needed.

5. Close the Registry Editor when you are finished.

6.6 Creating a Web Map with Content Analyzer

The following exercise shows you how to create a Web Map, and how to customize the options in Content Analyzer.

Estimated time: 25 minutes

1. Open Content Analyzer by going to Start, Programs, Windows NT 4.0 Option Pack, Microsoft Site Server Express 2.0, Content Analyzer. The Content Analyzer Welcome screen opens.

2. Click the New WebMap button. The New Map dialog box opens. You can create your WebMap from an URL (universal resource locator) or from a file. This exercise creates the site from an URL.

3. Select the URL radio button and click OK. Enter the URL to create the map from. You can tell it whether to map the entire site and whether to create reports. Clicking Options opens the Mapping from URL Options dialog box. These options allow you to control the behavior of Content Analyzer as it maps the site. Click OK to close the Options dialog box and then click OK to start creating the WebMap.

4. If you select the Create Reports option, you are prompted for a location for those files. Clicking OK opens a Web browser and displays the report as HTML. Use this report to determine where the site can be optimized, and remove broken links.

5. Close the report and you are returned to Content Analyzer and your completed WebMap.

6.7 Using the Ping Utility to identify Network Performance Issues

This exercise walks you through one way to identify network-related performance issues.

Estimated time: 10 minutes

1. Open the Command Prompt.

2. Type PING <the address of the subnet router> and hit ENTER. The results should look like this:

```
Pinging <router IP address> with 32 bytes of
data:
        Reply from <router IP address>:
        bytes=32 time<10ms TTL=128
        Reply from <router IP address>:
        bytes=32 time<10ms TTL=128
        Reply from <router IP address>:
        bytes=32 time<10ms TTL=128
```

```
        Reply from <router IP address>:
        bytes=32 time<10ms TTL=128
```

3. Check to see if those times are unusually long. To get a larger sample, type PING -n 100 and press ENTER. That will yield 100 pings for testing.

4. Finally, to PING the address until a break is sent, type PING -t and press ENTER.

Review Questions

1. You are the Web administrator for Exponent Mathematicians and you've been asked to produce a report showing the daily Web traffic to the Microsoft Internet Information Server 4.0 Internet Web site. Which IIS tool should you use? Can you automate this task?

2. You are an Internet consultant working for the Get Bux pawnshop chain. Get Bux uses IIS 4.0 to host an Internet Web site and FTP site. You are asked to track the number of anonymous users currently attached to the site. How can you do it?

3. You are the Windows NT administrator for Fly Away Travel. When administering Fly Away's internal IIS 4.0 server, you need to keep an eye on the system for potential bottlenecks. This server hosts all the daily travel specials, and Fly Away's agents need fast, reliable system access. What are some of the tools you can use to discover bottlenecks on the system?

4. You're the administrator of Little Faith Enterprise's of IIS 4.0-based Web site. You notice that the Web site is responding sluggishly during peak hours and you notice some inactive clients are staying connected even if there is no activity. You suspect these idle connections are using up critical system resources. How can you fix this?

APPLY YOUR KNOWLEDGE

5. You are administering the IIS 4.0 server for We Built It Computing. On your company's Web site, you use Microsoft Index Server to index all your online documents. You have between 100,000 and 150,000 documents stored on the server. How much RAM should you have for this number of documents?

6. You are doing some IIS consulting for Hunter's Sporting Goods, and the messaging administrator has asked for your help in setting up a smart host on her IIS 4.0 SMTP site. What is a smart host?

7. You are the news administrator for the Bug Off Software Corporation. The Microsoft NNTP news server you administer has been performing poorly due to over-subscription. Too many clients are connecting to it simultaneously. How can you limit the number of simultaneous users for Microsoft's NNTP Service?

8. What are the statistical measurements called that are used in Performance Monitor?

9. You are doing an audit of Kiss Me Quick dating services Internet Web site. To help with your audit, you use the Content Analyzer included with Microsoft Internet Information Server 4.0. Name three ways you can use this tool to optimize the site.

10. You are the NT administrator for the Get Well Soon hospital chain. You have had some complaints about performance on your IIS 4.0-based intranet server. You think you need to start looking for bottlenecks on your Microsoft Internet Information Server 4.0 server. What four categories of hardware do you monitor to find a bottleneck?

11. You have an IIS 4.0 server and you need to check processor utilization. What are three important counters to monitor when checking to see if processor utilization is too high?

Exam Questions

1. You administer an Internet site for the Shady Acre Retirement Village, running IIS 4.0's Web and FTP services. You plan to use Microsoft Index Server to index the site. The site contains over 500,000 documents to be indexed. What is the recommended amount of RAM your server should have to run Index Server?

   A. 32MB

   B. 64MB

   C. 128MB

   D. 256MB

2. On the same Index Server computer as discussed in Question 1, what is the minimum amount of RAM you need?

   A. 32MB

   B. 64MB

   C. 128MB

   D. 256MB

3. You are the Web administrator for Get Stuffed Taxidermy and you've been asked to produce a weekly site usage report for the Microsoft

APPLY YOUR KNOWLEDGE

Internet Information Server 4.0 Internet Web site. Which IIS tool should you use to generate this report?

A. Microsoft Excel

B. Microsoft Site Server Express Analysis Report Writer

C. Microsoft Site Server Express Analysis Usage Import

D. Crystal Reports

4. When setting up IIS 4.0 logging, you want to customize the type of data that is logged. Which logging option should you choose?

A. NCSA Common Log File Format

B. W3C Extended Log File Format

C. ODBC Logging

D. SQL Logging

5. IIS 4.0 is installed on a server with all IIS 4.0's default settings used. When you examine the Web Site tab on the Service Master Properties dialog box, what is the number of maximum connections listed in the Limited To field under the Connections area?

A. 0

B. 500

C. 1000

D. 100

6. The IIS 4.0 Web site you administer does not receive a large number of hits each day, but the server's performance is sluggish. Which one of the following statements is true?

A. The Performance Tuning slider setting on the WWW Service Master Properties Performance tab is too high.

B. The Performance Tuning slider setting on the WWW Service Master Properties Performance tab is too low.

C. The site could be operating at a TCP port other than the default.

D. You are probably using IDE drives rather than SCSI.

7. Scenario: You manage the IIS 4.0 servers for Screwed-Up Screwdriver Corporation. One of the IIS 4.0 servers you manage performs slowly and reports numerous hits reported for every client that connects to your site.

Required Result: Improve Site Performance.

Required Result: Reduce the number of hits each client makes when connecting to the server.

What should you do?

A. Enable Bandwidth Throttling

B. Enable Logging

C. Connection Timeout

D. HTTP Keep-Alives Enabled

8. To optimize the performance of your FTP site, you can set which of the following option(s) that you can also set for your Web site? Select all that apply.

A. Connection Timeout

B. Enable Bandwidth Throttling

C. Connection Limited To value

D. Home Directory Redirection to URL

APPLY YOUR KNOWLEDGE

9. You are the Collaborative Computing administrator for Talk to Me Telephone. Your company has IIS 4.0 installed with the Microsoft SMTP and Microsoft NNTP Services running. What is the default maximum size of news articles that can be posted to a Microsoft NNTP Service news server?

   A. Unlimited

   B. 2MB

   C. 1,000KB

   D. 512KB

10. You run Performance Monitor periodically to check your IIS 4.0's performance. Which of the following counters is not a valid item under the Internet Information Services Global object?

    A. Current Blocked Async I/O Requests

    B. File Listings

    C. Measured Async I/O Bandwidth Usage

    D. Objects

11. You are an IIS 4.0 consultant. A client calls to report that Microsoft Index Server has stopped running, and a message says that there is not enough free disk space available. From the following choices, you know what about the amount of disk space at this point?

    A. The free disk space has dropped to 100MB.

    B. The free disk space has dropped to 3MB.

    C. The free disk space is not 20 percent of the corpus.

    D. The free disk space is not 50 percent of the corpus.

12. When installing Microsoft Index Server, you need to calculate the amount of free disk space to set aside for it. What is the amount you should set aside?

    A. 20 percent of the corpus

    B. 30 percent of the corpus

    C. 40 percent of the corpus

    D. 50 percent of the corpus

13. In Question 11, the logging on the IIS 4.0 server had stopped. You need to restart it.

    What should you do?

    A. Free enough disk space for the service to run and reboot the server.

    B. Free enough disk space for the service to run and stop and start the WWW and FTP services using the Internet Service Manager.

    C. Free enough disk space for the service to run. It restarts automatically as soon as there is enough free disk space for the log files.

    D. Install a bigger hard drive. Reinstall IIS 4.0 so the logs are stored on the new drive.

14. You administer your company's IIS 4.0's Internet site. You need to create a report based on your server's data logs using Report Writer. Before running Report Writer, what should you do?

    A. Enable logging and install SQL Server or MS Access.

    B. Enable ODBC Logging file format.

    C. Run Usage Import and import the log file.

    D. Use Edit from the command line to convert the file to TXT.

APPLY YOUR KNOWLEDGE

15. You use the Scheduler in Report Writer and Usage Import. What is the name of the items placed in a new job?

    A. Job items

    B. Categories

    C. Subjobs

    D. Tasks

16. You're the administrator of your IIS 4.0 Web site. The Web site is responding sluggishly, and you notice some inactive clients are staying connected to your server. What is an appropriate response?

    A. From the Web site's Service Master Properties dialog box, set the Connection Timeout field to a higher number.

    B. From the Web site's Service Master Properties dialog box, enable the Unlimited Connection option.

    C. From the Web site's Service Master Properties dialog box, set the Connection Timeout field to a lower amount.

    D. From the Web site's Service Monitor Properties dialog box, set the Connection Timeout field to a lower amount.

17. On your company's Web site, you run Microsoft Index Server. You have between 100,000 and 150,000 documents stored on it. How much RAM is recommended for this number of documents?

    A. 32MB

    B. 64MB

    C. 128MB

    D. 256MB

18. You are an IIS 4.0 consultant working with a large company that has asked you to set up a smart host. What should you do to increase performance if you enter an IP address for the smart host?

    A. Use brackets to surround the IP address

    B. Use commas to separate octets

    C. Use percent signs to surround the IP address

    D. Use semicolons to separate octets

Answers to Review Questions

1. To create a report of daily Web site activity, enable logging for your site and use Report Writer to create a detailed report of the activity. You can use Scheduler in Report Writer or Usage Analyst to automate this task. See "Importing Log Files Into a Report Writer and Usage Import Database" for details.

2. Run Performance Monitor, select Edit, Add To Chart, and select the FTP Service from the Objects list. From the Counter list, select Current Anonymous Users and click Add. Click Done. See "Monitoring Performance of Various Functions Using Performance Monitor."

3. You can use Performance Monitor, Event Viewer, and Network Monitor. See "Analyzing Performance" for more information.

4. From the Web site's Service Master Properties dialog box, set the Connection Timeout field to a lower amount. See "Optimizing the Performance of IIS."

APPLY YOUR KNOWLEDGE

5. If you have between 100,000 and 150,000 documents, you should have 64 to 128MB of RAM. The minimum required is only 32MB, but the higher number is recommended. See "Optimizing the Performance of Index Server."

6. Instead of sending all outgoing messages in Microsoft SMTP Service directly to a remote domain, you can route all messages through a smart host. A smart host enables you to route messages over a more direct or less costly connection than via other routes. See "Optimizing the Performance of the SMTP Service."

7. On the NNTP Site Properties dialog box, click the Limited To option and fill in the connections field with the number of simultaneous connections you want to limit NNTP to handle. The default is 5,000. See "Changing Connection Settings."

8. Performance Monitor uses statistical measurements called counters. See "Interpreting Performance Data."

9. You can import usage data to review how users are using your site, export the tree view of your site's WebMap to be an HTML index or table of contents for your site, and assign helper applications to file types to edit source files. See "Optimizing a Web Site Using Content Analyzer."

10. CPU, Memory, Disk, and Network Utilization. See "Introduction to Performance Monitoring."

11. %Processor Time. To track the total processor utilization.

    %User Time. To find out the amount of processor time is being used by applications.

    %Privileged Time. To find out how much processor Windows NT is using.

Interrupts/Sec. To keep track of the number of hardware interrupts the CPU is servicing.

See "Introduction to Performance Monitoring."

Answers to Exam Questions

1. **D.** If you have over 500,000 documents, you must have 256MB. See the section "Optimizing the Performance of Index Server" for more information. With 32MB, you can only index 100,000 documents. 64MB to 128MB allows you to index between 100,000 and 250,000 documents. Although 128MB is the minimum amount of RAM needed for over 500,000 documents, 256MB is the recommended amount. See "Optimizing the Performance of Index Server."

2. **C.** If you have over 500,000 documents, you must have 128MB of RAM installed. 32MB is the minimum recommendation for up to 250,000 documents. 64MB is the minimum for up to 500,000 documents. There are no recommendations that reference 256MB for a minimum. See "Optimizing the Performance of Index Server."

3. **B.** Microsoft Site Server Express Analysis Report Writer is the recommended tool for generating this report. This tool is bundled with IIS 4.0 and can be used to analyze a variety of different log file formats. Microsoft Excel is used for spreadsheets. The Usage Import utility imports your log information into the reporting database, but does not analyze the information. Crystal Reports is a third-party reporting tool not suited for this purpose. See "Configuring Report Writer and Usage Import to Analyze Logs Created by the WWW Service or the FTP Service."

APPLY YOUR KNOWLEDGE

4. **B.** W3C Extended Log File Format enables you to customize the type of data that is logged. The NCSA log is a standard logfile type, but cannot be customized as required. ODBC logging places your information in an ODBC-compliant database like Microsoft SQL Server. You can customize the information you take out of the database, but you cannot configure the actual logging using ODBC. There is no option for SQL Logging. See "Configuring the Logging Features of the WWW Service."

5. **C.** 1000 is the default in the Limited To field. See "Optimizing the Performance of IIS."

6. **A.** The Performance Tuning slider on the WWW Service Master Properties Performance tab is set too high. This causes foreground processing to be favored over background applications like the Web site. If it is set too low, that can cause the server to act sluggish from the console. Setting the site at a nonstandard TCP port can make the site unavailable, but does not cause it to perform poorly. The difference between IDE and SCSI drives' performance is too subtle to display the symptoms described. See "Connections."

7. **D.** HTTP Keep-Alives Enabled can help alleviate the problem. Bandwidth throttling does not affect the number of hits reported. Logging has no impact at all on the number of hits reported. Setting the connection timeout might help the performance issue, but does not affect the number of hits per user. See "HHTP Keep-Alives."

8. **A, C.** The Connection Timeout and Connection Limited To value pertain to both FTP and WWW sites. You cannot enable bandwidth throttling for the FTP service, and you cannot redirect an URL for the FTP service. See "Connections."

9. **C.** The default maximum size of news articles that can be posted to a Microsoft NNTP Service news server is 1,000KB. See "Optimizing the Performance of the NNTP Service."

10. **A, C, D.** Only File Listings is a valid IIS Global object. See "Optimizing the Performance of IIS."

11. **B.** When free space drops below 3MB, Index Server stops running. To get it running again, just clear more disk space. It automatically restarts once there is enough available space. See "Optimizing the Performance of Index Server."

12. **B.** The amount of free space should be 40 percent of the corpus. See "Optimizing the Performance of Index Server."

13. **C.** When there is enough free space for the logging to run (greater than 3MB), IIS 4.0 automatically resumes logging. Although rebooting and restarting the server can't hurt the process, they are not necessary to get logging started again. Adding a hard drive also fixes the issue, but you do not need to reinstall IIS to move the logs to another drive. See "Optimizing the Performance of Index Server."

14. **C.** Run Usage Import and import the file in question. Although using databases is possible for logging, Report Writer needs the log files imported into the IIS 4.0 database before it can analyze the results. This eliminates the other selections. See "Importing Log Files into a Report Writer and Usage Import Database."

15. **D.** Items placed in a new job are called tasks. See "Automating the Use of Report Writer and Usage Import."

APPLY YOUR KNOWLEDGE

16. **C.** From the Web site's Service Master Properties dialog box, set the Connection Timeout field to a lower amount. A higher Connection Timeout allows inactive users to stay connected for an even longer period of time, wasting precious system resources. Enabling Unlimited Connections doesn't do anything to improve performance. There are no "Service Monitor" properties. See "Optimizing the Performance of IIS."

17. **B.** A minimum of 64MB is recommended for this many documents. 32MB only allows you to index 100,000 documents, and anything over 64MB is in excess of the minimum specified in the question. See "Optimizing the Performance of Index Server."

18. **A.** Use brackets to surround the IP address and increase performance. Microsoft SMTP then looks at the IP address as an actual IP address without looking at it as a string value first. See "Optimizing the Performance of the SMTP Service."

Suggested Readings and Resources

1. Edmead, Mark. *Windows NT Performance Monitoring.* New Riders Publishing: 1999.

2. Heywood, Drew. *Inside Windows NT 4.0 Server.* New Riders Publishing: 1997.

3. Howell, Nelson, and Forta, Ben. *Using Microsoft Internet Information Server 4 (Special Edition Using...).* Que Education and Training: 1997.

4. Siyan, Karanjit S. *Windows NT Server 4 Professional Reference.* New Riders Publishing: 1996.

This chapter will help you get ready for the Troubleshooting section of the exam. As with any product, there can be problems while installing or supporting an Internet Information Server 4 server. If you have provided any kind of computer support, you know that at least 50 percent of your time is spent figuring out why something isn't working the way that you think it should. Microsoft recognizes that a large part of an IIS support person's job will be providing that troubleshooting expertise, so this chapter will deal with troubleshooting a variety of issues that could arise during the installation and subsequent support of your IIS server(s). You can take Microsoft's recognition of the importance of this subject as an indication that it will be tested on heavily on this exam. For future reference, you should be aware that Microsoft emphasizes troubleshooting on most of their exams.

For the exam, Microsoft defines the Troubleshooting objectives as follows:

Resolve IIS configuration problems.

▶ After you have successfully installed IIS 4, the first step to resolve an issue is to make sure that IIS is configured correctly. For this objective, you should be familiar with all the configuration information we have discussed throughout the rest of this book, as well as understand where to look when problems occur.

Resolve security problems.

▶ Information security and resource access are two sides of the same issue. When you have a security issue, that means someone who should not be able to access a resource can access it. For this objective, you need to understand the mechanisms that IIS provides for securing resources and the steps for locating problems.

CHAPTER 7

Troubleshooting

Resolve resource access problems.

▶ This is the other side of the security objective. A resource access problem occurs when someone who should have access to a resource does not. This loss of access can be due to incorrect setup, improper security restrictions, or even incorrect user IDs or passwords. For this objective, you should know how to determine what access a user has and the IIS mechanisms for providing and restricting resource access.

Resolve Index Server query problems.

▶ Index Server provides the ability to search an IIS server for information. Problems will generally involve incorrect information being returned from a query or no information returned at all. To understand the requirements of this objective, be familiar with the process of submitting a query and receiving the result. Also, be sure you understand the functions of the various scripts used for these queries.

Resolve setup issues when installing IIS on a Windows NT Server 4.0 computer.

▶ This should probably be the first objective because you really won't see any of the other problems described in these objectives until IIS has been installed. But you'll notice that the objectives are tackled in the order in which Microsoft presents them. It goes without saying that although installing IIS can be a trouble-free process, there are sometimes problems that occur when installing any complex software product. Quite a few of the installation issues are related to inadequate or custom hardware that cannot support the application.

You also need an adequate processor and enough memory to complete the installation. For this objective, you should understand the minimum hardware requirements for IIS.

Use a WebMap to find and repair broken links.

▶ In a perfect world, every Web site you ever deployed would be perfectly designed and implemented. Every link would move you to the correct page and your site would be perfect—no nasty "404: File Not Found" errors for you customers. Unfortunately, there are occasionally problems with even the most perfectly designed site. For this objective, you should understand how to use the WebMap utility to find and correct issues with your site.

Resolve WWW service problems.

▶ Problems with WWW service are typically the first issues you will receive calls on with an IIS server because the WWW is the interface used to access the rest of an IIS server's resources. For this objective, you need to understand how the WWW service works, and how to locate a problem when there is one.

Resolve FTP service problems.

▶ If your IIS server is used for uploading and downloading files, problems with FTP are almost as quickly discovered as WWW problems. For this objective, you should be familiar with the common settings for the FTP service, as well as the steps you should take to troubleshoot an FTP issue.

In the previous chapters, we discussed study strategies that focused on portions of the objectives that Microsoft considered to be particularly important, generally based on the key concepts of a particular section. For example, in Chapter 1, "Planning," Microsoft considers the ability to choose the correct IIS service to address a customer requirement to be particularly important. If you are not able to select the best service, you probably aren't ready to be deploying IIS in a production environment. Microsoft ties their objectives to real-world requirements as much as possible in a testing environment. For that reason, it is very difficult to pick and choose sections of this particular chapter for you to concentrate on. Microsoft considers the ability to troubleshoot issues with its products to be extremely important in its entirety, and you should be prepared to see questions on virtually every facet of the process. One thing you should keep in mind when you are troubleshooting any technical issue is the following seven-step method:

1. **Determine the problem.** The first step in any troubleshooting process is problem determination. After you know exactly what the problem is, you can start to tackle the solution.

2. **Isolate the related components.** Whether you are troubleshooting hardware or software problems, you should determine what components are related to your problem. In a PC with no video, your related components are the monitor, the video adapter, and the cable. For a Web page that is displayed incorrectly, you must consider the browser and the WWW service, as well as the related HTML and graphic files. Know what's involved before you start trying to correct this issue.

3. **Figure out if anything has changed.** In a majority of technical issues with a product or service that has stopped working, the problem is not because something has failed, but because something has changed. Did one of the administrators install a patch to a different application? Did the network

group upgrade router software? The list of possibilities could go on indefinitely. If you can find something that has changed, you are usually on the track to a solution.

4. **Plan your resolution.** The worst thing you can do while troubleshooting a problem is to start throwing solutions at it. Many administrators have a tendency to give in to the urgency of a problem and rush to fix it and can inadvertently make things worse. Be methodical. Make a plan to resolve the issue and stick to it. Try to anticipate what your next step will be if your first attempt doesn't correct the issue.

5. **Fix it.** After you have completed your plan, it's time to fix the problem.

6. **Test it.** If your fix was effective, move on to step 7. If it didn't fix the problem, start over at step 1.

7. **Document it.** If the same problem occurs next year, it would be great to be able to refer to the solution you used the last time it occurred. Chances are you won't remember exactly how you did it. Or even better, if you are on the beach in Cancun, it would be nice if your backup could look up the solution rather than page you just as you were headed into the water.

The preceding steps apply to any situation in which you need to troubleshoot a problem. The main thing is to be methodical and take your time. Even in a critical situation, the person who can step back and analyze a problem will generally solve the problem before the person who rushes and starts applying patches and changing settings. The same can be said for the troubleshooting questions you may encounter on the exam. Step back and analyze the entire question. Make sure you understand exactly the problem being described and what the result needs to be. Then, read all the answers. Make your decision after you fully understand the question and the answers.

That being said, there are a few key items you might want to make sure you know as you go through the chapter. Concentrate on the following key concepts:

▶ Know the hardware and software requirements for a successful IIS implementation.

▶ Know the steps involved in troubleshooting a misbehaving service, especially the WWW and FTP services.

▶ Be sure you understand how to allow or deny access to the site by IP address. Pay close attention to whether the site is set to deny access to the listed addresses or permit access.

▶ Understand the NTFS permissions and how they apply to accessing IIS resources.

▶ Know what file type is used to query Index Server and what file type is used to format the results. You shouldn't need to memorize all the different variables used in the files. Debugging code is beyond the scope of this exam.

INTRODUCTION

This chapter discusses the different components of Microsoft Internet Information Server 4 and, unlike previous chapters, discusses how to fix them if they are broken. The chapter focuses on IIS configuration issues, starting with installation. Due to the integral nature of TCP/IP in an Internet/intranet environment and the many potential problems with TCP/IP configurations, potential issues, and troubleshooting techniques are discussed at length. Next, specific IIS services are covered, including WWW, FTP, Index Server, and ODBC connection issues. The chapter concludes with an examination of some other resources available when you have an issue, and using WebMaps to troubleshoot Web site issues.

RESOLVING IIS CONFIGURATION PROBLEMS

IIS problems can be broken down into three basic categories. First, there are installation problems. These always occur during the installation of IIS for the first time or when you try to add a service that you had skipped during the initial installation.

Next, there are service problems. These are frequently typified by one sort of service being available, whereas another is not. If you can open the home page in your browser, but can't FTP a file, for example, you should probably look at the FTP service.

Finally, and usually the most complex, are the configuration problems. These can be anything from issues with security to broken links on your Web site. Each of these types of problems, and the steps to resolve them, are discussed in this chapter. Jump right into it by looking at common installation problems.

Installation Problems

The first thing you need to consider if you are confronting installation issues is whether your hardware is up to the task. Before you set up IIS 4, your system must meet or exceed the hardware requirements described in Tables 7.1 and 7.2. Table 7.1 shows requirements for a system running an Intel x86 processor; Table 7.2 lists requirements for a system running a DEC Alpha processor.

TABLE 7.1

IIS 4 HARDWARE REQUIREMENTS FOR AN INTEL SYSTEM

Hardware Device	Requirements
CPU	Minimum of a 66MHZ 486 DX processor. For better performance, you need a Pentium 133 or higher processor.
Hard disk space	Minimum of 30MB, but it is recommended that you have at least 120MB. This does not include storage needed for files you plan to distribute via IIS.
Memory	Minimum of 32MB. For a Web site on which you will store multimedia files or expect a great deal of traffic, 48MB is the recommended minimum.
Monitor	Super VGA monitor with 800×600 resolution.

TABLE 7.2

IIS 4 HARDWARE REQUIREMENTS FOR AN ALPHA SYSTEM

Hardware Device	Requirements
CPU	Minimum of 150MHZ processor.
Hard disk space	Minimum of 120MB, but you should allocate up to 200MB for best performance.
Memory	Minimum of 48MB. For better performance, have at least 64MB.
Monitor	Super VGA monitor with 800×600 resolution.

While you are on the topic of hardware requirements, consider it an excellent idea to use hardware that is on Microsoft's Hardware Compatibility List (HCL), which you can find on Microsoft's Web site (http://www.microsoft.com) or on the Microsoft TechNet CD. Use of non-HCL hardware can lead to odd problems with the Windows NT operating system and, subsequently, on your IIS installation.

Before installing IIS, make sure the following software is installed:

♦ Windows NT Server 4.0

♦ Service Pack 3 for Windows NT Server 4.0

♦ Internet Explorer (4.01 or higher) (This is included on the Windows NT 4.0 Option Pack CD, should you not have a copy already installed.)

You also must be logged on to the Windows NT Server computer with Administrator privileges. Failing to have proper permissions or the required software installed almost always guarantees a failed installation.

Another place you may encounter an issue is when you try to install a service after the initial IIS installation is complete. For example, when you first installed IIS, you may not have needed Microsoft Transaction Server (MTS). Later, the manager of your Web Development group needs to deploy an application that relies on MTS. You break out your IIS media, go back into setup, and then have a problem installing MTS. Start with the basics. Make sure you still have enough disk space and enough memory to add the application—things might have changed since you originally installed IIS. You should also make sure you haven't loaded any additional applications or services to the server, which might have taken some of the resources originally allocated to IIS.

After you've gotten IIS successfully installed, it's time to look at the myriad of other issues that might crop up while you are using the server.

> **NOTE**
> **Revisiting Planning**   As was noted in Chapter 1, "Planning," before you install IIS 4, remove any installations of a previous version of IIS. You'll also need to disable other versions of FTP, Gopher, or World Wide Web services you have installed under Windows NT Server 4.0. This includes the Windows Academic Center service included with the Windows NT Resource Kit.

> **NOTE**
> **Installing SMTP**   To install the SMTP Service, you need to have an NTFS partition in which to install it.

TCP/IP Problems

A very common issue you will find with any server is the ability to get to the server over the network. This can be particularly troublesome with an IIS server because it is totally reliant on a stable, properly configured TCP/IP infrastructure. There are three main parameters that specify how TCP/IP is configured on a host with the ability to communicate beyond its local segment: the IP address, the subnet mask, and the default gateway (which is the address of a router on that subnet). The Protocols tab of Network applet lists all the installed protocols. Selecting the TCP/IP protocol and clicking on the Properties button

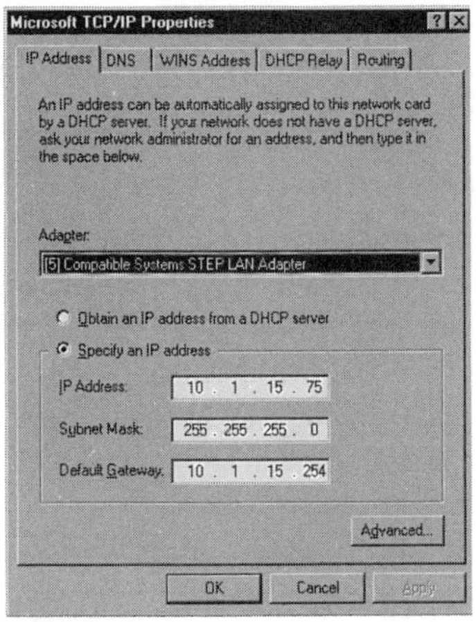

FIGURE 7.1
From this tab, you can make sure that the three components of the IP address are correctly configured. Pay close attention to the subnet mask; a misconfigured subnet mask might allow you to access some hosts but not others. It can be a very deceptive problem.

> **NOTE**
>
> **Client Configuration Problems**   While you are studying server issues in this section, keep in mind that clients can have the same problems. If you have a user who cannot access the server, it is generally a good idea to check the same items on the workstation as those discussed for the server.

---

will allow you to configure the protocol. The IP Address tab allows you to configure these parameters, as shown in Figure 7.1.

Although it's possible to receive an IP address from a DHCP server, that is not generally a good idea with a server. It is usually much easier to assign servers a static address, and then ensure that your DHCP server doesn't issue that address to another workstation. For more information, DHCP-related issues are discussed in the later section, "DHCP Client Configuration Problems."

These three TCP/IP parameters must be correctly configured for you to be able to connect with TCP/IP. An incorrect configuration can result from typographical errors; if you type the wrong IP address, subnet mask, or default gateway, you may not connect properly or even be able to connect at all. An easy way to think of this is to make a comparison to a telephone call. If you dial the wrong number when making a telephone call, you won't reach the person you want to talk to. If you read the wrong phone number out of the phone book, you won't ever make a correct call, even if you repeatedly dial the number you think is correct.

Whether the TCP/IP configuration parameters are wrong due to a typo or to a mistaken address, you will find it difficult to connect as you need to. Different types of problems occur when each of these parameters has a configuration error.

IP Address Configuration Problems

Although an incorrect TCP/IP address almost always causes problems, there are some instances when it does not. If you configure an IP address that's on the correct subnet but uses the wrong host ID and isn't a duplicate, the client may be able to communicate just fine. If, however, the correct IP address has been entered in a static file or database that resolves host names to IP addresses, such as an LMHOSTS file or a DNS database file, you will not connect to the intended server.

For more information on TCP/IP, see Chapter 1, or Appendix F, "TCP/IP and Subnetting."

The other side of this problem occurs when the correct address was entered in static files, such as a HOSTS file or a DNS database, but an incorrect address is entered elsewhere. In this case, no one can communicate with this client by name because the name resolution for this host always returns the correct address, which can't be used to contact the host because the address has been incorrectly typed. Basically, the problems you encounter with an incorrect host address are intermittent.

The bottom line for this type of an issue is to always double-check your addressing, including both the local address as well as the entries in a HOSTS file or in DNS.

Subnet Mask

The *subnet mask* specifies which portion of the IP address specifies the network address and which portion of the address specifies the host address. The subnet mask also can be used to take part of what would have been the host address and use it to further divide the network into subnets. If the subnet mask isn't correctly configured, your clients may not be able to communicate at all, or you may see partial communication problems.

Figure 7.2 shows a subnet on a TCP/IP network. The network uses a Class B network address of 138.13.x.x. However, the third octet is used in this case for subnetting, so all the clients in the figure should be on subnet 4, as indicated by the common addresses 138.13.4.x. Unfortunately, the subnet mask entered for one client is 255.255.0.0. When this client tries to communicate with other hosts on the same subnet, it should be able to contact them because the subnet mask indicates they are on the same subnet, which is correct.

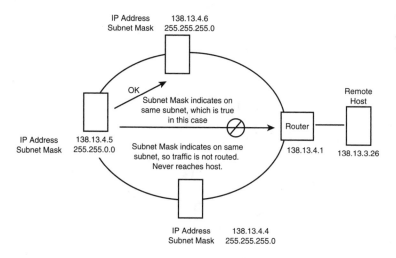

FIGURE 7.2
An incorrectly configured subnet mask (missing the third octet).

If the client tries to contact a host on another subnet, however, such as 138.13.3.x, the client fails. In this case, the subnet mask still interprets the destination host to be on the same subnet and the message is never routed. Because the destination host is on another subnet, the message never reaches the intended destination. The subnet mask is used to determine routing for outgoing communications, so the client with the incorrect subnet mask can receive incoming messages. However, when the client tries to return communications, the message isn't routed if the source host is on the same network but on a different subnet. So, in actuality, the client really can establish communications with only one side of the conversation. Contact with hosts outside the local network still works because those contacts are routed.

Figure 7.3 shows a subnet mask that masks too many bits. In this case, the subnet mask is 255.255.255.0. However, the network designers had intended the subnet mask to be 255.255.240.0, with four bits of the third octet used for the subnet and four bits as part of the host address. If the incorrect client tries to send a message to a local host and the third octet is the same, the message is not routed and reaches the local client. However, if the local client has an address that differs in the last four bits of the third octet, the message is routed and never reaches its destination. If the incorrect client tries to send a message to another client on another subnet, the message is routed because the third octet is different.

FIGURE 7.3
An incorrectly configured subnet mask (wrong third octet).

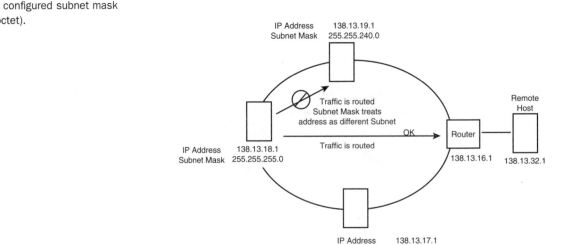

Default Gateway

The *default gateway* address is the address of the router, the gateway to the network beyond the local subnet. If the default gateway address is wrong, the client can contact local hosts but cannot communicate beyond the local subnet. It's possible for the incorrect client to receive a packet from another host because the default gateway is used only to send packets to other hosts. However, as soon as the incorrect client attempts to respond to the incoming packet, the response is unable to leave the local subnet due to the incorrect default gateway address.

So, if you can reach hosts on the local network, but not on networks beyond, the default gateway should be the first place you look.

NOTE **Subnet Mask Problems** Problems with the subnet mask might appear as intermittent connections. Sometimes the connection works, sometimes it doesn't. The problems show up when the IP address of the destination host causes a packet to be routed when it shouldn't or to remain local when the packet should be routed.

DHCP Client Configuration Problems

All the TCP/IP parameters previously mentioned can cause communication problems if they're not configured correctly. Using a DHCP server can greatly reduce these configuration problems. If the DHCP scope is set up properly, without any typos or other configuration errors, DHCP clients shouldn't have any configuration problems. It's impossible to completely eliminate human error, but using DHCP should restrict the points of potential errors to just the DHCP servers rather than every client on the network.

Even when there are no configuration problems with DHCP addresses, DHCP clients can obtain a duplicate IP address from a DHCP server. If you have multiple DHCP servers in your environment, you should have scopes on each DCHP server for different subnets. Usually, you have scopes with a larger number of addresses for the local subnet on which the DHCP server is located and smaller scopes for other subnets. Creating multiple scopes on one server provides backup for giving clients IP addresses. If the server on the local scope is busy or down, the client can still receive an address from a remote DHCP server. When the router forwards this DHCP request to another subnet's server, it includes the address of the subnet it came from. That way, the remote DHCP server knows from which subnet scope of addresses to lease an address to the remote client. Using this type of redundancy, however, can cause problems if you don't configure the scopes on all the DHCP servers correctly.

For more information on DHCP, check Appendix F. Also, keep in mind that this is a key concept for the TCP/IP exam, one of the more popular MCSE electives.

NOTE **Should Servers Also Be DHCP Clients?** It's important to mention that servers are generally not DHCP clients, due to their nature. DHCP will significantly reduce the number of client configuration issues you will see on your network.

The most important part of the configuration is to make sure you don't have duplicate addresses in the different scopes. On one server, for example, you could have a scope in the range 131.107.2.100 to 131.107.2.170. On the remote DHCP server, you could have a scope of 131.107.2.171 to 131.107.2.200. By setting up the scopes without overlap, you should not have any problems with clients receiving duplicate IP addresses. DHCP servers don't communicate with each other, so one server doesn't know anything about the addresses the other server has leased. Therefore, you must ensure that the servers never give out duplicate information by making sure the scopes for one subnet on all the different DHCP servers have unique IP addresses. One other thing: Any reservations you have made for hosts not using DHCP must exist on both DHCP servers.

Another common problem with having multiple scopes on one server is entering the configuration parameters correctly. For example, if you enter the default gateway as 131.107.3.1 (instead of 131.107.2.1) for the scope 131.107.2.100 to 131.107.2.170, the clients receiving these addresses won't be able to communicate beyond the local subnet because they have the wrong router address. With one scope on a DHCP server, you're usually quite sure of what all the configuration parameters should be. With multiple scopes on one server, however, it's easy to get confused about which scope you're editing and what the parameters should be for that scope. To avoid this type of problem, check each scope's parameters very carefully to make sure the parameters match the address of the scope, not the subnet where the DHCP server is located.

Also, if the client doesn't receive an address because the server is down, or doesn't respond in a timely manner, the client isn't able to contact anyone. Without an IP address, the IP stack doesn't initialize and the client can't communicate at all with TCP/IP. There are a number of ways to troubleshoot issues with the TCP/IP configuration that need to be discussed at this point.

Using IPCONFIG to Resolve DHCP Address Problems

When a DHCP client receives an IP that isn't configured correctly, or if the client doesn't get an IP address at all, IPCONFIG can be used to resolve these problems. If the client gets incorrect IP parameters, it should be apparent from the results of IPCONFIG /all. You should be able to see that some of the parameters don't match the IP address or that some parameters are completely blank. For example, you could have the wrong default gateway (in which case the entry would not appear), or the client might not be configured to be a WINS client.

When a DHCP client fails to receive an address, the results of IPCONFIG /all are different. In this case, the client has an IP address of 0.0.0.0—an invalid address—and the DHCP server is 255.255.255.255—a broadcast address.

To fix this problem, you can release the incorrect address with IPCONFIG /release and then try to obtain a new IP address with IPCONFIG /renew. The IPCONFIG /renew command sends out a new request for a DHCP address. If a DHCP server is available, the server responds with the lease of an IP address. If there is no response, then it sends a request for a new one.

In many cases, the DHCP client acquires the same address after releasing and renewing. That the client receives the same address indicates that the same DHCP server responded to the renewal request and gave out the address that had just been released back into the pool of available addresses. If you need to renew an address because the parameters of the scope are incorrect, you must fix the parameters in DHCP configuration before releasing and renewing the address. Otherwise, the client could receive the same address again with the same incorrect parameters.

NOTE **Fixing DHCP** Occasionally, a DHCP client won't acquire an address regardless of how many times you release and renew the address. One way to try to fix the problem is to manually assign a static IP address to the client. After the client is configured with this address, which you can verify by using IPCONFIG, switch back to DHCP.

Microsoft IP Configuration Troubleshooting Utilities

A number of tools come with TCP/IP when the protocol is installed on a Windows NT computer. After you have resolved any problems caused by the Windows NT network configuration, you can then focus on using the TCP/IP tools to solve IP problems. Some tools can be used to verify the configuration parameters. Other tools can be used to test the connectivity capabilities of TCP/IP as configured.

Using PING to Test an IP Configuration

PING is a command-line tool included with every Microsoft TCP/IP client (any DOS or Windows client with the TCP/IP protocol installed). You can use PING to send a test packet to the specified address. If things are working properly, the packet is returned. Figure 7.4 shows the results of a successful PING command. Note that four successful responses are returned. Unsuccessful pings can result in different messages, depending on the type of problem PING encounters while trying to send and receive the test packet.

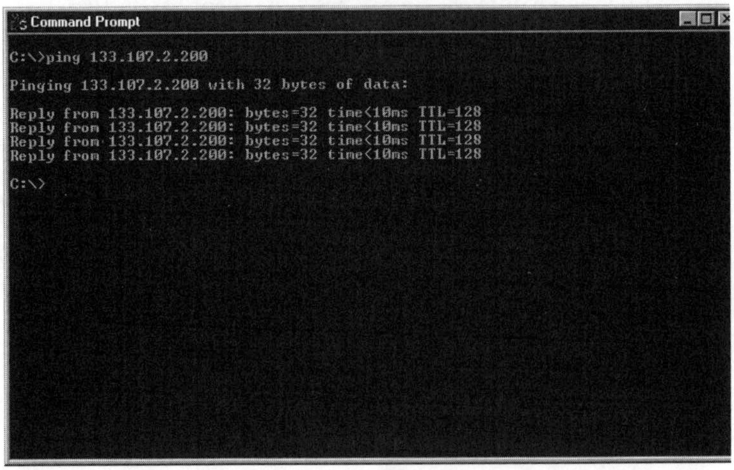

FIGURE 7.4
A successful PING of a host.

```
Command Prompt                                                    _ □ x

C:\>ping 133.107.2.200

Pinging 133.107.2.200 with 32 bytes of data:

Reply from 133.107.2.200: bytes=32 time<10ms TTL=128
Reply from 133.107.2.200: bytes=32 time<10ms TTL=128
Reply from 133.107.2.200: bytes=32 time<10ms TTL=128
Reply from 133.107.2.200: bytes=32 time<10ms TTL=128

C:\>
```

Although PING is a simple tool to use (from the command prompt, type **PING** with the IP address or host name you want to PING), choosing what to PING is the key to using it for successful troubleshooting. The remainder of this section covers which IP addresses or hosts you should ping to troubleshoot TCP/IP connectivity problems.

Troubleshooting IP Protocol Installation by PINGing the Loopback Address

The first step in troubleshooting many problems is to verify that TCP/IP installed correctly on the client. You can look at the configuration through the Network Properties dialog box or with IPCONFIG, but to actually test the working status of the protocol stack, you should try to PING the loopback address. The loopback address is 127.0.0.1. When you ping this address, a packet isn't sent on the network. PING simply sends a packet down through the layers of the IP architecture and then up the layers again. If TCP/IP is installed correctly, you should receive an immediate successful response. If IP isn't installed correctly, the response fails.

To correct problems of this type, you should verify that the NT network configuration and the protocol installation. You can check the following items:

◆ Make sure TCP/IP is listed on the installed protocols.

◆ Make sure the network adapter card is correctly configured.

◆ Make sure TCP/IP shows up in the bindings for the adapter card and that the bindings aren't disabled for TCP/IP.

◆ Check the system log for any errors indicating that the network services didn't start.

If you try the preceding steps, including rebooting the system, and have no success, you may have to remove TCP/IP and install it again. Sometimes, Windows NT gets hung up somewhere and thinks things are really installed when they are not. Removing the protocol and then installing it again can often resolve this halfway state.

Troubleshooting Client Address Configuration by PINGing Local Addresses

After you have verified that TCP/IP is installed correctly, you should PING the address of the local host. PING the IP address that you think is configured for the host you are having an issue with. You should receive an immediate successful reply if the client address is configured as specified in the PING command. You also can PING the name of the local host, but problems with name resolution are discussed later in the section "Diagnosing and Resolving Name Resolution Problems." For the moment, you are concerned with raw TCP/IP connectivity—the capability to communicate with another IP host by using its IP address.

Correcting a failure at this level concerns checking the way the client's address was configured. Was the address typed in correctly? Did the client receive the IP address from the DHCP server that you expected? Also, does the client have a connection on the network? PINGing the local host address doesn't cause a packet to be sent on the network, so if you have lost network connectivity, this PING won't indicate a network failure.

Troubleshooting Router Problems by PINGing the Default Gateway

If you can communicate with hosts on the same subnet but cannot establish communications with hosts beyond the subnet, the problem may be with the router or the way its address is configured. To communicate beyond the subnet, a router must be enabled with an address that matches the subnet address for the clients on the local subnet. The router also has other ports configured with different addresses, so it can send packets out to the network at large. PINGing the default gateway address tests the address you have configured for the router and tests the router itself.

If the default gateway PING fails, there are several possible sources for the error:

♦ **The router has failed or is down.** In this case, you cannot make connections outside the subnet until the router is brought up again. However, you should be able to communicate with hosts on the same subnet.

♦ **The client has lost a physical connection with the router or with the network.** You can test a network connection at a hardware level and also through the software by trying to establish a session with a server with another protocol, such as NetBEUI, for example. If you only have TCP/IP on your network, you can temporarily install NetBEUI on the client and on another computer on the same subnet. Test connectivity by connecting to a file share on the other computer. Remember, the computer should be on the same subnet because NetBEUI packets don't route (but may be bridged).

♦ **The IP address on the router may be configured incorrectly.** The router address must match the client's default gateway address so that packets can move outside the subnet.

♦ **The client has the wrong router address.** Of course, if you PING the correct router address and it works, you also want to make sure the default gateway address configured on the client matches the address you successfully pinged.

♦ **The wrong subnet mask is configured.** If the subnet mask is wrong, packets destined for a remote subnet may not be routed.

You should also PING each of the IP addresses used by the different ports on your router. It's possible that the local interface for your subnet is working but other interfaces on the router, which actually connect the router to the other subnets on the network, have some type of problem.

PINGing a Remote Host

As a final test in using PING, you can PING the IP address of a remote host, a computer on another subnet, or even the IP address of a Web server or FTP server on the Internet. If you can successfully PING a remote host, your problem doesn't lie with the IP configuration; you're probably having trouble resolving host names.

If PINGing the remote host fails, your problems may be with the router, the subnet mask, or the local IP configuration. However, if you have followed the earlier steps of PINGing the loopback, local host address, and the default gateway address, you have already eliminated many of the problems that could cause this PING to fail.

When a remote host PING fails after you have tried the other PING options, the failure may be due to other routers beyond the default gateway used for your subnet. If you know the physical layout of your network, you can PING other router addresses along the path to the remote host to see where the trouble lies. Remember to PING the addresses on both sides of the router: the address that receives the packet and the address that forwards the packet on. You also can use the Route command, as described in the following section to find the path used to contact the remote host.

It is also possible that there is not a physical path to the remote host due to a router problem, a disruption in the physical network, or a problem on the remote host.

Many troubleshooters prefer to simply try this last step when using PING to troubleshoot IP configuration and connectivity. If you can successfully PING a remote host, then the other layers of TCP/IP must be working correctly. In order for a packet to reach a remote host, IP must be installed correctly, the local client address must be configured properly, and the packet must be routed. If a PING to the remote host works, then you can look to other sources (usually name resolution) for your connection problems. If the PING fails, you can try each of the previous steps until you find the layer where the problem is located. Then you can resolve the problem at that layer.

You can either start by PINGing the loopback address and working up through the architecture, or you can PING the remote host. Of course, if PINGing the remote host works, you can stop. If not, you can work back through the architecture until you find a layer where PING succeeds. The problem must therefore be at the next layer.

Diagnosing and Resolving Name Resolution Problems

Name resolution problems are easily identified as such with the PING utility. If you can ping a host using its IP address, but cannot PING it by its host name, then you have a resolution problem. If you cannot PING the host at all, then the problem lies elsewhere.

Problems that can occur with name resolution and their solutions fit into the following categories:

◆ **The entry is misspelled.** Examine the HOSTS or LMHOSTS file to verify that the host name is correctly spelled. If you're using the HOSTS file on a system prior to Windows NT 4.0, capitalization is important because this file is case sensitive; LMHOSTS, on the other hand, is not case sensitive (regardless of the Windows NT version number).

◆ **Comment characters prevent the entry from being read.** Verify that a pound sign is not at the beginning of the line (with the exception of entries such as #PRE and #DOM, in LMHOSTS only) or anywhere on the line prior to the host name.

◆ **There are duplicate entries in the file.** Because the files are read in linear fashion, where there is duplication, only the first entry is read and all others are ignored. Verify that all host names are unique.

◆ **A host other than the one you want is contacted.** Verify that the IP address entered in the file(s) is valid and corresponds to the host name.

◆ **The wrong file is used.** Although similar in nature, HOSTS and LMHOSTS are really quite different, and not all that interchangeable. HOSTS is used to map IP addresses to host names, and LMHOSTS is used to map NetBIOS names to IP addresses.

In addition to PING, the all-purpose TCP/IP troubleshooting tool, useful name-resolution utilities include the following:

◆ TRACERT

◆ NETSTAT

◆ NBTSTAT

◆ HOSTNAME

TRACERT

TRACERT.EXE uses the same ICMP protocol as PING, but it uses it not only to determine if a device is active, but also to determine the path the packets take, by having each intermediate device respond. This is particularly useful in a large network, where you are trying to determine where delays or outages are between one device and another. Like PING, TRACERT has a number of options, which can be displayed by typing **TRACERT** with no options selected:

◆ **-d.** Do not resolve addresses to host names.

◆ **-h** *host-list.* Maximum number of hops to search for target.

◆ **-j** *host-list.* Loose source route along host-list.

◆ **-w** *timeout.* Wait timeout milliseconds for each reply.

NETSTAT

NETSTAT.EXE, although not used a great deal in day-to-day support, provides a great way to see what's happening with your TCP/IP packets. It can show you what your active connections are, as well as provide you with a number of statistics. The switches and the information they provide include the following:

◆ **-a.** Displays all connections and listening ports. (Server-side connections are normally not shown.)

◆ **-e.** Displays Ethernet statistics. This may be combined with the -s option.

◆ **-n.** Displays addresses and port numbers in numerical form.

◆ **-p** *proto.* Shows connections for the protocol specified by *proto*; *proto* may be tcp or udp. If used with the -s option to display per-protocol statistics, *proto* may be tcp, udp, or ip.

- ◆ **-r.** Displays the contents of the routing table.

- ◆ **-s.** Displays per-protocol statistics. By default, statistics are shown for TCP, UDP and IP; the -p option may be used to specify a subset of the default.

- ◆ *interval.* Redisplays selected statistics, pausing *interval* seconds between each display. Press Ctrl+C to stop redisplaying statistics. If omitted, NETSTAT will print the current configuration information once.

NBTSTAT

The NBTSTAT (NetBIOS over TCP/IP) utility displays protocol statistics and current TCP/IP connections. It is useful for troubleshooting NetBIOS name resolution problems, and has a number of parameters and options that can be used with it:

- ◆ **-a (adapter status).** Lists the remote machine's name table, given its name.

- ◆ **-A (Adapter status).** Lists the remote machine's name table, given its IP address.

- ◆ **-c (cache).** Lists the remote name cache, including the IP addresses.

- ◆ **-n (names).** Lists local NetBIOS names.

- ◆ **-r (resolved).** Lists names resolved by broadcast and via WINS.

- ◆ **-R (Reload).** Purges and reloads the remote cache name table.

- ◆ **-S (Sessions).** Lists sessions table with the destination IP addresses.

- ◆ **-s (sessions).** Lists sessions table converting destination IP addresses to host names via the LMHOSTS file.

HOSTNAME

The HOSTNAME.EXE utility, located in \systemroot\System32 returns the name of the local host. This is used only to view the name and cannot be used to change the name. The host name is changed from the Network Control Panel applet.

If you have configured TCP/IP correctly and the protocol is installed and working, then the problem with connectivity is probably due to errors in resolving host names. When you test connectivity with TCP/IP addresses, you are testing a lower level of connectivity than users generally use. When users want to connect to a network resource, such as mapping a drive to a server or connecting to a Web site, they usually refer to that server or Web site by its name rather than its TCP/IP address. In fact, users do not usually know the IP address of a particular server.

The name used to establish a connection must be resolved down to an IP address so that the networking software can make a connection. After you've tested the IP connectivity, the next logical step is to check the resolution of a name down to its IP address. If a name cannot be resolved to its IP address or if it is resolved to the wrong address, users won't be able to connect to the network resource with that name, even if you can connect to it using an IP address.

Two types of computer names are used when communicating on the network. A NetBIOS name is assigned to a Microsoft computer, such as a Windows NT server or a Windows 95 client. A host name is assigned to a non-Microsoft computer, such as a UNIX server. (Host names also can be assigned to a Windows NT server running Internet Information Server. For example, the name www.microsoft.com refers to a Web server on the Microsoft Web site. This server is running on Windows NT.) In general, when using Microsoft networking, such as connecting to a server for file sharing, print sharing, or applications, you refer to that computer by its NetBIOS name. When executing a TCP/IP-specific command, such as FTP or using a Web browser, you refer to that computer by its host name.

A NetBIOS name can be resolved to a TCP/IP address in several ways. Figure 7.5 shows an example of how NetBIOS names are resolved. The TCP/IP client initiating a session first looks in its local name cache. If the client cannot find the name in a local cache, a local Hosts, or an LMHosts file, it then queries a WINS server if it is configured to be a WINS client. If the WINS server cannot resolve the name, the client tries a broadcast that only reaches the local subnet, because routers, by default, aren't configured to forward broadcasts. Finally, if the client cannot resolve a name in any other way, it queries a DNS server if it has been configured to be a DNS client. However, if the client specifies a name longer than 15 characters (the maximum length of a NetBIOS name), the client first queries DNS before trying a HOSTS file or WINS.

FIGURE 7.5
Resolving NetBIOS names.

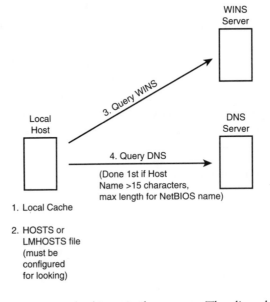

1. Local Cache

2. HOSTS or
   LMHOSTS file
   (must be
   configured
   for looking)

Host names are resolved in a similar manner. The client, however, checks sources that are used solely to resolve host names before trying sources that are used to resolve NetBIOS names. In resolving host names, the client first tries the local host name, then checks the HOSTS file next, followed by the DNS server (if it is configured to be a DNS client). These two sources only resolve host names. If the client cannot resolve the name, it checks the WINS server (if configured as a WINS client), tries a broadcast, then looks in the LMHOSTS file. The last three methods to resolve a name are used to resolve NetBIOS names, but it is possible for a host name to be listed in these sources.

Several tools are available to test name resolution. They are discussed in the following sections.

Testing Name Resolution with PING

Just as you can use PING to verify the TCP/IP configuration, you can also use PING to verify host name resolution. If you can successfully PING a host name, then you have verified TCP/IP communication from the Network Interface layer of the TCP/IP architecture to the Transport layer. When you PING a host name, a successful reply shows the IP address of the host. This shows that the name has been successfully resolved to an IP address and that you can communicate with that host.

Testing NetBIOS Name Resolution by Establishing a Session

The ultimate test of connectivity is to establish a session with another host. If you can establish a session through mapping a drive or by executing a Net Use command (which is the command-line equivalent of mapping a drive), you have made a NetBIOS connection. If you can FTP, Telnet, or establish a Web session with another host, you have made a Sockets connection. NetBIOS connection and Sockets connection are the two main types of connections made by a TCP/IP client.

After the drive has been mapped with Net Use, you can switch to the new drive letter, view files and directories, and do any other things that are specified in the permissions of the share mapped to the drive letter. To get more information about the syntax of the Net Use command, type **net help use** at a command prompt.

A common problem in making NetBIOS connections is that the wrong NetBIOS name is used. Verify that the destination host has the same name that you are using to make the connection.

Another potential problem with the name configuration occurs when NetBIOS scope IDs are used. Only NetBIOS hosts with the same scope ID can communicate with each other. The scope ID is configured through the advanced TCP/IP parameters. Incorrect share permissions can prevent you from establishing a NetBIOS session. When you try to connect a drive to a share where you have no access, you receive an Access Denied message. This message indicates that you can connect to the server, but your rights did not enable you to make a connection to this specific share. This type of failure has nothing to do with TCP/IP connectivity. Remember that if the administrator adds your account to a group that has access, and you want to try again, you must log out and log in again to receive a new access token with the updated permissions.

To resolve NetBIOS connectivity problems, you must know what sources are used to resolve NetBIOS names. The first place a client looks to resolve a NetBIOS name is the local cache. You can view the contents of the NetBIOS cache with the NBTSTAT command. You should verify that no incorrect entry is in the cache that maps the NetBIOS name to an incorrect IP address. If there is, however, you can remove the entry and then try to make another connection.

The next place to attempt NetBIOS name resolution is in a query to a WINS server. The client must be configured to be a WINS client. You can verify the address of the WINS server through the Advanced properties of TCP/IP or by using IPCONFIG /all. You can view the contents of the WINS database by using WINS Manager on the WINS server (or any computer where the management tools are installed). Verify that the host name is in the database and, if so, make sure it is mapped to the correct IP address.

If the WINS server is configured to do a DNS lookup, you have another way to get NetBIOS resolution. The WINS server queries DNS if the WINS server cannot resolve the name from its own database. You can view the contents of the DNS database files by using DNS Manager on the DNS server or by using the NSLOOKUP utility from any client.

Next, the client tries a broadcast to resolve NetBIOS names, although you cannot configure what the client finds through the broadcast. The next place the client looks for NetBIOS name resolution is the LMHOSTS file. You can configure the contents of this file. The client must be configured for LMHOSTS lookup in the advanced TCP/IP configuration. Also, the LMHOSTS file must be located in the correct directory path. On a Windows NT computer, the LMHOSTS file must be in the path <winnt root>\system32\drivers\etc.

Next, verify the entries in the LMHOSTS file. The correct host name and IP address must be entered in this file. If you have multiple entries in the file for a host name, only the first entry is used. If you added another entry for a host in the file, you must delete it so that it will not be used.

Domain names are another source of potential problems with LMHOSTS files in a non-WINS environment. The domain name must be registered with the IP address of the Primary Domain Controller (PDC) and #DOM (a switch that registers the server as a domain controller) on the same line. This entry is necessary to log on to the domain, as well as to see the domain in a browse list.

Another problem with LMHOSTS files doesn't prevent connectivity, but can greatly delay it. If you have #INCLUDE statements at the top of the LMHOSTS file, the files specified by #INCLUDE are included before any other entries lower in the LMHOSTS file are searched. You can speed connections to hosts entered in the LMHOSTS file by moving the #INCLUDE entries to the bottom of the LMHOSTS file.

Testing TCP Name Resolution by Establishing a Session

Typical TCP/IP connections from a Microsoft client, such as FTP or Telnet, use Windows Sockets. To test connectivity at this level, try establishing an FTP or Telnet session or try to connect to a Web server. When you successfully connect to a Web server, you see the site's Web page and you can navigate through the page. When the connection fails, you receive a message on your Internet browser that the connection has failed.

To resolve problems with a Windows Sockets connection, you must understand how a client resolves TCP/IP host names. The first place a client looks to resolve a host name is the local host name. You can see what TCP/IP thinks the local host name is by executing the HOSTNAME command. Verify the host name if the results of the HOSTNAME command confirm that the local host is not what you expect it to be. You can modify the host name in the DNS tab of the TCP/IP properties.

The next place the client looks is in a HOSTS file. This file must be located in the path <winnt root>\system32\drivers\etc. Verify that any entry in the file for the host is correct, with the correct host name and IP address. If multiple entries for the same host name are in the file, only the first name is used. The HOSTS file can also have links to HOSTS files on other servers. If links are specified in the local HOSTS file, you should make sure entries in the other HOSTS files also are correct.

The final place a client can use host name resolution is a DNS server. The client must be configured to use DNS on the DNS tab in the TCP/IP properties dialog box. The DNS server must have a zone file corresponding to the domain name specified in the host name, or it must be able to query another DNS server that can resolve the name.

RESOLVING SECURITY PROBLEMS

Security problems relate to a user or users being unable to utilize the resources you have made available to them—or to too many users being able to access what only a limited number should be able to access. There is an unlimited number of reasons why these situations could occur, based on what the resources are and how users access

N O T E

Security This section is not going to teach you how to be a security expert. Keep in mind that a truly secure environment is much more complicated than configuring IIS to keep users out of areas they shouldn't be in.

them. This section discusses a few of the more common problem areas in this section. For example, let's say your IIS server is also the office file server and the personnel files are on it. The last thing you want to have happen is someone inadvertently accessing the personnel files the week before you are up for your annual raise. It wouldn't do wonders for your increase.

Common Security Problems

This section covers a number of common problem areas with IIS security in this section. Keep in mind that some of these issues actually exist outside the IIS application.

In most Web server operations, you want to make the server available to as many users as possible. Unfortunately, this can lead to the risk of allowing in unwanted traffic. Some ways to combat this problem include using a firewall to restrict traffic, disabling anonymous access, or moving the Web server service to a port other than its default 80—essentially hiding it from the outside world (discussed in more detail in this chapter's section on resolving WWW service problems).

◆ **Firewalls.** Can be used to restrict incoming traffic to only those services you are choosing to allow in. Additionally, a firewall can be used to prevent all traffic from coming in. If you're attempting to make data available on the Web, consider putting the Web server outside the firewall and allowing traffic to pass to it but to nothing else on your network.

◆ **Anonymous usage.** A staple of most public Web sites. If you don't want to have a public Web site, however, consider disabling the logon. You can configure the Web server to use user authentication to verify that everyone accessing it has a valid Windows NT user account (they must give a username and password before being allowed to interact with the server).

◆ **Secure Sockets Layer (SSL) 3.0.** Included with IIS, its use should be mandatory on any site holding sensitive data (such as medical information, credit card information, and so on). SSL enables a secure connection to be established between the browser and the server, and encryption to be used between them.

◆ **Server Certificates.** A part of SSL, this can be created (unique digital identifications) to authenticate your Web site to browsers. This is used for public and private key (key pair) interactions of a secure nature.

◆ **NTFS permissions.** Can be used in conjunction with IIS to secure individual files and directories from those who should not access them. The five permission types follow:

   • **Change.** Users can read and modify files, including deleting them and adding new ones to a directory.

   • **Full Control.** The default for the Everyone group. Users can modify, move, delete, take ownership, and even change permissions.

   • **No Access.** Overrides everything and gives absolutely no access to the resource.

   • **Read.** As the name implies, users can read the data.

   • **Special Access.** User permissions have been set to something specific by the administrator.

From a security perspective, the No Access permission is the most powerful permission. When it is implemented, the user that has been assigned this permission has no access to that resource. It doesn't matter what other permissions have been assigned. The No Access permission overrides any other assigned permissions.

The Basic Steps in the Access Control Process

Solving most security problems involves using a great deal of common sense (if passwords are used, make them more than six characters in length and insist on mixed letters, numbers or characters, and so on) and understanding what is taking place. The following steps illustrate the access control process:

1. The Web server receives a request from the browser to perform an operation.

2. The Web server checks to see if the IP address is permitted. If there are no restrictions on IP address ranges, or the request is coming from a valid range, processing continues.

3. The Web server checks to see if the user is permitted. If anonymous access is not enabled, this means the user is prompted for a user ID and password. Avoid clear text authentications whenever possible.

4. The Web server checks to see if its own permissions will enable access.

5. A check is made to see if the NTFS permissions will enable access. This is based on the user ID and password used to authenticate. If anonymous access is permitted, the IUSR_*server name* user ID is used.

If any of the preceding steps fail, then the access is denied. If they all succeed, then access is granted.

RESOLVING WWW SERVICE ISSUES

This chapter has discussed at length how to deal with possible connectivity issues. Now take a look at what could be wrong when the WWW service has a problem.

The first place to look is in the Internet Service Manager application. This can be found in the Windows NT 4.0 Option Pack program group. Select the Microsoft Internet Information Server sub-group, and then select the Internet Service Manager application. This will open the Microsoft Management Console, shown in Figure 7.6.

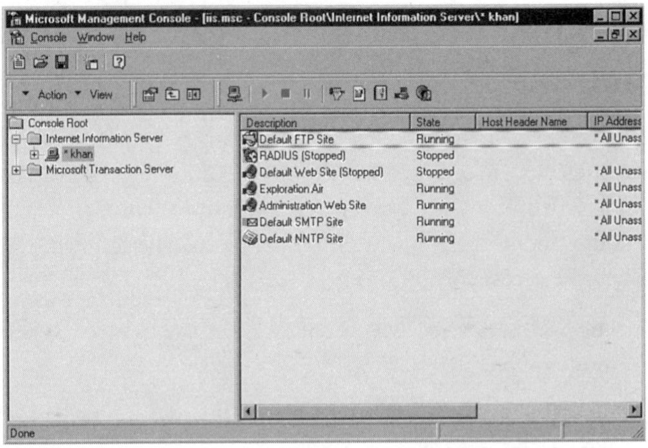

FIGURE 7.6
Use this application to troubleshoot the configuration of the IIS Server. In this case, be sure the WWW (or FTP) service for the site in question is actually running.

Verify that the service is running. Before you get into the service configuration, it's a good idea to be familiar with the errors you might see from a browser. These can be customized within IIS, but this list contains the default errors:

◆ **HTTP Error 400: 400 Bad Request.** Due to malformed syntax, the request could not be understood by the server. The client should not repeat the request without modifications.

◆ **HTTP Error 401 - 401.1 Unauthorized: Logon Failed.** This error indicates that the credentials passed to the server do not match the credentials required to log on to the server.

◆ **HTTP Error 401 - 401.2 Unauthorized: Logon Failed due to server configuration.** This error indicates that the credentials passed to the server do not match the credentials required to log on to the server. This is usually caused by not sending the proper WWW-Authenticate header field.

◆ **HTTP Error 401 - 401.3 Unauthorized: Unauthorized due to ACL on resource.** This error indicates that the credentials passed by the client do not have access to the particular resource on the server. This resource could be either the page or file listed in the address line of the client, or it could be another file on the server that is needed to process the file listed on the address line of the client.

◆ **HTTP Error 401 - 401.4 Unauthorized: Authorization failed by filter.** This error indicates that the Web server has a filter program installed to verify users connecting to the server. The authentication used to connect to the server was denied access by this filter program.

◆ **HTTP Error 401 - 401.5 Unauthorized: Authorization failed by ISAPI/CGI app.** This error indicates that the address on the Web server you attempted to use has an ISAPI or CGI program installed that verifies user credentials before proceeding. The authentication used to connect to the server was denied access by this program.

◆ **HTTP Error 403 - 403.1 Forbidden: Execute Access Forbidden.** This error can be caused if you try to execute a CGI, ISAPI, or other executable program from a directory that does not allow programs to be executed.

N O T E

Error Messages By default, these error messages can be found in HTML files in the WINNT\HELP\COMMON subdirectory.

◆ **HTTP Error 403 - 403.2 Forbidden: Read Access Forbidden.** This error can be caused if there is no default page available and directory browsing has not been enabled for the directory, or if you are trying to display an HTML page that resides in a directory marked for Execute or Script permissions only.

◆ **HTTP Error 403 - 403.3 Forbidden: Write Access Forbidden.** This error can be caused if you attempt to upload to, or modify a file in, a directory that does not allow Write access.

◆ **HTTP Error 403 - 403.4 Forbidden: SSL required.** This error indicates that the page you are trying to access is secured with Secure Sockets Layer (SSL). In order to view it, you need to enable SSL by typing **https://** at the beginning of the address you are attempting to reach.

◆ **HTTP Error 403 - 403.5 Forbidden: SSL 128 required.** This error message indicates that the resource you are trying to access is secured with a 128-bit version of Secure Sockets Layer (SSL). In order to view this resource, you need a browser that supports this level of SSL.

◆ **HTTP Error 403 - 403.6 Forbidden: IP address rejected.** This error is caused when the server has a list of IP addresses that are not allowed to access the site and the IP address you are using is in this list.

◆ **HTTP Error 403 - 403.7 Forbidden: Client certificate required.** This error occurs when the resource you are attempting to access requires your browser to have a client Secure Sockets Layer (SSL) certificate that the server recognizes. This is used for authenticating you as a valid user of the resource.

◆ **HTTP Error 403 - 403.8 Forbidden: Site access denied.** This error can be caused if the Web server is not servicing requests, or if you do not have permission to connect to the site.

◆ **HTTP Error 403 - 403.9 Access Forbidden: Too many users are connected.** This error can be caused if the Web server is busy and cannot process your request due to heavy traffic. Try to connect again later.

◆ **HTTP Error 403 - 403.10 Access Forbidden: Invalid Configuration.** There is a configuration problem on the Web server at this time.

◆ **HTTP Error 403 - 403.11 Access Forbidden: Password Change.** This error can be caused if the user has entered the wrong password during authentication. Refresh the page and try again.

◆ **HTTP Error 403 - 403.12 Access Forbidden: Mapper Denied Access.** Your client certificate map has been denied access to this Web site.

◆ **HTTP Error 404 - 404 Not Found.** The Web server cannot find the file or script you asked for. Check the URL to ensure that the path is correct.

◆ **HTTP Error 405 - 405 Method Not Allowed.** The method specified in the Request Line is not allowed for the resource identified by the request. Ensure that you have the proper MIME type set up for the resource you are requesting.

◆ **HTTP Error 406 - 406 Not Acceptable.** The resource identified by the request can only generate response entities that have content characteristics that are "not acceptable" according to the Accept headers sent in the request.

◆ **HTTP Error 407 - 407 Proxy Authentication Required.** You must authenticate with a proxy server before this request can be serviced. Log on to your proxy server and try again.

◆ **HTTP Error 412 - 412 Precondition Failed.** The precondition given in one or more of the Request-header fields evaluated to FALSE when it was tested on the server. The client placed preconditions on the current resource metainformation (header field data) to prevent the requested method from being applied to a resource other than the one intended.

◆ **HTTP Error 414 - 414 Request-URI Too Long.** The server is refusing to service the request because the Request-URI is too long. This rare condition is likely to occur only in the following situations:

• A client has improperly converted a POST request to a GET request with long query information.

- A client has encountered a redirection problem (for example, a redirected URL prefix that points to a suffix of itself).

- The server is under attack by a client attempting to exploit security holes present in some servers using fixed-length buffers for reading or manipulating the Request-URI.

◆ **HTTP Error 500 - 500 Internal Server Error.** The Web server is incapable of performing the request. Try your request again later.

◆ **HTTP Error 501 - 501 Not Implemented.** The Web server does not support the functionality required to fulfill the request.

◆ **HTTP Error 502 - 502 Bad Gateway.** The server, while acting as a gateway or proxy, received an invalid response from the upstream server it accessed in attempting to fulfill the request.

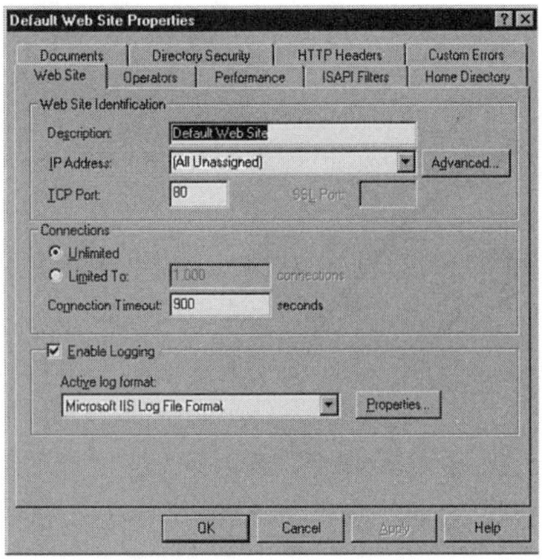

Now you have a reference for all the errors you might see on a client trying to access your Web server. Now take a look at some of the configuration options for the WWW service and see where problems might crop up. From the Microsoft Management Console shown in Figure 7.6, select the Web site you'd like to review. Right-click and select Properties. Figure 7.7 shows the resulting dialog box.

The Web Site tab offers a few areas of possible configuration issues. First, make sure that the TCP port is set to 80. It is extremely rare that you would need to set up your site on a non-standard port. This is occasionally done for Web-based management tools, but seldom for a public access Web site.

The second thing to check is whether you have selected the Limited To option button to limit the number of concurrent connections. If you have, be sure you have set the number high enough to allow all your users to connect as needed.

Figure 7.8 shows the Operators tab. If you have a user who needs to perform Web site maintenance and you keep finding they do not have the rights they need, this is where you can assign and alter rights.

FIGURE 7.7
The Web Site tab of the Properties dialog box contains all the pertinent information about the site identification and connection parameters.

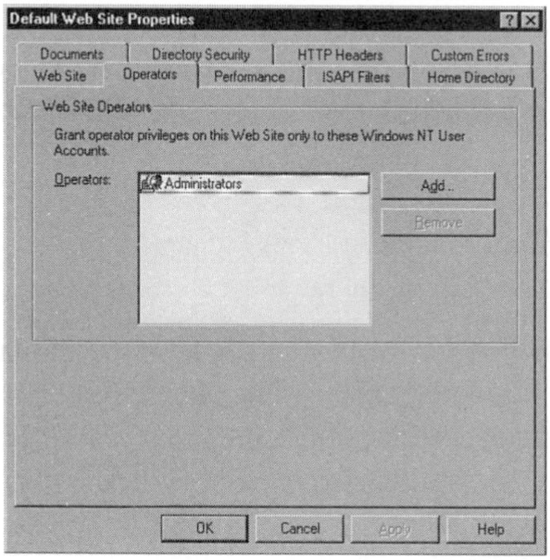

◀FIGURE 7.8
The Operators tab is used to grant operator privileges to NT users or groups.

Figure 7.9 shows the Performance tab. You can find that issues arise when you have under- or overestimated the number of hits your site is getting. Review your logs to ensure that the Performance Tuning slide is set appropriately. A second potential issue is the enabling of bandwidth throttling. If this is set too low, you will have users that are unable to access the site or who are having intermittent issues as the bandwidth used reaches the limit.

Figure 7.10 shows where the ISAPI filters are installed that were discussed in Chapter 5, "Running Applications." Make sure that if you have any filters installed, they are written properly, and the correct filter is installed.

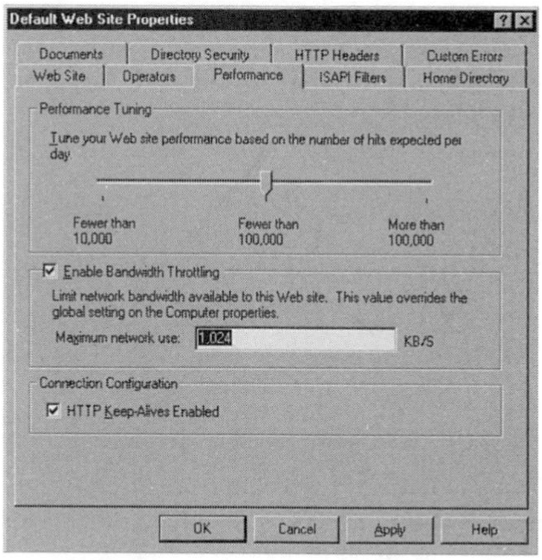

FIGURE 7.9▲
The Performance tab is used to tune the servers performance based on the client base and application requirements.

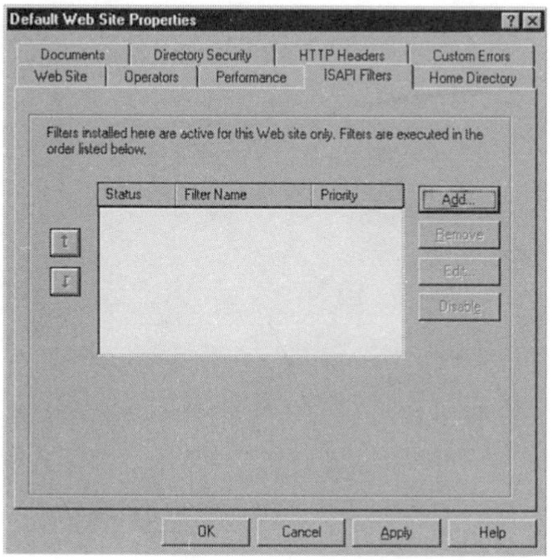

◀FIGURE 7.10
The ISAPI Filters tab is used to load ISAPI filters to be applied to the Web site.

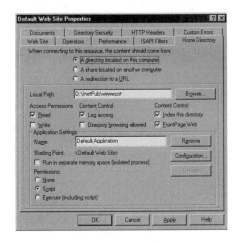

FIGURE 7.11▲
The Home Directory is especially important if you are receiving a lot of File Not Found errors when you try to load the home page.

FIGURE 7.12▶
The Documents tab determines what file name(s) and extension(s) are used as the default page to be opened in a directory.

Figure 7.11 shows the Home Directory tab. This is where you decide where the home directory for the site should be located. If problems arise, check the path, and if the home directory is located on another server, ensure that it is available and the mappings are still valid. You should also double-check your access permissions. If you are having an issue running an application, be sure to verify that the application settings at the bottom of the tab are set correctly.

Figure 7.12 shows the Documents tab, and this is another good place to look if you are receiving File Not Found or You Do Not Have Rights To Access This Directory errors. These errors are frequently caused by a mislabeled or missing default document. For example, if you are using INDEX.HTML as your default documents, and you accidentally name the file INDEX.HTM, the server will respond with an error. If the user is referencing the document specifically, you will receive a 404 (File Not Found) error. If the user is just trying to load based on the DNS name or IP address of the site, IIS will look for the default document. If IIS cannot find that document, it will try to list the directory. If your security is configured correctly, this will generate the You do not have rights error. Be sure the document(s) listed here exist in the site's home directory, and that they have the correct permissions set so they can be opened by your users.

Figure 7.13 shows the Directory Security tab. This is the place to start if you are having security issues. Remember, you should avoid sending clear text passwords (the Basic Authentication check box you see after clicking Edit) at all costs. That is a very dangerous configuration option from a security standpoint.

Clicking on the Edit button under Anonymous Access and Authentication Control opens the Anonymous User Account dialog box, shown in Figure 7.14. Here you can configure the user ID and password used for anonymous access. If you have a problem where no one can access your public Web site, you should check the configuration of the anonymous user, making sure the correct user ID is selected and the password for that account is correct.

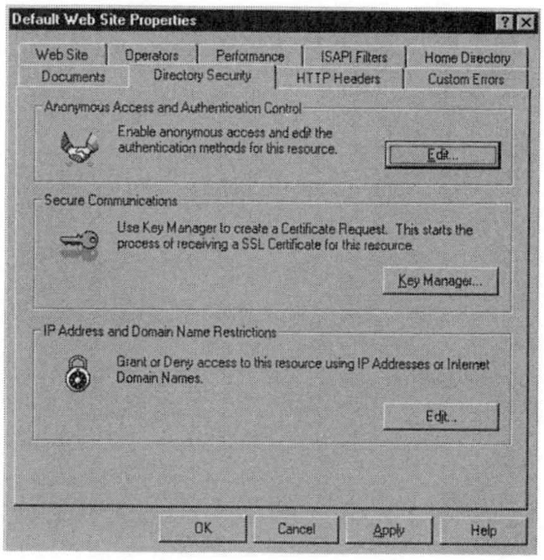

FIGURE 7.13▲
The Directory Security tab is where to go to configure and troubleshoot the file and directory security configurations for the site.

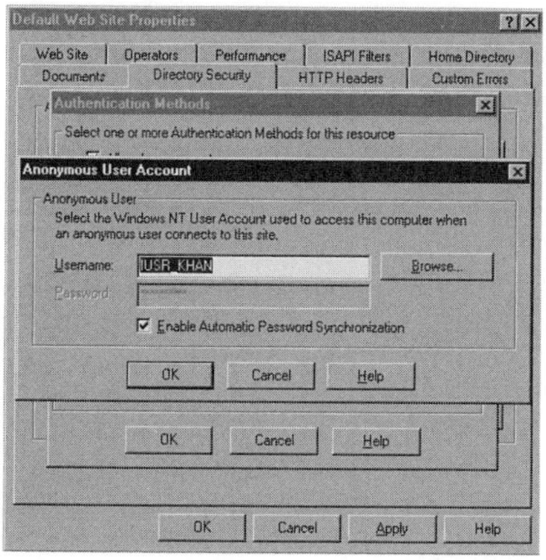

◀FIGURE 7.14
The Anonymous User Account dialog box allows you to set the user ID and password used by anonymous end users accessing your site.

Figure 7.15 shows the HTTP Headers tab. If you are having problems with custom headers or unknown MIME types, this is the screen you would need to investigate. Also, be very careful when rating sites. An inadvertent rating coupled with some strict client configurations can result in the site being blocked to certain users. This is also where you configure content expiration. Content expiration gives administrators the ability to control the life of the content in the browser cache. If you set this value too high, you may find end users viewing outdated, cached information, rather than the new content you have posted. If this is the case, have the users delete their browser's cache and they should be able to see the new content immediately. On the other hand, if you set this value too low, you may find that the proxy servers caching your site are continually accessing the site because the content is timing out so quickly.

The HTTP Headers tab can be used to set the life of content, content ratings, and the MIME file types that IIS can understand.

FIGURE 7.16▲
The Custom Errors tab shows the locations and file names of the files used when there are errors.

If you need to come up with a custom error for your site, Figure 7.16 shows you the tab used to do this. Custom errors can be used if you have a particular custom error you want to use with a custom application, or even if you want to be a little more creative with the error messages your users receive when there is an issue.

That covers issues you might see on the configuration of the WWW Service of IIS 4.0. Now, move on to the FTP Service, which is less complex.

RESOLVING FTP SERVICE ISSUES

FTP, or File Transfer Protocol, provides a simple but robust mechanism for copying files to or from remote hosts using the connection-oriented services of TCP/IP. FTP is a component of the TCP/IP protocol, and is defined in RFC 959. To use FTP to send or receive files, the following requirements must be met:

◆ The client computer must have FTP client software, such as the FTP client included with Windows NT.

◆ The user must have a username and password on the remote system. In some cases, a username of anonymous with no password suffices.

◆ The remote system must be running an FTP daemon or service (depending upon whether it is UNIX or NT).

◆ Your system and the remote system must be running the TCP/IP protocol.

You can use FTP in either a command-line mode or in a command-interpreter mode. The following options are available from the command line:

```
C:\>ftp ?
Transfers files to and from a computer running an FTP server
                service (sometimes called a daemon). Ftp
                ➥can be used interactively.

FTP [-v] [-d] [-i] [-n] [-g] [-s:filename] [-a]
➥[-w:windowsize] [host]

   -v              Suppresses display of remote server
                   ➥responses.
   -n              Suppresses auto-login upon initial
                   ➥connection.
   -i              Turns off interactive prompting during
                   ➥multiple
                   file transfers.
   -d              Enables debugging.
   -g              Disables filename globbing (see GLOB
                   ➥command).
   -s:filename     Specifies a text file containing FTP
                   ➥commands;
                   the commands will automatically run
                   ➥after FTP
                   starts.
   -a              Use any local interface when binding data
                   connection.
   -w:buffersize   Overrides the default transfer buffer size of
                   4096.
   host            Specifies the host name or IP address of the
                   remote host to connect to.
```

If you use FTP in a command-interpreter mode, some of the more frequently used options are as follows:

◆ **open.** Specifies the remote system to which you connect.

◆ **close.** Disconnects from a remote system. Bye or Quit works as well.

◆ **ls.** Obtains a directory listing on a remote system, much like the dir command in DOS. Note that the ls -l command provides file size and time stamps. In Windows NT you can use the old DOS DIR as well.

◆ **cd.** Changes directories on the remote system. This command functions in much the same way as the DOS cd command.

◆ **lcd.** Changes directories on the local system. This command also functions in much the same way as the DOS cd command.

- **binary.** Instructs FTP to treat all files transferred as binary.

- **ascii.** Instructs FTP to treat all files transferred as text. You need to choose a transfer type because certain files cannot be read correctly as binary, whereas ASCII is universally accepted.

- **get.** Copies a file from the remote host to your local computer.

- **put.** Copies a file from your local computer to the remote host.

- **debug.** Turns on debugging commands that can be useful in diagnosing problems.

Because remote host systems typically are based on UNIX, you will encounter a number of nuances relating to UNIX if you interact with these hosts in your FTP connections:

- The UNIX operating system uses the forward slash in path references rather than the backward slash. In UNIX, the file name \WINNT40\README.TXT would be /WINNT40/README.TXT.

- UNIX is case sensitive at all times—the command get MyFile and the command get MYFILE are not the same. Usernames and passwords also are case sensitive.

- UNIX treats wild card characters, such as the asterisk and the question mark, differently. The glob command within FTP changes how wild card characters in local file names are treated.

The biggest problems with FTP typically involve permissions in uploading and downloading files. To upload files, a user (whether specified by name or anonymous) must have Change permission for the directory. To download files, a user (again, either by name or anonymous) must have Read permission. These represent the very bare bones permissions required to perform these operations. If an anonymous user cannot get connected, verify that the anonymous user password is the same in both User Manager for Domains and Internet Service Manager. These are distinct logons and passwords, and unified logons work only if their values are the same. You can avoid this problem by enabling automatic password synchronization when you configure anonymous access.

To prevent anonymous users from logging on to your site, you can take advantage of this information about FTP. When FTP is running on the server, it constantly looks for activity on control port 21—its pre-assigned number. If you want to offer the service, yet hide its availability, you can do so by changing the port assignment from 21 to any open number greater than 1,023. Alternatively, or additionally, you can disable anonymous access by unchecking the Allow Anonymous Access check box in the Authentication Methods dialog box for each site.

FTP usage statistics can be gathered from Performance Monitor using the Connection Attempts and Logon Attempts counters. The former reports when a host attempts to connect to a target anonymously; the latter indicates those times a connection other than anonymous was attempted.

The FTP service is a much less complicated service to troubleshoot because it basically has one function; to transfer files to and from the server. Typical issues include incorrect user ID and password, overloaded site, or even something as simple as the service being stopped. Check the Internet Information Server Manager window (refer to Figure 7.6) for the list of available services. It is always a good idea to make sure the service is running before you get too far into troubleshooting.

Figure 7.17 shows the basic site information. As with the WWW Service, ensure the port and address are correct.

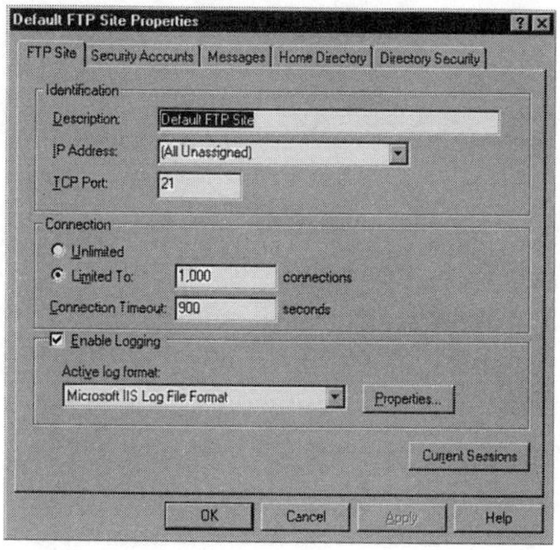

FIGURE 7.17
The FTP Site tab contains the information regarding the description, IP address, and port used by the site.

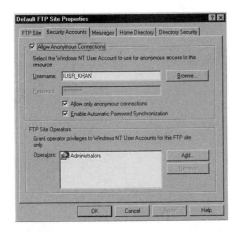

FIGURE 7.18▲
The Security Accounts tab is used to configure
the type of access allowed to the FTP site, as
well as the account used for anonymous
access.

FIGURE 7.19▶
Just like the WWW equivalent tab, the Home
Directory tab is used to set the location of the
FTP home directory.

Figure 7.18 shows the Security Accounts page. Be very careful as you
allow or deny anonymous access to your FTP server. If you are trying to distribute a patch or a form, anonymous access is probably
appropriate. If you have company-confidential information on the
server, you may want to restrict your anonymous access to the site.
Selecting Allow Only Anonymous Connections will prevent users
from inadvertently sending their clear-text user IDs and passwords
across the network. The FTP login sequence doesn't contain any
encryption. In order to configure the server to allow only anonymous connections, you must first enable anonymous access.
Otherwise, the Allow Only Anonymous Connections configuration
option will not be available.

If you are finding you can log on, but cannot change to the home
directory, check the configuration shown in Figure 7.19. Those types
of issues are almost always an incorrect home directory issue or a
permissions issue.

Figure 7.20 shows you where to set the ranges of allowed or denied
IP addresses or networks. If you are having issues in which some of
the hosts can access based on the IP address but others cannot, verify
that the subnet mask is set correctly on the permit. If you find that
everyone who has access is not supposed to, whereas the authorized
users can't get in, make sure you have selected the correct option
button for Granted Access or Denied Access. It is very easy to reverse
the two and throw a monkey wrench into your deployment.

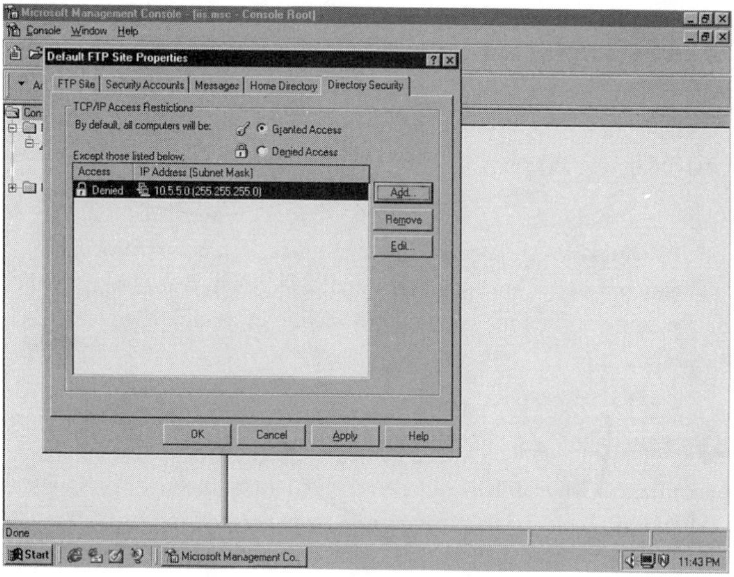

FIGURE 7.20
The Directory Security tab is used to permit or deny specific IP hosts or networks access to the site. WWW has a similar tab located off its Directory Security tab.

That sums up FTP configuration issues. It is really a subset of the WWW configuration we looked at in the previous section. Now we need to discuss troubleshooting Index Server issues.

RESOLVING INDEX SERVER PROBLEMS

Index Server works with IIS through queries that come in the form of .IDQ (Internet Data Query) files. It responds to those queries in the form of .IDQ files as well. To function properly, .IDQ files should always be placed in the Scripts directory, and they require Execute or Script permission.

As discussed in Chapter 4, "Integration and Interoperability," there are two sections to .IDQ files, with [Query] being required, and [Names] being optional (used only to define nonstandard column names that are referred to in a query). Refer to Chapter 4 for a listing of parameters, variables, and conditional expressions.

Most troubleshooting or trouble correction is automatically implemented with Index Server. For example, if the cache becomes corrupted, Index Server begins a recovery operation and no administrator interaction is required. For all events, messages are written to

EXAM TIP

Error Messages—Don't Panic
Before you kick into memorize
mode, you need to understand that
these errors will not be on the
Microsoft Internet Information
Server 4 exam. They are included in
this section as a reference for you
should you ever need to troubleshoot an Index Server issue in
your job. So, if you are preparing to
take the exam, relax and look over
Table 7.3 with that in mind.

the event log indicating the actions taking place, and administrators
can monitor their Index Server installations from there.

Query Errors

Errors can, and often do, occur when improper syntax is used in
queries, when files are corrupt, or when other problems occur. There
is a series of standard messages returned to alert you that query errors
are the cause of the problem, and this section examines those error
messages.

Syntax Errors

According to Microsoft's online documentation, the error messages,
as shown in Table 7.3, can be returned when executing a query.

TABLE 7.3

INDEX SERVER ERROR MESSAGES

Message	Explanation
Expecting closing parenthesis	Occurs when parentheses are mismatched.
Expecting closing square bracket	An opening square bracket was not followed by a closing square bracket. Usually, the result of an ill-formed weight.
Expecting comma	Occurs when a reserved token or end-of-string occurs before the closing brace of a vector property. Example: @VectorString = {A1, B@}.
Expecting currency	A currency value was expected but not found. Occurs when a property of type DBTYPE_CY is fed incorrect input. Correct format for currency is #.#.
Expecting date	A date was expected but not found. Occurs when a property of type DBTYPE_DATE is fed incorrect input. Allowed formats for dates are yyyy/mm/dd, yyyy/mm/dd hh:mm:ss, and relative dates (-#y, -#m, -#w, -#d, -#h, -#n, -#s).
Expecting end of string	A complete restriction has been parsed, and there is still more input. Example: (@size = 100) sample.

Message	*Explanation*
Expecting GUID	A GUID (Globally Unique Identifier) was expected but not found. Occurs when a property of DBTYPE_GUID is fed incorrect input. Property format for a GUID is XXXXXXXX-XXXX-XXXX-XXXX-XXXXXXXXXXXX.
Expecting integer	An integer was expected but not found. Occurs when a property of an integer type (DBTYPE_I4, for example) is fed a nonnumeric value, or a nonnumeric vector weight is entered.
Expecting phrase	A textual phrase was expected and not found. This error occurs in a variety of situations where the query parser is expecting plain text and is given a special token instead.
Expecting property name	Occurs when a correctly formed property name is not found after an @ sign.
Expecting real number	A real number was expected but not found. Occurs when a property of a real type (DBTYPE_R4, for example) is fed a nonnumeric value.
Expecting regular expression	Similar to Expecting phrase error. Used when in regular-expression parsing mode.
The file <file> is on a remote UNC share. .IDQ, .IDA, and .HTX files cannot be placed on a remote UNC share	An .IDQ, .IDA, or .HTX file was found on a remote UNC share. None of these files can be on a remote UNC share.
Invalid literal	Occurs only when a query property is formatted poorly. Almost all conditions are covered by the Expecting Integer, Expecting Date, and other errors.
No such property	Property specified after @, #, or $ does not exist. It is not a default property and is not specified in the [Names] section of the .IDQ file.
Not yet implemented	An unimplemented feature of Index Server.
Out of memory	The server ran out of memory processing the CiRestriction.
Regular expressions property of type string	A property of a nontextual a require type (DBTYPE_I4, DBTYPE_GUI DBTYPE_GUI, and so on) was selected for regular expression mode. For example, #size 100* would cause this error.

continues

TABLE 7.3	*continued*

INDEX SERVER ERROR MESSAGES

Message	*Explanation*
Unexpected end of string	There is a missing quotation mark in your query.
Unsupported property type	For future expansion. Will occur when a display-only property type is used in a query restriction.
Weight must be between 0 and 1000	Occurs when a query term weight is outside the legal range of 0 to 1,000.

IDQ File Errors

According to Microsoft's online documentation, the messages in Table 7.4 are returned by use of the CiErrorMessage variable, accessible from .htx error pages.

TABLE 7.4

IDQ FILE ERROR MESSAGES

Message	*Explanation*
The catalog directory cannot not be found in the location specified by 'CiCatalog=' in file <file>.	The catalog location specified by the CiCatalog parameter did contain a valid content index catalog.
DBTYPE_BYREF must be used with DBTYPE STR, DBTYPE_WSTR, DBTYPE_GUID, or DBTYPE UI1 types.	DBTYPE_BYREF must always be used in conjunction with an indirect type in the [Names] section.
DBTYPE_VECTOR or BYREF DBTYPE_BYREF used alone	The VECTOR and .property modifiers must always be used with a type. Example: DBTYPE_I4 ¦ DBTYPE_VECTOR
Duplicate column, possibly by column alias, found in the ' 'CiColumns= specification in file <file>.	The same property was named a more than once in the CiColumns line. It may have been mentioned with different friendly names that refer to the same property
Duplicate property name.	The same property was defined twice in the [Names] section.
Expecting closing parenthesis.	Opening parenthesis in [Names] section is not followed by closing parenthesis in .IDQ file.
Expecting GUID.	Incorrectly formatted entry in the [Names] section of .IDQ file.
Expecting integer.	Incorrectly formatted entry in the [Names] section of .IDQ file.
Expecting property name.	Incorrectly formatted entry in the [Names] section of .IDQ file.
Expecting property specifier.	Invalid or missing property specifier in [Names] section. Property is named either by PROPID (integer) or string.

Message	*Explanation*

Expecting SHALLOW or DEEP in .IDQ file <file>
on line 'CiFlags='.

The `CiFlags` parameter has a value other than SHALLOW or DEEP.

Expecting TRUE or FALSE in .IDQ file <file> on
line 'CiForceUseCi=1'.

The `CiForceUseCi` parameter has a value other than TRUE or FALSE.

Expecting type specifier.

Incorrectly formatted entry in the [Names] section of .IDQ file.

Failed to set property name.

A resource failure. Usually out of memory.

The file <file> is on a network share . .IDQ,
.IDA, and .HTX files cannot be placed on a
network share.

You must put these files into a virtual root on the local computer.

The .HTX file specified could not be found in
physical path.

The file specified in the `CiTemplate` parameter could any virtual or not be located.

The .IDQ file <file> contains a duplicate entry
on line<line>.

A parameter in the [Query] section of the .IDQ file was given more than once.

The .IDQ file <file> could not be found.

Check the path to the .IDQ file and then make sure the .IDQ file is in that path.

An invalid ÔCiScope=' or 'CiCatalog=' was
specified in file <file>.

The .IDQ file cannot contain invalid parameters. Correct the condition and try again.

Invalid GUID.

A poorly formatted GUID was found in the [Names] section.

An invalid locale was specified on the 'CiLocale='
line in .IDQ file <file>.

The locale ID specified by the `CiLocale` parameter was not recognized as a valid locale ID.

Invalid property found in the 'CiColumns='
specification in file <file>.

A property specified in the `CiColumns` parameter is not a standard property and is not listed in the [Names] section of the .IDQ file.

Invalid property found in the 'CiSort='
specification in file <file>.

A property specified in the `CiSort` parameter is not a standard property and is not listed in the [Names] section of the .IDQ file.

An invalid sort order was specified on the on the
'CiSort=' line in file <file>. Only [a] and [d]
are supported.

A sort-order specification following a property name in the `CiSort` parameter was unrecognized. Only [a] (for ascending). and [d] (for descending) are allowed.

One or more output columns must be specified in
the .IDQ file <file>.

The CiColumns parameter is missing or empty. At least one output column must be specified `file` for the query.

Operation on line number of .IDA file <file> is
invalid.

An unrecognized keyword was found in the .IDA file.

continues

<table>
<tr><td>**TABLE 7.4**</td><td>*continued*</td></tr>
</table>

IDQ FILE ERROR MESSAGES

Message	Explanation
The query failed because the Web server is busy processing other requests	The limit on the number of queries has been exceeded. To allow more ueries to wait in the queue for processing, increase the value of the otherRegistry key IsapiRequestQueueSize, and to allow more queries to be processed simultaneously, increase the value for the Registry key Isapi-RequestThresholdFactor.
Read error in file <file>.	I/O error occurred reading the file. Generally caused by hardware failure.
A restriction must be specified in the IDQ file <file>.	The CiRestriction parameter is missing or empty..Every query must have a restriction. A restriction such as #vpath *.* will match all pages.
A scope must be specified in the .IDQ file <file>.	The CiScope parameter is missing or empty. Every query must have a scope. The scope /(forward slash) will match every page in all virtual directories and the scope \ (backslash) will match every page on every physical path.
The template file cannot be found in the location specified by 'CiTemplate=' in file <file>.	An attempt to open a .HTX file the location specified by the CiTemplate parameter failed The path may be invalid, it may specify a directory, or it may resolve to NULL after parameter replacement.
A template file must be specified in the .IDQ file <file>.	The CiTemplate parameter is missing or empty. Every query must have a template (.HTX) file.
Template for .IDA file cannot have detail section.	A <%BeginDetail%> was <file> found in the .IDA file. Please remove it and the entire detail section.
Unrecognized type.	Type specifed is not one of the valid types (DBTYPE_I4, DBTYPE_GUID, and so on).
You must specify 'MaxRecordsPerPage' in the .IDQ file <file>.	The CiMaxRecordsPerPage parameter is missing or empty. Every query must specify the number of records per page.

Event Log Messages

Index Server system errors are reported in the application event log under the Ci Filter Service category. System errors reported here include page filtering (*indexing*) problems, out-of-resource conditions, index corruption, and so on.

The messages in Table 7.5 are written to the Windows NT application event log.

TABLE 7.5

EVENT LOG ERROR MESSAGES

Message	Explanation
Account user-id does not have interactive logon privileges on this computer. You can give user-id interactive logon privileges on this computer using the user manager administrative tool.	The specified user-id does not have interactive logon privileges on the computer running Index Server. Give the user-id interactive logon privileges through the User Manager for Domains.
The CI filter daemon has prematurely stopped and will be subsequently restarted.	The filter daemon (Cidaemon.exe) stopped unexpectedly. It will be automatically restarted. This can be caused by poorly written filters or experimentation with the Windows NT Task Manager.
CI has started on <catalog>.	An informational message logged when Index Server is started successfully.
Class for extension <extension> unknown. Sample file: <file>.	This is a warning that files with the specified extension are being filtered with the default (text) filter. This can lead to the addition of unnecessary data in the index. Consider turning off filtering for this extension. The full physical path of a representative file is included in the message. Generation of this message can be disabled by turning on a special flag in the ContentIndex Registry key.
Cleaning up corrupted content index metadata on <catalog>. Index will be automatically restored by refiltering all documents.	A catastrophic data corruption error was detected on the specified catalog. The catalog will be rebuilt. This is usually caused by hardware failure, but also can occur in rare circumstances because of abrupt shutdown or power failure. Recovery will occur automatically.
Content index on <catalog> could not be initialized. Error <number>.	Unknown, possibly catastrophic error. Please report the error number to Microsoft Technical Support. To recover, delete all files under <catalog> and re-index.
Content index on <catalog> is corrupted. Please shut down and restart Web server.	A catastrophic data corruption error was detected on the specified catalog. The catalog will be rebuilt. This is usually caused by hardware failure, but also can occur in rare circumstances because of abrupt shutdown or power failure. You must shut down and restart the Web server for recovery to occur.
Content index corruption detected in component <stack>.	The content index is corrupted. Delete the catalog and start <component>. Stack trace is over. If you keep getting this error, remove reinstall Index Server.
Content index corruption detected in component <component> in catalog <catalog>. Stack trace is <stack>.	The content index is corrupt. Delete the catalog and start over. If you keep getting this error, remove and reinstall Index Server.

continues

TABLE 7.5	*continued*

EVENT LOG ERROR MESSAGES

Message	*Explanation*
The content index could not filter file <file>. The filter operation was retried <number> times without success.	The specified document failed to successfully filter <number> times. This usually indicates a corrupted document or corrupted properties. In rare cases, filtering may fail because the document was in use for a long period of time.
Content index on drive is corrupted. Please shut down and restart the Content Index service (cisvc).	In the Windows NT Control Panel under Services, stop the Content Index service, and then restart it.
The content index filter for file <file> generated content data more than <size> times the file's size.	Filtering of the specified document generated more than the allowed maximum amount of output. This is usually caused by a poorly written filter, a corrupted document, or both.
The content index filter stopped while filtering <file>. The CI daemon was restarted. Please check the validity of the filter for objects of this class.	Filtering of the specified document was started, but did not finish before the timeout period expired. This is usually caused by a poorly written filter, a corrupted document, or both.
A content scan has completed on <catalog>.	A content scan of the catalog has been successfully completed.
An error has been detected on <catalog> that requires a full content scan.	The catalog lost a change notification, usually due to lack of resources (disk space) or hardware failure. The complete scope of the catalog will be scanned, and all documents will be refiltered. This action is deferred until a suitable time.
An error has been detected in content index on <catalog>.	The content index is corrupted. Delete the catalog and start over. If you keep getting this error, remove and reinstall Index Server.
An error has been detected on <catalog> that requires a partial content scan.	The catalog lost a change notification, usually due to lack of resources (disk space) or hardware failure. A partial scope of the catalog will be scanned, and some documents will be refiltered. This action is deferred until a suitable time.
Error <number> detected in content index on <catalog>.	Unknown, possibly catastrophic error. Please report error number to Microsoft Technical Support. To recover, delete all files under <catalog> and start over.
File change notifications are turned off for scope <scope> because of error <number>. This scope will be periodically rescanned.	An error prevented reestablishing automatic change notifications for the specified directory scope. To determine Documents that changed in the scope, periodic incremental scans will be done by Index Server. The rescan interval is specified in the Registry.
File change notifications for scope <scope> are not enabled because of error <number>. This scope will be periodically rescanned.	An error prevented establishment of automatic change notifications for the specified directory scope. This usually happens with virtual roots that point to remote shares on file servers that do not support automatic change notifications. To determine which documents changed in the scope, periodic incremental scans will be done by Index Server. The rescan interval is specified in the Registry.

Message	Explanation
The filter service could not run since file <file> could not be found on your system.	An executable or DLL required for filtering cannot be found, usually because Cidaemon.exe is not on the path.
A full content scan has started on <catalog>.	A complete rescan of the catalog has been initiated.
<number> inconsistencies were detected in PropertyStore during recovery of catalog <catalog>.	Corruption was detected in the property cache during startup. Recovery is automatically scheduled. Usually the result of hardware failure or abrupt shutdown.
Master merge cannot be restarted on <catalog> due to error <number>.	A master merge cannot be restarted on the specified catalog. The error code gives the reason.
Master merge cannot be started on <catalog> due to error <number>.	A master merge cannot be started on the specified catalog. The error code gives the reason.
Master merge has been paused on <catalog>. It will rescheduled later.	A master merge has been temporarily halted on the Specified be catalog. Often occurs when a merge runs out of system resources (disk space, memory, and so on).
Master merge has completed on <catalog>.	A master merge has been completed on the specified catalog. This is an informational message.
Master merge has restarted on <catalog>.	A paused master merge hasbeen restarted.
Master merge has started on <catalog>.	A master merge has been initiated on the specified catalog. This is an informational message.
Master merge was started on <catalog> because the amount of remaining disk space was less than <number>%.	A master merge was started because the amount of free space on the catalog volume dropped below a minimum threshold. The total free disk space should be increased after the master merge completes.
Master merge was started on <catalog> because more than <number> documents have changed since the last master merge.	A master merge was started because the number of documents changed since the last master merge exceeded the maximum threshold.
Master merge was started on <catalog> because the size of the shadow indexes is more than <number>% the disk.	A master merge was started because the amount of data in shadow indexes exceeded the maximum threshold.
Notifications are not enabled on <pathname> because this is a DFS aware share. This scope will be periodically scanned.	If a virtual root points to a distributed file system (DFS) share, notifications are disabled for the entire DFS share because DFS does not support notifications.
One or more embeddings in file <file> could not be filtered.	The specified file was filtered correctly, but several of the embedded objects could not be filtered. This is usually caused by embedded objects without a registered filter. Text within unfiltered embedded objects is not searchable. Generation of this message can be disabled by turning on a special flag in key Registry.
The path <pathname> is too long for Content Index.	The Content Index service detected a path that was longer than the maximum number of characters allowed for a path name as determined by the constant MAX_PATH (260 characters). As a result, no documents from that path will be returned or indexed.

continues

TABLE 7.5	*continued*

EVENT LOG ERROR MESSAGES

Message	*Explanation*
`Please check your system time. It might be set to an invalid value.`	This event is generated when the system time is invalid—for example, when set to a date before January 1, 1980. When the system time is invalid, the date may appear as 2096.
`<Process-Name> failed to logon <UserId> because of error <number>.`	The specified process (Index Server Search Engine or CiDaemon) failed to log on the specified user because of an error. The remote shares for which the UserId is used will not be filtered correctly. This can happen if either the password is wrong or the validity of the password could not be verified due to network errors.
`PropertyStore inconsistency detected in catalog <catalog>.`	Corruption was detected in the property cache. Recovery is automatically scheduled. Usually the result of hardware failure or abrupt shutdown.
`Recovery is starting on PropertyStore in catalog <catalog>.`	Corruption was detected in the property cache. Recovery is starting on the property cache. This can take a long time, depending upon the size of the property cache.
`Recovery was performed successfully on PropertyStore in catalog <catalog>.`	Corruption was detected in the property cache. The error has been fixed. Usually the result of hardware failure or abrupt shutdown.
`Very low disk space was detected on drive <drive>. Please free up at least <number> MB of space for content index to continue.`	Free space has fallen below the minimum threshold required for successful merge. This is just a warning, but no merges will be initiated until space is freed up. Filtering will also stop.

Virtual Roots

Table 7.6 describes the error messages that occur when there are virtual root problems.

TABLE 7.6

VIRTUAL ROOT ERROR MESSAGES

Message	*Explanation*
`Added virtual root <root> to index.`	The message `Mapped to <path>` is added to the event log when a virtual root is indexed.
`Removed virtual root <root> from index.`	This message is written to the event log when a virtual root is deleted from the index.
`Added scope <path> to index.`	This message is added to the event log when a new physical scope is indexed.
`Removed scope <path> from index.`	This message is written to the event log when a new physical scope is deleted from the index.

Other Index Server Issues

Other issues to be aware of with Index Server include the following:

◆ Index Server starting and stopping

◆ Word weighting

◆ Disk filling

Starting and Stopping Index Server

Index Server, by default, is set to automatically start when IIS does. If this is set to another value, such as manual, then IIS can be started from the Services icon in the Control Panel. This is the same utility that can be used to stop the Index Server service, although it automatically shuts down when IIS does.

If Index Server isn't running and a query comes in, Index Server automatically starts. Therefore, as an administrator, the starting of Index Server is not something you should ever need to do manually. The stopping of Index Server is something you should never need to do, either, but you can do it from the Services utility.

Weighting Words

Word weighting determines how words in the data are indexed. This process is done by the Waisindx.exe utility. It determines what to index, how much to weight words, how to optimize the server, and where to find the actual data. As a rule of thumb, seven indexes are created for each data file, with the combined size of the seven indexes being equal to 110% of the size of the data file.

The weighting factors that Waisindx.exe uses are as follows:

◆ **The actual weight of the word.** Whether it appears in a headline, capitalized, and so on, or just in the body of the data.

◆ **The term of the weight.** How many times it appears, and thus, how important it is to the data.

◆ **The proximity.** How close multiple words always appear to each other—for example, "computer publishing."

◆ **The density of the word.** Computed by taking the total of times the word appears and dividing it by the total number of all words in the data.

When Waisindx.exe is run, it creates the indexes that are then used to locate the data. As you add new records to the data, the indexes are not updated, and you must rerun Waisindx.exe to create new indexes incorporating the new data.

Running Out of Disk Space

One of the most common problems with using Index Server is that of running out of disk space. If the drive fills, indexing is paused, and the only method of knowing this is by a message written to the event log. The event log should be monitored routinely by an administrator for this and similar occurrences.

ODBC ERRORS

One other area in which you may see problems is that of your connection to an ODBC-compliant database.

ODBC Configuration was discussed in Chapter 4.

Some of the common errors you might run into include the following:

◆ ```
Microsoft OLE DB Provider for ODBC Drivers error
'80004005' [Microsoft][ODBC Driver Manager] Data source
name not found and no default driver specified.
```

This error occurs when the ODBC Data Source Name isn't set up so that database connections can be made.

◆ ```
Microsoft OLE DB Provider for ODBC Drivers error
'80004005' [Microsoft][ODBC SQL Server Driver][SQL
Server] Logon failed.
```

This error may occur if the account being used by IIS doesn't have the right Windows NT permissions to access the database file.

◆ ```
Microsoft OLE DB Provider for ODBC Drivers error
'80004005'[Microsoft][ODBC Microsoft Access 97 Driver]
Couldn't use '(unknown)'; file already in use.
```

The database cannot be locked correctly for multiple users.
```

◆ `Microsoft OLE DB Provider for ODBC Drivers error`
`'80004005'[Microsoft][ODBC Microsoft Access 97 Driver]`
`'(unknown)' isn't a valid path. Make sure that the path`
`name is spelled correctly and that you are connected to`
`the server on which the file resides.`

The specified path for the database being read by the IIS server is not valid.

◆ `Microsoft OLE DB Provider for ODBC Drivers error`
`'80004005'[Microsoft][ODBC SQL Server Driver][DBMSSOCN]`
`General network error. Check your network document.`

This can occur when the SQL server is renamed, and the IIS server is not updated to reflect the change.

If you can't find the specific ODBC error you received, there are myriad places you can go to find the information. The following sections discuss a few of the more useful places.

OTHER AVENUES FOR SUPPORT

There are probably issues that you will run into that are not covered in this chapter. There is just no way to foresee every issue you might run into using a complex product like IIS, and certainly not in a chapter like this one. Fortunately there are a number of places to find help, and they include the following:

◆ Windows NT Resource Kit

◆ Online help in both Windows NT and IIS

◆ Microsoft Technet

◆ CompuServe

◆ Microsoft Internet site

◆ IIS Resource Kit

The Microsoft Windows NT Resource Kit includes three volumes of in-depth information and a CD of utilities. The Resource Kit utilities add a large number of troubleshooting utilities and can help you isolate problems much easier.

The online help in Windows NT is available from the Start Menu, Help, or from almost anywhere else in the product by pressing F1. The IIS help is available at several locations, but most notably by selecting Product Documentation from the IIS section of the Programs menu.

Microsoft Technet is a monthly CD subscription that includes the latest service packs, drivers, and updates for all operating system products. After it is installed, you can run it at any time by choosing Microsoft TechNet from the Programs menu.

The CompuServe forums are not as well supported as they once were and almost everything is shifting to the Web, but these are still good locations to find interaction among users experiencing similar problems. The easiest method to use to find a forum supporting the problem you're experiencing is to click the stoplight icon on the main CompuServe menu (or type **GO** at a command prompt) and enter **NDEX**. This brings up an index of all the forums currently available. You can select a choice from the list, or—depending upon your version of CompuServe—choose **GO** again, and enter the abbreviation for the forum you want.

The Microsoft Internet site at http://www.microsoft.com makes all software updates and patches available. It also serves as an entry point to the KnowledgeBase, where you can find documentation on all known problems.

USING A WEBMAP TO FIND AND REPAIR BROKEN LINKS, HYPERLINK TEXTS, HEADINGS, AND TITLES

Content Analyzer's WebMaps can be used to administer Web site content to help you keep your Web site up to date and functioning correctly. You use the Link Info window, searches, and properties to help manage your site's content. In this section, you are shown how to use the Link Info windows to find and repair the following:

◆ Broken links

◆ Hyperlink text

◆ Headings

◆ Titles

To show the Link Info window, create a WebMap of your Web site.
Click the Object Links toolbar button, or right-click the page you
want to view and select Links. The Link Info window is displayed
(see Figure 7.21). In this window, you can display different types
of links on a page.

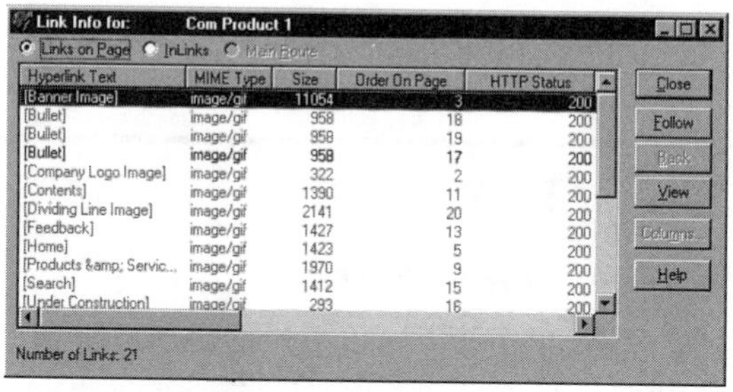

FIGURE 7.21
The Link Info Window.

Click the Links on Page option to display all links on a selected page.
This is handy if you want to review navigational paths on a page.

Click the InLinks option to display links that reference the page
you are reviewing. These are called InLinks, and can be from pages
on the same site as the page you're viewing or from another site.

When you click the Main Route option, the Link Info window
displays all ancestor links from the main page to the selected page.
If the page you're reviewing is your site's home page, for instance,
you won't see any other ancestors. However, if the page is one level
below the home page (that is, you can link to the page from the
home page), you'll see the home page displayed when selecting the
Main Route option. This is because the home page is the *parent* of
the page you're reviewing. Pages one level below the child page are
considered *grandchildren* to the home page, and so on. You'll find
this option handy when you're viewing a page that is buried deep
in the hierarchy and ancestry is not easy to discern.

Finally, to see the number of links for each type of link option you
can display, look at the bottom of the Link Info window.

Fixing Broken Links

As your Web site matures and content is upgraded, deleted, moved,
and renamed, you'll need to update links on your pages. Over time,
however, some of your page may contain broken links, those refer-

ences that lead nowhere. You can use a WebMap to discover broken links and then launch your Web page editor to fix the link.

You can use two methods to search for broken objects in your pages. One way is to conduct a search for all links that are broken. Another way is to search for broken objects or for objects based on a specific HTTP status.

To search for broken links, use Step by Step 7.1:

STEP BY STEP

7.1 Searching for Broken Links

1. Create a WebMap and select Tools, Custom Search (or click the Search toolbar button). The Search dialog box is displayed.

2. Configure the Search dialog box using the following parameters:
   - Object Type set to Links
   - Field set to Broken
   - Modifiers set to Equals
   - Value set to True

3. Click Search. The Search Results window displays all broken links, if any.

NOTE

Broken Versus Unavailable Links
Sometimes links are shown as broken (shown in red) but really aren't broken at all. A site may be unavailable because of repairs it is going through. There may be too much network traffic to enable you to connect to the server. You may need to try the site later to establish a connection to it.

To fix a broken link from the Search Results window, implement Step by Step 7.2:

STEP BY STEP

7.2 Fixing a Broken Link from the Search Results Window

1. Select the link.

2. Select the parent page (the page that includes the broken link) of the page you just selected.

3. Select Tools, Launch Helper App.

Checking and Modifying Hyperlink Text

Text that is used to describe a link (that is, the text that is *hyperlinked* to another object) also can be viewed using the Content Analyzer. Many sites use consistent wording and spellings for hyperlink text pointing to the same object. You can check the InLinks text to a particular object quickly with Content Analyzer. Then, if necessary, launch your editor to modify this text.

To review the hyperlink text, perform Step by Step 7.3:

STEP BY STEP

7.3 Reviewing Hyperlinked Text

1. Select the object that you want to see the InLinks text for.

2. Click the Object Links toolbar button. The Link Info window is displayed.

3. Click the InLinks option.

4. Scroll through the list of InLinks and view the hyperlink text in the Hyperlink Text column.

5. Select a link you want to change and click Follow. The page you want to change is displayed.

6. Right-click a page you want to modify and select Launch Helper App and the specific application to modify the page. Change the hyperlink text on that page.

> **NOTE**
>
> **Adding Hyperlink Text**   If Hyperlink Text is not a column in the Links Info window, add it by right-clicking any column header in the Links Info window. Use the Configure Columns dialog box to add the Hyperlink Text column to the Links Info window. Click Done.

Checking and Changing Headers

Content Analyzer can be used to check header information in pages. Headers are HTML tags used to set up sections in your Web pages.

To view headers on a page in Content Analyzer, implement Step by Step 7.4:

STEP BY STEP

7.4 Viewing Headers on a Page in Content Analyzer

1. Create a WebMap.

2. Right-click a page you want to check.

3. Select Properties to display the Properties dialog box.

4. Click the Page tab and review the Headings area.

5. Click OK to close the Properties dialog box.

If the page you just checked includes a header you want to change or does not include headers but you want to add them to the page, right-click the page in the WebMap and select Launch Helper App. Select the helper application that enables you to edit the source code of the page. Modify the page to include headers.

Checking Page Titles

You can use Content Analyzer to check page titles. Page titles are referenced by many index servers, and also are used by some browsers (such as Internet Explorer) in bookmark lists.

You'll probably want to check page titles as your Web page content changes or evolves. To check page titles, implement Step by Step 7.5:

STEP BY STEP

7.5 Checking Page Titles

1. Create a WebMap and perform a Custom Search for all pages.

2. Add the Title column to the Search Results window. This shows you the titles for each page displayed.

3. Double-click an object in the Search Results window. The associated browser launches, with the page displayed. Review the page to see if the title for it describes the content of the page. If a title is not shown, create a title for the page based on its content. You can then launch a helper application for editing Web pages to add or modify a page's title.

You should now be prepared to apply all the troubleshooting expertise to the following case study.

CASE STUDY: TROUBLESHOOTING AN IIS INSTALLATION AND DEPLOYMENT

ESSENCE OF THE CASE

▶ You need to install Microsoft Internet Information Server 4 on a 486 server for the Accounting Department, and you are having a problem getting it to run.

▶ The Sales Department set up their own Microsoft Internet Information Server 4 server on a new application server the department purchased. No one can access the Web site.

▶ There have been complaints about broken links on the company's Internet site. They need to be found and reported to the Webmaster.

SCENARIO

You are the network administrator for a thousand-person law firm and you are in the process of installing an IIS server for the Accounting Department. You are using an existing server, which has a Pentium 133 CPU, 28MB of available RAM, and 500MB of available hard drive. The Accounting Department wants you to install the entire Microsoft Internet Information Server 4 application, so you will be using every file.

After you complete the installation for the Accounting Department, the Sales Department had one of its employees decide that anyone could set up an IIS Server, so they set up one on their brand new Windows NT application server. The problem is no one can access the Web site they copied to the server. They have asked you to fix the problem.

After you fix the Sales Server, your manager asks you to look at the Internet site. There have been many complaints about broken links on the site, but no one has provided URLs for the broken links.

continues

CASE STUDY: TROUBLESHOOTING AN IIS INSTALLATION AND DEPLOYMENT

continued

ANALYSIS

You should attack each problem one at a time.

Problem 1

During the install you run into a problem. What should you look at?

First, consider the CPU. IIS 4 will run on a 66MHz 486DX CPU, so your Pentium 133, while not cutting-edge, should be adequate for the install. You have 500MB of hard drive space available. Because IIS 4 only requires 30MB and recommends 120MB, either way you have plenty of hard drive space. How about memory? IIS needs 32MB of available memory in order to run. The 28MB you have available is not sufficient to install this application.

Problem 2

The Sales Department has successfully loaded IIS 4.0 on the server. They created a new WWW site, but when users try to access it, they get no response. What should you do?

First, ensure that the service is actually running. In this scenario, it is. Next, ensure that the IP addressing is correctly configured. After some PING testing, you determine that it is. Verify that the files are in the correct location. They are. Finally, ensure that anonymous access is using a valid account name. When you look into this, you discover that the sales person who loaded IIS thought it would be more secure to disable any account she didn't recognize. She disabled the IUSR_*servername* account because she didn't recognize it. You re-enable the account and the server becomes accessible to all your users.

Problem 3

Finding the broken links on the Web site is an easy task. You load Content Analyzer and point it at the company's Internet Web site's URL. After creating a WebMap for the entire site, you make note of all the broken links, and pass the information on to the Webmaster so the links can be fixed.

CHAPTER SUMMARY

KEY TERMS

- Anonymous login
- Domain Name System (DNS)
- Dynamic Host Control Protocol (DHCP)

Take a moment to recap what you've learned in this chapter. You have looked at a number of different areas to consider while troubleshooting problems with an IIS server:

◆ **Installation Problems.** The key to installation issues is the hardware and software you are running on the server. Do you have the proper service packs loaded? Is the hardware up to Microsoft specifications? Do you have enough available RAM and hard disk space? You should be familiar with the requirements before going into the exam.

CHAPTER SUMMARY

◆ **Resolving WWW Service Issues.** You walked through the configuration screens of the WWW service and discussed a number of the common misconfigurations and errors you might see. A couple of the more obvious problems include setting the wrong port for browser access (it should be port 80), using the wrong account for anonymous access to the site, and making sure the service is actually running.

◆ **Resolving FTP Service Issues.** The FTP Service issues this chapter discusses are very similar to the WWW Service issues, although the FTP Service is quite a bit less complex. With this service as well you need to be sure you have the correct port configured, are using the correct user ID with the appropriate permissions, and, as always, be sure the service is running.

◆ **Common Security Problems.** Some of the more common security issues that arise with IIS include the following:

- Firewalls can be used to restrict incoming traffic to only those services you are choosing to allow in. Additionally, a firewall can be used to prevent all traffic from coming in. If you're attempting to make data available on the Web, consider putting the Web server outside the firewall and allowing traffic to pass to it but to nothing else on your network.

- Anonymous usage is a staple of most public Web sites. If you don't want to have a public Web site, however, consider disabling the logon. You can configure the Web server to use user authentication to verify that everyone accessing it has a valid Windows NT user account (they must give a username and password before being allowed to interact with the server).

- Secure Sockets Layer (SSL) 3.0 is included with IIS and its use should be mandatory on any site holding sensitive data (such as medical information, credit card information, and so on). SSL enables a secure connection to be established between the browser and the server, and encryption to be used between them.

continues

KEY TERMS

- File Transfer Protocol (FTP)
- HOSTS file
- Index Server
- Microsoft Management Console
- Secure Sockets Layer (SSL)
- TCP/IP
- World Wide Web (WWW)

CHAPTER SUMMARY (continued)

- Server Certificates, a part of SSL, can be created (unique digital identifications) to authenticate your Web site to browsers. This is used for public and private key (key pair) interactions of a secure nature.

- NTFS permissions can be used in conjunction with IIS to secure individual files and directories from those who should not access them. The five permission types follow:

  ◆ **Change.** Users can read and modify files, including deleting them and adding new ones to a directory.

  ◆ **Full Control.** The default for the Everyone group. Users can modify, move, delete, take ownership, and even change permissions.

  ◆ **No Access.** Overrides everything else and gives absolutely no access to the resource.

  ◆ **Read.** As the name implies, users can read the data.

  ◆ **Special Access.** User permissions have been set to something specific by the administrator.

◆ **Resolving Index Server Problems.** Be familiar with what each of the files used in conjunction with Index Server are used for, and be familiar with some of the more common errors.

◆ **ODBC Errors.** You studied some of the common ODBC errors and what they are about. The list includes the following:

  - `Microsoft OLE DB Provider for ODBC Drivers error '80004005' [Microsoft][ODBC Driver Manager] Data source name not found and no default driver specified.`

    This error occurs when the ODBC Data Source Name isn't set up so that database connections can be made.

  - `Microsoft OLE DB Provider for ODBC Drivers error '80004005' [Microsoft][ODBC SQL Server Driver][SQL Server] Logon failed.`

    This error may occur if the account being used by IIS doesn't have the right Windows NT permissions to access the database file.

CHAPTER SUMMARY

- Microsoft OLE DB Provider for ODBC Drivers error
  '80004005'[Microsoft][ODBC Microsoft Access 97 Driver]
  Couldn't use '(unknown)'; file already in use.

  The database cannot be locked correctly for multiple users.

- Microsoft OLE DB Provider for ODBC Drivers error
  '80004005'[Microsoft][ODBC Microsoft Access 97 Driver]
  '(unknown)' isn't a valid path. Make sure that the
  path name is spelled correctly and that you are connected to the server on which the file resides.

  The specified path for the database being read by the IIS server is not valid.

- Microsoft OLE DB Provider for ODBC Drivers error
  '80004005'[Microsoft][ODBC SQL Server Driver]
  [DBMSSOCN] General network error. Check your
  network document.

  This can occur when the SQL server is renamed and the IIS server is not updated to reflect the change.

◆ **Troubleshooting and Repairing a Web Site Using WebMaps.** Finally, you looked at using the Site Server WebMap capability to analyze and repair a Web site. You should be familiar with how to build a WebMap, how to use it to find broken links, and finally how to repair the broken links once they have been found.

This chapter also discussed a general method for troubleshooting any problems that may arise:

1. **Determine the problem.** The first step in any troubleshooting process is problem determination. After you know exactly what the problem is, you can start to tackle the solution.

2. **Isolate the related components.** Whether you are trou-bleshooting hardware or software problems, you should deter-mine what components are related to your problem. Know what's involved before you start trying to correct this issue.

continues

CHAPTER SUMMARY   (continued)

3. **Figure out if anything has changed.** In a majority of technical issues with a product or service that has stopped working, the problem is not because something has failed, it's because something has changed. If you can find something that has changed, you are oftentimes on the track to a solution.

4. **Plan your resolution.** The worst thing you can do while troubleshooting a problem is start throwing solutions at it. Be methodical. Make a plan to resolve the issue, and stick to it. Try to know what your next step will be if your first attempt doesn't correct this issue.

5. **Fix it.** After you have completed your plan, it's time to fix the problem.

6. **Test it.** If you've fixed the problem, move on to step 7. If it's still not working right, start over at step 1 and try to find what you've missed.

7. **Document it.** If the same problem occurs next year, it would be great to be able to refer to the solution you used the last time it occurred.

APPLY YOUR KNOWLEDGE

Exercises

7.1   Examine Your Windows 95 TCP/IP Configuration

To become familiar with how TCP/IP is configured, examine your TCP/IP configuration information on a Windows 95 system and implement the following steps:

Estimated time: 10 minutes

1. Choose Run from the Start menu.
2. Type **WINIPCFG** and press Enter.
3. Select the More Info button.
4. Note the Host and Adapter information that appears.

7.2   Examine Your Windows NT TCP/IP Configuration

To become more familiar with how TCP/IP is configured, examine your TCP/IP configuration information on a Windows NT Workstation or Server system that is manually configured. Implement the following steps:

Estimated time: 15 minutes

1. Right-click Network Neighborhood and choose Properties.
2. Select the Protocols tab.
3. Highlight TCP/IP and choose Properties.
4. Note the configuration information presented.

7.3   Setting NTFS Permissions

To set the NTFS Permissions on a directory or file object, the following steps must be completed:

Estimated time: 20 minutes

1. Right-click the NTFS Resource.
2. Select Properties from the pop-up menu for the object.
3. Switch to the Security Page of the object. This only appears if the resource is on an NTFS volume.
4. Click the Permissions button.
5. Click the Add Button to add new groups and users to assign NTFS permissions to the resource.
6. Click the local group or user that you want to assign permissions to and choose the NTFS permission you wish to assign from the bottom drop list.
7. Click the OK button to return to the Directory Permissions dialog box. From the top of the dialog box, choose whether you want to replace the permissions on all existing files in the directory and whether you want the changes to propagate to all subdirectories.
8. Click OK to make your changes to NTFS permissions effective.
9. Answer Yes to the dialog box that questions whether you want the change in security information to replace the existing security information on all files in all subdirectories.
10. Click OK to exit the Directory's properties dialog box.

APPLY YOUR KNOWLEDGE

7.4 Using NBTSTAT to View the Local NetBIOS Name Cache and Add Entries to the Cache from an LMHOSTS File

You should have installed TCP/IP and have another Windows client with TCP/IP installed and file sharing enabled.

Estimated time: 20–30 minutes

1. Use Notepad to open the file \WINNT\ SYSTEM32\DRIVERS\ETC\LMHOSTS.SAM.

2. Add an entry to the bottom of the file for the other Windows client, specifying the NetBIOS name and the IP address of the Windows client. Make sure that there's not a comment (#) in front of this line.

3. Save the file in the same directory as LMHOSTS (without an extension).

4. From a command prompt on your NT computer, type **nbtstat -c**. This displays the local cache.

5. From a command prompt, type **nbstat -R**. This purges the cache and loads the contents of the LMHOSTS file into the local cache.

6. From a command prompt, type **nbtstat -c** to display the new contents of the local cache.

7. Using Windows NT Explorer, map a network drive to the other Windows client. The local cache was used to resolve the NetBIOS name for this connection.

8. From a command prompt, type **nbtstat /?** to see all the switches available with the NBTSTAT command.

7.5 Examine Your Windows NT TCP/IP Configuration

To examine your TCP/IP configuration information on a Windows NT Workstation or Server system that is configured through static or dynamic IP addresses (DHCP), implement the following steps:

Estimated time: 15 minutes

1. From the Start menu, select Programs, and then Command Prompt.

2. Type **IPCONFIG**.

3. Note the information that appears. Now type **IPCONFIG /ALL**.

4. Note the information that appears.

7.6 Examine Your Windows NT Configuration with the Resource Kit

To examine your TCP/IP configuration information if the Windows NT Resource Kit CD has been installed on your system, implement the following steps:

Estimated time: 30 minutes

1. From the Start menu, Choose Programs, then Resource Kit 4.0.

2. Choose Internet Utils and then IP Configuration.

3. Select the More Info button.

4. Note the Host and Adapter information that appears.

APPLY YOUR KNOWLEDGE

7.7   Correcting a Network Configuration Error

Use this exercise to see the effects that an improperly configured network card has on other networking services and protocols. Before starting, make sure you have installed Windows NT Server with a computer that has a network adapter card and that TCP/IP has been installed.

Estimated time: 30–45 minutes

1. Clear the System Log in Event Viewer.

2. From the desktop, right-click on Network Neighborhood and choose Properties from the resulting menu.

3. From the Network Properties dialog box, select the Adapters tab.

4. Select your adapter card from the list and choose Properties.

5. Note the correct setting as it is and change the .IRQ of your adapter card to an incorrect setting.

6. Close this dialog box and choose to reboot your computer when prompted.

7. When your computer reboots, note the message received after the Logon prompt is displayed. The message should indicate A Dependency Service Failed to Start.

8. Log on and open Event Viewer.

9. Note the error message generated from the adapter card. Note the other error messages generated after the adapter card error.

10. Clear the System Log in Event Viewer.

11. From the command prompt, type **PING 127.0.0.1**. This PING fails because TCP/IP doesn't start if the adapter doesn't start.

12. From the Network Properties dialog box, change the .IRQ of your adapter card back to its proper setting and reboot.

13. Log on and check the System Log. There should be no adapter card errors or errors from networking services.

14. From the command prompt, type **PING 127.0.0.1**. This PING succeeds because TCP/IP is started now.

7.8   Using PING to Test an IP Configuration

This exercise uses PING to verify a TCP/IP installation and configuration. You should have installed Windows NT Server and TCP/IP.

Estimated time: 10 minutes

1. From the desktop, right-click on Network Neighborhood and choose Properties from the resulting menu.

2. From the Bindings tab, expand all the networking services.

3. Select TCP/IP and choose Disable.

4. Repeat step 3 until you have disabled TCP/IP for all the listed networking services.

5. Close the dialog box and, when prompted, choose to reboot your computer.

6. When the computer reboots, log in.

7. From a command prompt, type **PING 127.0.0.1**. This PING works because TCP/IP is installed.

APPLY YOUR KNOWLEDGE

8. From a command prompt, type **PING** *x.x.x.x*, where *x.x.x.x* is your default gateway address. This PING fails because you have disabled TCP/IP from all the networking services. There isn't a way for TCP/IP packets to be sent on the network.

9. From the Bindings tab in Network Properties, enable TCP/IP for all the networking services.

10. Close the dialog box and, when prompted, choose to reboot your computer.

11. When the computer reboots, log in.

12. From a command prompt, ping your default gateway. PING works this time because a path now exists by which TCP/IP communications can reach the network.

7.9   Using the Event Viewer to view Index Server Error Messages

This exercise uses the Log Viewer to find Index Server error messages. Note: These messages are listed in the chapter and will only be seen if there is a problem with Index Server.

Estimated time: 10 minutes

1. Open the Event Viewer from the Administrative Tools program group.

2. Switch to the Application Log by selecting Application under the Log menu.

3. Any informational messages for the Index Server will show under the CI source. Any error messages will show as Ci Filter Service.

4. When you are done viewing the Event Log, close the Event Viewer.

7.10   Verifying the Default WWW Port

This exercise shows you how to verify the WWW Service is using the correct port. This is a common error when you are having issues with the WWW Service.

Estimated time: 10 minutes

1. Open Internet Service Manager.

2. Select the WWW Site you want to check.

3. Right-click and select Properties.

4. Under the Web Site tab, verify that the TCP Port is set to 80.

7.11   Verifying the Default FTP Port

This exercise shows you how to verify the correct port is being used by the FTP Service. This is a common error when you are having issues with the FTP Service.

Estimated time: 10 minutes

1. Open Internet Service Manager.

2. Select the FTP Site you want to check.

3. Right-click and select Properties.

4. Under the FTP Site tab, verify that the TCP Port is set to 21.

7.12   Verifying the Service Pack Level of Your Windows NT Server

One of the keys to a successful IIS installation is verifying the correct Service Pack has been installed. This exercise shows you how to verify that Service Pack 3 or greater has been installed.

Estimated time: 10 minutes

APPLY YOUR KNOWLEDGE

1. Open the Windows NT Diagnostics application by going to Start -> Run -> WINMSD.

2. Under the version tab, there will be a line for the operating system (e.g., Windows NT). The next line will be the version of the operating system. At the end of this line will be the Service Pack Level, in parentheses (e.g., Service Pack 4).

3. This application can also be used to verify available memory, hard drive, and other useful configuration information.

4. When you are done, close the application by clicking OK.

Review Questions

1. You are a new administrator at Asp Snakes and Reptiles. You have been asked to install and configure TCP/IP on an new Windows NT server, which will eventually run Microsoft Internet Information Server 4. What are the three main values that must be entered to configure TCP/IP on a host with the ability to communicate beyond the local network?

2. You are the Windows NT Administrator for Little Faith Enterprises and you have been asked to configure NTFS on the IIS Web Server to allow users to view documents without being able to change them. What NTFS permission enables a user to view any documents that are stored in a share, but does not enable them to make any changes to the documents?

3. You are an end user at Exponent Mathematics and you need to see what the address of the DHCP server you are receiving your IP address

information from, so you can get some support from your Help Desk. You are running Windows NT Workstation 4.0. What command-line command should be given at your workstation to see the address of the DHCP server from which the client received its IP address?

4. You are working on passing the IIS 4.0 exam for your MCSE. One of the people in your study group is stumped on an Index Server question. She can't figure out when Index Server starts running. You offer to help her out. By default, when does Index Server start?

5. You are the Webmaster for Hatter's Hats and Fine Clothing and you have been tasked with upgrading your IIS 3.0 server to IIS 4.0. To upgrade IIS 3.0 to IIS 4.0, what must you do?

6. What tool, new to IIS 4.0, can be used to administer Web site content to help you keep your Web site up to date and functioning correctly?

7. You are the Intranet Administrator at CIC Enterprises, and after doing some Windows NT user account updates, you suddenly find no one can access your Web site, even though you have enabled anonymous access. Where should you look to find this problem?

8. You are the Web site administrator for Oui Gyp U Loansharks. You have posted an updated listing of your interest rates, but you are receiving complaints that the old information is still showing up when people reach the site. Where should you look for the problem?

9. You run the Microsoft Internet Information Server 4-based FTP Server for Little Faith Enterprises. You remember reading somewhere

APPLY YOUR KNOWLEDGE

that to make your FTP site secure, you should set the port number to something greater than 1,023. Suddenly, none of your users can access the FTP site. Why not?

10. You are using Microsoft Index Server to index your intranet site. You come in to work one day and notice that it has stopped indexing. You also notice that you are out of disk space on the server you are running Index Server on. What happened and how can you fix it?

Exam Questions

1. You are the Network Administrator for Little Faith Enterprises, and you need to enable a user to view and navigate through the contents of a directory, but nothing more. Which of the following NTFS Directory permissions enables the user to view the contents of a directory and to navigate to its subdirectories?

   A. No Access

   B. List

   C. Read

   D. Add

   E. Change

2. You are the Network Administrator for Mad Hatter Hats. You have a user that has been given access to a directory by user account, but still cannot access the directory. You suspect that one of the groups he is a member of is blocking his access, even though you have given him explicit access. Which of the following NTFS Directory permissions overrides all other permissions?

   A. No Access

   B. List

   C. Read

   D. Add

   E. Change

3. Which of the following NTFS Directory permissions enables the user to do the most data manipulation?

   A. No Access

   B. List

   C. Read

   D. Add

   E. Change

4. Which of the following NTFS Directory permissions enables the user to navigate the entire directory structure, view the contents of the directory, view the contents of any files in the directory, and execute programs?

   A. No Access

   B. List

   C. Read

   D. Add

   E. Change

5. You are the IIS Administrator for Little Faith Enterprises. One of your users surfs out to the URL of your new intranet server and instead of opening to the index.html home page, she is presented with a listing of the directory instead. What's happened? Select all that apply.

APPLY YOUR KNOWLEDGE

A. They don't have permission to load the index.html document.

B. The List Directory permission has been granted to the site.

C. The index.htm file has not been configured as a default document.

D. The IUSR_*HOSTNAME* account has been granted the Full Access permission for the site.

6. Which set of permissions enable a user to add new files to the directory structure and, once the files have been added, ensures that the user has read-only access to the files? Select all that apply.

A. No Access

B. List

C. Read

D. Add

E. Change

7. HOSTS file entries are limited to how many characters?

A. 8

B. 255

C. 500

D. Unlimited

8. The entries in the HOSTS file are limited to what number?

A. 8

B. 255

C. 500

D. Unlimited

9. Which of the following files is case sensitive on NT 3.5 systems?

A. HOSTS

B. LMHOSTS

C. ARP

D. FQDN

10. Which of the following files is used for NetBIOS name resolution?

A. HOSTS

B. LMHOSTS

C. ARP

D. FQDN

11. Index Server error messages can be viewed with which of the following? Select the best answer.

A. Server Manager

B. User Manager for Domains

C. Event Viewer

D. Disk Administrator

12. Index Server error messages are written to what log file?

A. System

B. Server

C. Security

D. Application

APPLY YOUR KNOWLEDGE

13. To run IIS 4.0 on NT, which Service Pack must be installed?

    A. None

    B. 1

    C. 2

    D. 3

Answers to Review Questions

1. The IP address, the subnet mask, and the default gateway are the three values that must be entered at each host to configure TCP/IP. See "Resolving IIS Configuration Problems."

2. With the Read permission, users can view any documents that are stored in the share, but they cannot make any changes to the documents. See "Resolving Security Problems."

3. IPCONFIG/ALL shows the DHCP server as well as all IP configuration information. See "Resolving Resource Access Problems."

4. By default, Index Server starts when IIS starts. If, for some reason, it has not started, Index Server starts with the first query. See "Resolving Index Server Query Problems."

5. To upgrade IIS 3.0 to IIS 4.0, you must first delete all traces of the IIS 3.0 operating files before installing 4.0. See "Resolving Setup Issues When Installing IIS on a Windows NT Server 4.0 Computer."

6. Content Analyzer's WebMap can be used to administer site content. It is new to IIS 4.0 and can help you keep your site up-to-date and functioning correctly. See "Use a WebMap to Find and Repair Broken Links, Hyperlink Texts, Headings, and Titles."

7. Check the configuration of the IUSR_*HOST-NAME* account. You probably changed the password or disabled the account IIS uses to grant anonymous access to the Web site. See "Resolving Security Problems."

8. Check the content expiration settings for the site. This problem is probably caused by a long time period before site content expires, and users are seeing cached information. See "Resolving WWW Service Issues."

9. Because your users are still trying to access the site on the default port of 21, they cannot access the FTP site. See "Resolving FTP Service Issues."

10. When available disk space falls below 3MB, Index Server automatically stops running. To restart the service, simple free up some disk space. After available disk space is greater then 3MB, Index Server will automatically restart. See "Resolving Index Server Problems."

Answers to Exam Questions

1. **B.** List enables the user to view the contents of a directory and to navigate to its subdirectories. No Access will prevent any access form occurring. Choices C, D, and E all allow more access than just listing the directory and navigating. See "Common Security Problems."

2. **A.** No Access overrides all other permissions. See "Common Security Problems."

3. **E.** Change enables the user to perform the most data manipulation. No Access offers the least

APPLY YOUR KNOWLEDGE

amount of permissions. List allows you to get a directory listing, but no more. Read allows you to see what's in a file, but not manipulate it. Add allows you to add a file or directory to the directory, but no more. Change allows you to do all this, plus modify files and directories. See "Common Security Problems."

4. **C.** Read enables the user to navigate the entire directory structure, view the contents of the directory, view the contents of any files in the directory, and execute programs. See "Common Security Problems."

5. **B, C.** Directory Listing has been enabled, and the index.htm has not been configured as a default document. See "Resolving WWW Service Issues."

6. **C, D.** Read and Add enable a user to add new files to the directory structure and, once the files have been added, the user then has only read-only access to the files. See "Common Security Problems."

7. **B.** HOSTS file lines are limited to 255 characters in length. See "IP Address Configuration Problems."

8. **D.** The HOSTS file can be an unlimited number of lines long. See "IP Address Configuration Problems."

9. **A.** The HOSTS file, prior to NT 4.0, was case sensitive and remains so on non-NT systems. See "IP Address Configuration Problems."

10. **B.** LMHOSTS is the static file used for NetBIOS name resolution. See "IP Address Configuration Problems."

11. **C.** Index Server system errors can be viewed with Event Viewer. See "Resolving Index Server Problems."

12. **D.** Index Server error messages are written to the application log. See "Resolving Index Server Problems."

13. **D.** To run IIS 4.0 on NT, Service Pack 3 must be installed. See "Installation Problems."

Suggested Readings and Resources

1. Comer, Douglas. *Internetworking With TCP/IP: Principles, Protocols, and Architecture, Third Edition.* Prentice Hall: 1998.

2. Heywood, Drew. *Networking With Microsoft TCP/IP, Third Edition.* New Riders Publishing: 1998.

3. Howell, Nelson and Forta, Ben. *Special Edition Using Microsoft Internet Information Server 4.* Que Education and Training: 1997.

4. Siyan, Karanjit S. *Windows NT TCP/IP.* New Riders Professional Library: 1998.

5. Tulloch, Mitch. *Administering Internet Information Server 4 (Windows NT Technical Expert).* Computing McGraw-Hill: 1998.

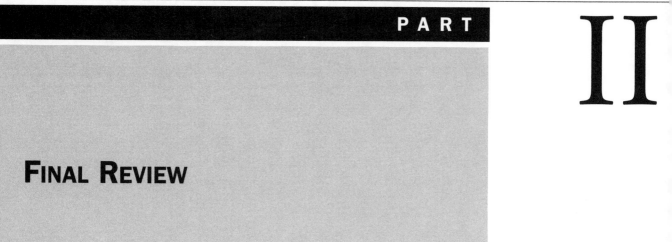

PART

II

Final Review

Fast Facts

Study and Exam Prep Tips

Practice Exam

The seven chapters of this book have covered the objectives and components of the Microsoft IIS 4.0 exam. After reading all of that, what is it that you really need to know? What should you read as you sit and wait in the parking lot of the testing center—right up until the hour before going in to pass the test and finish one more step towards your first (or next) Microsoft certification?

The following material covers the significant points of the previous seven chapters as well as provides some insight into the information that makes particularly good material for exam questions. Although there is no substitute for real-world, hands-on experience, knowing what to expect on the exam can go a long way towards a passing score. The information that follows is equivalent to *Cliffs Notes*, providing the information you must know in each of the seven sections to pass the exam. Don't just memorize the concepts given; attempt to understand the reason why they are so, and you will have no difficulties passing the exam.

PLANNING

As with previous IIS exams, the WWW service and FTP service are the core ones the exam focuses on. IIS can be installed on a standalone machine or in almost any other configuration. It can be installed on a workstation or server, but a workstation should be used only as a test environment and is not for exam preparation.

For the most secure configuration, IIS should be installed on a standalone server, with only data that is supposed to be made available through IIS on it. Placing IIS on a domain controller can expose your user database, and using a file and print or application server as an IIS server can expose additional data not meant to be served through IIS. For additional security, data should always be stored on an NTFS partition.

Fast Facts

Exam 70-087

Remember that IIS automatically creates a user account upon installation, with the user name of IUSR_computername. This is the account used for anonymous access and granted Log on Locally user rights by default. The account is necessary for anonymous logon access to your Web site, and permissions applied to it control the permissions for the anonymous user. You even can go so far as to disable anonymous access if security is a concern.

For the WWW service, available authentication methods are as follows:

◆ **Allow Anonymous Access.** Enables clients to connect to your Web site without requiring a user name or password by using the default account of IUSR_computername.

◆ **Basic Authentication.** This method is used if you do not specify anonymous access and you want a client connecting to your Web site to enter a valid Windows NT user name and password to log on. This sends a password in clear text format, with the passwords being transmitted in an unencrypted format.

◆ **Windows NT Challenge/Response.** This setting is used if you want the Windows NT Challenge/ Response feature to authenticate the client attempting to connect to your Web site. The only Web browsers that support this feature include Internet Explorer 2.0 and later. During the challenge/ response procedure, cryptographic information is exchanged between the client and server to authenticate the user.

For the FTP service, available authentication methods include the ability to specify that anonymous connections are allowed or only anonymous connections are allowed, or the administrator can configure user and group accounts. Although it makes perfect sense, you cannot specify on the exam that only anonymous connections

are allowed until you have first allowed anonymous connections.

Know the basics of TCP/IP (including what WINS and DNS are) and IP values, namely the number of hosts available per IP address class, as recapped in Table 1.

TABLE 1
ADDRESS CLASSES

Class	Address	Number of Hosts Available	Default Subnet Mask
A	01-126	16,777,214	255.0.0.0
B	128-191	65,534	255.255.0.0
C	192-223	254	255.255.255.0

The WINS service is used for dynamic resolution of NetBIOS names to IP addresses, and DNS is used for dynamic resolution of host names to IP addresses. The static versions of each are the LMHOSTS and HOSTS files, respectively.

The Secure Sockets Layer (SSL) enables you to protect communications over a network, whether that network is an intranet or the Internet. It does so by establishing a private (and encrypted) communication link between the user and the server. SSL can be used not only to authenticate specific users, but also the anonymous user. If SSL is enabled and a user attempts anonymous access, the Web server looks for a valid certificate on the client and rejects those lacking one. To use SSL, you must obtain a digital certificate from an authentication authority and use Key Manager to generate keys. SSL URLs begin with https:// instead of http://.

Memorize these subnet addresses and the corresponding number of hosts that each makes available on a C-level network (see Table 2).

TABLE 2
SUBNET ADDRESSES AND NUMBER OF HOSTS

Last Digits of Subnet Address	Number of Addresses in Range
128	128
192	64
224	32
240	16
248	8
252	4
254	2
255	1 (not used)

You should also be familiar with the following different components of IIS and what each of them can do for you:

♦ **Microsoft Management Console (MMC).** The MMC provides the next-generation management framework for managing Windows NT servers and services. Through the use of management applications known as *snap-ins*, the MMC provides a single interface for IIS 4.0 today.

♦ **WWW.** The World Wide Web (WWW) service in IIS 4.0 is the service that allows you to include HTML (Hypertext Markup Language) documents on your site.

♦ **FTP.** The File Transfer Protocol (FTP) service provides clients attaching to your server the ability to transmit files to and from the server.

♦ **Microsoft Transaction Server.** Microsoft Transaction Server (MTS) is a transaction processing system for developing and managing server applications.

♦ **Microsoft SMTP Service.** Microsoft SMTP Service uses the Simple Mail Transfer Protocol (SMTP) to send and receive e-mail.

♦ **Microsoft NNTP Service.** The Microsoft NNTP Service supports the Network News Transport Protocol and enables clients to access newsgroups.

♦ **Microsoft Index Server.** Microsoft Index Server indexes the full text and properties of documents stored on an Internet or intranet Web site.

♦ **Microsoft Certificate Server.** Microsoft Certificate Server enables you to increase the security of your site by issuing certificates (digital identifiers) that use public-key encryption. Certificates enable you to verify that you have secure communication across the network, whether that network is an intranet or the Internet.

♦ **Site Server Express.** The Site Server Express component of IIS 4.0 brings site management to IIS. Where earlier versions of IIS allowed you to log usage, Site Server Express provides the ability to analyze that usage.

♦ **Active Server Pages and Microsoft Script Debugger.** Active Server Pages (ASP) can be used to create dynamic HTML pages or build powerful Web applications. Microsoft Script Debugger is exactly what it sounds like. It is a tool that allows you to test ASP scripts.

♦ **Internet Connection Services for Remote Access Services.** Microsoft Internet Connection Services for Remote Access Services provides enhanced Internet connection capabilities, including a dial-up service, and Virtual Private Networking (VPN) capabilities.

♦ **Microsoft Message Queue.** Microsoft Message Queue Server (MSMQ) allows applications to communicate with other applications by providing a reliable mechanism for sending and receiving messages.

♦ **Microsoft Data Access Components.** Microsoft Data Access Components are a bundle of components that allow easier access to a variety of data types. Microsoft Data Access Components consist of ActiveX Data Objects (ADO) and Remote Data Service (RDS), the Microsoft OLE DB Provider for ODBC, and Open Database Connectivity (ODBC).

◆ **Additional Support for Internet Standards.** In addition to new services and components, IIS 4.0 also adds support for a number of Internet standards, including the following:

• **HTTP 1.1 Support.** The latest version of the HTTP protocol adds the following features:

◆ **Pipelining.** HTTP version 1.0 processes client requests one at a time, waiting until the request is completed before servicing the next request. Pipelining can be used to provide improved Web server performance by allowing clients to send many requests before receiving a response from the Web server. This can provide a significant performance boost, depending on the types of requests being made.

◆ **Persistent Connections.** Also known as *Keep-Alives*, persistent connections can be used to reduce the number of connections a client uses to make multiple requests to a Web server. When a browser connects to a Web server and requests a resource, a connection is established with the server. When the request is completed, the connection is dropped. Because this is an expensive process in terms of server processing, persistent connections can be used to reduce or eliminate the need for multiple connections when clients make multiple requests for resources. This is a configurable parameter that is discussed in Chapter 2, "Installation and Configuration."

◆ **HTTP PUT and DELETE.** HTTP PUT and DELETE can be used to post and delete files to and from a Web site using any HTTP 1.1-compliant browser. This is similar to the RFC 1867 support mentioned shortly, but is not the same thing.

◆ **Transfer Chunk Encoding.** Transfer Chunk Encoding (also known as *chunked transfers)* allows Active Server Pages (ASP) to transmit variable-length documents more efficiently. Because ASP can be used to build pages on-the-fly, these pages can be a variable length. Transfer Chunk Encoding allows these pages to be broken into "chunks" for more efficient transfers.

◆ **RFC 1867 Support.** RFC 1867 defines the mechanism for allowing file uploads, such as posting content from a browser directly to a Web server.

◆ **HTTP Redirects.** Support for HTTP Redirects means that IIS 4.0 site administrators can redirect requests for files to a different Web site, directory, or file.

INSTALLATION AND CONFIGURATION

To install IIS 4.0, you must first remove any previous versions of IIS (IIS 3.0 or version 2.0 that came with Windows NT 4.0). During the installation of it, you are prompted to select the services you want to install.

IIS 4.0 includes the features listed in Table 3.

TABLE 3
IIS 4 SERVICES AND FEATURES

Component	Subcomponent	Description
Certificate Server	Certificate Server Certificate Authority	Enables you to create certificate authority on the IIS server to issue digital certificates to users accessing your Web.
	Certificate Server Documentation	Documents to help you install and configure certificate authorities.
	Certificate Server Web Client	Enables you to post Web pages on your server to submit requests and retrieve certificates from a certificate authority.
FrontPage 98 Server Extensions	FrontPage Server Extensions Files	Enables you to author Web pages and administer Web sites using Microsoft FrontPage and Visual InterDev.
Internet Information Server (IIS)	Common Program Files	Files used by several IIS components.
	Documentation	Product documentation for IIS.
	File Transfer Protocol (FTP) Server	Provides FTP support to set up an FTP site to allow users to upload and download files from your site.
	Internet News Server	Installs the Microsoft Internet News Server for NNTP news.
	Internet Service Manager	Provides a snap-in for the Microsoft Management Console (MMC) to administer IIS.
	Internet Service Manager (HTML)	Provides an HTML-based administrative tool for IIS. You use IE 4 with this manager to administer IIS.
	SMTP Server	Installs the SMTP (Simple Mail Transfer Protocol) Server for e-mail.
	World Wide Web Samples	Installs sample IIS Web sites and other samples.
	World Wide Web Server	Installs the Web server so clients can access your Web site.
Microsoft Data Access Components 1.5	Data Sources	Installs the drivers and providers to access common data sources, including Jet and Access (ODBC), Oracle, and SQL Server data sources.
	MDAC, ADO, ODBC, and OLE	Installs the ActiveX Data Objects and other OLE DB and ODBC files.
	Remote Data Service 1.5 (RDS/ADC)	Installs Remote Data Service. Click the Show Subcomponents button to see options for this subcomponent.
Microsoft Index	Index Server System Files	Installs the files for the Index Server system.
	Language Resources	Installs Index Server language resources. Click the Show Subcomponents button to see a list of these languages. U.S. English Language is the default setting.
	Online Documentation	Installs Index Server documentation.

continues

TABLE 3   *continued*

Component	Subcomponent	Description
	Sample Files	Installs sample files on how to use the Index Server.
Microsoft Management Console (MMC)	Management Console	Allows management of the IIS Services through the new console.
Microsoft Message (MSMQ)	HTML Documentation	Installs the MSMQ Queue Administration Guide.
	Administration Tools	Enables you to control and monitor your message queuing enterprise.
	Microsoft Message Queue (Core)	Installs the required MSMQ files.
	Software Development Kit	Installs the MSMQ SDK for creating MSMQ applications with C or C++ APIs, or with ActiveX components.
Microsoft Script Debugger	Microsoft Script Debugger	Installs the Microsoft Script Debugger to debug Active Server Pages scripts and applications.
Microsoft Site Server Express 2.0	Analysis—Content	Enables you to analyze your site with content, site visualization, link management, and reporting tool.
	Analysis—Usage	Enables you to analyze your site usage.
	Publishing—Posting Acceptor 1.01	Enables IIS to receive files uploaded to it using the HTTP POST protocol.
	Publishing—Web Publishing Wizard 1.52	Automatically uploads new or revised content to Web servers.
Remote Access Services	Connection Manager Administration Kit	Sets up dial-up profiles in Connection Manager.
	Connection Point Services	Provides administration and services to phone books.
	Internet Authentication Services	Installs the Internet Authentication Service.
	Product Documentation	Installs documentation for Remote Access Services.
Transaction Server	Microsoft Management Console	Installs MMC, which is an interface for systems management applications.
	Transaction Server (MTS) Core Components	Installs MTS files.
	Transaction Server Core Documentation	Installs MTS product documentation.
	Transaction Server Deployment	Installs headers, libraries, and samples to help you create transaction components.
Visual InterDev RAD	Visual InterDev RAD Remote Deployment Support	Enables you to deploy applications remotely on the Web server.
Windows Scripting Host	Windows Scripting Host Files	Installs executable files for the Windows Scripting Host.
NT Option Pack Common Files		Files shared by all components of the NT Option Pack.

If you choose not to install a service at this time, you can restart the installation routine at any time and choose only the additional services you want to add. IIS 4.0 hardware requirements for an Intel system are:

Hardware Device	Requirements
CPU	Minimum of a 66MHz 486 processor. For better performance, you need a Pentium 33-or-higher processor.
Hard disk space	Minimum of 30MB, but it is recommended you have at least 120MB. This does not include storage needed for files you plan to distribute via IIS.
Memory	Minimum of 32MB. For a Web site on which you will store multimedia files or expect a great deal of traffic, 48MB is the recommended minimum.
Monitor	Super VGA monitor with 800×600 resolution.

TCP port settings are used by clients to connect to your FTP or WWW site. Memorize the default port settings:

Service	Port
FTP	21
SMTP	25
WWW	80
NNTP	119
SSL	443
NNTP with SSL	563

You can change the settings to unique TCP port numbers, but you must announce this setting to all clients who want to access your server.

An FTP directory listing style is the way in which your server displays a directory listing. The two choices are DOS (such as C:\folder\subfolder) and UNIX format (such as C:/directory/subdirectory/). Use UNIX format for the greatest compatibility on the Internet. (The default is MS-DOS.)

Limiting bandwidth is known as *bandwidth throttling*, and it can be used to limit the bandwidth used by a single Web site or the entire Web server. The WWW service is the only service on IIS that can use bandwidth throttling. IIS 4.0 provides support for HTTP 1.1 Host Headers to allow multiple host names to be associated with one IP address. With this feature, a separate IP address is not needed for every virtual server you support. Microsoft Internet Explorer 3.0 and later and Netscape Navigator 2.0 and later support this feature, but many other browsers do not.

IIS 4.0's support for HTTP Keep-Alives enables clients to maintain open connections. This way, a client does not need to re-establish connections for each request. By enabling Keep-Alives, you decrease the amount of time a client waits to connect to another document or application on your site. But you also increase the amount of resources devoted to this client.

CONFIGURING AND MANAGING RESOURCE ACCESS

The Microsoft Management Console is the primary utility used for most configuration and management tasks. Accessed by choosing Internet Service Manager from the Programs menu, it is used for almost everything, including creating and sharing new directories or virtual directories, or servers. If there is only one thing you need to learn for the exam, it is everything you possibly can about MMC.

Access permissions for directories include the following:

◆ Allow Read Access

◆ Allow Script Access

◆ Allow Execute Access

◆ Allow Write Access

◆ Allow Directory Browsing

The five rights that you can select for IIS access work in conjunction with all other rights. Like share rights, the IIS rights are *in addition to* NTFS rights and of greatest value when you are using anonymous access. Allowing Read access lets users view a file if their NTFS permissions also allow it. Taking away Read, however, prevents users from viewing the file, regardless of what the NTFS permissions may be.

The names of the rights give you a fair assessment of what they enable a user to do on the server. Keep in mind that Read and Script access are assigned by default, and Execute is a superset of Script access.

With virtual directories, you can get around issues such as disk space, determining where best to store files, and so forth. Virtual directories *must* exist on a server in the same authentication domain as the IIS 4.0 server being used to serve them. There are two downfalls to using virtual directories:

◆ There is a slight decrease in performance because files must be retrieved from the LAN rather than being centralized.

◆ Virtual directories do not show up in WWW listings and must be accessed through explicit links within HTML files or in the URL itself, such as `http://www.microsoft.com/train_cert`.

You should also have a scripts directory under every virtual home directory to handle any executable files to be run from that home directory.

If you want to serve information on a Novell NetWare server, you should map a drive to the NetWare volume from a Windows NT machine in the same authentication domain as the IIS 4.0 server. Then, map your virtual directory to the mapped drive on the Windows NT computer.

The Internet Service Manager (HTML) enables you to manage the FTP and WWW service remotely (the WWW service must first be running to use it). Remotely, you can do almost everything you can locally, with the exception of making MIME Registry changes or stopping and starting services (if you stopped WWW, you would be disconnected).

MIME is used to define the type of file sent to the browser based upon the extension. If your server is supplying files in multiple formats, it must have a MIME mapping for each file type, or browsers will most likely be unable to retrieve the file. Mappings can be added or changed with REGEDIT or REGEDT32.

INTEGRATION AND INTEROPERABILITY

Databases such as Oracle or Microsoft SQL (Structured Query Language) Server can be used with IIS to supply the information to fulfill a query, update information, and add new data through the Web almost as easily as if a user were sitting on a local area network.

Open Database Connectivity (ODBC) is an API (Application Programming Interface) that provides a simple way to connect to an existing database (whether that database is by SQL or is any ODBC-compliant database). It was designed by Microsoft to address the issue of any number of applications needing to interface with SQL Server. Authentication can be done by NT or SQL. If SQL is chosen, it uses standard logon security, and a SQL Server user ID and password must be given for all connections. If you choose to use Windows NT authentication, the Windows NT user account is associated with a SQL Server user account, and integrated security is used to establish the connection, regardless of the current security mode at the server.

The greatest advantage that ODBC offers is that it defines a clear distinction between the application and the database, and thus does not require any specific programming. To use it, you create a query and template for how the output is to look.

The following are four major components to IIS's implementation of ODBC:

- **.HTM.** The file containing the hyperlink for a query. The request comes from the browser and merely specifies the URL for the .IDC (Internet Database Connector) file on IIS.

- **.HTX.** A file of HTML extensions containing the template document with placeholders for the result. Database fields that it receives are known as containers and are identified by field names surrounded by percent signs (%) and braces (<>). Thus, the employeeno field that comes from the SQL database is known as <%employeeno%> here. All processing is done in loops that start with <%begindetail%> and end with <%enddetail%>. Logic can be included with <%if ...%> and <%endif%>, as well as <%else%> statements.

- **.IDC.** The file containing the data source file information and SQL statement. Four required parameters are Datasource, Username, Template, and SQLStatement. SQLStatement is the list of commands you want to execute. Parameter values can be used if they are enclosed in percent signs (%); if multiple lines are required, a plus sign (+) must be the first character on each line.

- **HTTPODBC.DLL.** The dynamic link library included with the server.

Index Server differs from the ODBC discussion in the files used to hold the queries. Rather than using the .IDC file, Index Server uses an .IDQ (Internet Data Query) file. The .IDQ file should always be placed in the Scripts directory, and it requires Execute or Script permission to function properly.

There are two sections to the file: It begins with a tag of [Query] (the first section), followed by the [Names] section. The Names section is purely optional and not used most of the time. If it is used, it defines nonstandard column names that are referred to in a query. The Query section of the file is all that is required, and it can contain parameters, variables, and conditional expressions.

Restrictions are that lines must start with the variable you are trying to set, and only one variable can be set per line. Additionally, percent signs (%) are used to identify the variables and references.

The variables that can be used in .IDQ files are as follows:

- **CiCatalog.** Sets the location for the catalog. If the value is already set, the value here overrides that one.

- **CiCodepage.** Sets the server's code page. Again, if the value is already set, the entry here overrides the previous one.

- **CiColumns.** Defines a list of columns that will be used in the .HTX file.

- **CiDeferNonIndexedTrimming.** Is not used by default, but can be set if the scope of the query must be limited.

- **CiFlags.** Query flags can be set to DEEP or SHALLOW to determine whether only the directory listed in CiScope is searched or more.

- ◆ **CiForceUseCi.** By setting to TRUE, you can force the query to use the content index even if it is out of date.

- ◆ **CiLocale.** Specifies the locale used to issue the query.

- ◆ **CiMaxRecordsInResultSet.** Specifies the maximum number of results that can be returned from the query.

- ◆ **CiMaxRecordsPerPage.** Specifies the maximum number of records that can appear on a display page.

- ◆ **CiRestriction.** A restriction that you are placing on the query.

- ◆ **CiScope.** Specifies the starting directory for the search.

- ◆ **CiSort.** Specifies whether the results should be sorted in ascending or descending order.

- ◆ **CiTemplate.** Specifies the full path of the .HTX file from the root. Index Server is bound by the Windows NT shell limit of 260 characters per path.

As with most script files, a pound sign (#) can be used to specify a comment. At whatever point the # is in the line, from there on the line is ignored. The conditional expressions that can be used in .IDQ files are the following:

- ◆ **CONTAINS.** Is true if any part of the first value is found in the second value

- ◆ **EQ.** Equal to

- ◆ **GE.** Greater than or equal to

- ◆ **GT.** Greater than

- ◆ **ISEMPTY.** Is true if the value is null

- ◆ **LE.** Less than or equal to

- ◆ **LT.** Less than

- ◆ **NE.** Not equal to

RUNNING APPLICATIONS

ISAPI (Internet Server Application Programming Interface) can be used to write applications that Web users can activate by filling out an HTML form or clicking a link in an HTML page on your Web server. The user-supplied information can then be responded to and the results returned in an HTML page or posted to a database.

ISAPI was a Microsoft improvement over popular CGI (common gateway interface) scripting and offers much better performance over CGI because applications are loaded into memory at server runtime. This means that they require less overhead and each request does not start a separate process. Additionally, ISAPI applications are created as DLLs on the server and allow preprocessing of requests and post-processing of responses, permitting site-specific handling of HTTP requests and responses.

ISAPI filters can be used for applications for such functions as customized authentication, access, or logging. You can create complex sites by combining ISAPI filters and applications.

ISAPI works with OLE connectivity and the Internet Database Connector. This allows ISAPI to be implemented as a DLL (in essence, an executable) or as a filter (translating another executable's output). If ISAPI is used as a filter, it is not called by the browser's accessing an URL, but rather summoned by the server in response to an event (which could easily be an URL request). Common uses of ISAPI filters include the following:

- ◆ Tracking URL usage statistics
- ◆ Performing authentication
- ◆ Adding entries to log files
- ◆ Compression

You don't need to be an ISAPI programmer to pass the exam, but there are several things you need to know:

◆ ISAPI applications effectively extend server applications to the desktop.

◆ ISAPI is similar to CGI but offers better performance; CGI needs a new process for every execution.

◆ Although created by Microsoft, ISAPI is an open specification that third parties can write to.

◆ ISAPI filters can do pre- or post-processing.

◆ Execute, but not necessarily read, permission is required for CGI or ISAPI script execution.

MONITORING AND OPTIMIZATION

The Active Log Format drop-down list enables you to select the type of log format you want to create. The following are the supported log file formats:

◆ **Microsoft IIS Log Format.** This is a fixed ASCII format that records basic logging items, including user name, request date, request time, client IP address, number of bytes received, HTTP status code, and other items. This is a comma-delimited log file, making it easier to parse than other ASCII formats.

◆ **NCSA Common Log File Format.** This is a fixed ASCII format endorsed by the National Center for Supercomputing Applications (NCSA). The data it logs includes remote host name, user name, HTTP status code, request type, and the number of bytes received by the server. Spaces separate different items logged.

◆ **ODBC Logging.** This is a fixed format that is logged to a database. This log includes client IP address, user name, request date, request time, HTTP status code, bytes received, bytes sent,

action carried out, and the target. When you choose this option, you must specify the database for the file to be logged to. In addition, you must set up the database to receive that log data.

◆ **W3C Extended Log File Format.** This is a customizable ASCII format endorsed by the World Wide Web Consortium (W3C). This is the default setting. You can set this log format to record a number of different settings, such as request date, request time, client IP address, server IP address, server port, HTTP status code, and more. Data is separated by spaces in this format. Details of this format are presented in Table 4.

TABLE 4
W3C EXTENDED LOG FILE FORMAT LOGGING OPTIONS

Option	Description
Date	Date the activity occurred
Time	Time the activity occurred
Client IP Address	IP address of the client attaching to your server
User Name	User name of the user who accessed your server
Service Name	Client computer's Internet service
Server Name	Server name where the log entry was created
Server IP	Server IP address where the log entry was created
Server Port	Port number to which the client is connected
Method	Action the client was performing
URI Stem	Logs the resource the client was accessing on your server, such as an HTML page, CGI program, and so on
URI Query	Logs the search string the client was trying to match
HTTP Status	Status (in HTTP terms) of the client action
Win32 Status	Status (in Windows NT terms) of the client action

continues

TABLE 4 *continued*

Option	Description
Bytes Sent	Number of bytes sent by the server
Bytes Received	Number of bytes received by the server
Time Taken	Amount of time to execute the action requested by the client
User Agent	Browser used by the client
Cookie	Content of any cookies sent or received by the server
Referrer	URL of the site from where the user clicked to get to your site

In the New Log Time Period section of the site's configuration, you set when you want IIS to create a new log file for the selected Web site. The default is Daily, but you can select Weekly, Monthly, Unlimited File Size, or When File Size Reaches. If you select the last option, you need to set a maximum file size the log file can reach before a new file is created. The default is 19MB. The default directory in which you store log files is %WinDir\System32\LogFiles.

The Report Writer and Usage Import Database help you analyze and create reports based on logs created by IIS. The main difference between Report Writer and Usage Import is that Report Writer creates analysis reports based on the log file data. Usage Import, on the other hand, reads the log files and places the data into a relational database.

Performance Monitor is used when you want to see trends and patterns of your site's usage. When you install IIS, new objects relating to Web and FTP services are added to Performance Monitor along with specific counters for those services. Objects are individual occurrences of a system resource, such as Web Service, FTP Service, Active Server Pages, Browser, and other items. Counters, on the other hand, are statistics relating to the objects, such as Debugging Requests, Memory Allocated, and Request Wait Time (all of which relate to the Active Server Pages object).

Bottlenecks occur when one (or several) hardware resource(s) is being used too much, causing other components to have to wait for the lagging resource. The result is a performance reduction of the entire system. A bottleneck can occur due to insufficient server memory or because of too little bandwidth available to the connected users.

Start looking for bottlenecks by running Performance Monitor to create a baseline of activities for your site. You also can use Event Viewer to record events and audit situations on your computer that might require your attention. Another useful tool to use to locate bottlenecks is Task Manager, which shows you all the ongoing tasks and threads on your computer.

For medium-to-very busy sites, you can expect IIS to saturate a 10MB Ethernet network adapter. This certainly causes bottlenecks to occur that are network-related. To check for network saturation, check for CPU % Utilization on both the client and server. To prevent the server from becoming network-bound, try one of the following solutions:

◆ Use multiple 10MB ethernet cards.

◆ Install a 100MB ethernet or FDDI network card. (This only works on a 100MB or FDDI network.)

CPU bottlenecks can be identified by measuring the amount of the server CPU that is being utilized. If the CPU % Processor Time value is high, try the following remedies:

◆ Upgrade the CPU to a faster one.

◆ Add additional CPUs to your server.

◆ Move any CPU-intensive applications (such as database applications) you run on the Web server to another computer.

◆ Add more computers on which you replicate your site and then distribute traffic across them.

To optimize the performance of Index Server, you should start by looking at the configuration of the computer on which it resides. The following are the factors you need to measure to set this configuration:

◆ Number of documents in the corpus, which is the collection of documents and HTML pages indexed by Index Server

◆ Corpus size

◆ Rate of search requests

◆ Kind of queries

You'll find that the amount of memory you have installed greatly affects the performance of Index Server. For sites that have fewer than 100,000 documents stored in the corpus, a minimum of 32MB is required and recommended. However, if you have 100,000 to 250,000 documents, the recommended amount of memory jumps to 64-128MB, whereas the minimum required still is 32MB. For sites with 250,000 to 500,000 documents, you need a minimum of 64MB of RAM, but it is recommended that you have 128-256MB. Finally, if you have over 500,000 documents, you must have 128MB of RAM installed, but at least 256MB is recommended. The corpus size is 40 percent of the total.

TROUBLESHOOTING

Content Analyzer's WebMaps can be used to administer Web site content to help you keep your Web site up-to-date and functioning correctly. You use the Link Info window, searches, and properties to help you manage your site's content.

The following are three main parameters that specify how TCP/IP is configured:

◆ The IP address (the network address and host address of the computer)

◆ The subnet mask (specifies what portion of the IP address specifies the network address and what portion of the address specifies the host address)

◆ The default gateway (most commonly, the address of the router)

Using a DHCP server can greatly reduce TCP/IP configuration problems. Scopes are ranges of available addresses on a DHCP server. The most important part of the configuration is to make sure you don't have duplicate addresses in the different scopes.

Most Index Server troubleshooting and correction is automatically implemented without administrator interaction.

If Index Server is not running and a query comes in, Index Server automatically starts. Therefore, as an administrator, the starting of Index Server is not something you should ever need to do manually. As an administrator, the stopping of Index Server is something you should never need to do either, but you can do it from the Services utility.

One of the most common problems with using Index Server is running out of disk space. If the drive fills, indexing is paused, and the only way of knowing this is by a message written to the event log. The event log should be monitored routinely by an administrator for this and similar occurrences.

When you are using ODB to connect to a SQL database, you should be aware of some of the more common errors you might see:

◆ Microsoft OLE DB Provider for ODBC Drivers error '80004005' [Microsoft][ODBC Driver Manager] Data source name not found and no default driver specified

This error occurs when the ODBC Data Source Name isn't set up so that database connections can be made.

◆ Microsoft OLE DB Provider for ODBC Drivers error '80004005' [Microsoft][ODBC SQL Server Driver][SQL Server] Logon failed

This error might occur if the account being used by IIS doesn't have the right Windows NT permissions to access the database file.

◆ Microsoft OLE DB Provider for ODBC Drivers error '80004005'[Microsoft][ODBC Microsoft Access 97 Driver] Couldn't use '(unknown)'; file already in use.

The database cannot be locked correctly for multiple users.

◆ Microsoft OLE DB Provider for ODBC Drivers error '80004005'[Microsoft][ODBC Microsoft Access 97 Driver]   '(unknown)' isn't a valid path.

Make sure that the path name is spelled correctly and that you are connected to the server on which the file resides.

The specified path for the database being read by the IIS server is not valid.

◆ Microsoft OLE DB Provider for ODBC Drivers error '80004005'[Microsoft][ODBC SQL Server Driver][DBMSSOCN]

General network error. Check your network document. This can occur when the SQL server is renamed, and the IIS server is not updated to reflect the change.

Also, pay attention to potential security issues with your site. They are common in real life and on the IIS exam. Some of the more common security issues that arise with IIS include the following:

◆ Firewalls can be used to restrict incoming traffic to only those services you are choosing to allow in. Additionally, a firewall can be used to prevent all traffic from coming in. If you're attempting to make data available on the Web, consider putting the Web server outside the firewall and allowing traffic to pass to it but to nothing else on your network.

◆ Anonymous usage is a staple of most public Web sites. If you don't want to have a public Web site, however, consider disabling the logon. You can configure the Web server to use user authentication to verify that everyone accessing it has a valid Windows NT user account (they must give a user name and password before being allowed to interact with the server).

◆ Secure Sockets Layer (SSL) 3.0 is included with IIS and its use should be mandatory on any site holding sensitive data (such as medical information, credit card information, and so on). SSL enables a secure connection to be established between the browser and the server such that encryption can be used between them.

◆ Server Certificates, a part of SSL, can be created (unique digital identifications) to authenticate your Web site to browsers. This is used for public and private key (key pair) interactions of a secure nature.

◆ NTFS permissions can be used in conjunction with IIS to secure individual files and directories from those who should not access them. The five permission types follow:

- **Change.** Users can read and modify files, including deleting them and adding new ones to a directory.

- **Full Control.** The default for the Everyone group. Users can modify, move, delete, take ownership, and even change permissions.

- **No Access.** Overrides everything else and gives absolutely no access to the resource.

- **Read.** As the name implies, users can read the data.

- **Special Access.** User permissions have been set to something specific by the administrator.

Study and Exam Prep Tips

This chapter provides you with some general guidelines for preparing for the exam. It is organized into three sections. The first section addresses your pre-exam preparation activities and covers general study tips. This is followed by an extended look at the Microsoft Certification Exams, including a number of specific tips that apply to the Microsoft exam format. Finally, changes in Microsoft's testing policies and how they might affect you are discussed.

To better understand the nature of preparation for the test, it is important to understand learning as a process. You probably are aware of how you best learn new material. You might find that outlining works best for you, or you might need to "see" things as a visual learner. Whatever your learning style, test preparation takes place over time. Obviously, you can't start studying for these exams the night before you take them; it is very important to understand that learning is a developmental process. Understanding it as a process helps you focus on what you know and what you have yet to learn.

Thinking about how you learn should help you recognize that learning takes place when we are able to match new information to old. You have some previous experience with computers and networking, and now you are preparing for this certification exam. Using this book, software, and supplementary materials will not just incrementally add to what you know; as you study, you actually change the organization of your knowledge as you integrate new information into your existing knowledge. This will lead you to a more comprehensive understanding of the tasks and concepts outlined in the objectives (and of computing in general). Again, this happens as a repetitive process rather than a singular event. Keep this model of learning in mind as you prepare for the exam, and you will make better decisions concerning what to study and how much more studying you need to do.

STUDY TIPS

There are many ways to approach studying, just as there are many different types of material to study. However, the tips that follow should work well for the type of material covered in the certification exams.

Study Strategies

Although individuals vary in the ways they learn information, some basic principles of learning apply to everyone. You should adopt some study strategies that take advantage of these principles. One of these principles is that learning can be broken into various depths. Recognition (of terms, for example) exemplifies a more surface level of learning in which you rely on a prompt of some sort to elicit recall. Comprehension or understanding (of the concepts behind the terms, for example) represents a deeper level of learning. The ability to analyze a concept and apply your understanding of it in a new way represents a further depth of learning.

Your learning strategy should enable you to know the material at a level or two deeper than mere recognition. This will help you do well on the exams. You will know the material so thoroughly that you can easily handle the recognition-level types of questions used in multiple-choice testing. You will also be able to apply your knowledge to solve new problems.

Macro and Micro Study Strategies

One strategy that can lead to this deeper learning includes preparing an outline that covers all the objectives and subobjectives for the particular exam you are working on. You should delve a bit further into the material and include a level or two of detail beyond the stated objectives and subobjectives for the exam. Then expand the outline by coming up with a statement of definition or a summary for each point in the outline.

An outline provides two approaches to studying. First, you can study the outline by focusing on the organization of the material. Work your way through the points and subpoints of your outline with the goal of learning how they relate to one another. For example, be sure you understand how each of the main objective area is similar to and different from one another. Then do the same thing with the subobjectives; be sure you know which subobjectives pertain to each objective area and how they relate to one another.

Next, you can work through the outline, focusing on learning the details. Memorize and understand terms and their definitions, facts, rules and strategies, advantages and disadvantages, and so on. In this pass through the outline, attempt to learn detail rather than the big picture (the organizational information that you worked on in the first pass through the outline).

Research has shown that attempting to assimilate both types of information at the same time seems to interfere with the overall learning process. Separate your studying into these two approaches, and you will perform better on the exam.

Active Study Strategies

The process of writing down and defining objectives, subobjectives, terms, facts, and definitions promotes a more active learning strategy than merely reading the material. In human information-processing terms, writing forces you to engage in more active encoding of the information. Simply reading over it exemplifies more passive processing.

Next, determine whether you can apply the information you have learned by attempting to create examples and scenarios on your own. Think about how or where you could apply the concepts you are learning. Again, write down this information to process the facts and concepts in a more active fashion.

The hands-on nature of the Step by Step tutorials and the exercises at the end of each chapter provide further active learning opportunities that will reinforce concepts.

Common-Sense Strategies

Finally, you should also follow common-sense practices when studying. Study when you are alert, reduce or eliminate distractions, take breaks when you become fatigued, and so on.

Pre-Testing Yourself

Pre-testing allows you to assess how well you are learning. One of the most important aspects of learning is what has been called meta-learning. Meta-learning has to do with realizing when you know something well or when you need to study some more. In other words, you recognize how well or how poorly you have learned the material you are studying.

For most people, this can be difficult to assess objectively on their own. Practice tests are useful in that they reveal more objectively what you have learned and what you have not learned. You should use this information to guide review and further studying. Developmental learning takes place as you cycle through studying, assessing how well you have learned, reviewing, and assessing again until you feel you are ready to take the exam.

You might have noticed the practice exam included in this book. Use it as part of the learning process. The Top Score software on the CD-ROM also provides a variety of ways to test yourself before you take the actual exam. By using the Top Score Practice Exam, you can take entire practice tests. By using the Study Cards, you can also take entire practice tests, or you might choose to focus on a particular objective area, such as planning, troubleshooting, or monitoring and optimization. By using the Flash Cards, you can test your knowledge at a level beyond that of recognition; you must come up with the answers in your own words.

The Flash Cards also enable you to test your knowledge of particular objective areas.

You should set a goal for your pre-testing. A reasonable goal would be to score consistently in the 90 percent range.

See Appendix D, "Using the Top Score Software," for a more detailed explanation of the test engine.

EXAM PREP TIPS

Having mastered the subject matter, the final preparatory step is to understand how the exam will be presented. Make no mistake, a Microsoft Certified Professional (MCP) Exam will challenge both your knowledge and test-taking skills. This section starts with the basics of exam design, reviews a new type of exam format, and concludes with hints targeted to each of the exam formats.

The MCP Exam

Every MCP exam is released in one of two basic formats. What's being called exam format here is really little more than a combination of the overall exam structure and the presentation method for exam questions.

Each exam format uses the same types of questions. These types or styles of questions include multiple-rating (or scenario-based) questions, traditional multiple-choice questions, and simulation-based questions. It's important to understand the types of questions you will be asked and the actions required to properly answer them.

Understanding the exam formats is key to good preparation because the format determines the number of questions presented, the difficulty of those questions, and the amount of time allowed to complete the exam.

Exam Format

There are two basic formats for the MCP exams: the traditional fixed-form exam and the adaptive form. As its name implies, the fixed-form exam presents a fixed set of questions during the exam session. The adaptive form, however, uses only a subset of questions drawn from a larger pool during any given exam session.

Fixed-Form

A fixed-form computerized exam is based on a fixed set of exam questions. The individual questions are presented in random order during a test session. If you take the same exam more than once you won't necessarily see the exact same questions. This is because two or three final forms are typically assembled for every fixed-form exam Microsoft releases. These are usually labeled Forms A, B, and C.

The final forms of a fixed-form exam are identical in terms of content coverage, number of questions, and allotted time, but the questions are different. You might notice, however, that some of the same questions appear on, or rather are shared among, different final forms. When questions are shared among multiple final forms of an exam, the percentage of sharing is generally small. Many final forms share no questions, but some older exams may have a 10 to 15 percent duplication of exam questions on the final exam forms.

Fixed-form exams also have a fixed time limit in which you must complete the exam. The Top Score software on the CD-ROM that accompanies this book carries fixed-form exams.

Finally, the score you achieve on a fixed-form exam, which is always reported for MCP exams on a scale of 0 to 1,000, is based on the number of questions you answer correctly. The exam's passing score is the same for all final forms of a given fixed-form exam.

The typical format for the fixed-form exam is as follows:

- ◆ 50–60 questions.
- ◆ 75–90 minutes of testing time.
- ◆ Question review is allowed, including the opportunity to change your answers.

Adaptive Form

An adaptive-form exam has the same appearance as a fixed-form exam, but its questions differ in quantity and process of selection. Although the statistics of adaptive testing are fairly complex, the process is concerned with determining your level of skill or ability with the exam subject matter. This ability assessment begins by presenting questions of varying levels of difficulty and ascertaining at what difficulty level you can reliably answer them. Finally, the ability assessment determines if that ability level is above or below the level required to pass that exam.

Examinees at different levels of ability will see quite different sets of questions. Examinees who demonstrate little expertise with the subject matter will continue to be presented with relatively easy questions. Examinees who demonstrate a high level of expertise will be presented progressively more difficult questions. Individuals of both levels of expertise may answer the same number of questions correctly, but because the higher-expertise examinee can correctly answer more difficult questions, he or she will receive a higher score and is more likely to pass the exam.

The typical design for the adaptive-form exam is as follows:

- ◆ 20–25 questions.
- ◆ 90-minute testing time, although this is likely to be reduced to 45–60 minutes in the near future.
- ◆ Question review is not allowed, providing no opportunity to change your answers.

The Adaptive-Exam Process

Your first adaptive exam will be unlike any other testing experience you have had. In fact, many examinees have difficulty accepting the adaptive-testing process because they feel that they were not provided the opportunity to adequately demonstrate their full expertise.

You can take consolation in the fact that adaptive exams are painstakingly put together after months of data gathering and analysis and are just as valid as a fixed-form exam. The rigor introduced through the adaptive-testing methodology means that there is nothing arbitrary about what you'll see. It is also a more efficient means of testing, requiring less time to conduct and complete.

As you can see from Figure 1, there are a number of statistical measures that drive the adaptive-examination process. The most immediately relevant to you is the Ability estimate. Accompanying this test statistic are the Standard Error of Measurement, the Item Characteristic Curve, and the Test Information curve.

The Standard Error of Measurement, which is the key factor in determining when an adaptive exam will terminate, reflects the degree of error in the Examinee Ability estimate. The Item Characteristic Curve reflects the probability of a correct response relative to Examinee Ability. Finally, the Test Information statistic provides a measure of the information contained in the set of questions the examinee has answered, again relative to the ability level of the individual examinee.

When you begin an adaptive exam, the standard error has already been assigned a target value it must drop below for the exam to conclude. This target value reflects a particular level of statistical confidence in the process. The Examinee Ability is initially set to the mean possible exam score (500 for MCP exams).

As the adaptive exam progresses, questions of varying difficulty are presented. Based on your pattern of responses to these questions, the Ability estimate is recalculated. Simultaneously, the Standard Error of Measurement estimate is refined from its first estimated value of one toward the target value. When the Standard Error of Measurement reaches its target value, the exam terminates. Thus, the more consistently you answer questions of the same degree of difficulty, the more quickly the Standard Error of Measurement estimate drops, and the fewer questions you will end up seeing during the exam session. This situation is depicted in Figure 2.

As you might suspect, one good piece of advice for taking an adaptive exam is to treat every exam question as if it is the most important. The adaptive scoring algorithm attempts to discover a pattern of responses that reflects some level of proficiency with the subject matter. Incorrect responses almost guarantee that additional questions must be answered (unless, of course, you get every question wrong). This is because the scoring algorithm must adjust to information that is not consistent with the emerging pattern.

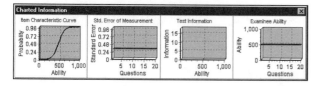

FIGURE 1
Microsoft's Adaptive Testing Demonstration Program.

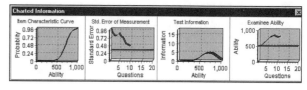

FIGURE 2
The changing statistics in an adaptive exam.

New Question Types

A variety of question types can appear on MCP exams. Examples of multiple-choice questions and scenario-based questions appear throughout this book and the Top Score software. Simulation-based questions are new to the MCP exam series.

Simulation Questions

Simulation-based questions reproduce the look and feel of key Microsoft product features for the purpose of testing. The simulation software used in MCP exams has been designed to look and act, as much as possible, just like the actual product. Consequently, answering simulation questions in an MCP exam entails completing one or more tasks just as if you were using the product itself.

The format of a typical Microsoft simulation question consists of a brief scenario or problem statement along with one or more tasks that must be completed to solve the problem. An example of a simulation question for MCP exams is shown in the following section.

A Typical Simulation Question

It sounds obvious, but the first step when you encounter a simulation question is to carefully read the question (see Figure 3). Do not go straight to the simulation application! You must assess the problem being presented and identify the conditions that make up the problem scenario. Note the tasks that must be performed or outcomes that must be achieved to answer the question, and review any instructions on how to proceed.

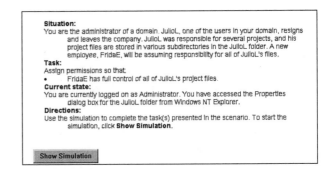

Situation:
You are the administrator of a domain. JulioL, one of the users in your domain, resigns and leaves the company. JulioL was responsible for several projects, and his project files are stored in various subdirectories in the JulioL folder. A new employee, FridaE, will be assuming responsibility for all of JulioL's files.
Task:
Assign permissions so that:
• FridaE has full control of all of JulioL's project files.
Current state:
You are currently logged on as Administrator. You have accessed the Properties dialog box for the JulioL folder from Windows NT Explorer.
Directions:
Use the simulation to complete the task(s) presented in the scenario. To start the simulation, click **Show Simulation**.

[Show Simulation]

FIGURE 3
A typical MCP exam simulation question with directions.

The next step is to launch the simulator by using the button provided. After clicking the Show Simulation button, you will see a feature of the product, as shown in the dialog box in Figure 4. The simulation application will partially cover the question text on many test center machines. Feel free to reposition the simulation or move between the question text screen and the simulation by using hotkeys, point-and-click navigation, or even clicking the simulation launch button again.

FIGURE 4
Launching the simulation application.

It is important to understand that your answer to the simulation question is not recorded until you move on to the next exam question. This gives you the added ability to close and reopen the simulation application (using the launch button) on the same question without losing any partial answer you might have made.

The third step is to use the simulator as you would the actual product to solve the problem or perform the defined tasks. Again, the simulation software is designed to function, within reason, just as the product does. But don't expect the simulation to reproduce product behavior perfectly. Most importantly, do not allow yourself to become flustered if the simulation does not look or act exactly like the product.

Figure 5 shows the solution to the example simulation problem.

There are two final points that will help you tackle simulation questions. First, respond only to what is being asked in the question; do not solve problems that you are not asked to solve. Second, accept what is being asked of you. You might not entirely agree with conditions in the problem statement, the quality of the desired solution, or the sufficiency of defined tasks to adequately solve the problem. Always remember that you are being tested on your ability to solve the problem as it is presented.

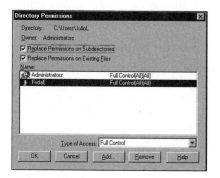

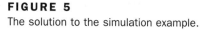

FIGURE 5
The solution to the simulation example.

The solution to the simulation problem shown in Figure 5 perfectly illustrates both of those points. As you might recall from the question scenario (refer to Figure 3), you were asked to assign appropriate permissions to a new user, Frida E. You were not instructed to make any other changes in permissions. Thus, if you had modified or removed the Administrator's permissions, this item would have been scored wrong on an MCP exam.

Putting It All Together

Given all these different pieces of information, the task is to assemble a set of tips that will help you successfully tackle the different types of MCP exams.

More Pre-Exam Preparation Tips

Generic exam-preparation advice is always useful. Tips include the following:

◆ Become familiar with the product. Hands-on experience is one of the keys to success on any MCP exam. Review the exercises and the Step by Steps in the book.

◆ Review the current exam-preparation guide on the Microsoft MCP Web site. The documentation Microsoft makes available over the Web identifies the skills every exam is intended to test.

◆ Memorize foundational technical detail, but remember that MCP exams are generally heavy on problem solving and application of knowledge rather than just questions that require only rote memorization.

◆ Take any of the available practice tests. We recommend the one included in this book and the ones you can create using the Top Score software on the CD-ROM. Although these are fixed-form exams, they provide preparation that is just as valuable for taking an adaptive exam. Because of the nature of adaptive testing, these practice exams cannot be done in the adaptive form. However, fixed-form exams use the same types of questions as adaptive exams and are the most effective way to prepare for either type. As a supplement to the material bound with this book, try the free practice tests available on the Microsoft MCP Web site.

◆ Look on the Microsoft MCP Web site for samples and demonstration items. These tend to be particularly valuable for one significant reason: They help you become familiar with any new testing technologies before you encounter them on an MCP exam.

During the Exam Session

The following generic exam-taking advice you've heard for years applies when taking an MCP exam:

◆ Take a deep breath and try to relax when you first sit down for your exam session. It is very important to control the pressure you might naturally feel when taking an exam.

◆ You will be provided scratch paper. Take a moment to write down any factual information and technical detail that you committed to short-term memory.

◆ Carefully read all information and instruction screens. These displays have been put together to give you information relevant to the exam you are taking.

◆ Accept the Non-Disclosure Agreement and preliminary survey as part of the examination process. Complete them accurately and quickly move on.

◆ Read the exam questions carefully. Reread each question to identify all relevant detail.

◆ Tackle the questions in the order they are presented. Skipping around won't build your confidence; the clock is always counting down.

◆ Don't rush, but also don't linger on difficult questions. The questions vary in degree of difficulty. Don't let yourself be flustered by a particularly difficult or verbose question.

Fixed-Form Exams

Building from this basic preparation and test-taking advice, you also need to consider the challenges presented by the different exam designs. Because a fixed-form exam is composed of a fixed, finite set of questions, add these tips to your strategy for taking a fixed-form exam:

◆ Note the time allotted and the number of questions appearing on the exam you are taking. Make a rough calculation of how many minutes you can spend on each question and use this to pace yourself through the exam.

◆ Take advantage of the fact that you can return to and review skipped or previously answered questions. Record the questions you can't answer confidently, noting the relative difficulty of each question, on the scratch paper provided. After you've made it to the end of the exam, return to the more difficult questions.

◆ If there is session time remaining after you have completed all questions (and if you aren't too fatigued!), review your answers. Pay particular attention to questions that seem to have a lot of detail or that require graphics.

◆ As for changing your answers, the general rule of thumb here is *don't*! If you read the question carefully and completely and you felt like you knew the right answer, you probably did. Don't second-guess yourself. If, as you check your answers, one clearly stands out as incorrectly marked, however, of course you should change it in that instance. If you are at all unsure, go with your first impression.

Adaptive Exams

If you are planning to take an adaptive exam, keep these additional tips in mind:

◆ Read and answer every question with great care. When reading a question, identify every relevant detail, requirement, or task that must be performed and double-check your answer to be sure you have addressed every one of them.

◆ If you cannot answer a question, use the process of elimination to reduce the set of potential answers, then take your best guess. Stupid mistakes invariably mean additional questions will be presented.

◆ Forget about reviewing questions and changing your answers. After you leave a question, whether you've answered it or not, you cannot return to it. Do not skip any questions either; when you do, it's counted as incorrect.

Simulation Questions

You might encounter simulation questions on either the fixed-form or adaptive-form exam. If you do, keep these tips in mind:

◆ Avoid changing any simulation settings that don't pertain directly to the problem solution. Solve the problem you are being asked to solve and nothing more.

◆ Assume default settings when related information has not been provided. If something has not been mentioned or defined, it is a non-critical detail that does not factor into the correct solution.

◆ Be sure your entries are syntactically correct, paying particular attention to your spelling. Enter relevant information just as the product would require it.

◆ Close all simulation application windows after completing the simulation tasks. The testing system software is designed to trap errors that could result when using the simulation application, but trust yourself over the testing software.

◆ If simulations are part of a fixed-form exam, you can return to skipped or previously answered questions and change your answer. However, if you choose to change your answer to a simulation question or even attempt to review the settings you've made in the simulation application, your previous response to that simulation question will be deleted. If simulations are part of an adaptive exam, you cannot return to previous questions.

FINAL CONSIDERATIONS

Finally, there are a number of changes in the MCP program that affect how frequently you can repeat an exam and what you will see when you do:

◆ Microsoft has instituted a new exam retake policy. This new rule is "two and two, then one and two." That is, you can attempt any exam twice with no restrictions on the time between attempts. But after the second attempt, you must wait two weeks before you can attempt that exam again. After that, you are required to wait two weeks between subsequent attempts. Plan to pass the exam in two attempts or plan to increase your time horizon for receiving an MCP credential.

◆ New questions are being seeded into the MCP exams. After performance data is gathered on new questions, the examiners will replace older questions on all exam forms. This means that the questions appearing on exams will be regularly changing.

◆ Many of the current MCP exams will be republished in adaptive form in the coming months. Prepare yourself for this significant change in testing as it is entirely likely that this will become the preferred MCP exam format.

These changes mean that the brute-force strategies for passing MCP exams may soon completely lose their viability. So if you don't pass an exam on the first or second attempt, it is entirely possible that the exam's form will change significantly the next time you take it. It could be updated to adaptive form from fixed form or have a different set of questions or question types.

The intention of Microsoft is clearly not to make the exams more difficult by introducing unwanted change, but to create and maintain valid measures of the technical skills and knowledge associated with the different MCP credentials. Preparing for an MCP exam has always involved not only studying the subject matter but also planning for the testing experience itself. With the recent changes, this is now truer than ever.

Practice Exam

This exam consists of 70 questions that are representative of the multiple-choice questions that you should expect on the actual exam. The answers appear following the last question. It is strongly suggested that when you take this exam, you treat it just as you would the actual exam at the test center. Time yourself, read carefully, and answer all the questions to the best of your ability.

> **NOTE**
>
> **Simulations** Example simulation questions are available on the CD-ROM. Also, as you have been advised throughout this book, make sure you are familiar with Microsoft Management Console before you take the exam.

Some of the questions are vague and require deduction on your part to come up with the best answer from the possibilities given. Many of them are verbose, requiring you to read thoroughly before you encounter a question. These are skills you should acquire before attempting the actual exam. Run through the test, and if you score less than 750 (missing more than 17), try rereading the chapters containing information on which you were weak (use the Index to find keywords to point you to appropriate locations).

EXAM QUESTIONS

Questions 1–3 refer to Figure 1.

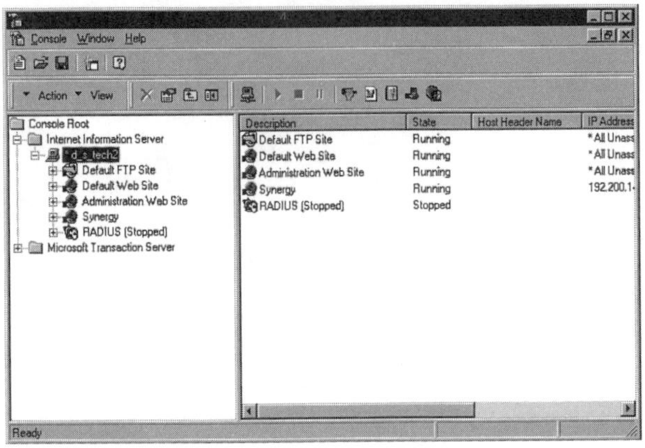

FIGURE 1
Refer to this figure for questions 1–3.

1. The utility shown in Figure 1 is known as which of the following?

    A. Internet Service Manager

    B. Internet Service Console

    C. Microsoft Console Manager

    D. Microsoft Management Console

2. It is the goal of all the Microsoft BackOffice products to use the management utility shown in Figure 1. The ability to plug and unplug management applications into this framework is provided by which of the following?

    A. Plug-ins

    B. Snap-ins

    C. Add-ons

    D. ADO

3. Several icons are shown in the utility's main menu (refer to Figure 1) representing links to other utilities available in NT. On the far right, there is an icon representing a globe with people in front of it. This is a link to which of the following?

    A. Server Manager

    B. User Manager for Domains

    C. Performance Monitor

    D. Key Manager

4. You are the Webmaster for Little Faith Enterprises. Your Web server runs Microsoft Internet Information Server. The Graphic Design department in your company maintains a file server running Novell NetWare. This file server contains logo designs in the LOGOS subdirectory of the DATA volume. The Marketing department wants to make these logo designs available to customers by means of the corporate Internet site.

    You do not have space for the logo design files on your Web server computer running Microsoft Internet Information Server 4.0. However, you want to make the logo design files available through Microsoft Internet Information Server.

    What should you do?

    A. Configure a virtual directory pointing to the physical path \\DATA\LOGOS on the Novell NetWare file server.

    B. Load a Novell NetWare-based Web server on the Novell NetWare file server. Configure your Web site running Microsoft Internet Information Server to link to the DATA:\LOGOS directory.

    C. a drive from a computer running Microsoft Windows NT Server in the same authentication domain as your Web server. Configure a virtual directory that points to the mapped drive.

    D. Back up the file server running Novell NetWare. Uninstall Novell NetWare. Load Microsoft Windows NT 4.0 and Microsoft Internet Information Server 4.0. Restore the data to the file server.

5. You are the Web site administrator for your company's Intranet. The Human Resources department has a Web server and needs to restrict access to Human Resources users only. The HR department uses the IP address range 192.18.27.1 and 192.18.27.62.

   To restrict access to Human Resources department users only, you open the Using IP and Domain Name Restrictions dialog box and select the Group option. The first IP address you enter is 192.18.27.1. What subnet mask should you enter?

   A. 255.255.255.192

   B. 255.255.255.0

   C. 255.255.255.252

   D. 255.255.255.224

Questions 6–8 refer to Figure 2.

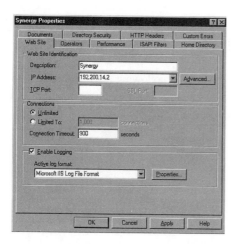

FIGURE 2
Refer to this figure for questions 6–8.

6. The TCP port shown for Synergy in Figure 2 is blank. By default, this value should be which of the following?

   A. 21

   B. 25

   C. 80

   D. 110

7. To hide the Synergy site shown in Figure 2, which of the following TCP ports should be considered?

   A. 80

   B. 100

   C. 1,000

   D. 5,000

8. You are the network administrator for Little Faith Enterprises and you need to implement bandwidth throttling to ensure that bandwidth is available to all your users. You want to prevent the IIS server from saturating the network segment. Which of the following tabs (shown in Figure 2) should you select to enable bandwidth throttling?

   A. Performance

   B. Directory Security

   C. Custom Errors

   D. Home Directory

9. You are the security administrator for Little Faith Enterprises and you are attempting to implement security on your IIS-based intranet Web site. You have decided to use session keys between the clients and the server to encrypt and decrypt the transmissions. Session keys are typically of what length?

   A. 16-bit

   B. 32-bit

   C. 40-bit

   D. 128-bit

10. With public-key encryption, how many keys are involved?

    A. 1

    B. 2

    C. 3

    D. 4

Questions 11–14 refer to Figure 3.

FIGURE 3
Refer to this figure for questions 11–14.

11. Figure 3 shows the properties for a Web site log file. Which log file format must the administrator choose to have these properties logged?

    A. SQL Logging

    B. ODBC Logging

    C. W3C Extended Log File Format

    D. NCSA Common Log File Format

    E. Microsoft IIS Log File Format

12. You are the Web site administrator for Little Faith Enterprises. You have been asked to determine from which sites users are connecting to your IIS server. Which of the following items (refer to Figure 3) would add to the log file the site from which the user is connecting?

    A. URI Stem

    B. Referrer

    C. Client IP Address

    D. User Agent

    E. Method

13. As the Web site administrator, you need to know what action the client is performing when users connect to your server. Which of the following items in Figure 3 would add to the log file the action the client was performing?

    A. URI Stem

    B. Referrer

    C. Client IP Address

    D. User Agent

    E. Method

14. Which of the following items in Figure 3 would add to the log file the resource the user is accessing on your server?

    A. URI Stem

    B. Referrer

    C. Client IP Address

    D. User Agent

    E. Method

15. You are the network administrator for Generic Recordings, a very small independent recording label. Your network has very few machines (clients or servers) on the network. You have just added a new database server, and you need to update the static name resolution file so the other hosts will be

able to access the server by name rather than by the TCP/IP address. What should you do?

A. Update the HOSTS file.

B. Update the HOSTNAME file.

C. Update the LMHOST file.

D. Update the HOST file.

16. You are the Webmaster for XYZ Plumbing, and one of your Web developers needs you to add a MIME type to your IIS 4.0 Web Server for a new document format she is developing. After you've added the MIME type to IIS, she asks you where that information is stored. Where is MIME information stored?

A. In the metabase

B. In the Registry

C. In the INETPUB\MIME subdirectory

D. In the MIME.INI file

17. Jerry and Jennifer have finished installing IIS 4. Jennifer needs to verify some information about the installation. Jerry tells her that there is a hierarchical database that stores the IIS 4 settings. In that database, there are keys that correspond to IIS elements, and each key has properties that affect the configuration of the element. This database is known as which of the following?

A. Bindery

B. NDS

C. Registry

D. Metabase

18. You are the FTP site administrator for Generic Recordings. You are hosting a Microsoft Internet Information Server 4 to provide sample MPEG files from your artists over the Internet. You have been receiving complaints about slow

performance on the site during peak utilization times. Bandwidth does not appear to be the issue; it seems to be server related. You need to improve site performance. What should you do?

A. Enable SSL.

B. Enable Event Logging.

C. Increase the number of permitted concurrent connections.

D. Decrease the connection timeout interval.

19. You are the network administrator for Exponent Mathematics and you are using a server running Microsoft Internet Information Server 4 to host your Internet Web page. There are 100 remote consultants with the company that need to send in their monthly billing records at the end of each week. These are business-critical files that must be passed securely, but are too large to be sent via e-mail. You want to use your existing Microsoft Internet Information Server 4 as an FTP server to receive their monthly reports. What should you do?

A. Start Internet Service Manager. Create a new FTP Site, leaving Allow Anonymous Connections enabled. Under the Home Directory tab of the site properties, select the Write permission.

B. Start Internet Service Manager. Create a new FTP Site, disabling Allow Anonymous Access. Enable NT Challenge/Response authentication and give each user the Write permission for the FTP site.

C. Start Internet Service Manager. Create a new FTP Site, disabling Allow Anonymous Access. Enable NT Challenge/Response authentication and give each user the Write permission for the FTP site. Enable SSL to encrypt the files during transfer.

D. This cannot be done using the FTP service.

20. What version of Microsoft Internet Explorer must you be running before you can begin the IIS 4 installation process?

   A. 2.0

   B. 3.0

   C. 4.0

   D. 4.01

Questions 21–24 refer to Figure 4.

FIGURE 4
Refer to this figure for questions 21–24.

21. In Figure 4, not everyone is allowed access to this site. Web site access has been denied to which of the following?

   A. All IP addresses except 193.100.100.1

   B. Only the IP address 193.100.100.1

   C. A number of IP addresses, beginning with 193.100.100.1

   D. All IP addresses except a small set beginning with 193.100.100.1

22. The significance of the subnet mask shown in Figure 4 is that the number of hosts affected is which of the following?

   A. 1

   B. 8

   C. 16

   D. 32

   E. 64

23. To change the subnet mask shown in Figure 4 to effectively remove subnetting, which of the following would be the new value?

   A. 0.0.0.0

   B. 1.1.1.1

   C. 255.255.255.255

   D. 255.255.255.0

24. To change the subnet mask shown in Figure 4 to make 128 sites affected, which of the following would be the new value?

   A. 255.255.255.128

   B. 255.255.255.224

   C. 255.255.255.240

   D. 255.255.255.248

   E. 255.255.255.255

25. You are the NT administrator for Little Faith Enterprises, and you have been asked to set up a new NT server as a Microsoft Internet Information Server 4 Web server. You have the Windows NT Server 4 media, and you are connected to the Internet. What do you need to do to install IIS 4?

   A. Install Windows NT Server. When asked if you want to install IIS, select Yes. IIS 4.0 ships with the latest version of Windows NT 4.0 Server, so you are done.

   B. Obtain the Enterprise version of Windows NT 4.0. This version includes IIS 4.0. Install Windows NT Server, and when prompted, install IIS.

C. Install Windows NT Server. When prompted, install IIS 3.0. Download the Windows NT 4.0 Option Pack from the Microsoft Web site. Upgrade from IIS 3.0 to IIS 4.0 using the Option Pack.

D. Install Windows NT 4.0. When prompted to install IIS, select No. Download the Windows NT 4.0 Option Pack from the Microsoft Web site. Install IIS 4.0 using the Option Pack.

26. In reference to question 25, if you choose to install IIS during the installation of Windows NT Server, which of the following user accounts will be created on the server? Select all that apply.

A. Administrator

B. Guest

C. IUSR_computername

D. IIS_Administrator

27. You are the new network administrator for Generic Recordings and your first task is to install IIS 4 on an Intel server that has been sitting in a closet for some time. You need to verify that the equipment will support IIS 4.0. What is the minimum CPU required?

A. 50MHz

B. 66MHz

C. 133MHz

D. 150MHz

28. You are the network administrator for Little Faith Enterprises and you are planning to install a new IIS server on the network. To access the new server, you also need to install TCP/IP on all the clients. What should you consider implementing to simplify the configuration of TCP/IP on the client machines?

A. DNS

B. WINS

C. DHCP

D. HOSTS

29. You are the security administrator for Generic Recordings and your company is running its intranet server on IIS 4.0. One of your responsibilities is file-level security on that server. In order to obtain this granularity, you will need to use which file system?

A. FAT

B. NTFS

C. DNS

D. Any NT-supported file system

Questions 30–32 refer to Figure 5.

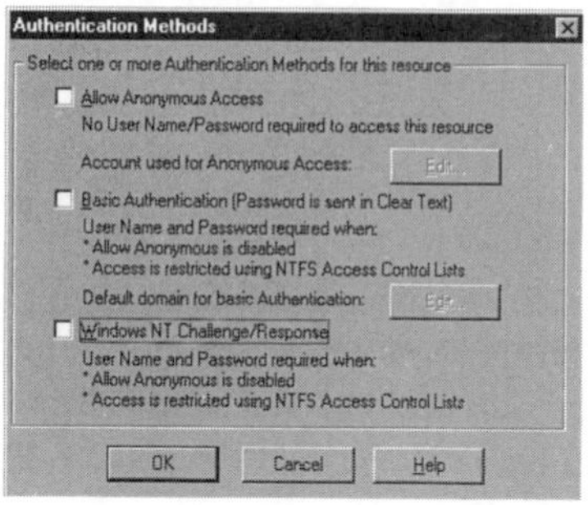

FIGURE 5
Refer to this figure for questions 30–32.

30. Figure 5 shows the authentication methods available at a particular Web site. This box is obtained by selecting which tab from the Web site's properties?

A. Web Site

B. Operators

C. Home Directory

D. Directory Security

E. Documents

31. If the Allow Anonymous Access check box is checked in Figure 5, what account is used on a server named Synergy for the anonymous account?

    A. Synergy

    B. Synergy_anonymous

    C. Anoymous_Synergy

    D. IUSR_Synergy

32. Connie selects Windows NT Challenge/Response for the authentication method to be used at her site (as shown in Figure 5). She must now ensure that all her users' Internet Explorer browsers are at least what version?

    A. 1.0

    B. 2.0

    C. 3.0

    D. 4.0

    E. 4.01

33. You are the head Web designer for Too Cool Web Design. You keep all your sample Web sites on your Internet Web site. Because you don't always have access to the Internet when you do sales presentations, you want to download a copy of the Web site to your laptop, so you can show it to potential customers as an example of your work.

You want to include all the files that are on the Web server, as well as files that are currently referred by an HTML file on your Web site. What should you do?

    A. Copy the files using Site Server Express to a map based on URL.

    B. Copy the files using Site Server Express to a map based on the file system.

    C. Copy the files using the FTP service.

    D. Map a drive to the root of the server and manually copy the files to your laptop.

34. You are the systems administrator for Generic Recordings and you need to be able to monitor the activity of your IIS 4.0 Web server. What standard NT utility includes 75 counters and can be used to track IIS services?

    A. User Manager for Domains

    B. Server Manager

    C. Performance Monitor

    D. Task Manager

35. When using the FTP service, if users type in only a slash (/) as an URL, to what directory do they default? (Assume that IIS is installed on the C: drive.)

    A. C:\

    B. C:\inetpub\Ftproot

    C. C:\Ftproot\Inetpub

    D. C:\Winnt\System32

Questions 36–38 refer to Figure 6.

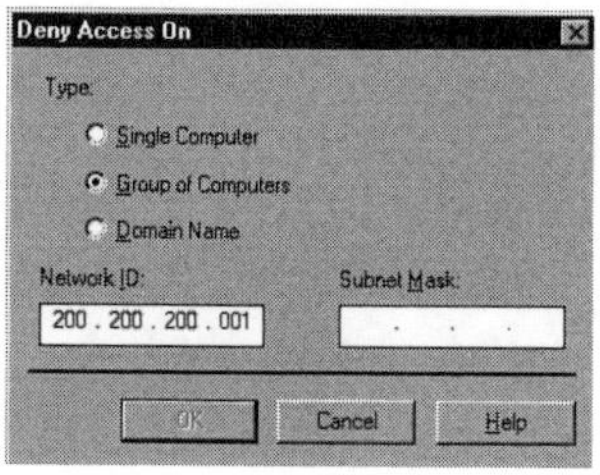

FIGURE 6
Refer to this figure for questions 36–38.

36. Mike has chosen to deny access to a group of computers in order to keep the sales staff from accessing the Human Resources intranet. In Figure 6, he has entered a starting IP address and now must enter the corresponding subnet. What value should he enter if he wants to keep 16 hosts out?

   A. 255.255.255.240

   B. 255.255.255.224

   C. 255.255.255.248

   D. 255.255.255.252

37. In reference to question 36 and Figure 6, what should the subnet value be if Mike wants to keep eight hosts out?

   A. 255.255.255.240

   B. 255.255.255.224

   C. 255.255.255.248

   D. 255.255.255.252

38. In reference to question 36 and Figure 6, what should the subnet value be if Mike wants to keep 32 hosts out?

   A. 255.255.255.240

   B. 255.255.255.224

   C. 255.255.255.248

   D. 255.255.255.252

39. You are using Microsoft Internet Information Server 4 to host three Web sites: SALES, MARKETING, and ENGINEERING. You have enabled bandwidth throttling to control bandwidth usage, and have limited the total bandwidth utilization for the server to 8,192KB/sec. Because the SALES site is the most popular of the three sites, you want to ensure that it is permitted to use twice the total bandwidth of the other two. What should you do?

   A. Enable site-level bandwidth throttling for the SALES site and set it to 4,096KB/sec. Allow MARKETING and ENGINEERING to use bandwidth as needed.

   B. Enable site-level bandwidth throttling for the MARKETING and ENGINEERING sites at 2,048KB/sec and allow the SALES site to use bandwidth as needed.

   C. Set the server-level bandwidth throttling to 16,384KB/sec.

   D. Do nothing; SALES will automatically use bandwidth as needed.

40. Jodi has a number of users accessing her Web site without specifying an URL to a document. Therefore, Jodi decides to implement default document pages. When specifying more than one default page, which page will the user see?

   A. The topmost document in the list

   B. The bottommost document in the list

   C. The page specific to his or her IP Address

   D. The page specific to his or her referring Web site

Questions 41–43 refer to Figure 7.

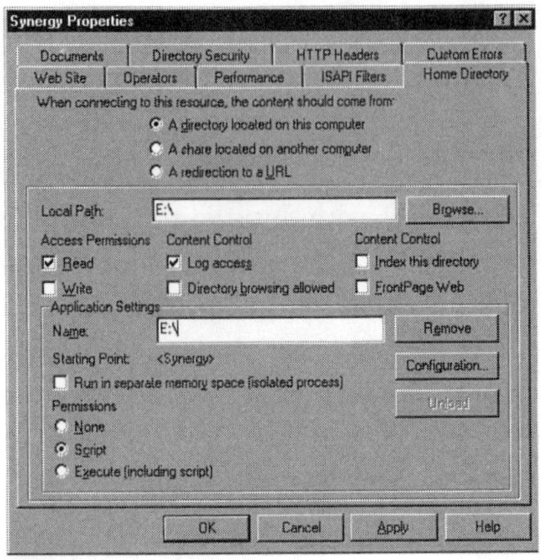

FIGURE 7
Refer to this figure for questions 41–43.

41. There are a number of action buttons displayed on the Home Directory tab shown in Figure 7. Which of those buttons, when selected, will change its text to Create?

   A. Browse

   B. Remove

   C. Configuration

   D. Unload

42. If the home directory depicted in Figure 7 is changed to a share located on another computer, which of the following is a valid choice for the path specification?

   A. E:\

   B. \\synergy\website

   C. http://www.synergy.com

   D. 192.5.6.7

43. Which access permission is required to view the parent directory of whatever subdirectory you begin in?

   A. Read

   B. Write

   C. Directory Browsing Allowed

   D. None

44. You are the administrator of the Your Net ISP Services IIS Server. You have only a single IP address for that server, but you need to support multiple sites, each with a different host name. Multiple host names can be associated with a single IP address through the use of which of the following?

   A. Multihomed hosts

   B. HTTP 1.1 host headers

   C. HTTP Keep-Alives

   D. Virtual directories

45. You are the network administrator for Comfortable Shoes, Inc. You are running the NNTP service on your Microsoft Internet Information Server 4 server to provide newsgroup access for 500 users. Approximately 100 users access the server from your internal network; the other 400 access the server via the Internet. The corporate standard newsreader does not support Windows NT Challenge/Response authentication. All your users have the same security privileges for the newsgroups. How should you configure security so that you can provide secure access to both the Internet and intranet users?

   A. Create a Windows NT domain account for all users. Enable Basic Authentication for the NNTP service.

B. Create a Windows NT domain account for all users. Configure NNTP to use Allow Anonymous Access.

C. Configure SSL client authentication for all users. Require SSL client authentication to access the newsgroups.

D. Configure a Windows NT domain account for all Internet users. Create SSL client certificates for all Internet users. Map all of the certificates to the Windows NT domain account.

46. Clients can maintain open connections to reduce the amount of time re-establishing connections for requests taken through the use of which of the following?

A. Multihomed hosts

B. HTTP 1.1 host headers

C. HTTP Keep-Alives

D. Virtual directories

Questions 47–49 refer to Figure 8.

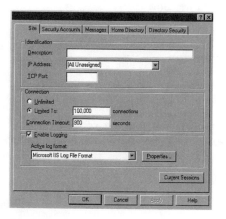

FIGURE 8
Refer to this figure for questions 47–49.

47. The properties shown in Figure 8 are for what type of site?

A. WWW

B. FTP

C. NNTP

D. Gopher

48. Which of the following is the default port that should appear in the TCP field shown in Figure 8?

A. 21

B. 25

C. 80

D. 110

49. To hide the site shown in Figure 8, which of the following TCP ports should be considered?

A. 80

B. 100

C. 1,000

D. 5,000

50. You are the Web administrator for Great Books Publishing. You need to use IIS to set up an FTP server for authors to upload their files to. A directory will be created for each book the publishing company is working on, and the authors will log in using anonymous access. Which permission is needed for anonymous users under these circumstances?

A. Only the Read permission

B. Only the Write permission

C. The Read and Write permissions

D. The Execute permission

51. Ann and Joyce are setting up the SMTP service and need to complete reams of paperwork to document the process and keep their ISO certification. In the paperwork, they must detail what TCP port the

service is using. If defaults are used, the service is using which of the following ports?

A. 21

B. 25

C. 80

D. 110

52. By default, the FTP service is limited to how many connections?

A. Unlimited

B. 900

C. 10,000

D. 100,000

53. By default, the connection timeout for the FTP service is set to how many seconds?

A. Unlimited

B. 900

C. 10,000

D. 100,000

Questions 54–56 refer to Figure 9.

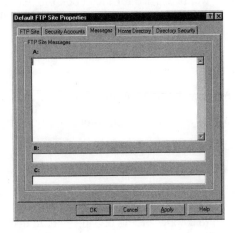

54. The FTP service can be configured to display three messages based upon events that occur. Refer to Figure 9. The message that would appear at the location marked C: would be which of the following?

A. On welcome

B. On exit

C. On error

D. On maximum connections reached

55. Referring to Figure 9, what message would appear at the location marked A:?

A. On welcome

B. On exit

C. On error

D. On maximum connections reached

56. Referring to Figure 9, what message would appear at the location marked B:?

A. On welcome

B. On exit

C. On error

D. On maximum connections reached

57. You are the Web administrator for Little Faith Enterprises and you have configured your IIS server to use daily log files to keep track of the activity on the FTP site. What will the log file name syntax be?

A. inetsv#.log

B. inyymmdD.log

C. inyymmdD.txt

D. yymmddlog.txt

FIGURE 9
Refer to this figure for questions 54–56.

Questions 58–60 refer to Figure 10.

FIGURE 10▲
Refer to this figure for questions 58–60.

58. Which of the following are two possible directory listing styles available to a Web site, as shown by the markings A: and B: in Figure 10?

A. LFN

B. UNIX

C. NTFS

D. FAT

E. MS-DOS

59. In reference to question 58 and Figure 10, which of the following is the default style?

A. LFN

B. UNIX

C. NTFS

D. FAT

E. MS-DOS

60. If the home directory depicted in Figure 10 is changed to a share located on another computer, which of the following are valid locations for the directory?

A. A volume on a NetWare file server

B. A drive mapped to a NetWare file server from the IIS server

C. Any server in the same domain as the IIS Server

D. Any server on the same network as the IIS server

Questions 61–63 refer to Figure 11.

FIGURE 11▲
Refer to this figure for questions 61–63.

61. Not everyone is allowed access to the site in Figure 11. FTP site access has been denied to which of the following?

A. All IP addresses except 202.1.1.1

B. Only the IP address 202.1.1.1

C. A number of IP addresses, beginning with 202.1.1.1

D. All IP addresses except a small set of those beginning with 202.1.1.1

62. The subnet mask shown in Figure 11 causes how many hosts to be affected?

   A. 1

   B. 8

   C. 16

   D. 32

   E. 64

63. To change the subnet mask shown in Figure 11 to affect only two hosts, what would the new value be?

   A. 255.255.255.128

   B. 255.255.255.224

   C. 255.255.255.240

   D. 255.255.255.248

   E. 255.255.255.254

64. You are the Web administrator for Generic Recordings and you are preparing to implement Microsoft Index Server on your intranet running IIS 4.0. You need to estimate how much hard disk space will be needed on the server after the site is indexed. The size of the Index Server data is approximately what percentage of the size of the corpus?

   A. 40 percent

   B. 30 percent

   C. 20 percent

   D. 10 percent

65. If the hard drive space available to Index Server drops below a certain amount, Index Server will stop operating. What is that minimum amount?

   A. 100MB

   B. 30MB

   C. 10MB

   D. 3MB

66. Sven is adding comments to a number of files and scripts so that the person who inherits his job will be able to understand the flow of data. Which of the following is a comment character that Sven should use in all cases?

   A. %

   B. @

   C. #

   D. \\

67. You are the application developer for Little Faith Enterprises. You have been asked to provide information from a legacy SQL database through the company's IIS-based Intranet. What will be the extension for the file that governs the results of the ODBC calls?

   A. HTX

   B. HTM

   C. IDC

   D. IDQ

68. When you are working with IIS's implementation of ODBC, what file extension is necessary to stipulate how data is accessed?

   A. HTX

   B. HTM

   C. IDC

   D. IDQ

69. How is ISAPI implemented in IIS?

    A. As a plug-in

    B. As a snap-in

    C. As an add-on

    D. As a dynamic link library

70. With Index Server, what is the minimum amount of RAM you should have on the server if you are indexing more than 600,000 documents?

    A. 128MB

    B. 256MB

    C. 512MB

    D. 1GB

ANSWERS TO EXAM QUESTIONS

1. **D.**   The utility shown in Figure 1 is the Microsoft Management Console. The MMC is the framework for all IIS management utilities.

2. **B.**   Interfaces are loaded and unloaded in MMC through the use of snap-ins.

3. **B.**   User Manager for Domains is depicted by the icon of the globe with users in front of it. This application can also be opened from the Administrative Tools (Common) program group.

4. **C.**   Map a drive from a computer running Microsoft Windows NT Server in the same authentication domain as your Web server. Configure a virtual directory that points to the mapped drive. You cannot point to a share located directly on the Novell server.

5. **A.**   The correct subnet mask for this is 255.255.255.192.

6. **C.**   The default port for a WWW site is 80.

7. **D.**   To make a Web site hidden, its TCP port should be changed to a value greater than the known ports (approximately 1,023). An example of this would be the HTML administrator that ships with IIS 4. It is installed at a port higher than 1,023.

8. **A.**   Bandwidth throttling is enabled on the Performance tab of the site's properties. Keep in mind that you can configure bandwidth throttling on each site, or for the entire server.

9. **C.**   Sessions employ 40-bit encryption. This is commonly referred to as the International or Export version because it is the length that can be exported legally. 128-bit keys are also an option when both parties are in the US and/or Canada.

10. **B.**   With public-key encryption, two keys are used: one public and one private. Messages encrypted with the public key can be decrypted only with the private key. This ensures that the data sent can be read only by the owner of the private key.

11. **C.**   The extended properties are available with only W3C Extended Log File Format.

12. **B.**   The Referrer option will denote the Web site from which the user is connecting.

13. **E.**   The Method option will denote the action the client was performing.

14. **A.**   URI Stem will denote the resource the user is accessing on your server.

15. **A.**   The HOSTS file is used for static host name-to-IP address resolution. Although not commonly used today, the HOSTS file was the precursor to DNS.

16. **B.** Although the metabase is used to store IIS configuration information, the Registry stores the MIME-type information.

17. **D.** The metabase stores values and variables unique to IIS 4.

18. **D.** By decreasing the connection timeout interval, inactive connections will be dropped faster, freeing server resources for active connections.

19. **D.** You cannot pass files securely using the standard IIS FTP Service, or any standard FTP service for that matter.

20. **D.** The IIS 4.0 installation will prompt you to install IIS version 4.01.

21. **C.** Site access is denied to a number of computers, beginning with 193.100.100.1.

22. **E.** A subnet mask of 192 denotes that 64 hosts are denied access to the site.

23. **D.** The default subnet mask for a Class C network is 255.255.255.0. This will change the access so that all the hosts on the 193.100.100 network are affected.

24. **A.** To deny access to 128 sites, the subnet mask used must be 255.255.255.128.

25. **D.** You need the Windows NT 4.0 Option Pack to install IIS 4.0. You cannot install on a system with an older version of IIS without first uninstalling the old version.

26. **A, B, C.** Administrator and Guest accounts are always created during NT installation. IUSR_computername is created if IIS is installed as well.

27. **B.** The minimum CPU requirement on an Intel machine is 66MHz.

28. **C.** DHCP (Dynamic Host Configuration Protocol) will ease the burden of TCP/IP implementation and administration.

29. **B.** NTFS partitions are required on a server for file-level security. This should be the default for any IIS implementation, due to the security limitations of the FAT file system.

30. **D.** The Authentication Methods dialog box is accessed through the Directory Security tab.

31. **D.** IUSR_Synergy is the account created for anonymous user access on an IIS server named Synergy.

32. **B.** NT Challenge/Response requires Internet Explorer browsers of version 2.0 or greater.

33. **A.** Use Site Server Express to copy the site based on its URL. This will allow you to navigate the site from a Web browser without broken references.

34. **C.** Performance Monitor includes over 75 counters and can be used to track IIS services. It is the tool included with Windows NT for monitoring system performance. The installation of IIS adds a number of counters to the default Performance Monitor configuration to assist in planning and maintenance of the server.

35. **B.** When the slash (/) is used as an URL with FTP, the directory defaulted to is C:\Inetpub\Ftproot.

36. **A.** A subnet value of 255.255.255.240 is required to deny access to 16 hosts.

37. **C.** A subnet value of 255.255.255.248 is required to deny access to eight hosts.

38. **B.** A subnet value of 255.255.255.224 is required to deny access to 32 hosts.

39. **B.** Enable site-level bandwidth throttling for the MARKETING and ENGINEERING sites at 2048KB/S. The SALES site will use the remaining bandwidth available to the site: 4096KB/sec.

40. **A.** With multiple default documents, the topmost one of the list is used unless it is unavailable, in which case the next one in the list is used.

41. **B.** The Remove button changes to Create after it is clicked.

42. **B.** Share names are always given as \\server\share.

43. **C.** Directory Browsing Allowed is needed to see parent directories and other directories.

44. **B.** Multiple host names can be associated with a single IP address (virtual servers) through HTTP 1.1 host headers.

45. **C.** HTTP Keep-Alives allow users to make multiple requests without having to disconnect and reconnect for each request.

46. **C.** Configure SSL client authentication for all users. Require SSL client authentication to access the newsgroups.

47. **B.** The properties shown in Figure 9 are for an FTP site.

48. **A.** The default TCP port for an FTP site is 21.

49. **D.** To hide the site, its TCP port should be changed to one above the known ports (approximately 1,023).

50. **B.** Write permission best fits the scenario; it allows authors to upload files, but not see other files or download files.

51. **B.** SMTP's default TCP port is 25.

52. **D.** By default, FTP is limited to 100,000 connections.

53. **B.** By default, FTP connections timeout after 900 seconds.

54. **D.** The C: location in Figure 10 is used for messages when maximum connections are reached.

55. **A.** The A: location in Figure 10 is used for messages upon welcome.

56. **B.** The B: location in Figure 10 is used for messages upon exit.

57. **B.** The syntax for daily logs is inyymmdd.log.

58. **B, E.** The two possible FTP listing styles are UNIX and MS-DOS.

59. **E.** MS-DOS is the default FTP listing style used.

60. **B, C.** IIS can point to a mapped drive on the local machine, whether the actual share is on NetWare or Windows NT, and can point at a share on a server in the same authentication domain.

61. **D.** In Figure 12, all hosts are denied access to the site except a small group of those beginning with the IP address 202.1.1.1.

62. **C.** The subnet value 255.255.255.240 limits the number of hosts to 16.

63. **E.** Changing the subnet value to 255.255.255.254 limits the number of hosts that can access the site to two.

64. **A.** The Index Server data is approximately 40 percent of the corpus.

65. **D.** Below 3MB of free space, Index Server stops indexing (and functioning).

66. **C.** The pound sign (#) is used to denote comments.

67. **A.** HTX files are used for data presentation.

68. **C.** IDC files are used to define data access.

69. **D.** ISAPI is implemented in IIS as a DLL (Dynamic Link Library).

70. **A.** With 600,000 documents, Index Server needs 128MB of RAM. 256MB of RAM, however, is highly recommended and should be considered.

APPENDICES

Glossary

.HTX file   This file contains the information for formatting the results of the query in an HTML document that can be read by the user's browser.

.IDQ file   The file containing the data source file information and SQL statements for the query.

A

Active Server Pages (ASP)   A dynamically created Web page that contains either Visual Basic or JavaScript programming, with an .ASP extension.

ActiveX Data Objects (ADO)   Language-independent interfaces for entering or retrieving data through a Web page. ADO provides a general data interface that can be used to access a variety of data types, including Web pages, text documents, spreadsheets, and other data types.

anonymous login   A type of FTP login that allows access to any user by logging in using "anonymous" as the user ID. Usually, your e-mail address is requested as a password.

B-G

Certificate Authority (CA)   A third party (VeriSign or CyberTrust, for example) who issues certificates and verifies the identity of the person or company the certificate is issued to.

Certificate Server   Microsoft's application for creating and issuing certificates.

common gateway interface (CGI)   A specification for transferring data between a World Wide Web server and a CGI application.

Domain Name System (DNS)   A TCP/IP service for resolving host names to IP addresses and IP addresses to host names.

Dynamic Host Control Protocol (DHCP)
A TCP/IP service used to dynamically configure TCP/IP addressing information. DHCP defines a method for dynamically allocating IP addresses on a network segment.

File Transfer Protocol (FTP)   A TCP/IP application protocol used for transferring files.

H-L

HOSTS file   A static file used by TCP/IP hosts to resolve host names to IP addresses.

HTTP Keep-Alives   A request to a Web server used to keep an HTTP connection open across multiple client requests.

HyperText Markup Language (HTML)   A textual document markup language used to facilitate navigating through a document.

HyperText Transfer Protocol (HTTP)   The TCP/IP application protocol used to access World Wide Web services.

Index Server   Microsoft Internet Information Server 4.0 application used to index Web site documents.

Internet Database Connector (IDC)   The IDC is an ISAPI DLL (HTTPODBC.DLL) and provides the link for connecting IIS to a variety of ODBC-compliant databases.

Internet Explorer   Microsoft's Web browser; used to access Web pages.

Internet Server Application Programming Interface (ISAPI)   An API for Microsoft Internet Information Server used for the development of Web-based applications. ISAPI applications run much faster than conventional CGI programs because of their tight integration with IIS.

Internet service provider (ISP)   A company that provides access to the Internet.

M-N

Microsoft Management Console Management Framework used to manage Microsoft Internet Information Server 4.0.

Microsoft Transaction Server (MTS)   A transaction processing system for developing and managing server applications.

Multipurpose Internet Mail Extensions (MIME)   A specification for formatting non-ASCII messages so that they can be sent over the Internet. Used by most mail hosts for file attachments.

Network News Transfer Protocol (NNTP)   A TCP/IP application protocol used to transfer information from news server to news server. This is the Internet standard protocol for transferring Usenet news.

newsfeed   An Internet feed of all the available Usenet newsgroups.

O-R

Open Database Connectivity (ODBC) A Microsoft-developed database access method designed to make it possible to access any data from any application.

Performance Monitor   Tool used to monitor Windows NT and IIS 4.0 performance for a variety of objects and counters.

persistent connections   After a Web browser connects to a Web server, it can receive multiple files through the same persistent connection. This feature of HTTP can improve performance by as much as 15 to 20 percent.

Remote Data Services (RDS)   A feature of ADO (ActiveX Data Objects), RDS allows developers to create data-centric applications.

S-T

Secure Sockets Layer (SSL)   An encrypted TCP/IP application protocol used for secure communications across a network.

Simple Mail Transfer Protocol (SMTP)   A TCP/IP application protocol used to transfer mail from server to server.

TCP/IP   The suite of network protocols used to communicate across the global Internet. Also used in most corporate environments.

U-Z

Usage Import and Report Writer   A Web site analysis tool included with Microsoft Internet Information Server 4.0.

WebMap   A graphical representation of a Web site generated by Content Analyzer.

Whois   A TCP/IP application service used to identify the owner of a DNS domain.

World Wide Web (WWW)   The TCP/IP service that uses the HTTP protocol to serve documents to client computers running Web browsers.

Overview of Certification

You must pass rigorous certification exams to become a Microsoft Certified Professional. These closed-book exams provide a valid and reliable measure of your technical proficiency and expertise. Developed in consultation with computer industry professionals who have experience with Microsoft products in the workplace, the exams are conducted by two independent organizations. Sylvan Prometric offers the exams at more than 1,400 Authorized Prometric Testing Centers around the world. Virtual University Enterprises (VUE) testing centers offer exams at over 500 locations.

To schedule an exam, call Sylvan Prometric Testing Centers at 800-755-EXAM (3926) or VUE at 888-837-8616 (or register online with VUE at http://www.vue.com/student-services/). Currently, Microsoft offers seven types of certification, based on specific areas of expertise.

TYPES OF CERTIFICATION

◆ **Microsoft Certified Professional (MCP).** Qualified to provide installation, configuration, and support for users of at least one Microsoft desktop operating system, such as Windows NT Workstation. Candidates can take elective exams to develop areas of specialization. MCP is the base level of expertise.

◆ **Microsoft Certified Professional+Internet (MCP+Internet).** Qualified to plan security, install and configure server products, manage server resources, extend service to run CGI scripts or ISAPI scripts, monitor and analyze performance, and troubleshoot problems. Expertise is similar to that of an MCP, but with a focus on the Internet.

◆ **Microsoft Certified Professional+Site Building (MCP+Site Building).** Qualified to plan, build, maintain, and manage Web sites using Microsoft technologies and products. The credential is appropriate for people who manage sophisticated, interactive Web sites that include database connectivity, multimedia, and searchable content.

◆ **Microsoft Certified Database Administrator (MCDBA).** Qualified to derive physical database designs, develop logical data models, create physical databases, create data services by using Transact-SQL, manage and maintain databases, configure and manage security, monitor and optimize databases, and install and configure Microsoft SQL Server.

◆ **Microsoft Certified Systems Engineer (MCSE).** Qualified to effectively plan, implement, maintain, and support information systems with Microsoft Windows NT and other Microsoft advanced systems and workgroup products, such as Microsoft Office and Microsoft BackOffice.

◆ **Microsoft Certified Systems Engineer+Internet (MCSE+Internet).** Qualified in the core MCSE areas, and also qualified to enhance, deploy, and manage sophisticated intranet and Internet solutions that include a browser, proxy server, host servers, database, and messaging and commerce components. A MCSE+Internet-certified professional is able to manage and analyze Web sites.

◆ **Microsoft Certified Solution Developer (MCSD).** Qualified to design and develop custom business solutions by using Microsoft development tools, technologies, and platforms. The new track includes certification exams that test users' ability to build Web-based, distributed, and commerce applications by using Microsoft's products, such as Microsoft SQL Server, Microsoft Visual Studio, and Microsoft Component Services.

◆ **Microsoft Certified Trainer (MCT).** Instructionally and technically qualified by Microsoft to deliver Microsoft Education Courses at Microsoft-authorized sites. An MCT must be employed by a Microsoft Solution Provider Authorized Technical Education Center or a Microsoft Authorized Academic Training site.

NOTE

For up-to-date information about each type of certification, visit the Microsoft Training and Certification World Wide Web site at http://www.microsoft.com/train_cert. You also can contact Microsoft through the following sources:

- Microsoft Certified Professional Program: 800-636-7544
- mcp@msource.com
- Microsoft Online Institute (MOLI): 800-449-9333

CERTIFICATION REQUIREMENTS

An asterisk following an exam in any of the lists below means that it is slated for retirement.

How to Become a Microsoft Certified Professional

Passing any Microsoft exam (with the exception of Networking Essentials) is all you need to do to become certified as an MCP.

How to Become a Microsoft Certified Professional+Internet

You must pass the following exams to become an MCP specializing in Internet technology:

◆ Internetworking Microsoft TCP/IP on Microsoft Windows NT 4.0, #70-059

◆ Implementing and Supporting Microsoft Windows NT Server 4.0, #70-067

◆ Implementing and Supporting Microsoft Internet Information Server 3.0 and Microsoft Index Server 1.1, #70-077

  OR Implementing and Supporting Microsoft Internet Information Server 4.0, #70-087

How to Become a Microsoft Certified Professional+Site Building

You need to pass two of the following exams to be certified as an MCP+Site Building:

- ◆ Designing and Implementing Web Sites with Microsoft FrontPage 98, #70-055

- ◆ Designing and Implementing Commerce Solutions with Microsoft Site Server 3.0, Commerce Edition, #70-057

- ◆ Designing and Implementing Web Solutions with Microsoft Visual InterDev 6.0, #70-152

How to Become a Microsoft Certified Database Administrator

You must pass four core exams to become an MCDBA. You must pass one elective exam as well.

Core Exams

The core exams include the following:

- ◆ Administering Microsoft SQL Server 7.0, #70-028

- ◆ Designing and Implementing Databases with Microsoft SQL Server 7.0, #70-029

- ◆ Implementing and Supporting Microsoft Windows NT Server 4.0, #70-067

- ◆ Implementing and Supporting Microsoft Windows NT Server 4.0 in the Enterprise, #70-068

Elective Exams

The elective exams include the following:

- ◆ Designing and Implementing Distributed Applications with Microsoft Visual C++ 6.0, #70-015

- ◆ Designing and Implementing Data Warehouses with Microsoft SQL Server 7.0 and Microsoft Decision Support Services 1.0, #70-019

- ◆ Internetworking with Microsoft TCP/IP on Microsoft Windows NT 4.0, #70-059

- ◆ Implementing and Supporting Microsoft Internet Information Server 4.0, #70-087

- ◆ Designing and Implementing Distributed Applications with Microsoft Visual Basic 6.0, #70-175

How to Become a Microsoft Certified Systems Engineer

You must pass four operating system exams and two elective exams to become an MCSE. The MCSE certification path is divided into two tracks: Windows NT 3.51 and Windows NT 4.0.

The following lists show the core requirements (four operating system exams) for both the Windows NT 3.51 and 4.0 tracks and the electives (two exams) you can take for either track.

Windows NT 3.51 Track

The Windows NT 3.51 Track will probably be retired with the release of Windows NT 5.0. The Windows NT 3.51 core exams are scheduled for retirement at that time.

Core Exams

The four Windows NT 3.51 Track Core Requirements for MCSE certification are as follows:

◆ Implementing and Supporting Microsoft Windows NT Server 3.51, #70-043*

◆ Implementing and Supporting Microsoft Windows NT Workstation 3.51, #70-042*

◆ Microsoft Windows 3.1, #70-030*

   OR Microsoft Windows for Workgroups 3.11, #70-048*

   OR Implementing and Supporting Microsoft Windows 95, #70-064

   OR Implementing and Supporting Microsoft Windows 98, #70-098

◆ Networking Essentials, #70-058

Windows NT 4.0 Track

The Windows NT 4.0 track is also organized around core and elective exams.

Core Exams

The four Windows NT 4.0 Track Core Requirements for MCSE certification are as follows:

◆ Implementing and Supporting Microsoft Windows NT Server 4.0, #70-067

◆ Implementing and Supporting Microsoft Windows NT Server 4.0 in the Enterprise, #70-068

◆ Microsoft Windows 3.1, #70-030*

   OR Microsoft Windows for Workgroups 3.11, #70-048*

OR Implementing and Supporting Microsoft Windows 95, #70-064

OR Implementing and Supporting Microsoft Windows NT Workstation 4.0, #70-073

OR Implementing and Supporting Microsoft Windows 98, #70-098

◆ Networking Essentials, #70-058

Elective Exams

For both the Windows NT 3.51 and the 4.0 track, you must pass two of the following elective exams for MCSE certification:

◆ Implementing and Supporting Microsoft SNA Server 3.0, #70-013

   OR Implementing and Supporting Microsoft SNA Server 4.0, #70-085

◆ Implementing and Supporting Microsoft Systems Management Server 1.0, #70-014*

   OR Implementing and Supporting Microsoft Systems Management Server 1.2, #70-018

   OR Implementing and Supporting Microsoft Systems Management Server 2.0, #70-086

◆ Microsoft SQL Server 4.2 Database Implementation, #70-021

   OR Implementing a Database Design on Microsoft SQL Server 6.5, #70-027

   OR Implementing a Database Design on Microsoft SQL Server 7.0, #70-029

◆ Microsoft SQL Server 4.2 Database Administra-tion for Microsoft Windows NT, #70-022

OR System Administration for Microsoft SQL Server 6.5 (or 6.0), #70-026

OR System Administration for Microsoft SQL Server 7.0, #70-028

◆ Microsoft Mail for PC Networks 3.2-Enterprise, #70-037

◆ Internetworking with Microsoft TCP/IP on Microsoft Windows NT (3.5-3.51), #70-053

OR Internetworking with Microsoft TCP/IP on Microsoft Windows NT 4.0, #70-059

◆ Implementing and Supporting Microsoft Exchange Server 4.0, #70-075*

OR Implementing and Supporting Microsoft Exchange Server 5.0, #70-076

OR Implementing and Supporting Microsoft Exchange Server 5.5, #70-081

◆ Implementing and Supporting Microsoft Internet Information Server 3.0 and Microsoft Index Server 1.1, #70-077

OR Implementing and Supporting Microsoft Internet Information Server 4.0, #70-087

◆ Implementing and Supporting Microsoft Proxy Server 1.0, #70-078

OR Implementing and Supporting Microsoft Proxy Server 2.0, #70-088

◆ Implementing and Supporting Microsoft Internet Explorer 4.0 by Using the Internet Explorer Resource Kit, #70-079

How to Become a Microsoft Certified Systems Engineer+Internet

You must pass seven operating system exams and two elective exams to become an MCSE specializing in Internet technology.

Core Exams

The seven MCSE+Internet core exams required for certification are as follows:

◆ Networking Essentials, #70-058

◆ Internetworking with Microsoft TCP/IP on Microsoft Windows NT 4.0, #70-059

◆ Implementing and Supporting Microsoft Windows 95, #70-064

OR Implementing and Supporting Microsoft Windows NT Workstation 4.0, #70-073

OR Implementing and Supporting Microsoft Windows 98, #70-098

◆ Implementing and Supporting Microsoft Windows NT Server 4.0, #70-067

◆ Implementing and Supporting Microsoft Windows NT Server 4.0 in the Enterprise, #70-068

◆ Implementing and Supporting Microsoft Internet Information Server 3.0 and Microsoft Index Server 1.1, #70-077

OR Implementing and Supporting Microsoft Internet Information Server 4.0, #70-087

◆ Implementing and Supporting Microsoft Internet Explorer 4.0 by Using the Internet Explorer Resource Kit, #70-079

Elective Exams

You must also pass two of the following elective exams for MCSE+Internet certification:

◆ System Administration for Microsoft SQL Server 6.5, #70-026

◆ Implementing a Database Design on Microsoft SQL Server 6.5, #70-027

◆ Implementing and Supporting Web Sites Using Microsoft Site Server 3.0, # 70-056

◆ Implementing and Supporting Microsoft Exchange Server 5.0, #70-076

  OR Implementing and Supporting Microsoft Exchange Server 5.5, #70-081

◆ Implementing and Supporting Microsoft Proxy Server 1.0, #70-078

  OR Implementing and Supporting Microsoft Proxy Server 2.0, #70-088

◆ Implementing and Supporting Microsoft SNA Server 4.0, #70-085

How to Become a Microsoft Certified Solution Developer

The MCSD certification is undergoing substantial revision. Listed here are the requirements for the new track (available fourth quarter 1998) as well as the old.

New Track

For the new track, you must pass three core exams and one elective exam. The three core exam areas are listed here as well as the elective exams from which you can choose.

The core exams include the following:

Desktop Applications Development (One Required)

◆ Designing and Implementing Desktop Applications with Microsoft Visual C++ 6.0, #70-016

  OR Designing and Implementing Desktop Applications with Microsoft Visual Basic 6.0, #70-176

Distributed Applications Development (One Required)

◆ Designing and Implementing Distributed Applications with Microsoft Visual C++ 6.0, #70-015

  OR Designing and Implementing Distributed Applications with Microsoft Visual Basic 6.0, #70-175

Solution Architecture (Required)

◆ Analyzing Requirements and Defining Solution Architectures, #70-100

You must pass one of the following elective exams:

◆ Designing and Implementing Distributed Applications with Microsoft Visual C++ 6.0, #70-015

  OR Designing and Implementing Desktop Applications with Microsoft Visual C++ 6.0, #70-016

  OR Microsoft SQL Server 4.2 Database Implementation, #70-021*

◆ Implementing a Database Design on Microsoft SQL Server 6.5, #70-027

  OR Implementing a Database Design on Microsoft SQL Server 7.0, #70-029

◆ Developing Applications with C++ Using the Microsoft Foundation Class Library, #70-024

◆ Implementing OLE in Microsoft Foundation Class Applications, #70-025

◆ Designing and Implementing Web Sites with Microsoft FrontPage 98, #70-055

◆ Designing and Implementing Commerce Solutions with Microsoft Site Server 3.0, Commerce Edition, #70-057

◆ Programming with Microsoft Visual Basic 4.0, #70-065

   OR Developing Applications with Microsoft Visual Basic 5.0, #70-165

   OR Designing and Implementing Distributed Appli-cations with Microsoft Visual Basic 6.0, #70-175

   OR Designing and Implementing Desktop Appli-cations with Microsoft Visual Basic 6.0, #70-176

◆ Microsoft Access for Windows 95 and the Microsoft Access Development Toolkit, #70-069

◆ Designing and Implementing Solutions with Microsoft Office (Code-named Office 9) and Microsoft Visual Basic for Applications, #70-091

◆ Designing and Implementing Web Solutions with Microsoft Visual InterDev 6.0, #70-152

Old Track

For the old track, you must pass two core technology exams and two elective exams for MCSD certification. The following lists show the required technology exams and elective exams needed to become an MCSD.

Core Technology Exams

You must pass the following two core technology exams to qualify for MCSD certification:

◆ Microsoft Windows Architecture I, #70-160*

◆ Microsoft Windows Architecture II, #70-161*

Elective Exams

You must also pass two of the following elective exams to become an MSCD:

◆ Designing and Implementing Distributed Applications with Microsoft Visual C++ 6.0, #70-015

◆ Designing and Implementing Desktop Applications with Microsoft Visual C++ 6.0, #70-016

◆ Microsoft SQL Server 4.2 Database Implementation, #70-021*

   OR Implementing a Database Design on Microsoft SQL Server 6.5, #70-027

   OR Implementing a Database Design on Microsoft SQL Server 7.0, #70-029

◆ Developing Applications with C++ Using the Microsoft Foundation Class Library, #70-024

◆ Implementing OLE in Microsoft Foundation Class Applications, #70-025

◆ Programming with Microsoft Visual Basic 4.0, #70-065

   OR Developing Applications with Microsoft Visual Basic 5.0, #70-165

   OR Designing and Implementing Distributed Appli-cations with Microsoft Visual Basic 6.0, #70-175

   OR Designing and Implementing Desktop Appli-cations with Microsoft Visual Basic 6.0, #70-176

◆ Microsoft Access 2.0 for Windows-Application Development, #70-051

  OR Microsoft Access for Windows 95 and the Microsoft Access Development Toolkit, #70-069

◆ Developing Applications with Microsoft Excel 5.0 Using Visual Basic for Applications, #70-052

◆ Programming in Microsoft Visual FoxPro 3.0 for Windows, #70-054

◆ Designing and Implementing Web Sites with Microsoft FrontPage 98, #70-055

◆ Designing and Implementing Commerce Solutions with Microsoft Site Server 3.0, Commerce Edition, #70-057

◆ Designing and Implementing Solutions with Microsoft Office (Code-named Office 9) and Microsoft Visual Basic for Applications, #70-091

◆ Designing and Implementing Web Solutions with Microsoft Visual InterDev 6.0, #70-152

How to Become a Microsoft Certified Trainer

To understand the requirements and process for becoming an MCT, you need to obtain the Microsoft Certified Trainer Guide document from the following Web site:

```
http://www.microsoft.com/train_cert/mct/
```

At this site, you can read the document as Web pages or display and download it as a Word file. The MCT Guide explains the four-step process of becoming an MCT. The general steps for the MCT certification are as follows:

1. Complete and mail a Microsoft Certified Trainer application to Microsoft. You must include proof of your skills for presenting instructional material. The options for doing so are described in the MCT Guide.

2. Obtain and study the Microsoft Trainer Kit for the Microsoft Official Curricula (MOC) courses for which you want to be certified. Microsoft Trainer Kits can be ordered by calling 800-688-0496 in North America. Those in other regions should review the MCT Guide for information on how to order a Trainer Kit.

3. Take the Microsoft Certification Exam for the product you want to be certified to teach.

4. Attend the MOC course featuring the course for which you want to be certified. This is done so you can understand how the course is structured, how labs are completed, and how the course flows.

WARNING

Be Sure to Get the MCT Guide
You should consider the preceding steps a general overview of the MCT certification process. The precise steps you need to take are described in detail on the website mentioned earlier. Do not misinterpret the preceding steps as the exact process you need to undergo.

If you are interested in becoming an MCT, you can obtain more information by visiting the Microsoft Certified Training website at `http://www.microsoft.com/train_cert/mct/` or by calling 800-688-0496.

What's on the CD-ROM

This appendix is a brief rundown of what you'll find on the CD-ROM that comes with this book. For a more detailed description of the newly developed Top Score test engine, exclusive to Macmillan Computer Publishing, please see Appendix D, "Using the Top Score Software."

TOP SCORE

Top Score is a test engine developed exclusively for Macmillan Computer Publishing. It is, we believe, the best test engine available because it emulates the format of the standard Microsoft exams. In addition to providing a means of evaluating your knowledge of the exam material, Top Score features several innovations that help you improve your mastery of the subject matter.

For example, the practice tests allow you to check your score by exam area or category to determine which topics you need to study further. Other modes allow you to obtain immediate feedback on your responses, explanations of correct answers, and even hyperlinks to the chapter in an electronic version of the book where the topic is covered. Again, for a complete description of the benefits of Top Score, see Appendix D.

Before running the Top Score software, be sure that AutoRun is enabled. If you prefer not to use AutoRun, then you can run the application from the CD by double-clicking the START.EXE file from Explorer.

EXCLUSIVE ELECTRONIC VERSION OF TEXT

As referred to above, the CD-ROM also contains the electronic version of this book in Portable Document Format (PDF). In addition to the links to the book that are built into Top Score, you can use this version to help search for terms you need to study or other book elements. The electronic version comes complete with all figures as they appear in the book.

COPYRIGHT INFORMATION AND DISCLAIMER

Macmillan Computer Publishing's Top Score Test Engine. Copyright 1998, New Riders Publishing. All rights reserved. Made in the U.S.A.

Using the Top Score Software

GETTING STARTED

The installation procedure for the Top Score software is very simple. Put the CD into the CD-ROM drive. The AutoRun function starts and, after a moment, you will see the opening screen. Click Exit to quit or Continue to proceed. If you click Continue, you will see a window offering you the choice of launching any of the four Top Score applications.

> **NOTE**
> **Getting Started Without AutoRun**
> If you have disabled the AutoRun function, you can start the Top Score Software suite by viewing the contents of the CD-ROM in Explorer and double-clicking START.EXE.

At this point, you are ready to use the Top Score software.

INSTRUCTIONS ON USING THE TOP SCORE SOFTWARE

Top Score software consists of the following four applications: Study Cards, Flash Cards, Practice Exam, and Simulator.

Study Cards serve as a study aid organized around the specific exam objectives, arranged in multiple-choice format. Flash Cards, another study aid, require responses to open-ended questions, testing knowledge of the material at a deeper level than simply recognition memory. The practice exam simulates the Microsoft Certification Exams. Simulator emulates elements of the Windows NT interface to provide you with hands-on experience and practice with simulation questions like those now appearing in new and revised certification exams.

To start the Study Cards, Flash Cards, or Practice Exam applications, click the application you would like to use. On the next screen, click the button that appears centered near the bottom of the screen. The initial screen of the application will appear and you will be ready to go.

To start Simulator, click the button, then follow the instructions to install it. When Simulator is installed, it will appear in your Programs menu.

Further details on using the four specific applications follow.

Using Top Score Practice Exams

The Practice Exam interface is simple and straightforward. Its design simulates the look and feel of the Microsoft Certification Exams. If you followed the preceding two steps which start the Practice Exam application, you should see an opening screen similar to the one shown in Figure D.1.

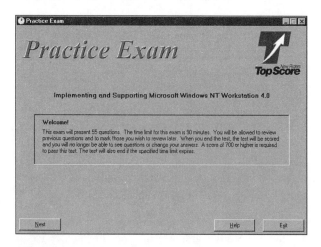

FIGURE D.1▲
Top Score Practice Exam opening screen.

Click Next to see a disclaimer and copyright screen, read the information, and click Top Score's Start button. A notice appears indicating that the program is randomly selecting questions for the practice exam from the exam database (see Figure D.2). Practice exams include the same number of items as the Microsoft exam.

> **NOTE**
> **Some Exams Follow a New Format**
> The number of questions on the practice exam is the same for traditional exams. However, this is not the case for exams that incorporate the new "adaptive testing" format. In that format, there is no set number of questions. See "Study and Exam Prep Tips" for more details on this new format.

The items are selected from a larger set of 150 to 900 questions. The random selection of questions from the database takes some time to retrieve. Don't reboot; your machine is not hung!

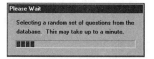

FIGURE D.2▲
Top Score's Please Wait notice.

After the questions have been selected, the first test item appears. See Figure D.3 for an example of a test item screen.

FIGURE D.3▲
A Top Score test item requires a single response.

Notice the several important features in this window. The question number, out of the total number of retrieved questions, is located at the top-left corner of the window in the control bar. Immediately below this is a check box labeled Mark, which enables you to mark any exam item as one you would like to return to later. Across the screen from the check box, you will see the total time remaining for the exam.

The test question is located in a colored section (gray in the figure). Directly below the test question, in the white area, are response choices. Be sure to note that immediately below the responses are instructions about how to respond, including the number of responses required. You might notice that questions requiring a single response, such as that shown in Figure D.3, have radio buttons next to the choices. Items requiring multiple responses have check boxes (see Figure D.4).

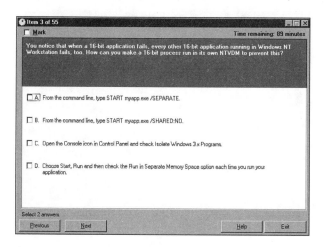

FIGURE D.4▲
A Top Score test item requiring multiple responses.

Some questions and responses do not appear on the screen in their entirety. In these cases, a scrollbar appears to the right of the question or response. Use the scrollbar to reveal the rest of the question or response item.

The buttons at the bottom of a window enable you to return to a previous test item, proceed to the next test item, or exit Top Score Practice Exams.

Some items require you to examine additional information called *Exhibits*. These screens typically include graphs, diagrams, or other types of visual information needed to respond to the test question. Exhibits can be accessed by clicking the Exhibit button also located at the bottom of the window.

After you complete the practice test by moving through all the test questions, you arrive at a summary screen titled Item Review (see Figure D.5).

FIGURE D.5▲
The Top Score Item Review window.

This window enables you to see all of the question numbers, your responses to each item, any questions you have marked, and any left incomplete. The buttons at the bottom of the screen enable you to review all the marked items and incomplete items in numeric order.

If you want to review a specific marked or incomplete item, simply type the desired item number in the box at the lower-right corner of the window and click the Review Item button. After you review the item, you can respond to the question. Notice that the item window also offers the Next and Previous options. You can also select the Item Review button to return to the Item Review window.

NOTE   **Your Time Is Limited**   If you exceed the time allotted for the test, you do not have the opportunity to review any marked or incomplete items. The program moves to the next screen.

After you complete your review of the practice test questions, click the Grade Now button to find out your score. An Examination Score Report is generated for your practice test (see Figure D.6). This report provides you with the required score for this particular certification exam, your score on the practice test, and a grade. The report also breaks down your performance on the practice test by the specific objectives for the exam. Click the Print button to print out the results of your performance.

![Examination Score Report window]

FIGURE D.6▲
The Top Score Examination Score Report window.

You also have the option of reviewing those items that you incorrectly answered. Click the Show Me What I Missed button to receive a summary of those items. Print out this information if you need further practice or review; the printouts can be used to guide your use of Study Cards and Flash Cards.

Using Top Score Study Cards

To start the software, begin from the main screen. Click on the Study Cards button, then on the smaller button displayed in the next screen. After a moment, an initial screen similar to that of the Practice Exams appears.

Click Next to see the first Study Cards screen (see Figure D.7).

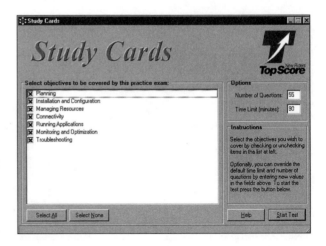

FIGURE D.7▲
The first Study Cards screen.

The interface for Study Cards is similar to that of Practice Exams. However, you have several important options that enable you to prepare for an exam. The Study Cards material is organized using the specific objectives for each exam. You can choose to receive questions on all of the objectives or use the check boxes to select coverage of a limited set of objectives. For example, if you have already completed a practice exam and your score report indicates that you need to work on planning, you can choose to cover only the Planning objectives for your Study Cards session. You can also determine the number of questions to be presented by typing it in the option box at the right of the screen. You can also control the amount of time allowed for a review by typing the number of minutes into the Time Limit option box on the right side.

When you click the Start Test button, Study Cards randomly select the indicated number of questions from the question database. A dialog box appears, informing you that this process could take some time. After the questions are selected, you will see a first item that looks similar to the one in Figure D.8.

FIGURE D.8▲
A Study Cards item.

Respond to the questions in the same manner as you did to Practice Exam questions. Radio buttons signal that a single answer is required, whereas check boxes indicate that multiple answers are expected.

Notice the menu options at the top of the window. The File option pulls down to allow you an exit from the program. Edit allows you to use the copy function and even copy questions to the Windows Clipboard. The Options pull-down menu allows you to take notes on a

particular question. When you pull it down, choose Open Notes. After Notepad opens, type and save your notes. Options also allows you to start over with another exam.

This application provides you with immediate feed back as to whether you answered the question correctly. Click the Show Answers button to see the correct answer(s) highlighted on the screen, as shown in Figure D.9.

FIGURE D.9▲
The correct answer(s) is highlighted.

Study Cards also includes Item Review, Score Report, and Show Me What I Missed features that are essentially the same as those in Practice Exams.

Using Top Score Flash Cards

Flash Cards are a third way to use the exam question database. The Flash Cards items do not offer you multiple-choice answers; instead, they require you to respond with a short answer or essay format. Flash Cards help you learn the material well enough to respond with the correct answer in your own words. If you have the depth of knowledge to answer questions without prompting, you will certainly be prepared to pass a multiple-choice exam.

Flash Cards are started in the same fashion as Practice Exams and Study Cards. Click the icon next to Flash Cards, and then click Start the Program. Click the button for the exam you want and the opening screen appears. It looks similar to the example in Figure D.10.

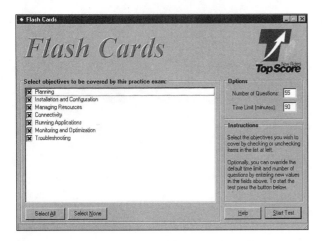

FIGURE D.10▲
The Flash Cards opening screen.

You can choose Flash Cards by various objectives, just as in Study Cards. Select the objectives you want to cover, the number of questions you want, and the amount of time you want to spend. Click the Start Test button to start the Flash Cards session; you will see a dialog box notifying you that questions are being selected.

The Flash Cards items appear in an interface similar to that of Practice Exams and Study Cards (see Figure D.11).

Notice, however, that although a question is presented, no answer choices appear. You must type your answer in the white space below the question (see Figure D.12).

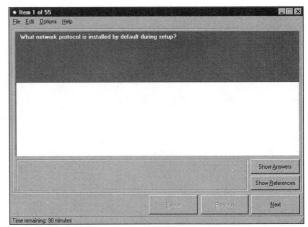

FIGURE D.11▲
A Flash Cards item.

FIGURE D.12▲
A typed answer in Flash Cards.

Compare your answer to the correct answer by clicking the Show Answers button (see Figure D.13).

appropriate tool button to complete the task (see Figure D.14).

FIGURE D.13▲
The correct answer is shown.

You can also use the Show References button in the same manner as described earlier in the Study Cards sections.

The pull-down menus provide nearly the same functionality as they do in Study Cards, with the exception of Paste on the Edit menu rather than Copy Question.

Flash Cards provide simple feedback. They do not include an Item Review or Score Report. They are intended to provide an alternative way to assess your level of knowledge that encourages you to learn the information more thoroughly than with other methods.

Using Top Score Simulator

Top Score Simulator is simple to use. Just choose Start, Program and click on the Simulator program name. After the application opens, go to Options, Question Set and choose one of the three sets of questions. You are presented with a task or question in the Task window and asked to type in an answer or choose the

FIGURE D.14▲
An example of a Simulator task.

After choosing the tool, you have to complete the task by choosing the correct tabs and settings or entering the correct information required by the task (see Figure D.15).

FIGURE D.15▲
Completing the task.

To find out if you chose correctly, click the Grade button. You receive immediate feedback about your choice in the Result window (see Figure D.16). To move on to the next question, simply click Next. You can use the Previous button to go back over questions you might have missed or want to review. The Exit button allows you to quit the program.

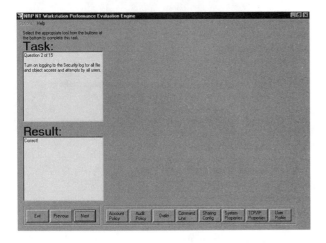

FIGURE D.16
You got it correct!

SUMMARY

The Top Score software suite of applications provides you with several approaches toward exam preparation. Use Practice Exams not only to assess your learning but also to prepare yourself for the test-taking situation. The same can be said of the Simulator application. Use Study Cards and Flash Cards as tools for more focused assessment, review, and to reinforce the knowledge you are gaining. You will find that these four applications are the perfect way to complete your exam preparation.

Modifying IIS 4 with the Registry

Many of the customization choices available to you with IIS 4 can be made from the Internet Service Manager. However, you also can make changes directly in the Windows NT Registry that affect IIS 4's performance.

Table E.1 lists and describes some of the common Registry changes you can make to the Web service settings that appear under the following Registry path:

```
HKEY_LOCAL_MACHINE\SYSTEM\CurrentControlSet\Services
➥\W3SVC\Parameters
```

> **NOTE**
>
> **Back Up the Registry!** Don't make any Registry changes until you've made a backup. You can learn how to do this, and more about the Registry in general, by reading *Windows NT Registry Troubleshooting* or *Windows NT Registry*, both published by New Riders.

TABLE E.1

REGISTRY ENTRIES FOR THE WEB SERVICE

Property	Data Type	Default Setting	Range Value	Description
AcceptByte Ranges	REG_DWORD	1 (enabled)	1, 0	When enabled, the Web server sends the Accept-Range:bytes header field to accept range requests.
AllowGuest Access	REG_DWORD	1 (enabled)	1, 0	Enables guest services on the service. This entry is available for the FTP service (MSFTPSVC) as well. Change this entry to 0 to disable guest access on your server.
AllowSpecial CharsInShell	REG_DWORD	0 (disabled)	1, 0	Enables batch files (.BAT and .CMD) to use special characters, including ;, ,, |, (, %, and <>. Keep this setting to 0 to reduce the threat of hackers using these characters to hack into your site. If you enable this setting, users can pass these characters (except | and <>) to CGI scripts. When disabled, however, users cannot send these characters to CGI scripts.
DLCCookie NameString	REG_STRING	none	string	Denotes the cookie string that is sent to downlevel clients.

continues

| TABLE E.1 | *continued* |

REGISTRY ENTRIES FOR THE WEB SERVICE

Property	Data Type	Default Setting	Range Value	Description
DLCHost NameString	REG_STRING	none	string	Specifies the Web site's name where the downlevel host menu document is stored. You can find the downlevel host menu name by looking at the DLCCookieMenu DocumentString Registry entry.
DLCCookie	REG_STRING	none	string	Indicates the host menu file name for clients that do not support HOST header, but do support cookies.
DLCMunge MenuDocument String	REG_STRING	none	string	Indicates the host menu file name for clients that do not support cookies.
DLCMenu String	REG_STRING	none	string	Specifies the special prefix of URLs requested by downlevel clients.
DLCSupport	REG_DWORD	0 (disabled)	1, 0	Enables downlevel client support.
EnableSvc Loc	REG_DWORD	1 (enabled)	1, 0	Registers IIS services so the Internet Service Manager can locate the service. This entry is supported by the FTP service as well.
Language Engines*	REG_STRING	none	string	Specifies a scripting language that does not support the Active Server Pages Object Method syntax.
LogError Requests	REG_DWORD	1 (enabled)	1, 0	Enables or disables error logging.
LogSuccess Requests	REG_DWORD	1 (enabled)	1, 0	Enables or disables the logging of successful activities.
SSIEnable CmdDirective	REG_DWORD	1 (enabled)	1, 0	Setting this value to 0 increases security for sites wanting to disable the #exec cmd directive the server-side includes when shell commands are executed.
TryExcept Disable	REG_DWORD	0 (disabled)	1, 0	When ISAPI applications run, this setting enables or disables exception caching when Http Extensionproc() is called. Set this entry to 1 when you want to perform JIT debugging. Otherwise, set it to 0 so ISAPI applications do not bring the server down in the event of an error in the ISAPI application.
UploadRead Ahead	REG_DWORD	48KB	0-0x80000000	Specifies the default amount of data posted by a client that the server reads before passing control to the application. Higher values require more server RAM.

*To use the LanguageEngines entry, you must create the following key under the W3SVC key:
    \ASP\LanguageEntries\Name_of_Language

TCP/IP and Subnetting

Before we dive right into the details of the TCP/IP protocol, a little background on TCP/IP networking is in order. If you have passed the Networking Essentials or TCP/IP exams, this should be review for you.

An *internet* or *internetwork* is a group of computers linked together using TCP/IP technology. An internet can be either a portion of the Internet (the worldwide network of publicly interconnected TCP/IP networks) or a private corporate or enterprise internetwork. Such private internetworks are usually called *intranets* to show that they are internal to an enterprise and not part of the Internet.

One unique characteristic of the Internet (and any TCP/IP network) is the way that computers are identified. When the TCP/IP protocol specification was first written, the designers wanted an identification scheme that was independent of any one type of computer, router, or any other network equipment. It also needed to be vendor neutral to avoid some of the issues with the other proprietary protocols that were around at the time, like IBM's SNA protocol. They established an addressing mechanism using *IP addresses*. IP addresses are written in an octet-based (coming from eight binary numbers) form, like 100.34.192.212. The first octet (you learn about the others later) dictates the *class* of network that is being referred to. The following are the three classes of IP addresses commonly used:

Network Address	Address Class	Default Mask
01-126	Class A	255.0.0.0
128-191	Class B	255.255.0.0
192-223	Class C	255.255.255.0

> **NOTE**
>
> **Other Classes of IP Addresses**
> There are also Class D and Class E networks, but they are reserved for research purposes and are not used on the public network.

Thus, an address of 100.34.192.212 is a Class A address, and the address 220.34.192.212 is a Class C address. The class is important, because it indicates the maximum number of hosts that a network can have. The breakout of numbers of hosts looks like this:

Class A	16,777,214 hosts
Class B	65,534 hosts
Class C	254 hosts

Although the existing shortage of addresses has made it impossible to obtain a class A address for some time, imagine the difficulties in trying to network 16 million hosts at a single site—it is virtually impossible. Even 254 hosts can present a challenge in today's networks. Typically, hosts are spread out across several physical locations, often within the same building, campus, or other geographical area.

For that reason, and to make routing practical, subnets are used to divide the network (and network numbers) into smaller portions. This appendix assumes some familiarity with the basics of TCP/IP and addressing and concentrates on *subnetting*—one of the most misunderstood components of addressing.

Simply put, subnetting is a mechanism for using some bits in the host ID octets as a subnet ID. Without subnetting, an IP address is interpreted as two fields:

> netid + hostid

With subnetting, an IP address is interpreted as three fields:

> netid + subnetid + hostid

This topic is examined thoroughly in the following sections:

- ◆ Subnet Masks, Host IDs, and Network IDs

- ◆ Purpose of Subnet Masks

- ◆ Default Subnet Masks

- ◆ Subdividing a Network

SUBNET MASKS, HOST IDS, AND NETWORK IDS

Subnets are created in a TCP/IP internetwork by choosing the IP addresses and subnet masks used, a process known as *subnet addressing* or *subnetting*. The term network is used when it is not necessary to distinguish between individual subnets and internetworks. A subnet is simply a subdivision of a network. The term *subnetworking* or subnetting is used when a single network ID is subdivided into multiple network IDs by applying a custom subnet mask.

> **NOTE** **Phone Number Analogy** An analogy for a subnet is a phone number. The area code equates to a network, the prefix equates to a subnet, and the last four digits equate to the actual host.

The *subnet mask*, like the IP address, is a 32-bit number, often shown in dotted decimal notation. When shown in binary notation, the subnet mask has a 1 bit for each bit corresponding to the position of the network ID in the IP address and a 0 bit for each bit corresponding to the position of the host ID in the IP address (in binary notation). An example of a subnet mask is

> 11111111.11111111.00000000.00000000

or 255.255.0.0 in dotted decimal notation.

BINARY

A binary number is made up of bits. A bit can be either a 1 or a 0, where 1 represents TRUE and 0 represents FALSE. All computer operations are performed using binary numbers because the bits are easily represented by electrical charges. Huge binary numbers are usually fairly meaningless to the average person, so the computer converts them to more human-friendly states, such as decimal numbers and characters.

Any decimal number is represented in binary notation, using 1s and 0s. Each bit with a 1 represents 2 raised to the power of $n-1$ ($2^{(n-1)}$), in which n is the position of the bit from the right. Each bit with a 0 represents a 0 in decimal notation as well. The decimal number results from adding together all the 1 bits after converting each to $2^{(n-1)}$.

For example, the binary number 100 is 2^2, which means the decimal equivalent is 4.

The binary number 101 is 2^2+0+2^0, or 5 in decimal notation.

With TCP/IP, you often use 8-bit binary numbers, also called octets or bytes in IP addresses. An example is

11111111

Each bit in position *n* from the right gives a value of $2^{(n-1)}$. Therefore, the first bit represents a 1, the second bit a 2, the third a 4, the fourth an 8, and so forth, so that you have the following:

1 1 1 1 1 1 1 1 (binary)

128+64+32+16+8+4+2+1 = 255 (decimal)

Keep in mind that any 0 bits do not add to the total, so the following are equal:

1 1 0 0 1 0 0 1 (binary)

128+64+0+0+8+0+0+1 = 201 (decimal)

Memorizing the decimal equivalent number of each character in the 8-bit number, as in the following, makes it extremely easy to convert between binary and decimal quickly:

Decimal to Binary

1	1	1	1	1	1	1	1
128	64	32	16	8	4	2	1

For example, the number

01111111

should be easily recognized as 127 by taking the maximum value (255) and subtracting the missing digit (128). Likewise, the number

11011111

is quickly converted to 223 by subtracting the value of the missing digit (32) from the maximum value (255).

The 0 bit of the subnet mask essentially mask out, or cover up, the host ID portion of an IP address. Thus, the subnet mask is used to determine on which network or subnet the address being referred to is found. When one host sends a message to another host, the TCP/IP protocol must determine whether the hosts are on the same subnet and can communicate directly, or whether they are on different subnets and the message

should be sent via a router to the other subnet. It is impossible to determine whether two IP addresses are on the same subnet just by looking at the IP addresses without the subnet mask. For example, if the host at 192.20.1.5 sends a message to the host at 192.20.6.8, should it be sent directly or to a router connecting to another subnet?

The answer depends on the subnet mask being used on the network. If the subnet mask was 255.255.255.0, the network ID of the first host would be 192.20.1, and the network ID of the second host would be 192.20.6. The hosts would be on different subnets, and therefore they must communicate via a router. On the other hand, if the subnet mask was 255.255.0.0, both hosts would be on subnet 192.20 and could communicate by using local broadcasts and local address resolution.

When the subnet mask is one of 255.0.0.0, 255.255.0.0, or 255.255.255.0, it is fairly obvious which part of the IP address is the network ID (these are the defaults for class A, B, and C networks, respectively). Yet, it becomes less apparent which part of the IP address is the network when other subnet masks are used (such as 255.255.248.0). In this case, if both the IP address and subnet mask are converted to binary, it becomes more apparent (the 1 bit of the subnet mask corresponds to the network ID in the IP address).

By figuring out what subnet a host is on from the IP address and subnet mask, it becomes easier to route a packet to the proper destination. Fortunately, all you have to do is supply the proper IP addresses with one subnet mask for the entire internetwork, and the software determines which subnet the destination is on. If the destination address is on a different subnet than the sender, it is on a remote network and the packet is routed appropriately, usually by being sent to the default gateway.

If a network has a small number of hosts, all on the same segment without any routers, they are likely given the same network ID (the network portion of an IP address). If the network is larger, however, with remote segments connected by routers (an internetwork), each individual subnet needs a different network ID. Therefore, when assigning IP addresses and subnet masks, the network administrator must know how many subnets are required and the maximum number of hosts that are on each subnet.

Depending on the subnet mask chosen, the internetwork can have either a lot of different network IDs with a smaller number of hosts on each subnet or a smaller number of network IDs with a larger number of hosts on each subnet. It will become clearer why the results are the way they are as you read further; Table F.1 shows the maximum number of hosts and subnets available per the number of bits used.

Purpose of Subnet Masks

By specifying the correct subnet mask for addresses, you are letting the TCP/IP software know which part of the address refers to the host and which part refers to the specific subnet the host is located on. As mentioned

previously, the IP address and subnet mask are made up of four 8-bit octets that are most often shown in decimal rather than binary format for ease of reading. As an example, an IP address and subnet mask in binary format could be

```
IP Address:      11000000 00010100 00010000
➥00000101
Subnet Mask:     11111111 11111111 11111111
➥00000000
Network ID:      11000000 00010100 00010000
➥00000000
Host ID:         00000000 00000000 00000000
➥00000101
```

Notice that the network ID is the portion of the IP address corresponding to a bit value of 1 in the subnet mask.

In the preceding example, you could have a maximum of 254 different hosts on the network 192.20.16 (192.20.16.1 through 192.20.16.254). If you want to have more hosts on one network, you have to use a different addressing scheme. For example, using a subnet mask of 255.255.0.0 gives the following results:

```
IP Address       192.20.16.5
Subnet Mask      255.255.0.0
Network ID       192.20
Host ID           16.5
```

TABLE F.1

HOSTS AND SUBNETS

Subnet Address	Additional Bits Required	Maximum Number of Subnets	Maximum Number of Hosts—C Network	Maximum Number of Hosts—B Network	Maximum Number of Hosts—A Network
0	0	0	254	65,534	16,777,214
192	2	2	62	16,382	4,194,302
224	3	6	30	8,190	2,097,150
240	4	14	14	4,094	1,048,574
248	5	30	6	2,046	524,286
252	6	62	2	1,022	262,142
254	7	126	invalid	510	131,070
255	8	254	invalid	254	65,534

Because the host ID in this example is a 16-bit value, it allows you to have (256×256) -2 hosts on the network 192.20. The two addresses that must be subtracted from the possibilities are 0 (consisting of all 0s) and 255 (consisting of all 1s)—both reserved addresses. Zero is used to define the network and 255 is a broadcast address for all computers in the network.

> **NOTE Omitting Zeros** It is common in TCP/IP to omit the trailing zero octets in a network ID and the leading zero octets in a host ID. Therefore, the network ID 192.20 really represents 192.20.0.0, and the host ID 16.5 really represents 0.0.16.5.

A host ID cannot have all bits set to either 1 or 0 because these addresses would be interpreted to mean a broadcast address or "this network only," respectively. Thus, the number of valid addresses is $(2^n)-2$, where n is the number of bits used for the host ID.

You might also notice that the second scheme allows fewer combinations of network IDs than the first scheme. Although the second sample scenario might seem preferable for most networks, you might not have the freedom to use such a scheme. For example, if the hosts are on the Internet, you must assign a certain set of IP addresses by the Internet address assignment authority, InterNIC (the Internet Network Information Center). Because the number of IP addresses available today is limited, you usually do not have the luxury of choosing a scheme that gives so many combinations of available host addresses. Suppose you are assigned the network ID 192.20.5 and have a total of 1,000 hosts on three remote networks. A Class C network using the default subnet mask of 255.255.255.0 has only one network (192.20.5) and 254 hosts (192.20.5.1 through 192.20.5.254).

> **NOTE Ones and Zeros as Address Bits** Common practice dictates that address bits cannot be all 1s or 0s. In reality, if—and only if—the routers on the network support extended prefixing addressing, it is possible to have addresses of all 1s or 0s. Both the software and the routers must support RIP V2, and you must disallow the possibility of traffic over any older, noncompatible routers.
>
> Cisco routers, NetWare 4.x, and Windows NT all support the extended prefixing address (they often call it a *zero network*). Although going against the principles of RFC 950, they permit the use of the all-0s and all-1s subnets. Just one NetWare 3.x system anywhere on your network, or any older router, means that the zero-network option cannot be used. For all practical purposes, however, you should consider 0s and 1s off limits.

Now look at how a subnet mask is used to determine which part of the IP address is the network ID and which part is the host ID. TCP/IP does a binary calculation using the IP address and the subnet mask to determine the network ID portion of the IP address. Microsoft refers to this calculation as the AND*ing process.*

The computation TCP/IP performs is a logical bitwise AND of the IP address and the subnet mask. The calculation sounds complicated, but all it means is that the octets are converted to binary numbers and a logical AND is performed whose result is the network ID. To make it simpler, recall that in the preceding example, the network ID is the portion of the IP address corresponding to a bit value of 1 in the subnet mask.

Performing a bitwise AND on 2 bits results in 1 (or TRUE) if the two values are both 1. If either or both of the values are not 1, the result is 0 (or FALSE).

Any logical AND with a 0 results in 0. For example:

1 AND 1 results in 1.

1 AND 0 results in 0.

0 AND 1 results in 0.

0 AND 0 results in 0.

In the first example of this section, the IP address 192.20.16.5 is ANDed with the subnet mask 255.255.255.0 to give a network ID of 192.20.16. The calculation that is performed is illustrated in Table F.2.

TABLE F.2

EXAMPLE OF A BITWISE AND OPERATION

	Decimal Notation	Binary Notation
IP address	192.20.16.5	11000000.00010100.00010000.00000101
Subnet mask	255.255.255.0	11111111.11111111.11111111.00000000
IP address AND subnet mask	192.20.16.0	11000000.00010100.00010000.00000000

Determining the network ID is very easy if the subnet mask is made up of only 255 and 0 values. Simply mask, or cover up, the part of the IP address corresponding to the 0 octet of the subnet mask. For example, if the IP address is 15.6.100.1 and the subnet mask is 255.255.0.0, the resulting network ID is 15.6. You cannot use a subnet mask with only 255 and 0 values if you need to subdivide your network ID into individual subnets.

Default Subnet Masks

There are default masks, usually assigned by the vendor, based upon the class of network in question.

Table F.3 shows the subnet mask that appears in the subnet mask field when an IP address is selected.

TABLE F.3

DEFAULT SUBNET MASKS

Class	IP Address	Default Subnet Mask
A	001.y.z.w to 126.y.z.w	255.0.0.0
B	128.y.z.w to 191.y.z.w	255.255.0.0
C	192.y.z.w to 223.y.z.w	255.255.255.0

Thus, using the default mask, the emphasis is on the number of hosts available and nothing more, as Table F.4 illustrates.

TABLE F.4

MAXIMUM NUMBER OF NETWORKS AND HOSTS PER NETWORK IN TCP/IP

Class	Using Default Subnet Mask	Number of Networks	Number of Hosts per Network
A	255.0.0.0	126	16,777,216
B	255.255.0.0	16,384	65,534
C	255.255.255.0	2,097,152	254

If the hosts on your internetwork are not directly on the Internet, you are free to choose the network IDs that you use. For the hosts and subnets that are a part of the Internet, however, the network IDs you use must be assigned by InterNIC.

It must be noted that if you are using network IDs assigned by InterNIC, you do not have the choice of choosing the address class you use (and you can bet that you will be given Class C addresses). In this case, the number of subnets you use is normally limited by the number of network IDs assigned by InterNIC, and the number of hosts per subnet is determined by the class of address. Fortunately, by choosing the proper subnet mask, you can subdivide your network into a greater number of subnets with fewer possible hosts per subnet.

Today, many companies with Internet requirements are avoiding the addressing constraints and security risks of having hosts directly on the Internet by setting up private networks with gateway access to the Internet. Having a private network means that only the Internet gateway host needs to have an Internet address. For security, a firewall can be set up to prevent Internet hosts from directly accessing the company's network.

Subdividing a Network

Internetworks are networks comprised of individual segments connected by routers. Following are the reasons for having distinct segments:

◆ They permit physically remote local networks to be connected.

◆ A mix of network technologies are connected, such as ethernet on one segment and token ring on another.

◆ They allow an unlimited number of hosts to communicate, whereas the number of hosts on each segment are limited by the type of network used.

◆ Network congestion is reduced as broadcasts and local network traffic are limited to the local segment.

Each segment is a subnet of the internetwork and requires a unique network ID. If you have only one network ID that is used—for example, if you have an InterNIC-assigned Internet network ID—you have to subdivide that network ID into subnets.

Following are the steps involved in subnetting a network:

1. Determine the number of network IDs required for planning future growth needs.

2. Determine the maximum number of host addresses that are on each subnet, again allowing for future growth.

3. Define one subnet mask for the entire internetwork that gives the desired number of subnets and allows enough hosts per subnet.

4. Determine the resulting subnet network IDs that are used.

5. Determine the valid host IDs and assign IP addresses to the hosts.

DYNAMIC HOST CONTROL PROTOCOL

Dynamic Host Control Protocol (DHCP) is the successor to the BOOTP protocol. BOOTP was the first protocol in the TCP/IP suite that allowed a central server to dynamically allocate IP addresses on a network. Although it worked, there were some limitations. What DHCP does is defines a method for dynamically allocating IP addresses on a network segment while addressing the shortcomings of the BOOTP protocol. Don't be surprised if you run across a BOOTP implementation out in the business world. It was used extensively in some places, and when it works, people are hesitant to remove it.

> **NOTE**
>
> **What Is BOOTP?** BOOTP (Bootstrap Protocol) is an Internet protocol that enables a diskless workstation to discover its own IP address, the IP address of a BOOTP server on the network, and a file to boot (bootstrap) the machine. This enables the workstation to boot without requiring a hard or floppy disk drive. The protocol is defined by RFC 951.

Why would you use DHCP? Let's say you have decided to add TCP/IP to your network and you have 250 end users. Your objective is to get a unique IP address assigned to each workstation. Now you can go to each workstation and manually assign an IP address and then come up with a spreadsheet or database to track what IPs have been assigned and what's available, as well as who is using that address in case there's a problem. Keep in mind that you need to set the mask, gateway, and DNS information on each machine as well. Or you could configure each machine to use DHCP for addressing and set the subnet mask, gateway, and DNS information on the DHCP server instead. Then, when TCP/IP is installed on each workstation, you select Use DHCP and, when the system reboots, it's on the network with valid addressing and network information.

DHCP is used extensively in larger networks, as well as networks with a large mobile population and a limited number of IP addresses. Imagine being able to walk into any office in a national corporation, plug a laptop into the network, and be on the network ready to work as soon as the system boots.

If you need to run DHCP in a routed environment, there are a few caveats to be aware of. Most routers are configured not to forward broadcasts. DHCP requires broadcasts to exchange information between the client and server. This means that you need a DHCP server on every segment that needs DHCP services. One way around this requirement is to have a DHCP relay agent that forwards on the client's broadcast request for an IP address to a DHCP server on another segment. Windows NT 4.0 has the capability to act as a DHCP relay. You can configure this parameter in the TCP/IP properties section of the Network applet.

One final point about DHCP: If you connect to the Internet using an ISP and a modem, you are probably using DHCP whether you know it or not. ISPs use DHCP to allow a large population of dial-up users to share a (relatively) small pool of IP addresses. That's why you generally end up with a different IP address every time you connect.

DOMAIN NAME SERVICE

The Domain Name Service (DNS) is a service used on the Internet for resolving names to IP addresses. For example, let's say you want to order a copy of this book to give to your best friend at the office. You need to go out to the Macmillan Computer Publishing Web site and order it. Which do you think is easier to remember? http://www.mcp.com or http://198.70.146.70? Most people would say www.mcp.com, and the Internet community recognized this as they were building the original architecture. Thus, DNS was born. DNS is a hierarchical database containing names and addresses for IP networks and hosts, and is generally represented as a tree. Because it is hierarchical, the same host names can coexist in the database as long as they are located in different branches of the tree. We could spend another hundred pages talking about DNS, but that level of detail isn't on the exam.

NOTE

Sound Familiar? If you have been keeping track of the industry, this description of DNS might sound familiar. That's because Novell's Novell Directory Services Directory and Microsoft's Active Directory are both similar to DNS. In fact, Active Directory is based on DNS.

NOTE

Using a HOSTS File Instead of DNS You can duplicate the function of a DNS server by setting up a local HOSTS file. This file contains entries in an <ip address> <host name> format. For a scenario, info.generic.com could be placed in the HOSTS file in the following manner:

```
10.1.35.100 info.generic.com
```

The hosts file can be found in the \%systemroot%\system32\drivers\ etc subdirectory.

NOTE

Domain Name Service or Domain Name System? You might have noticed that DNS has been identified as an acronym for Domain Name Service and Domain Name System. Both are accurate. Microsoft refers to DNS as a system. The Internet community generally refers to it as a service.

FOR FURTHER INFORMATION

The best possible sources of subnet information are the following two RFCs that define the concept:

◆ **RFC 950.** Internet Standard Subnetting Procedure

◆ **RFC 1219.** On the Assignment of Subnet Numbers

These can be found at a number of locations on the Internet.

Another excellent reference on Microsoft's TCP/IP implementation of TCP/IP is New Riders' *Networking with Microsoft TCP/IP*, by Drew Heywood (ISBN: 0-7357-0014-1). In its third edition, this book is an essential part of your library if you work with Microsoft's implementation of TCP/IP. You should also check out *DNS and Bind*, by Paul Albitz, Cricket Liu, and Mike Loukides. This is considered the definitive reference for DNS and the Bind implemantation. You would also benefit from the addition of New Riders' *Windows NT DNS*, by Michael Masterson and Herman L. Knief to your library.

Index

C

W-Z

NEW RIDERS CERTIFICATION TITLES

TRAINING GUIDES
NEXT GENERATION TRAINING

MCSE Training Guide:
Networking Essentials,
Second Edition

1-56205-919-X,
$49.99, 9/98

MCSE Training Guide:
TCP/IP, Second
Edition

1-56205-920-3,
$49.99, 10/98

A+ Certification
Training Guide

1-56205-896-7,
$49.99, Q4/99

MCSE Training Guide:
Windows NT Server 4,
Second Edition

1-56205-916-5,
$49.99, 9/98

MCSE Training Guide:
SQL Server 7
Administration

0-7357-0003-6,
$49.99, 5/99

TRAINING GUIDES
FIRST EDITIONS

MCSE Training Guide: Systems Management
Server 1.2, 1-56205-748-0

MCSE Training Guide: SQL Server 6.5
Administration, 1-56205-726-x

MCSE Training Guide:
Windows NT Server 4
Enterprise, Second
Edition

1-56205-917-3,
$49.99, 9/98

MCSE Training Guide:
SQL Server 7 Database
Design

0-7357-0004-4,
$49.99, 5/99

MCSE Training Guide: SQL Server 6.5
Design and Implementation, 1-56205-830-4

MCSE Training Guide: Windows 95, 70-064
Exam, 1-56205-880-0

MCSE Training Guide: Exchange Server 5,
1-56205-824-x

MCSE Training Guide: Internet Explorer 4,
1-56205-889-4

MCSE Training Guide: Microsoft Exchange
Server 5.5, 1-56205-899-1

MCSE Training Guide:
Windows NT
Workstation 4,
Second Edition

1-56205-918-1,
$49.99, 9/98

MCSD Training Guide:
Solution Architectures

0-7357-0026-5,
$49.99, 3/99

MCSE Training Guide: IIS 4, 1-56205-823-1

MCSD Training Guide: Visual Basic 5,
1-56205-850-9

MCSD Training Guide: Microsoft Access,
1-56205-771-5

Microsoft Corporation is a registered
trademark of Microsoft Corporation in
the United States and other countries.
New Riders Publishing is an independent
entity from Microsoft Corporation, and is
not affiliated with Microsoft Corporation
in any manner.

MCSE Training Guide:
Windows 98

1-56205-890-8,
$49.99, 2/99

MCSD Training Guide:
Visual Basic 6 Exams

0-7357-0002-8,
$69.99, 3/99

NEW RIDERS CERTIFICATION TITLES

FAST TRACKS

The Accelerated Path to Certification Success

Fast Tracks provide an easy way to review the key elements of each certification technology without being bogged down with elementary-level information.

These guides are perfect for when you already have real-world, hands-on experience. They're the ideal enhancement to training courses, test simulators, and comprehensive training guides.

No fluff—simply what you really need to pass the exam!

MCSE Fast Track: Networking Essentials
1-56205-939-4, $19.99, 9/98

MCSE Fast Track: Windows 98
0-7357-0016-8, $19.99, 12/98

MCSE Fast Track: TCP/IP
1-56205-937-8, $19.99, 9/98

MCSE Fast Track: Windows NT Server 4
1-56205-935-1, $19.99, 9/98

MCSE Fast Track: Windows NT Server 4 Enterprise
1-56205-940-8, $19.99, 9/98

MCSE Fast Track: Windows NT Workstation 4
1-56205-938-6, $19.99, 9/98

A+ Fast Track: Core/Hardware Exam & DOS/Windows Exam
0-7357-0028-1, $29.99, 3/99

MCSE Fast Track: Internet Information Server 4
1-56205-936-X, $19.99, 9/98

MCSE Fast Track: SQL Server 7 Administration
0-7357-0041-9, $19.99, Q2/99

MCSE/MCSD Fast Track: SQL Server 7 Database Design
0-7357-0040-0, $19.99, Q2/99

MCSD Fast Track: Visual Basic 6 Exam 70-175
0-7357-0018-4, $19.99, 12/98

MCSD Fast Track: Visual Basic 6 Exam 70-176
0-7357-0019-2, $19.99, 12/98

MCSD Fast Track: Solution Architectures
0-7357-0029-x, $29.99, Q3/99

TESTPREPS

PRACTICE, CHECK, PASS!

Questions. Questions. And more questions. That's what you'll find in our New Riders *TestPreps*. They're great practice books when you reach the final stage of studying for an exam. We recommend them as supplements to our *Training Guides*.

What makes these study tools unique is that the questions are the primary focus of each book. All the text in these books support and explain the answers to these questions.

✓ **Scenario-based questions** challenge your experience.

✓ **Multiple-choice questions** prep you for the exam.

✓ **Fact-based questions** test your product knowledge.

✓ **Exam strategies** assist you in test preparation.

✓ **Complete yet concise explanations of answers** make for better retention.

✓ **Two practice exams** prepare you for the real thing.

✓ **Fast Facts** offer you everything you need to review in the testing center parking lot.

Practice, practice, practice—pass with New Riders TestPreps*!*

MCSE TestPrep: Networking Essentials, Second Edition

0-7357-0010-9, $19.99, 12/98

MCSE TestPrep: Windows 98

1-56205-922-x, $19.99, 11/98

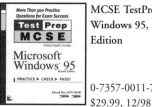

MCSE TestPrep: Windows 95, Second Edition

0-7357-0011-7, $29.99, 12/98

MCSE TestPrep: Windows NT Server 4, Second Edition

0-7357-0012-5, $19.99, 12/98

MCSE TestPrep: Windows NT Server 4 Enterprise, Second Edition

0-7357-0009-5, $19.99, 11/98

MCSE TestPrep: Windows NT Workstation 4, Second Edition

0-7357-0008-7, $19.99, 11/98

MCSE TestPrep: TCP/IP, Second Edition

0-7357-0025-7, $19.99, 12/98

A+ Certification TestPrep

1-56205-892-4, $19.99, 12/98

MCSD TestPrep: Visual Basic 6 Exams

0-7357-0032-x, $29.99, 1/99

TESTPREPS

FIRST EDITIONS

MCSE TestPrep: SQL Server 6.5 Administration, 0-7897-1597-X

MCSE TestPrep: SQL Server 6.5 Design and Implementation, 1-56205-915-7

MCSE TestPrep: Windows 95 70-64 Exam, 0-7897-1609-7

MCSE TestPrep: Internet Explorer 4, 0-7897-1654-2

MCSE TestPrep: Exchange Server 5.5, 0-7897-1611-9

MCSE TestPrep: IIS 4.0, 0-7897-1610-0

HOW TO CONTACT US

IF YOU NEED THE LATEST UPDATES ON A TITLE THAT YOU'VE PURCHASED:

1) Visit our Web site at www.newriders.com.

2) Click on the Product Support link and enter your book's ISBN number, which is located on the back cover in the bottom right-hand corner.

3) There you'll find available updates for your title.

IF YOU ARE HAVING TECHNICAL PROBLEMS WITH THE BOOK OR THE CD THAT IS INCLUDED:

1) Check the book's information page on our Web site according to the instructions listed above, or

2) Email us at support@mcp.com, or

3) Fax us at 317-817-7488 ATTN: Tech Support.

IF YOU HAVE COMMENTS ABOUT ANY OF OUR CERTIFICATION PRODUCTS THAT ARE NON-SUPPORT RELATED:

1) Email us at certification@mcp.com, or

2) Write to us at New Riders, 201 W. 103rd St., Indianapolis, IN 46290-1097, or

3) Fax us at 317-581-4663.

IF YOU ARE OUTSIDE THE UNITED STATES AND NEED TO FIND A DISTRIBUTOR IN YOUR AREA:

Please contact our international department at international@mcp.com.

IF YOU WISH TO PREVIEW ANY OF OUR CERTIFICATION BOOKS FOR CLASSROOM USE:

Email us at pr@mcp.com. Your message should include your name, title, training company or school, department, address, phone number, office days/hours, text in use, and enrollment. Send these details along with your request for desk/examination copies and/or additional information.

WE WANT TO KNOW WHAT YOU THINK

To better serve you, we would like your opinion on the content and quality of this book. Please complete this card and mail it to us or fax it to 317-581-4663.

Name _____

Address _____

City _____ State _____ Zip _____

Phone_____ Email Address _____

Occupation _____

Which certification exams have you already passed? _____
_____
_____
_____

Which certification exams do you plan to take? _____
_____
_____
_____

What influenced your purchase of this book?
❏ Recommendation   ❏ Cover Design
❏ Table of Contents   ❏ Index
❏ Magazine Review   ❏ Advertisement
❏ Reputation of New Riders ❏ Author Name

How would you rate the contents of this book?
❏ Excellent   ❏ Very Good
❏ Good   ❏ Fair
❏ Below Average   ❏ Poor

What other types of certification products will you buy/have you bought to help you prepare for the exam?
❏ Quick reference books   ❏ Testing software
❏ Study guides   ❏ Other

What do you like most about this book? Check all that apply.
❏ Content   ❏ Writing Style
❏ Accuracy   ❏ Examples
❏ Listings   ❏ Design
❏ Index   ❏ Page Count
❏ Price   ❏ Illustrations

What do you like least about this book? Check all that apply.
❏ Content   ❏ Writing Style
❏ Accuracy   ❏ Examples
❏ Listings   ❏ Design
❏ Index   ❏ Page Count
❏ Price   ❏ Illustrations

What would be a useful follow-up book to this one for you?_____

Where did you purchase this book? _____

Can you name a similar book that you like better than this one, or one that is as good? Why?_____
_____
_____

How many New Riders books do you own? _____

What are your favorite certification or general computer book titles? _____
_____

What other titles would you like to see us develop?_____
_____

Any comments for us? _____
_____
_____

MCSE TRAINING GUIDE: INTERNET INFORMATION SERVER 4   0-7357-0865-7

Fold here and tape to mail

Place
Stamp
Here

New Riders
201 W. 103rd St.
Indianapolis, IN 46290

By opening this package, you are bound by the following agreement:

Some of the software included with this product may be copyrighted, in which case all rights are reserved by the respective copyright holder. You are licensed to use software copyrighted by the publisher and its licensors on a single computer. You may copy and/or modify the software as needed to facilitate your use of it on a single computer. Making copies of the software for any other purpose is a violation of the United States copyright laws.

This software is sold "as is" without warranty of any kind, either expressed or implied, including, but not limited to, the implied warranties of merchantability and fitness for a particular purpose. Neither the publisher nor its dealers or distributors assumes any liability for any alleged or actual damages arising from the use of this program. (Some states do not allow for the exclusion of implied warranties, so the exclusion may not apply to you.)

NEW RIDERS TOP SCORE TEST SIMULATION SOFTWARE SUITE

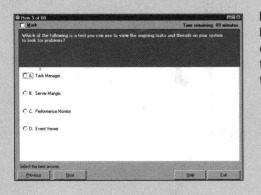

Practice Exams simulate the actual Microsoft exams. Option buttons and check boxes indicate whether there is more than one correct answer. All test questions are presented randomly to create a unique exam each time you practice—the ideal way to prepare.

The **Item Review** shows you the answers you've already selected and the questions you need to review before grading the exam.

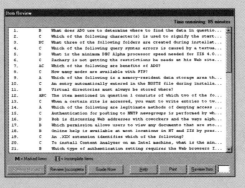

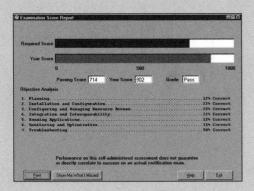

The **Score Report** displays your score for each objective category, helping you to define which objectives you need to study more. It also shows you what score you need to pass and your total score.

Study Cards allow you to test yourself and receive immediate feedback and an explanation for the correct answer. Links to the text are provided for more in-depth explanations.